The
Canadian
Rockies

An Altitude SuperGuide
by
Graeme Pole

The
Canadian
Rockies

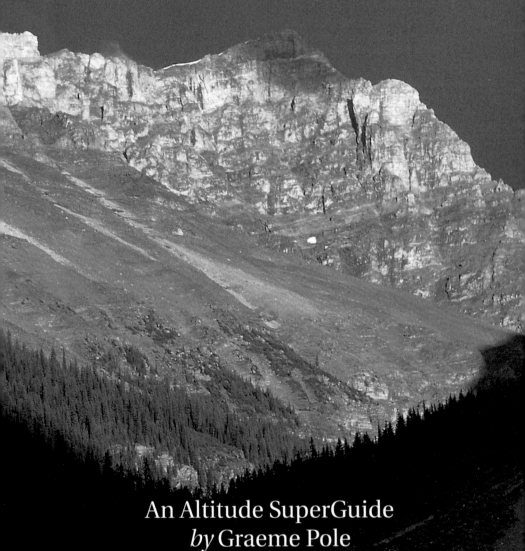

An Altitude SuperGuide
by Graeme Pole

Publication Information

Altitude Publishing Canada Ltd.

1500 Railway Avenue,
Canmore, Alberta T1W 1P6

Copyright © 1991/1997/1999 Altitude Publishing Canada Ltd.
Text copyright © 1991/1997 /1999 Graeme Pole
Second revised edition 1997
First edition 1991

Extreme care has been taken to ensure that all information presented in this book is accurate and up-to-date, and neither the author nor the publisher can be held responsible for any errors.

Canadian Cataloguing in Publication Data

Pole, Graeme, 1956–
The Canadian Rockies SuperGuide

ISBN 1-55153-632-3

1. Rocky Mountains, Canadian (B.C. and Alta.)--
Guidebooks.
2. Natural history--Rocky Mountains, Canadian (B.C. and Alta.)--Guidebooks. I. Title.
FC219.P64 1997 917.1104'4 C97-910436-X F1090.P64 1997

The topographic maps are based on information taken from the National Topographic System map sheet numbers MCR 221, Jasper National Park © 1985 and MCR 220, Banff National Park © 1985. Her Majesty the Queen in Right of Canada with permission of Energy, Mines and Resources.

10 9

Dedication
For Charlotte:
Welcome to a wonderful world.

Front cover photo:
Moraine Lake, Banff National Park
Inset front cover:
Bill Peyto, 1895
Frontispiece:
Cathedral Mountain & Cathedral Crags
Back cover photo:
Cascade Mountain in Banff

Project Development

Concept and design	Stephen Hutchings
Town maps	Catherine Burgess
Layout	Sharon Komori,
	Kelly Stauffer
Editorial	Sabrina Grobler/Joel Reimer
Index	Elizabeth Bell

We acknowledge the financial support of the Government of Canada through the Book Industry Development Program (BPIDP) for our publishing endeavors.

A Note from the Publisher

The world described in *Altitude SuperGuides* is a unique and fascinating place. It is a world filled with surprise and discovery, beauty and enjoyment, questions and answers. It is a world of people, cities, landscape, animals and wilderness as seen through the eyes of those who live in, work with, and care for this world. The process of describing this world is also a means of defining ourselves.

It is also a world of relationship, where people derive their meaning from a deep and abiding contact with the land–as well as from each other. And it is this sense of relationship that guides all of us at Altitude to ensure that these places continue to survive and evolve in the decades ahead.

Altitude SuperGuides are books intended to be used, as much as read. Like the world they describe, *Altitude Super-Guides* are evolving, adapting and growing. Please write to us with your comments and observations, and we will do our best to incorporate your ideas into future editions of these books.

Stephen Hutchings
Publisher

Altitude GreenTree Program

Altitude Publishing will plant twice as many trees as were used in the manufacturing of this product.

Made in Western Canada

Printed and bound in Canada by Friesen Printers

www.altitudepublishing.com

Contents

The *Canadian Rockies SuperGuide* is organized according to the following colour scheme:

Information and introductory sections . . . .

Banff National Park . . . .

Yoho National Park . . . .

Kootenay National Park . . . .

The Icefields Parkway . . . .

Jasper National Park . . . .

Waterton National Park . . . .

Reference . . . .

Canadian Rockies SuperGuide Maps

REFERENCE LEGEND

Use the following legend as a reference for all the topographic highway maps in this book.

TRANSPORTATION

Dual highway.......................................
Road, hard surface, all weather....................
Road, loose surface, all weather...................
Road, loose surface, dry weather...................
Trail ....
Route marker, Trans-Canada.........................   11
Railway, single track..............................
Railway, multiple track............................
Railway, station, stop.............................
Bridge...
Tunnel...
Airfield...

BOUNDARIES

Provincial...
County or District.................................
National Park......................................
Provicial Park, Special Area ....

HYDROGRAPHY

Rapids, Falls, Dam.................................
Intermittent stream, lake..........................
Lake elevation..................................... 1320±
Marsh or Swamp....................................
Glacier, Icefield..................................

RELIEF

Contours... 1000
Depression contours...............................
Spot elevation.................................... •3058
Moraine...

OTHER FEATURES

Settlements, 0-500, > 500........................   o   ●
Built up area.....................................
Building..   ■

Scale 1: 200 000

4   0   4   8   12   16

kilometres   kilomètres

Preface

Bighorn lambs perch on a ledge

How to Use this *SuperGuide*

The *Canadian Rockies SuperGuide* is your guide to understanding and appreciating the national parks and provincial parks in the Canadian Rockies—one of the most spectacular mountain environments in the world. The *Canadian Rockies SuperGuide* will be useful to first-time visitors as well as those on return visits. Whether you are looking for a guidebook or for a souvenir of the Rockies, you need look no further.

The introductory chapters describe the landscape, geology, ecology, wildlife, preservation, human history, recreation and climate of the Rockies. The bulk of the *SuperGuide*'s information follows in chapters that describe the highways and the townsites. You can use these chapters as road guides while you travel. The focus shifts constantly: historical events and personalities; scenery; natural processes; features of climate and ecology; glaciers; wildlife; and recreational opportunities. Each topic is described in detail at appropriate locations.

For each park, there is a sidebar entitled *SuperGuide* Recommendations. Refer to the index for detailed descriptions of the sightseeing options mentioned.

If you come across an unfamiliar term in the text, please refer to the index for references to explanations. Each of the highway chapters contains maps. The legend for these maps is on p. 6. The Reference section of *Canadian Rockies SuperGuide* provides useful phone numbers, contacts and other material to help make your visit to the Rockies more enjoyable.

In this *SuperGuide,* "the Rockies" refers to Banff, Jasper, Yoho, Kootenay and Waterton Lakes national parks; Mt. Assiniboine, Mt. Robson and Hamber provincial parks; and Kananaskis Country. Some of the references to climate, ecology, geology and park policy refer specifically to the "four mountain park block" of Banff, Jasper, Yoho and Kootenay national parks.

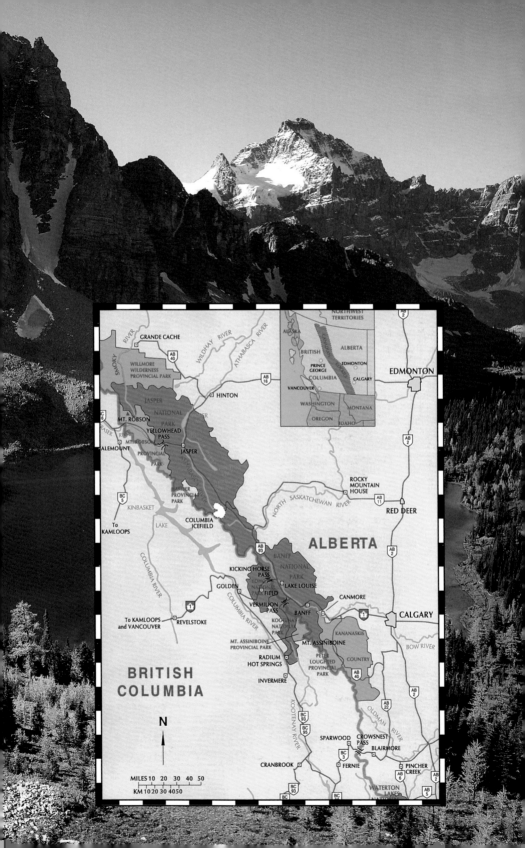

GRANDE CACHE

SMOKY RIVER

WILDHAY RIVER

ATHABASCA RIVER

WILLMORE WILDERNESS PROVINCIAL PARK

AB 40

HINTON

JASPER

NATIONAL

PARK

MT. ROBSON

YELLOWHEAD PASS

BC 16

MT. ROBSON PROVINCIAL PARK

VALEMOUNT

JASPER

BC 5

HAMBER PROVINCIAL PARK

KINBASKET

LAKE

COLUMBIA ICEFIELD

COLUMBIA RIVER

To KAMLOOPS

NORTHWEST TERRITORIES

ALASKA

BRITISH COLUMBIA

PRINCE GEORGE

VANCOUVER

WASHINGTON

OREGON

IDAHO

MONTANA

ALBERTA

EDMONTON

CALGARY

AB 2

EDMONTON

ROCKY MOUNTAIN HOUSE

AB 11

RED DEER

NORTH SASKATCHEWAN RIVER

ALBERTA

AB 93

BANFF

NATIONAL

PARK

AB 2

KICKING HORSE PASS

GOLDEN

FIELD

YOHO NATIONAL PARK

LAKE LOUISE

CANMORE

AB 1

CALGARY

VERMILION PASS

BANFF

To KAMLOOPS and VANCOUVER

REVELSTOKE

KOOTENAY NATIONAL PARK

KANANASKIS

BOW RIVER

MT. ASSINIBOINE PROVINCIAL PARK

MT. ASSINIBOINE

PETER LOUGHEED PROVINCIAL PARK

COUNTRY

AB 40

RADIUM HOT SPRINGS

INVERMERE

BRITISH COLUMBIA

N

AB 22

AB 2

KOOTENAY RIVER

BC 93

BC 95

SPARWOOD

CROWSNEST PASS

BLAIRMORE

BC 3

FERNIE

OLDMAN RIVER

AB 6

PINCHER CREEK

AB 2

CRANBROOK

BC 93

BC 95

WATERTON LAKES

AB 5

MILES 10 20 30 40 50

KM 10 20 30 40 50

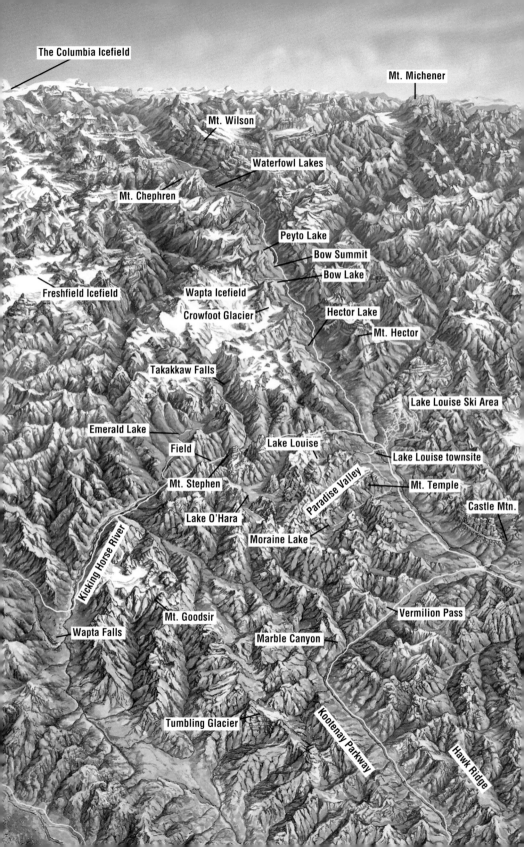

The Canadian Rockies

looking north from Banff to the Columbia Icefield

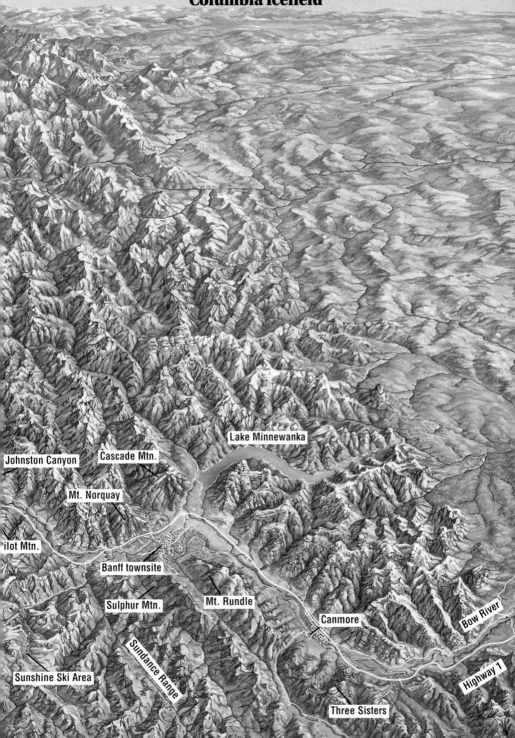

Lake Minnewanka

Johnston Canyon

Cascade Mtn.

Mt. Norquay

Pilot Mtn.

Banff townsite

Sulphur Mtn.

Mt. Rundle

Canmore

Bow River

Sundance Range

Sunshine Ski Area

Three Sisters

Highway 1

Mt. Robson

Pyramid Mtn.

Jasper townsite

Yellowhead Hwy

Maligne Canyon

Medicin

The Whistlers

Marmot Sk Area

Athabasca Falls

Mt.Edith Cavell

Mt Kerkeslin

Mt. Fryatt

Mt.

Mt. Christie

Sunwapta Falls

Dragon Peak

Fortress Lake

Athabasca River

Chaba Icefield

Clemenceau Icefield

The Canadian Rockies

looking north from the Columbia Icefield to the town of Jasper

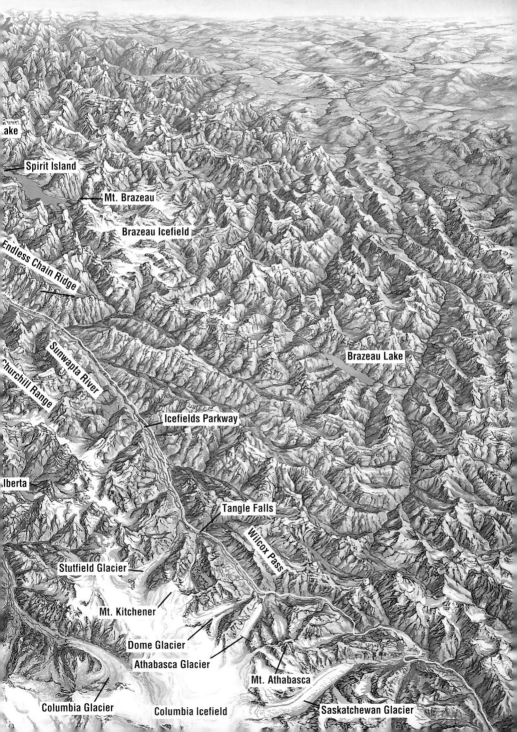

ake

Spirit Island

Mt. Brazeau

Brazeau Icefield

Endless Chain Ridge

Sunwapta River

Brazeau Lake

Churchill Range

Icefields Parkway

lberta

Tangle Falls

Wilcox Pass

Stutfield Glacier

Mt. Kitchener

Dome Glacier

Athabasca Glacier

Mt. Athabasca

Columbia Glacier

Columbia Icefield

Saskatchewan Glacier

Highlights of Nature

Welcome to the Canadian Rockies. The Rockies are part of a continuous chain of mountains that forms the backbone of North America, from Mexico to the Yukon. The Canadian Rockies are different in appearance and origin from the American Rockies,

and from mountains farther west in B.C. They are justly renowned for their impressive scenery, for their wildlife and for the wilderness they preserve.

The *Canadian Rockies SuperGuide* focuses on Banff, Jasper, Yoho and Kootenay national parks. It also includes Mt. Robson, Hamber and Mt. Assiniboine provincial parks in B.C., Waterton Lakes National Park in southwestern Alberta and Kananaskis Country.

The grain or strike of the Rockies is oriented southeast to northwest, along the continental divide. This height of land is the boundary between Alberta and B.C. It also separates rivers that flow to the Atlantic Ocean via Hudson Bay some 1,700 km away, and to the Arctic Ocean 2,200 km away, from rivers that flow to the Pacific Ocean 525 km away.

Although the Rockies are only 120 km wide, they feature diverse scenery. During the drive from Calgary to Golden on Highway 1, you pass through seven distinct landscapes, each with its own physical characteristics and climate, and resulting distributions of vegetation and wildlife. These landscapes are: prairie, foothills, front ranges, eastern main ranges, western main ranges, western ranges and Rocky Mountain Trench.

The Prairies

Calgary lies on the Interior Plains, the flat area that covers much of central North America. The Interior Plains are popularly known as the prairies. The original vegetation was scrubby woodland and open grassland. Little of this remains, as most of the land has been cleared for agriculture. The climate features hot, dry summers and cold, dry winters. The prairies are windy. Thunderstorms are common in summer.

The Foothills

Highway 1 enters the foothills 38 km west of Calgary, at Jumpingpound Creek. The elevation here is about 1,150 m. If you look at the rock cuts at roadside in this vicinity, you will notice that some of the rock layers are tilted vertically. This marks the easternmost manifestation of the compressive forces of mountain building. In the fields nearby, parallel ridges of rock protrude through the ground's surface. These are the upturned edges of thrust sheets. There are many glacial landforms in the foothills, close to the mountain front.

The fertility of the land in this area is due to the water that flows from the glaciers and icefields of the Rockies and into the soil material that has been eroded from the mountains and deposited here. River courses in the area are wide and meandering, a product of the relatively flat terrain. The rivers show considerable seasonal variation in volume due to their glacial sources. During winter, the climate is frequently moderated by warm winds called chinooks that blow eastward from the mountain front. Chinooks, in combination with the overall windiness, keep the foothills relatively snow-free.

The Front Ranges

The front ranges rise dramatically above the foothills near Exshaw, 80 km west of Calgary. Many visitors marvel at the wall-like appearance of these mountains, the summits of which tower more than 1,000 m above the foothills. The lack of any gradual transition is due to the manner in which the Rockies were created, and to the relative resistances of the rock types that comprise the foothills and the front ranges.

During mountain building,

Foothills

Front ranges

the rock formations that became the Rockies were compressed from southwest to northeast, until some layers broke and slid along thrust faults. The front ranges mark the easternmost location of such a fault in the Rockies—the McConnell Thrust Fault. The rocks that comprise the front ranges slid upward and northeastward along this fault, over rocks that later became the foothills. This created a common feature of Rockies geology—older rocks over younger rocks. In this case, rocks with an age difference of 400 million years lie atop one another.

The exaggerated difference in height between the front ranges and the foothills is the product of differential erosion. The limestones of the front ranges are less susceptible to erosion than the shales and sandstones of the foothills. Consequently, more of the original foothills have been weathered away. But keep in mind that many kilometres of height have been eroded from both the foothills and front ranges in the tens of millions of years since they were created.

The thrust sheets of mountain building also influenced the overall pattern of the front range landscape. The erosion-resistant, leading edges of the thrust sheets have become mountain ranges. At the base of these edges, fault valleys have been eroded into the weaker, underlying formations. Thus, there is a symmetry to the front ranges. Individual ranges are oriented along the southeast/northwest grain of the Rockies, and are separated by parallel valleys—like shingles on a roof.

This symmetry is broken by major rivers: the Bow, the Red Deer, the Clearwater, the North Saskatchewan, the Brazeau and the Athabasca. Each of these rivers cuts directly across the grain of the front ranges and foothills to exit onto the prairies. It is thought that these rivers are as old as the Rockies themselves, and initiated their courses before the mountains were created. As the mountains were thrust skyward, these rivers were able to keep pace eroding down. You can see this best on the drive north and east from Jasper on the Yellowhead Highway, where the Athabasca River bisects four mountain ranges before reaching the foothills.

The climate in the front ranges is dry. These mountains lie in the rain shadow of higher mountains to the west. Chinook winds are common. The annual temperature range is the greatest of any region in the Rockies: –54 °C to +38 °C. Vegetation is sparse above valley bottoms, and the soils of mountainsides have little ability to retain water. When rains do fall, flash floods may result. The montane ecoregion is found in valley bottoms. The montane is important range for the larger mammals, especially in winter.

Most of the rocks in the front ranges are limestone, so the mountains are a drab colour of gray. The average elevation of the front ranges is 2,850 m. The highest point is the 3,470 m summit of Mt. Brazeau, south of Maligne Lake in Jasper National Park. As a rule, the front range peaks in Jasper show more severe faulting and folding than those in Banff. The mountains in Waterton Lakes National Park are all in the front ranges.

The Eastern Main Ranges

The eastern main ranges are the meat and potatoes of the Rockies—the glacier-capped, lake-studded peaks famed

Eastern main ranges

Western main ranges

world-wide. The first prominent examples are visible looking west from Banff townsite. Highway 1 enters the eastern main ranges slightly east of Castle Junction, about halfway between Banff and Lake Louise.

These mountains contain some of the hardest rocks in the Rockies: quartzite, limestone and dolomite. The rock formations lie mostly in horizontal layers. This makes eastern main range mountains more resistant to erosion. They are higher than most front range peaks as a result. The rocks also tend to be more colourful than those of the front ranges.

Most mountains in the eastern main ranges rest on compressed rocks at the base of broad downward folds called synclines. The major valleys have been eroded into the weaker rocks at the crests of upward folds called anticlines. The 20 highest summits in the Rockies, all more than 3,353 m, are in the eastern main ranges. The highest of the high is Mt. Robson (3,954 m), visible from the Yellowhead Highway in Mt. Robson Provincial Park.

The horizontal orientation of the rock layers and the alternation of tough layers of limestone and dolomite with weak layers of shale produce the "layer-cake" shape of the castellated mountain. Castle Mountain is one of the best examples. Horn mountains are also common. The summits of these mountains have been sharpened by cirque glaciers eroding into two or more flanks.

Glaciers and icefields abound in the heavy snowfall areas at high elevations along the continental divide. The meltwaters of many glaciers empty directly into tarns and glacial lakes, of which there are hundreds. A majority of these lakes are on north and east aspects—the slopes most prone to glaciation. The combination of altitude and proximity to ice keeps the air in the eastern main ranges cool. The average annual temperature at treeline (2,200 m) is –4°C. The surfaces of most lakes, such as Lake Louise, are frozen for seven months during autumn, winter and spring.

Rivers in the eastern main ranges have significant erosive power because of the large amount of glacial sediment that they carry. River levels fluctuate greatly with the seasonal and daily glacial melt patterns, complicating the establishment of valley-bottom vegetation. High-water level for most rivers occurs from late May to mid-June. A second high-water level occurs in early August, at the peak of the glacial melt season.

The eastern main ranges lack the symmetry of the front ranges. The southeast/northwest alignment is present, but the local drainage patterns are irregular. This is due to more extensive glaciation, and the horizontal nature of the rock formations. The principal passes on the continental divide—Vermilion, Kicking Horse and Yellowhead—cut across the grain of the mountains. It is thought that these passes were first scoured by glacial ice sheets nearly two million years ago.

Eastern main range valleys support an abundance of vegetation and wildlife. However, growing seasons are short. The average temperature in the lower valleys is near the freezing point. Here, as elsewhere in the Rockies, some mammals hibernate. Mountainsides are covered with subalpine forest. Avalanche paths are a prominent feature on steep slopes. Alpine meadows and tundra occur above tree-

Rocky Mountain Trench, Columbia Valley

line. Most mountain summits are boulderfields and scree slopes that support little vegetation.

The Western Main Ranges

Just west of Field, Highway 1 enters the western main ranges. The rocks here were created from sediments deposited in deep waters that were almost devoid of life. As a result, limestone is uncommon. Weak slates and shales comprise more than 90 per cent of the rocks. Consequently, western main range mountains are more easily eroded and have a less angular appearance than eastern main range mountains. There are few glaciers and icefields. Typical summit elevations are close to 3,000 m.

The Rockies' largest outcrop of igneous (once molten) rock occurs in the western main ranges of Yoho and Kootenay national parks. (It is not visible from the highway.) Several mountain groups also have underlying layers of the tough limestone and dolomite of the Ottertail Formation. The Ottertail Formation forms the 900-metre-high Rockwall that

extends for 53 km through Kootenay and Yoho. There are many small glaciers along the Rockwall.

The mountains and valleys of the western main ranges are oriented along the southeast/ northwest axis of the Rockies, but not in such an orderly fashion as in the front ranges. Many western slope rivers initially cut across this grain as they leave the continental divide. Because these rivers do not have as far to travel to reach sea level as rivers on the eastern slopes, their courses are initially much steeper. Many leave the continental divide in narrow canyons or gorges. Western slope valleys have sections that are distinctly V-shaped as a result. You can see this in the upper Kicking Horse Valley and in the Kicking Horse Canyon west of Yoho.

Valley bottoms in the western main ranges are at lower elevations than those in the eastern main ranges. They receive more precipitation. The more moderate climate supports diverse wildlife and vegetation, including several species of trees uncommon in the Rockies, such as the western red cedar, western hemlock and western yew.

The Western Ranges

The western ranges comprise the western edge of the

Rockies between Golden and Radium. These are the oldest mountains in the Rockies. The rock is similar to that of the western main ranges, but the appearance of these mountains is even less uniform.

The weak shales of the western ranges absorbed a great deal of the forces of compression during mountain building. Some of the rock layers were tipped upwards and overturned past the vertical, creating a complex landscape. These mountains escaped significant glaciation during the last ice age, so troughs, cirques and hanging valleys are less common. There are no glaciers in these mountains in the present day. V-shaped valleys are more common here than elsewhere in the Rockies. The western ranges are visible from the Kootenay Parkway south of Kootenay Crossing, and on the south side of Highway 1 between Hoodoo Creek Campground and Golden.

The Rocky Mountain Trench

The last landscape is not part of the Rockies proper, but forms the western boundary of the range, dividing it from the older Columbia Mountains. The Rocky Mountain Trench is a broad rift valley that parallels the western slope of the Canadian Rockies for their entire length. You descend into it at Golden, Radium and Tete Jaune Cache. The Trench was created after the Rockies, when rocks subsided along the plane of a normal fault. The Trench has since been widened by glacial erosion, and is now home to the Columbia River, whose most southerly source is

45 km south of Radium.

Summers in the Rocky Mountain Trench are warm and dry. Winters are relatively mild. There are almost 100 more frost-free days than in valley bottoms in the eastern main ranges. When the weather is dreary in Banff or Lake Louise, Rocky Mountain locals flock to communities in the Rocky Mountain Trench.

There are extensive wetlands along the Columbia River south of Golden. Dry coniferous forests dominated by Douglas fir cover the lower mountainsides.

Geology

The history of the Rockies is written in the rocks. The language of rocks—geology—is unfamiliar to many. By acquainting yourself with a few concepts and terms of this new language, you will be able to better understand the appear-ance of the Rockies, and you will become aware of the natural forces, both obvious and subtle, that have created this exceptional landscape.

The creation of the Canadian Rockies involves three accounts:
• how the rocks were made (deposition)
• how the mountains were built (uplift)
• how the mountains have been weathered (erosion).

A Simple Geological Description of the Rockies

Deposition: The creation of sedimenary rock

Unlikely as it may seem, the Canadian Rockies were created from particles of sediment deposited on the floors of ancient seas. One and a half billion years ago, the area which is now the Rockies lay slightly off the western shore of North America, on the sloping edge of the continental plate. Sediments transported by prehistoric rivers collected there, and hardened into sedimentary rock under the weight of accumulated deposits above. The distinctive layers we see on mountainsides today are called sedimentary formations. Each formation records a particular episode during this process of deposition.

The most common sedimentary rocks in the Rockies are limestone, shale, dolomite and quartzite.

Uplift: Mountains created from the floors of ancient seas

How did nearly flat sea bottom become high mountain and deep valley? About 200 million years ago, the continental plate underlying North America reversed its eastward direction of drift. Off the western shore was a series of island and reef-like land masses. It was the collision between the plate and these land masses which supplied the compressive force to initiate mountain building, the process which created the Rockies.

About 120 million years ago, the compression began to deform the western edge of the Rockies. For the next 35 million years, the sedimentary formations were compressed horizontally. Below the earth's surface, the warm rock was pliable, and bowed under the pressure into folds. The stress was so great, some of the folds eventually fractured. Huge sheets of formations broke free and slid over underlying layers along ramp-like thrust faults, from west to east. Some of these thrust sheets moved 40-60 kilometres. The Rockies piled upwards.

Glaciation

Ever since the Rockies first started to poke their summits above sea level 120 million years ago, they have been subject to processes of erosion, which break down rock and carry the fragments away. Before the last ice age (the Wisconsin Glaciation of 75,000-11,000 years ago), the Rockies were rounded and gentle in appearance (1). Ancient streams (3) sculpted the landscape. The hallmark of this water-worn landscape was the V-shaped valley (2).

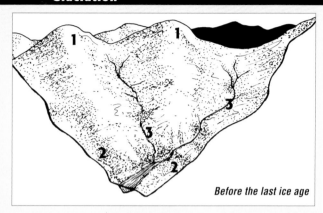

Before the last ice age

During the three advances of the Wisconsin Glaciation, ice sheets covered all but the highest of the Rockies' summits, sending massive glaciers into the surrounding valleys (4). Alpine valley glaciers (5) widened the V-shaped valleys into U-shaped troughs, and niche glaciers (6) formed on upper mountainsides, sharpening the profile of the peaks.

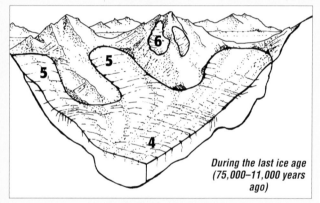

During the last ice age (75,000–11,000 years ago)

When the ice receded, it left behind the blueprint of the Rockies: broad, U-shaped valleys (7), with tributary valleys hanging above the main valley floors (8). It is at the mouths of these hanging valleys that the Rockies' famous waterfalls and canyons are found. Hanging glaciers (12) and niche glaciers (11) still occupy the shaded north and east aspects of many mountainsides, eroding the horn mountain shape (14). Horn mountains feature triangular faces separated by narrow ridges called arêtes (13). Cirque glaciers (9) nestle in the bowl-shaped cirques they have eroded. Meltwater from these and other glaciers collects in depressions or behind moraine dams, creating tarns (10)—the glacial lakes for which the Rockies are renowned.

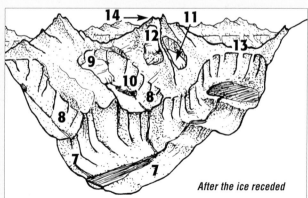

After the ice receded

Although glaciation has been the most significant force of erosion in the Rockies, there are many other processes which are constantly turning rock into rubble. Together, they are wearing down the Rockies at a rate of about 1 metre every 17,000 years.

The Blueprint of the Rockies

Ancient streams were the principal sculptors of the initial landscape of the Rockies. Rainwater and runoff are naturally slightly acidic, and break down limestone easily. Sediment carried by water acts like an aqueous sandpaper, grinding away at every surface it contacts. The hallmark of a water-worn landscape is the V-shaped valley.

Ice has an even more pronounced effect on landscape.

Ice ages have occurred many times in the Rockies since mountain building commenced. Each glacial advance erased most evidence of the one previous, so there is not much certainty as to the overall historic record. However, some evidence of the most recent glacial advances is well preserved. It is with certainty that we can say that the Rockies owe much of their appearance to glaciation.

The hallmark of the glaciated landscape is the U-shaped valley, or trough.

When they advanced, ice age glaciers readily followed the existing V-shaped valleys. In doing so, they undercut the surrounding slopes and caused mountainsides to collapse. Side valleys entering into main valleys were shorn and left as hanging valleys. Many of the Rockies' famous limestone canyons and waterfalls are at the mouths of hanging valleys.

Glaciers on mountainsides eroded downward and backward into niches in the rock, creating bowl-shaped depres-

Avalanches

Although they look like ski runs, the treeless swaths on mountains like Dolomite Peak are caused by snow avalanches. On the Icefields Parkway, snow avalanches occur when one or more layers within the snowpack release from other layers, or when the entire snowpack separates from the underlying slope. Avalanches are caused by a complex interplay of temperature, humidity, wind, snow depth, slope aspect and steep-

ness. People and animals travelling on a susceptible slope may trigger an avalanche. Loud noises cannot trigger an avalanche unless they originate in an explosion that also vibrates the ground.

Although they appear destructive, avalanches are simply another of nature's tools for ensuring biodiversity. They remove large vegetation and create open habitat that supports shrubs and

wildflowers. These are important foods for moose, elk, bears and deer.

In many places in the Rockies, as at Dolomite Peak, avalanche paths reach the road. In winter and spring, park wardens periodically close the roads and use explosive charges to trigger avalanches. This reduces the possibility of traffic being caught in a large slide. It is illegal to stop in posted avalanche areas.

Mountain Types

In the Rockies, the combined effects of mountain building and the processes of erosion have produced some basic mountain shapes that you can easily recognize. Familiarity with these shapes will give you a greater understanding of the Rockies' geology. This should help you create some order from the apparent chaos of mountains, allow you to distinguish the various mountain ranges that comprise the Rockies and identify some of the processes that created them.

Overthrust Mountain

Typified by the front ranges, overthrust mountains (Mt. Rundle, Endless Chain Ridge, Sunwapta Peak) feature a tilted southwest-facing slope and a steep northeast-facing cliff. This "writing desk" shape gives a graphic representation of how the thrust sheets slid upwards and over each other from southwest to northeast during mountain building. Overthrust mountains frequently contain niche glaciers on their northeast aspects.

Dogtooth Mountain

Found in the front ranges and western main ranges, dogtooth mountains (Mt. Louis, Mt. Edith, Mt. Birdwood, Cinquefoil Mountain, Spike Peak) contain sedimentary formations which were thrust towards the vertical during mountain building. Now they stand as relatively resistant spires. The surrounding rock has been weathered away.

Sawtooth Mountain

Another mountain type common in the front ranges, sawtooth mountains (Mt. Ishbel, Sawback Range, Colin Range, Queen Elizabeth Ranges) are the upturned edges of thrust sheets. Their ridges are angled perpendicular to the prevailing winds. Precipitation and mechanical weathering have eroded hourglass-shaped gullies into shale formations on their southwestern aspects to produce the sawtooth shape. Sawtooth mountains are very photogenic at sunset or when dusted with snow.

Castellated Mountain

Castellated mountains (Castle Mountain, Pilot Mountain, Mt. Temple, Mt. Chephren, Mt. Saskatchewan, Mt. Amery, Castleguard Mountain) are the trademark peaks of the Rockies, and are found in the eastern main ranges. Other examples (Mt. Crandell, Mt. Blakiston) can be observed in the front ranges of Waterton. Resistant limestone, dolomite and quartzite rocks are separated by weak layers of shale. The resistant formations become cliffs, whereas the weak layers are eroded to become ledges, creating the "layer-cake" appearance. All of these formations remained largely horizontal during mountain building. Castellated mountains frequently contain cirque glaciers on their east aspects, and alpine valley glaciers on their north aspects.

Horn Mountain

Most common in the eastern main ranges, horn mountains (Mt. Chephren, The White Pyramid, Mt. Athabasca, Mt. Fryatt, Mt. Assiniboine, Mont des Poilus, Mt. Stephen, Mt. King, Mt. Carnarvon) were created where several cirque glaciers eroded different sides of a mountain simultaneously. The narrow ridges that separate the cirques are called arêtes (ah-RETTS), and frequently offer mountaineering routes to the summit.

sions called cirques, and horn mountains. Troughs, hanging valleys and cirques are the blueprints of the Rockies. Areas that do not follow this pattern are few.

Raindrops and Tumbling Blocks

There are many other processes of erosion at work in the Rockies. Falling raindrops hit the earth's surface at speeds of up to 32 km per hour. The impact dislodges soil and rock particles, and the runoff carries these away. Groundwater seeps into cracks in rocks. Since water expands nine percent when frozen, the

cracks are wedged open and eventually the rock breaks apart. When this happens on cliffs, the broken rock falls, dislodges other material upon impact and shatters itself. The rubble is called talus (TAY-luss), and often forms cone-shaped piles at the bases of cliffs.

Snow avalanches sweep mountainsides with tremendous force, dislodging rock, rending large trees from the ground and removing surface vegetation and soils. Springtime avalanches have the greatest impact, as the entire depth of the winter's snowpack is often released in a single slide.

Rockslides pulverize objects lying in their path. They are often caused by expansion and contraction of rock as it heats and cools, or by the splitting apart of rock along naturally weak layers. Earthquakes are not common in the Rockies, but they may also trigger rockslides and avalanches.

One of the greatest agents of erosion in the Rockies is also one of the most imperceptible—biological action. Rock lichens and mosses break down the surface of rocks, forming thin, acidic soils in which less hardy plants can take hold. Tree roots lever

Synclines and Anticlines

The folds created during mountain building have greatly influenced erosion in the Rockies. U-shaped folds are called synclines (SIN-clines). At the base of a syncline, the rock was compressed and became relatively resistant to erosion. On either side of a syncline there were usually corresponding arch-shaped folds called anticlines. The rock at the crest of an anticline was stretched and rendered more susceptible to erosion. So synclines have often endured, whereas many anticlines have eroded away. Synclines and anticlines may be a few metres across—such as those commonly seen in rock cuts at roadside—or they may be as wide as valleys and mountain ranges.

Many of the major valleys in the Rockies have been eroded through anticlines. You can see this clearly looking north from Bow Summit into the Mistaya Valley. Synclines underlie the axes of many mountain ranges. The

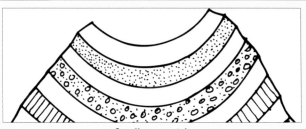

Syncline mountain

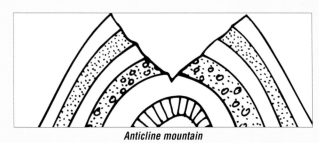

Anticline mountain

Castle Mountain Syncline extends 260 km through Banff and Jasper national parks. Its U-shaped fold is prominent in Castle Mountain, Mt. Hector, Cirrus Mountain, Nigel Peak and Mt. Kerkeslin.

Mountains that contain synclines and anticlines are called

complex mountains. There are many good examples along the Yellowhead Highway east of Jasper townsite, and on the west side of the Kootenay Parkway in the Kootenay Valley. Cascade Mountain near Banff is also a complex mountain.

23

rocks apart. Animals and birds burrow in soil and trees, create trails, and build dens, hastening the decay of the landscape.

Wind scours exposed sands and soils and redistributes fallen snow, creating dunes, glaciers, and areas devoid of vegetation. Soil saturated with ice and water creeps slowly downhill under the influence of gravity. Slumps, mudflows and landslides sometimes result.

The picture is clear: the Rockies have been on the road to ruin since their creation. These lofty mountains are being constantly whittled away. However, they are not about to disappear. It has been estimated that their height is being reduced about one metre every 17,000 years.

Glaciation

Glacial ice forms in areas where more snow falls in winter than melts in summer. As the fallen snow crystals age, they change shape from flakes to grains. When 30 m of snow has accumulated, the grains near the bottom compact under the weight and are transformed into glacial ice. When ice formed from compacted snow begins to flow downhill, it becomes a glacier (GLAY-seer).

There are thousands of glaciers and sixteen icefields in the Canadian Rockies. Icefields are remnants of past ice ages when most of Canada was covered by ice sheets a kilometre thick. The formation and motion of glaciers and their effects on the Rockies are discussed in detail in the chapter on Columbia Icefield. You can see displays concerning glaciation at the park information centres at Lake Louise and at Columbia Icefield.

Ecology

The simplicity of the concept of ecology—the interrelationship of all living things—belies

Prominent Glaciers in the Canadian Rockies

Glacier Type and Name	Where Visible	Glacier Type and Name	Where Visible
Icefield		Lefroy	Plain of Six Glaciers
Waputik	Hector Lake viewpoint	Horseshoe	Paradise Valley
Wapta	Hector Lake, Bow Lake,	Hector	Icefields Parkway
	Peyto Lake viewpoints		at Bow Lake
Mons	Howse River viewpoint	Balfour	Hector Lake viewpoint
Wilson	Mt. Wilson viewpoint	Kerkeslin	Mt. Kerkeslin,
Columbia	Parker Ridge, Athabasca		from Jasper townsite
	Glacier, Sunwapta Flats	Summit	Mt. Robson
Outlet Valley Glacier		Cathedral	Kicking Horse Pass
Athabasca	Columbia Icefield	Bath	Highway 1 at Lake Louise
	Information Centre	Cavell	Mt. Edith Cavell
Bow	Bow Glacier viewpoint	**Niche Glacier**	
Peyto	Bow Summit	Macdonald	North face of Mt. Temple
Saskatchewan	Parker Ridge	Snowbird	Mt. Patterson
Dome	Columbia Icefield	Howse Peak, Aries,	Howse Peak
	Information Centre	Stairway	viewpoint
Stutfield	Stutfield Glacier viewpoint	Chephren, White	Mt. Wilson viewpoint
Yoho	Yoho Valley Road	Pyramid, Epaulette,	Mt. Wilson viewpoint
Vulture	Hector Lake viewpoint	Kaufmann, Sarbach	Mt. Wilson viewpoint
Alpine Valley Glacier		Stephen	Yoho Valley Road
Crowfoot	Crowfoot Glacier viewpoint	Angel	Mt. Edith Cavell
Boundary	Sunwapta Pass	**Cirque Glacier**	
Hilda	Hilda Creek	Waputik Range	Hector Lake viewpoint
Stanley	Vermilion Pass	Crowfoot Mountain	Crowfoot Glacier viewpoint
Fay	Moraine Lake	Mt. Patterson	Mistaya Valley
Victoria	Lake Louise	Mt. Jimmy Simpson	Bow Pass
Aberdeen	Lake Louise	Mt. Amery	Graveyard Flats

Freshfield Icefield

the complexity of the many factors that link climate, landscape, vegetation and wildlife. Plants and animals in the Rockies occupy specific niches in the environment where their needs are met, and where their characteristics best ensure survival. In turn, they become food for other species, or provide assistance, both subtle and obvious, that helps other species to survive. Thus is created the balance from which springs the biodiversity of the Canadian Rockies.

The fascinating thing about this interdependence is that it holds true throughout the ecology of the Rockies, regardless of species or scale. From the tiniest plants on upper mountainsides to the largest free-roaming mammals, every living thing plays a key role in ensuring this balance is main-

tained. The elimination or unnatural reduction in the population of a single species upsets the balance and begins a chain reaction with effects that ultimately influence the ecosystem.

In the world today, we are constantly reminded of such effects. The clear-cutting of tropical and coastal rainforests, the pollution of the Great Lakes, the clearing of native prairie grasslands, the damming of wild rivers—each of these actions has tremendous environmental costs. They affect the quality and the supply of air and water, the availability of habitat and the diversity of species. They impoverish the natural heritage of the earth.

The beauty of the Rocky Mountain national parks is that a century of preservation has spared much of the land-

scape from the wanton actions of man. Most of the natural relationships, although stressed, are still present. We as visitors have the privilege of viewing the natural order close at hand—an opportunity that has sadly been lost in many areas of the world.

This privilege comes at a price. Our presence here interferes with natural relationships. The services and developments we demand are accelerating the decline of the ecosystem of which the Rockies are part. It has recently become apparent that many of the relationships in this ecosystem are on a scale that extends beyond the boundaries of the Rocky Mountain parks. Activities and attitudes on surrounding lands, both near and far, also undermine the integrity of the Canadian Rockies ecosystem.

Ecology at Riverside

Let's look at the complexity of ecology on the small scale, in a quiet side channel of the Bow River just west of Banff townsite. In this backwater is a metre-high mound of sticks and mud. This structure is a lodge, home to a family of beavers.

Beavers are aquatic rodents that require slow moving waters. In an incredible display of industry, the beaver family has taken advantage of this side channel and dammed the downstream end with tree trunks, mud and rocks, creating a pond. From their lodge near the centre of the pond, the nocturnal beavers emerge each evening. They swim to shore to fall aspens, birch and poplars that they use in maintaining the lodge and dam. The beavers eat the inner bark, buds and greens of these and other trees and shrubs. What they do not eat, the beavers cache underwater to tide them through the winter.

Trout are washed into the pond during periods of high water in the river. They flourish in the nutrient-rich, silt-free waters. Fish-eating birds such as osprey, belted kingfisher and great blue heron take up residence nearby. A pair of muskrats, which enjoy similar habitat to beaver, have built their own den on the shore of the pond. They will not compete with the beaver for food, preferring instead to eat the lush aquatic vegetation that grows near shore: horsetails, cattails, sedges and rushes. A shrub thicket grows on the river bank. The willows, alder and red osier dogwood provide food for moose, elk and deer.

Mosquitoes use the still pond waters for breeding. These insects are food for dragonflies and a host of songbirds. Among these, and easily recognized by its beautiful song (KONK-lah-REEEE), is the red-winged blackbird, which nests in the cattails and willows at the pond's edge. A pair of Canada geese make the pond their summer home, raising their goslings on its quiet waters.

When the pond freezes, wolf, coyote and lynx will walk across the ice to the lodge, seeking a winter meal. The natural concrete of the lodge is usually adequate defence for the beaver against this threat. Inside the lodge, the beaver does not hibernate. It remains active, venturing beneath the ice to eat from its food cache.

In creating a safe habitat for themselves, the beavers have rendered many other animals a great service, offering additional range and sources of food. In time, when the beavers have eaten all nourishing vegetation within safe range of the pond, they will move on. Without the beavers' maintenance, the dam may break and the pond once again become an active river channel. Or, the shoreline vegetation may proliferate and spread into the pond, transforming it into marsh. Over the course of many decades as larger vegetation takes root, this marsh will slowly become a shoreline forest, reclaimed from the river. Thus the actions of the beaver will not only have benefited a diverse array of wildlife and vegetation, but will have produced a transformation in the landscape itself.

Ecoregions

The mountain environment graphically assists us in understanding its complex ecology. Take a look at any mountainside around Banff or Jasper townsites. You will notice that the vegetation is generally dense and varied in the valley bottom and lower mountainsides, becoming more sparse as elevation increases. On the high ridges and summits, vegetation is almost absent. Biologists have used these natural transitions to describe three life zones or ecoregions: the montane, the subalpine and the alpine.

How Green are the Parks?

The following figures give approximate percentages of the combined area of Banff, Jasper, Yoho and Kootenay national parks occupied by each ecoregion:

Montane:	5%
Lower subalpine:	33%
Upper subalpine:	20%
Alpine:	6%
Glacial ice (mostly alpine elevations):	6%
Bedrock, moraine, river gravel:	30%

These are species counts for plants, animals and insects:

Plants:	approximately 1,300
Mammals:	69
Insects:	approximately 20,000
Fish:	40
Amphibians and reptiles:	16
Birds:	277

This photograph of Mt. Rundle and the Bow Valley shows three ecoregions:
1 - Alpine; 2 - Supalpine; 3 - Montane

In terms of growing season, the effect of moving from Banff townsite to a high mountainside nearby is the same as travelling to northern Alberta: each metre of elevation gained is equivalent to moving one km north, with a consequent shortening of the growing season. The duration of the growing season in the *SuperGuide*'s area ranges from six months in some of the lower valley bottoms, to less than two months on the upper mountainsides. Thus, the distribution of vegetation and wildlife and the extent of the ecoregions are largely governed by elevation and its associated effects.

1. The Alpine Ecoregion

The alpine ecoregion occurs above treeline and is characterized by diminutive and hardy vegetation—wildflowers, mosses, grasses and lichens.

Soils are generally rocky. Most of the precipitation in the alpine falls as snow. The mean annual temperature is the lowest of the ecoregions: –4°C is typical at treeline. The range of temperature extremes is the least. Vegetation patterns are often directly influenced by the manner in which snow accumulates or is removed by the actions of ever-present wind.

2. The Subalpine Ecoregion

The subalpine ecoregion occupies mountainsides between the montane and treeline, and also occurs in valley bottoms at high elevations. Treeline is the upper limit of the forest, which is generally 2,200 m on south-facing slopes. Treeline may be considerably lower on north-facing slopes, on cliff edges and near glaciers. Precipitation in the subalpine is heavier than in the montane. Most falls as

snow, some of this in summer. Winds are generally light and are influenced by ridges and valleys. Near glaciers, pools of cold air called frost hollows are common. These prolong the effects of winter and stunt the growth of vegetation.

The subalpine is the most extensive ecoregion in the Rockies and has been subdivided to allow ease of description. In the lower subalpine ecoregion, there is a mix of cone-bearing evergreen trees: lodgepole pine, Engelmann spruce, white-Engelmann spruce hybrids, and scattered subalpine fir. Balsam and cottonwood poplars grow in scattered stands. Engelmann spruce and subalpine fir trees dominate the upper subalpine forest. Whitebark pine grows in windswept locations. All these trees become krummholz (stunted forest) towards treeline. South of Bow Pass, pure stands of Lyall's larch frequently comprise the treeline forest.

3. The Montane Ecoregion

The montane ecoregion occupies the major valley bottoms and sun-exposed slopes of lower mountainsides, especially in the front ranges. (Montane is from the Latin word *montanus*, which means "of a mountain.") The annual temperature range in the montane is the greatest of the mountain ecoregions: –54 °C to +38 °C. Average precipitation in the montane on the eastern slopes is relatively low, and is split roughly equally between summer and winter. Precipitation is slightly higher in the montane on the western slopes, and is significantly higher in the Mt. Robson area.

The montane is the windiest ecoregion. Sections of the large valley bottoms are oriented parallel to the prevailing southwesterly winds. On the eastern slopes, this orientation also allows warm air masses and cold air masses to back up into the Rockies from the prairies and foothills. The warm chinook wind—the "snow eater"—is a common winter feature of the front ranges and foothills, and contributes to relatively sparse snow cover. Easier winter travel in montane valley bottoms and the relative abundance of food make this ecoregion important winter range for many animals, especially deer, bighorn sheep and elk.

The characteristic trees of the montane are: Douglas fir, lodgepole pine, white spruce, white birch, trembling aspen,

Hiker at Sunshine Meadows

balsam poplar and cottonwood poplar. Limber pine occurs in Banff, Yoho, Kootenay and Waterton. Grasslands and wetlands occupy areas adjacent to rivers. The montane is home to more species of vegetation and wildlife than any other ecoregion. But although important, the montane comprises very little of the total area of the Rocky Mountain parks— approximately five percent. Much of the montane has sustained severe impacts from the construction of townsites, railways and roads.

Other Life Zones

Because of the chilling effect that glaciers have on the surrounding areas, valley bottoms nearby often exhibit characteristics and vegetation of the alpine ecoregion, even though the elevation may seem too low.

In Waterton Lakes National Park, there are three other ecoregions: prairie, foothills transition and aspen parkland. These are all low-elevation life zones found in the northeast-

ern part of the park. They bolster the vegetation species counts, giving Waterton the greatest biodiversity of the Rocky Mountain parks.

The Effects of Landscape on Climate

Although elevation is used to roughly assign the limits of the ecoregions, the local climate produced by the landscape also influences the distribution of vegetation and wildlife. The local factors are: mean temperature; type and amount of precipitation; sunshine and shade; soil type; drainage; slope orientation or aspect; slope steepness; avalanche paths; proximity to water or glacial ice; and wind.

These factors interact to produce a myriad of variations on what might "normally" be expected for a particular location at any given elevation. The localized ecoregions that result are called ecosites. More than 130 ecosites have been identified in the Rocky Mountain parks. Δ

Succession

When we look at the landscape, we tend to think that a forest will always remain a forest, that a meadow will remain a meadow, and that a marsh will remain a marsh. In the short term, this may be true. However, over a period of decades, ecosites proceed through a successional sequence from youth to maturity. The lower subalpine forest best demonstrates this sequence.

A young, lower subalpine forest is not so much a forest as a charred mass of burned timber, the product of a forest fire. The lodgepole pine depends on forest fires to crack open its resin-sealed cones and allow for effective seeding. Consequently, this tree regenerates prolifically after a fire. The lodgepole loves the sun. It thrives in the open burn amid patches of common fireweed, wildflowers and scattered stands of white birch, trembling aspen and balsam poplar—deciduous trees that grow well on disturbed ground. This open habitat is a good one for wildlife, offering two blessings: access to food in the new growth of the recently burned area, and shelter in the unburned forest nearby.

The lodgepole pines fare too well under these conditions. Their dense seeding results in a thick growth of uniform age—a doghair forest. The forest floor becomes shaded and the undergrowth dies off. The food supply dwindles and the forest loses its appeal to most wildlife. However, because the lodgepoles do not grow well in shade, they effectively eliminate themselves by overcrowding. As the trees weaken, windstorms topple them.

Forest floor

Meanwhile, the shade-tolerant species of Engelmann spruce and subalpine fir have been growing beneath the lodgepole canopy. As the lodgepoles dwindle, these trees succeed them and become the most prevalent. More sunlight reaches the forest floor, and the undergrowth becomes more diverse. The forest is at its prime usefulness to most wildlife.

The last stage in the cycle of the fire-succession forest is the climax forest, when additional generations of spruce and fir trees take seed. When these seedlings mature, the forest attains old-growth status. If old-growth develops in an area that does not soon burn, it becomes a refuge for species such as woodpeckers and caribou. In most areas in the Rockies, extensive old-growth does not develop. Nature wipes the slate clean with another fire.

Not all of the successional cycles in the Rockies are fire-related. Some, such as the succession from montane wetland to white spruce forest, rely on floods, log

jams in rivers and the work of beavers. These cycles may require centuries. The primary succession of barren mountain top to alpine meadow is the work of erosion and biological action, and may well require thousands of years.

The absence of major forest fires in the last 70 years has greatly affected the balance of successional habitats in the Rockies. Doghair forests fill the major valley bottoms. Following extensive fire history studies, park wardens are igniting prescribed burns to initiate regeneration and increase the biodiversity of various ecosites.

Climate change affects the process of succession. Longterm changes in temperature or precipitation can speed up, slow down or preclude the establishment of species. Climatologists are paying special attention to protected areas like the Rocky Mountain parks, for it is here that the effects of climate change on biodiversity will first become evident.

Bighorn ram

Wildlife

S ince the first visits of Euro-Canadians 200 years ago, the Canadian Rockies have been renowned for wildlife. Today, the opportunity to view wild animals in their natural habitat is a key facet of the national park experience. Visitors are fortunate that good habitat for many of the

larger mammals exists at roadside. You have an excellent chance of seeing deer, elk, moose, coyote, mountain goat, bighorn sheep, grizzly bear and black bear—especially in early morning and late evening.

The history of man's interaction with wildlife in the Rockies chronicles the evolution of changing perceptions of the natural world, and highlights the responsibilities of park managers and visitors in ensuring that representative wildlife populations survive.

The Not-so-Happy Hunting Grounds

The days of the fur trade in the 1700s and early 1800s saw very little hunting and trapping in this part of the Rockies. Most of the pelts were harvested farther west in B.C. As the fur traders crossed the Rockies, they reported abundant wildlife. Half a century later, the total animal population, although still far greater than today, was evidently in decline. James Hector of the Palliser Expedition recorded few observations of wildlife

during his travels of 1857–60.

With the completion of the Canadian Pacific Railway in 1885, the frontier of the Wild West was thrown open to anyone who could pay the fare. By the late 1890s, hunters from Europe and eastern North America were making annual trips to the Rockies. These clients became the mainstay of guiding and outfitting operations such as those established by Tom Wilson, Jim Brewster and Jimmy Simpson.

Many of us cringe today when we read accounts of three grizzly bears shot in one

Gray (timber) wolf

Decades of Transition

With the proclamation of the National Parks Act in 1930, the awareness dawned that animals should be protected in the wild rather than in cages. The zoos were discontinued. However, the outlook on certain species remained unchanged. The mandate of the first national park wardens included the eradication of unwanted wildlife. Between 1924 and 1941, more than 80 cougars were exterminated in Banff and Jasper. Sightings of cougars are rare in these parks today. The wolf was exterminated as part of an anti-rabies program in the 1950s. It took more than three decades for this animal to return in numbers to the Rockies.

As a consequence of these predator-eradication programs, the populations of some animals went unchecked, and wardens found themselves having to kill the prey in the same manner as they had killed the predator. A mass killing of the burgeoning elk population between 1941 and 1970 was unpopular with the public. Not so the earlier eradication of the wolf—an act that directly contributed to the overpopulation of elk!

During the last two decades, the concept of managing the mountain national parks as an integrated ecosystem has become established. The dire situation now facing many animals outside of the national parks has driven home the realization that any act that tampers with wildlife habitat or population balances affects many species. After

afternoon, 500 fish hauled from a lake, or pack horses loaded down with more trophy sheep heads than could be carried. However, during the first few years of its existence, Rocky Mountains Park (Banff) had no regulations governing hunting and fishing. Even after regulations were established, enforcement was difficult. Hunters continued the wholesale slaughter both within and beyond the park boundaries.

Some observers were concerned. In 1911, surveyor and mountaineer A.O. Wheeler wrote: "It will readily be seen that to preserve these wild animals in their native habitat will prove of infinitely greater value to the country than to advertise them as spoils of the chase, when they will soon cease to exist."

It wasn't only over-hunting that threatened the natural balance. The late Victorian concept of the animal kingdom was markedly different from that of today. Animals were categorized as "good" and "bad." The good animals were the game that offered prospects to the hunter, or that could be viewed safely at close range in zoos: deer, elk, bear, moose, bighorn sheep and mountain goat. The bad animals were the predators: cougar, lynx, wolverine, owl, hawk, eagle, coyote and wolf. These last two were particularly persecuted. The concept of the balance between predator and prey was still many years away.

Early visitors had a tremendous desire to see animals, but did not want to risk encountering them on their own turf in the wild. To fulfill the visitors' desires, the Dominion Parks Branch established zoos at the Buffalo Paddock and at the Banff Park Museum.

Wildlife in the SuperGuide

Rodents

Members of the rodent family are small mammals whose character-istic behaviours are gnawing and hyperactivity. They have two prominent incisor teeth on both the upper and lower jaws. Most rodents are active only in daytime. Many species hibernate in winter.

- Least chipmunk, p. 174
- Golden-mantled ground squirrel, p. 174
- Columbian ground squirrel, p. 174
- Red squirrel, p. 174
- Hoary marmot, p. 225
- Porcupine, p. 148
- Beaver, p. 88

Rabbits

Members of the rabbit family are gnawing mammals that have two pairs of incisor teeth on the upper jaw. Only two species are present in the Rockies: the pika and the snowshoe hare.

- Pika, p. 126

Weasels

The nine members of the weasel family in the Rockies are charac-terized by long, slender bodies, short ears and legs and anal scent glands. Weasels are carniv-orous, agile and adept hunters. They do not hibernate. Most species are nocturnal.

- American marten, p. 145

Ungulates

Ungulates are animals that have hooves. In the Rockies, two fami-lies are represented. Members of the deer family have cloven hooves and antlers that are branched and shed each year. The bovid family has cloven hooves and horns that are not branched and never shed.

Deer Family

- Mule deer, p. 104
- White-tailed deer, p. 104
- Elk, p. 69
- Moose, p. 236
- Woodland (mountain) caribou, p. 208

Bovid Family

- Mountain goat, p. 210
- Bighorn sheep, p. 91
- Bison, p. 260

Wild Cats

There are three members of the cat family in the Rockies: cougar, lynx and bobcat. Wild cats are carnivorous, nocturnal and seldom seen. Their tracks show four toes with claws retracted.

- Cougar, p. 254

Wild Dogs

The three species of wild dogs are primarily carnivores. Tracks show four toes with claws visible on all feet. The red fox is rare.

- Wolf, p. 108
- Coyote, p. 108

Bears

Bears are the largest carnivores in the Rockies. They have five clawed toes on the front and rear feet.

- Black bear, p. 169
- Grizzly bear, p. 168

Birds

Approximately 40 per cent of North American bird species occur in the Rockies. These can be roughly grouped into four categories: songbirds, waterfowl, raptors (birds of prey) and ground-dwelling birds. The avid birder will see fewer species and numbers of birds than are common in areas of North America that have longer and milder summers. Nonetheless, there are some fine bird-watch-ing locations in the Rockies.

Those near Jasper offer especially good prospects for photography.

Songbirds

Banff and Jasper townsites; Cave and Basin; the Bow, Kicking Horse, Miette and Athabasca valleys.

Waterfowl

Vermilion Lakes; Fenland Trail; Cave and Basin; the Bow, Mistaya and Kicking Horse valleys; lakes in the vicinity of Jasper; the Athabasca Valley east of Jasper; Miette Valley.

Raptors

Foothills; Vermilion Pass; the Bow, Athabasca, Kootenay and Kicking Horse valleys; alpine ecoregion; upper and lower subalpine forest.

Ground-dwelling birds

Kootenay Valley, upper and lower subalpine forest, Parker Ridge, The Whistlers, Cavell Meadows, glacial forefields, alpine ecore-gion.

Some of the more common and interesting birds are profiled in the *SuperGuide*:

Resident songbirds

- Common raven, p. 208
- Clark's nutcracker, p. 106
- Gray jay, p. 106

Migratory songbirds

- Horned lark, p. 231

Raptors

- Golden eagle, p. 57
- Bald eagle, p. 57
- Osprey, p. 246

Ground-dwelling birds

- White-tailed ptarmigan, p. 186

Black bear

Grizzly bears

Wildlife Tips

The following will help protect both you and wildlife:

- Do not feed animals. Although it is tempting to offer a crumb to a squirrel or a bird, this practice establishes a dangerous dependency on unnatural food sources. Some of the foods that you may offer are very harmful, especially to animals that hibernate. Animals accustomed to being fed will expect this treatment from all visitors, and will become a nuisance or even a danger.
- Do not leave food or garbage unattended. If eaten, the packaging on some foods may kill an animal. Bears will frequent campgrounds and townsites if they are accustomed to easily obtainable food or garbage. A fed bear is a dead bear. Place all garbage in the animal-proof receptacles provided. Store food in the trunk of your vehicle.
- Do not approach or entice wildlife. Take photographs

from a distance, and use a telephoto lens.
- Do not interfere with the relationship between a mother and its young.
- Observe posted speed limits. Reduce speed at night. Pay special attention when driving through areas frequented by animals. Do not expect animals to get out of the way of your vehicle. Be prepared to stop instead.
- Elk, deer, moose, sheep and goats are highly unpredictable during their mating season of September to November. It is best to avoid them completely at these times.
- Bears are unpredictable. If you are fortunate enough to see a bear, remain in your vehicle. Report your sighting to a park information centre.
- Keep pets restrained on a leash or confined in a vehicle. Do not take dogs into the backcountry.

decades of manipulating wildlife in the Rockies, park managers today are for the most part leaving matters alone in an attempt to allow natural balances and cycles to return. If they are to be successful, park managers will require the cooperation of visitors and those who manage the adjoining provincial lands.

A Troubled State of Grace

Today, wildlife biologists, park wardens and researchers use the mountain national parks as a living laboratory in which they study wildlife. Some animals are fitted with radio collars by which they can be tracked, and their habits, range and life cycles monitored. Elk, bear, wolf, moose and mountain caribou have been studied in this fashion.

Wildlife in the Rockies is currently in a troubled state of grace. They are protected, but pressures from both within

33

Moose

Mountain goat

and outside the parks are causing a decline of many species. Animal death caused by collisions with automobiles and trains is one of the most pressing issues. Please slow down in posted wildlife areas, and drive with extra care at dawn and dusk.

Most wildlife species are normally fearful of people, but have come to realize that the average park visitor poses no threat to their well-being. What may appear to you as approachability is nonchalance. Do not forget that these animals are wild. When pressured or intimidated, their natural instincts will take over. At roadside in these very parks, people have paid for this education with their lives.

Amendments to the National Parks Act in 1988 provided stiff penalties for those convicted of hunting in the national parks. Nonetheless, poaching—the illegal hunting of wildlife (especially elk and bighorn sheep)—continues to be a problem. If you suspect behaviour that may indicate poaching, do not betray your suspicions. Discreetly record a description of the persons and their vehicle, and report your information promptly to the nearest park warden or RCMP officer.

Preservation

In recent years, the concept of ecology—the interrelationship of all living things—has been universally embraced. Unfortunately, we have arrived at this perception the hard way, by discovering that to a large extent, paradise has been lost. In the urban areas of the world, natural relationships have been so disrupted that it is impossible for us to conceptualize, let alone experience, the many facets of nature's balance. Most of us have been living out of touch and out of step with the earth beneath our feet.

Canada's 38 national parks are ecological touchstones that provide opportunities to observe, explore and understand the integral roles that natural processes, wildlife and vegetation play in creating and sustaining biodiversity. The positive and negative effects of our influence are highlighted. In the national parks, we can begin to re-establish our connection to the natural order, appreciate its workings and learn from our past mistakes.

We can take this awareness with us when we leave, to apply to the betterment of life in our homes and in the other places where we travel.

The concept of national parks was new when the reserve at Banff was proposed in 1885. In the debate concerning the pros and cons of establishing the world's third national park, there was a mixture of rationale. Many thought wilderness was worthless. Few wished to preserve the land unspoiled. Most saw a national park as an opportunity to make money. Certainly the gift horse was there—hot springs, a new railway, the great unknown and some of the most spectacular mountain scenery in the world.

In the end, economics prevailed in the establishment of Banff and Yoho national parks. Preserved areas and the means and intent to exploit them arrived on the Canadian scene simultaneously. The contradictory aims of preservation and development were entrenched. The debate between preservationists and developers, and the impacts on the Rockies ecosystem, have continued for more than a century.

Mule deer

Elk

Preservation of the Rocky Mountain parks might be a relatively simple matter if the only pressures came from developers within. However, added to the scenario of conflicting views on land use inside the parks are the effects of commercial, recreational and industrial developments outside park boundaries.

The opportunity to create buffer zones on adjacent lands has already been lost, due to provincial policies that give precedence to "multi-use" over genuine protection. Logging roads lead to formerly remote park boundaries. Clearcuts, mines, agriculture and petroleum exploration have destroyed adjacent habitat. This habitat is required seasonally by animals that range inside the parks. Suddenly, the Rocky Mountain parks are not big enough to protect grizzly bears, wolves, wolverines, caribou and cougars. Some of these species may become extinct within these parks in the next few decades. The park boundaries, established for political and economic reasons in 1930, afford little protection from contemporary pressures.

Within the parks, transcontinental railways and highways, carrying ever-increasing volumes of traffic through the park, slice the wilderness into smaller pieces. These pieces may be damaged irrevocably if the internal and external pressures continue to mount. The lesson we are painfully learning outside the parks applies within the boundaries too. Namely, that no arbitrary area or individual species stands alone; in a world of cause and effect, all things interrelate.

An Evergreen Opportunity

As a visitor to the Rocky Mountain parks, you have an opportunity to make contact with a natural landscape, the exceptional quality of which has largely disappeared from many other areas in the world. Even with the many battles fought over the endless array of development ideas, the Rocky Mountain parks clearly demonstrate the value of preservation. What would these mountains now look like if they had been unprotected this past century? Your voice, added to the many others urgently requesting that the

completion of the national park system be given priority, will help generate the necessary political will to achieve that aim and shortcut the negotiations.

Your experience of the Canadian Rockies—the fresh water, the lower incidence of pollution, the wildlife and the opportunities for recreation and solitude—can inspire you toward incorporating environmentally supportive practices into your daily life. Perhaps the greatest environmental challenge that faces each of us is to achieve a unity of thought and action that will move us closer to harmony with the natural world, and in turn, with each other.

The Reference section provides addresses of organizations working to preserve natural areas in Canada. Similar organizations exist in other countries. By joining these organizations, learning about the issues and expressing your views to politicians, businesses and manufacturers, you will help establish new protected areas and ensure that existing protected areas such as the Rocky Mountain parks will not be lost. △

Highlights of Human History

This short chronology lists some of the prominent and noteworthy events in the human history of the Canadian Rockies. From the time of the first inhabitants, the Rockies have been the home territory of countless societies which have flourished in the alpine landscape.

The First Inhabitants

11,000 BC The ice sheets of the Wisconsin Glaciation began to recede. The glaciers that filled the valleys of the Rockies retreated to their sources along the continental divide. By 6000 BC, all the major valleys in the Rockies were ice-free. Native peoples subsequently travelled through these valleys on hunting and trading journeys. Some natives may have stayed in the Rockies year-round.

1700 AD The stability of native life in the Rockies was shattered by an influx of natives from the east. These natives were fleeing the persecution of Euro-Canadians and diseases to which they had no immunity. The Stoney tribe came to the Rockies as part of this migration.

The Fur Trade

1754 Fur trader Anthony Henday was the first Euro-Canadian to see the Rockies.

1799 The North West Company and the Hudson's Bay Company each built outposts near Rocky Mountain House.

1800 David Thompson and Duncan McGillivray of the North West Company explored the Bow Valley. Two fur trade scouts crossed Howse Pass and established a fur trade route. The same scouts probably also crossed South Kootenay Pass and saw the area that is now Waterton Lakes National Park.

1807 David Thompson of the North West Company crossed Howse Pass and built Kootenae House in the Columbia Valley, near the present town of Invermere.

1810 Hostile Peigan Natives closed the Howse Pass route to fur traders.

1811 David Thompson established the Athabasca Pass route. Henry House was built at what is now Jasper—the first Euro-Canadian inhabitation in the Rockies.

1813 The North West Company built Jasper House at Brûlé Lake in the foothills of the Athabasca Valley.

1820s Yellowhead Pass was briefly incorporated into the fur trade route.

1821 The rival Hudson's Bay Company and North West Company amalgamated.

1827 Botanist David Douglas crossed Athabasca Pass and assigned erroneous elevations to Mt. Hooker and Mt. Brown.

1829 Jasper House was moved to a site near Jasper Lake.

1841 Sir George Simpson crossed the Rockies on his way around the world, and made the first recorded visit by a Euro-Canadian to the hot springs at Radium. James Sinclair led a group of 200 settlers through the Rockies to the Oregon Territory. He took a dip in the Radium Hot Springs, too.

1844 and 1847 Methodist missionary Robert Rundle preached to Stoney Natives in the Bow Valley.

1845-46 Jesuit missionary Jean Pierre de Smet crossed and recrossed the Rockies. At Jasper House he baptized 54 people.

1850s The western territories had been over-trapped. What furs remained were shipped from the west coast rather than packed overland. The fur trade began to decline.

1857 The last wood bison in the Rockies was seen in the Pipestone Valley.

Exploration

1857-60 The Palliser Expedition explored central and western Canada for the British Government. James Hector crossed Vermilion Pass, Kicking Horse Pass, Bow Pass and Howse Pass. Thomas Blakiston crossed South Kootenay Pass and recorded the first description of the area that is now Waterton Lakes National Park.

1859 The first tourist arrived. James Carnegie, the Earl of Southesk, travelled through

Historic buildings in Banff

the front ranges of what are now Jasper and Banff.

1862 Drawn by the Cariboo gold rush west of the Rockies, a group of immigrants known as The Overlanders made an epic crossing of western Canada by wagon, horse, raft and foot. They used Yellowhead Pass and the Fraser Valley to reach the Cariboo Mountains.

1863 Bungling tourists Milton and Cheadle crossed the Rockies via Yellowhead Pass, and barely survived the ordeal.

1865 John Kootenai Brown first saw the Waterton Lakes.

1867 Canada was granted independence from Britain under the terms of Confederation.

1870s The Cavell Advance (Little Ice Age) ended. At this time, the Athabasca Glacier blocked the Sunwapta Valley. Most glaciers in the Rockies began to recede rapidly.

The Canadian Pacific Railway

1871 B.C. joined Canada, and Prime Minister John A. Macdonald promised the new province a railway connection to the rest of the country, to be completed within a decade.

1872 Sir Sandford Fleming, the proposed railway's engineer-in-chief, chose Yellowhead Pass as the route for the railway. He then travelled across Canada on foot to examine the route.

1873 Scandal plagued John A. Macdonald's government and its plans for the railway. In November, the government resigned.

1874 Two American prospectors made a visit to hot springs on the slopes of Sulphur Mountain near Banff. One of them built a shack and wintered in the area in the hope of developing a claim to the springs.

1878 John A. Macdonald was returned to power, and the

push began in earnest to organize and complete a Canadian trans-continental railway. John Kootenai Brown homesteaded at Middle Waterton Lake.

1881 The charter establishing the Canadian Pacific Railway received Royal Assent. William Cornelius Van Horne, an American, was appointed general manager of the railway. Tom Wilson arrived in the Rockies.

1882 The Yellowhead Pass route was abandoned. Major Rogers, in charge of surveying the route for the railway through the mountains, discovered the pass in the Selkirks now named for him. Tom Wilson discovered Lake Louise and Emerald Lake, and crossed Howse Pass.

1883 The CPR tracks reached Calgary. Workers laid 11 km of track in a single day. Later in the summer, the end of steel reached Lake Louise. Surveyor G.M. Dawson discovered coal

Reverend Rundle

The Basin Pool

east of Banff. Three railway workers stumbled onto the hot springs at Banff while prospecting for minerals, and attempted to file a claim.

1884 A.P. Coleman, a geology professor from Toronto, made his first trip to the Rockies and climbed Castle Mountain. The railway boom town of Silver City flourished nearby. Tom Wilson discovered ore on Mt. Stephen.

Parks, Peaks & Pack Trains

1885 After a century of over-hunting, the plains bison was virtually extinct in the wild. The last spike of the CPR was driven at Craigellachie, B.C. The Hot Springs Reserve was established at Banff.

1886 The first passenger train rolled through the Rockies. The Mt. Stephen Reserve was established, forerunner of Yoho National Park. The CPR constructed Mt. Stephen House at Field. Development of the Cave and Basin hot springs began.

1887 Surveyor J.J. McArthur climbed Mt. Stephen near Field. National park status was bestowed on the reserve at Banff. It became known as

Rocky Mountains Park.

1888 The Banff Springs Hotel opened. A.P. Coleman made the first attempt to find the mythic giant peaks reported by David Douglas in 1827—Mt. Hooker and Mt. Brown.

1888 Hunting and fishing regulations were imposed in Rocky Mountains Park, but could not be enforced due to lack of staff. Stoneys were brought to Banff to entertain stranded tourists—the first of many Banff Indian Days. Dave White built the first cabin on the shore of Lake Louise, and Tom Wilson cut a trail to the lake.

1890 The CPR built its first chalet at Lake Louise. Roland Stuart obtained a lease at Radium Hot Springs.

1892 The area around Lake Louise was added to Rocky Mountains Park. A.P. Coleman headed north in quest of Mt. Hooker and Mt. Brown, but reached Fortress Lake instead.

1893 Pioneer outfitter and guide Tom Wilson set up shop in Banff. Bill Peyto began guiding with Wilson's company. American expatriate Lewis Swift settled in the Athabasca Valley east of Jasper. The chalet at Lake Louise burned.

While exploring near Lake Louise, Walter Wilcox and Samuel Allen obtained a distant view of Moraine Lake, and made an attempt to climb Mt. Temple. A.P. Coleman reached Athabasca Pass and stated that Mt. Hooker and Mt. Brown were frauds—they were mountains of average stature.

1894 Wilcox and Allen returned to Lake Louise with other school fellows and formed the Yale Lake Louise Club. They succeeded in climbing Mt. Temple and exploring more of the surrounding area. Samuel Allen visited Lake O'Hara.

1895 Wilcox made the first of several trips to Mt. Assiniboine and explored north towards Bow Pass. Samuel Allen also explored near Mt. Assiniboine. Mt Hector was climbed by members of the Appalachian Mountain Club. The forerunner of Waterton Lakes National Park was established.

1896 Wilcox attempted to find Mt. Hooker and Mt. Brown and helped pioneer part of the route of the present-day Icefields Parkway. Mountaineer P.S. Abbot was killed in a fall on Mt. Lefroy near Lake Louise—the first

L to R: Jim Brewster, Walter Wilcox and Tom Wilson

James Outram

recorded fatality in North American mountaineering.

1897 The first Swiss Guide, Peter Sarbach, was brought to Canada. He led a party of nine climbers who avenged Abbot's death by making the first ascent of Mt. Lefroy. Mt. Victoria was climbed two days later. Jean Habel explored the Yoho Valley and "discovered" Takakkaw Falls. Bison were donated to the park at Banff, and the Buffalo Paddock was established. Outfitter and guide Jimmy Simpson began work with Tom Wilson's company.

1898 John Norman Collie and party headed north from Lake Louise in quest of the elusive Mt. Hooker and Mt. Brown. Collie climbed Mt. Athabasca and "discovered" Columbia Icefield. Upon returning to England, Collie put the myth of Mt. Hooker and Mt. Brown to rest.

1900 Bill and Jim Brewster began guiding and outfitting at Banff. Eventually, they wrested the guiding market from Tom Wilson. Elk, which had been killed off by hard winters and over-hunting, were reintroduced to the Rockies.

1901 Edward Whymper, con-queror of the Matterhorn, made the first of five heralded visits to the Rockies. Mt. Assiniboine, the "Canadian Matterhorn," was climbed by James Outram. German explorer Jean Habel was the first to visit the north edge of Columbia Icefield. An oil well was established on Cameron Creek in Waterton.

1902 James Outram climbed Mt. Columbia, the second highest peak in the Rockies. Rocky Mountains Park (Banff) was expanded to its maximum size. Canada's second trans-continental railway, the Grand Trunk Pacific, was proposed.

1903 Photographer Byron Harmon arrived in Banff. The CPR began mining coal at Bankhead. The Banff Park Museum was constructed.

1906 Surveyor and moun-taineer A.O. Wheeler founded the Alpine Club of Canada—in Winnipeg, of all places. The Club held its first annual camp in Yoho Pass.

1907 A.P. Coleman and Reverend George Kinney made the first reconnaissance of the Rockies' highest peak, Mt. Robson. Jasper Forest Park reserve was established. Explorer Mary Schäffer jour-neyed to the headwaters of the Athabasca River.

1908 Coleman and Kinney returned to Mt. Robson, but poor weather thwarted their mountaineering ambitions. Coal was discovered on the slopes of Roche Miette in Jasper. Mary Schäffer reached Maligne Lake.

1909 George Kinney and out-fitter Curly Phillips almost reached the summit of Mt. Robson. Kinney claimed the first ascent. The Spiral Tunnels were completed. An avalanche destroyed many buildings in Field.

Parks and Prosperity

1910 A highway linking Banff and Invermere was proposed. Development of Miette Hot Springs began. The Pocahontas mine opened.

1911 A.O. Wheeler organized the joint ACC- Smithsonian Institution expedition to Yellowhead Pass, Mt. Robson and Maligne Lake. The town of Jasper (then named Fitzhugh) sprang up as a divisional point on the Grand Trunk Pacific Railway, which was completed across Yellowhead Pass. J.B. Harkin became the first

Moraine Lake

Teepee at Bow Lake

Commissioner of National Parks, a post he would hold for 25 years. Construction of the Kootenay Parkway began. It would be 12 years before it was completed. Waterton Lakes and Yoho national parks were officially established.

1912 The first dam at Lake Minnewanka was built.

1913 The first ascent of Mt. Robson was accomplished from an ACC camp. Mt. Robson Provincial Park was established. A third Canadian trans-continental railway, the Canadian Northern, was completed through Yellowhead Pass. The Interprovincial Boundary Survey began.

1914 Walter Painter's design for the Cave and Basin hot pools was built, as was his $2-million-dollar tower at the Banff Springs Hotel.

1915 Mt. Edith Cavell was named, and the first ascent accomplished.

1920 British Columbia conveyed the lands of Kootenay, Canada's 10th national park. Jimmy Simpson began building a cabin at Bow Lake.

1920s With the establishment of the automobile in the mountain parks, the CPR began constructing "auto bungalow camps" at Johnston Canyon, Castle Mountain, Storm Mountain, Radium, the Kootenay Valley, Wapta Lake, the Yoho Valley, Lake O'Hara, Moraine Lake and Emerald Lake.

1921 The Pocahontas mine closed.

1922 Jasper Park Lodge opened. The Bankhead mine closed and the town was removed. The dam at Lake Minnewanka was enlarged. Mt. Assiniboine Provincial Park was established. The federal government expropriated Roland Stuart's lease at Radium Hot Springs. Abbot Pass Hut was completed. The Grand Trunk Pacific and Canadian Northern railways amalgamated as the Canadian National Railway.

1923 The Kootenay Parkway opened. The first ascent of North Twin, the third highest mountain in the Rockies, was accomplished by J.M. Thorington and party.

1924 The National Geographic Society mounted an expedition to Columbia Icefield and Maligne Lake. Most of the Chateau Lake Louise burned.

The National Parks Association was founded—Canada's first environmental group.

1925 Mt. Alberta, one of the most difficult mountains in the Rockies, was climbed for the first time by a Japanese mountaineering party. The Interprovincial Boundary Survey was completed.

1927 A gravel road called the Kicking Horse Trail was completed from Lake Louise to Golden. The Prince of Wales Hotel opened in Waterton.

1928 Construction of the main building at the Banff Springs Hotel was completed.

Preservation and Development

1930 The National Parks Act was passed. The boundaries of the four Rocky Mountain parks were finalized.

1931 Construction of the Icefields Parkway began.

1932 The Waterton-Glacier International Peace Park was proclaimed.

1936 Skiing began at Sunshine. The present park administration building was built in Banff.

1937 The Miette Hot Springs

The Cave & Basin

Brass band at the Banff Springs Hotel

were developed.

1939 The Icefields Parkway was completed.

1940 The Survey Peak burn engulfed much of the forest near Saskatchewan River Crossing, forcing the closure of the recently opened Icefields Parkway.

1941 A third dam was constructed at Lake Minnewanka.

1945 The first ski lift was installed at Sunshine. A gravel road was completed between Jasper and McBride.

1952 Commercial snowmobile rides began at Columbia Icefield. Jasper Park Lodge burned and was soon rebuilt.

1956 Highway 1 was completed through Yoho. The era of steam ended on the CPR in the Rockies.

1961 Upgrading of the original Icefields Parkway was completed.

1968 A forest fire blazed through Vermilion Pass. Redevelopment of the Aquacourt at Radium Hot Springs was completed. The Whyte Museum of the Canadian Rockies opened.

1970 The Yellowhead Highway officially opened.

1973 Mt. Assiniboine

Provincial Park was enlarged.

1977 The Alberta Government established Kananaskis Country.

1979 Waterton-Glacier was proclaimed an International Biosphere Reserve.

1980 The Sunshine Gondola began winter operation.

1981 The Burgess Shale was proclaimed a World Heritage Site.

1985 The national parks celebrated their centennial. The refurbished Cave and Basin opened. The Duke of Edinburgh unveiled a monument at Lake Louise, proclaiming the Rocky Mountains a World Heritage Site. Redevelopment of Lake Louise townsite began.

1986 Emerald Lake Lodge was redeveloped.

1988 The Winter Olympic Games were hosted by Calgary. Nakiska at Mt. Allan was site of the alpine skiing events. The nordic skiing events were held in Canmore. New management plans for the four mountain parks were approved. The first amendments to the National Parks Act were passed. The Glacier Wing was completed at

Chateau Lake Louise. The first prescribed burn at Lake Minnewanka was ignited.

1989 The upgraded Bow Valley Parkway was officially opened. The Kicking Horse, Athabasca and North Saskatchewan rivers were designated Canadian Heritage Rivers. The Visitor Centre at Field opened. Redevelopment of the Mt. Norquay ski area began. Residents of Banff voted "yes" in a referendum for self-government, and elected their first town council.

1990 Banff became a self-governing community. The Lake Louise Visitor Centre opened. Daily passenger train service through the Rockies was discontinued. Mt. Assiniboine, Mt. Robson and Hamber provincial parks in B.C. were added to the Rocky Mountains World Heritage Site.

1993 The Sawback prescribed burn consumed forest in the Bow Valley west of Banff. The Whyte Museum was redeveloped.

1994 The swimming facility at the Cave and Basin was closed.

1997 The Buffalo Paddock at Banff was closed. Δ

Life in the Canadian Rockies

T he management plans for the Rocky Mountain parks identify "driving for pleasure" as the principal activity of most visitors. This is not surprising. The highways in the Rockies offer close-up views of some of the most spectacular mountain scenery in the world. However, many

other recreational activities are possible. Your experience of the Rockies will broaden greatly if you make an effort to walk, paddle or ski away from the highway—even if only for an afternoon. Don't worry if you don't have the necessary equipment with you. You can rent everything from boots to backpacks in Banff, Lake Louise and Jasper. Guides are available for walking, hiking, rafting, horseback riding, fishing, photography and mountaineering.

Refer to the *SuperGuide* Recommendations in the text. Use the phone numbers provided to make arrangements for many of the activities described below.

Fees are charged at all roadside campgrounds. Some campgrounds require self-registration. The maximum length of stay allowed is 14 nights. About three quarters of the campgrounds have flush toilets. All sites have picnic tables and access to drinking water. Most campgrounds have cook shelters. There are interpretive theatres at approximately one half of the campgrounds. Firewood is provided for a fee. Please use firewood sparingly. Do not gather firewood from the forest floor or from riverbeds.

BC Parks operates three roadside campgrounds in Mt. Robson Provincial Park— Robson Meadows, Robson River and Lucerne—totalling 178 sites. These have water, toilets and firewood, but no hook-ups. A sani-station is provided at Robson Meadows.

Camping

Parks Canada operates 32 roadside campgrounds in the Rocky Mountain parks, with 5,338 campsites. Although this seems to be a large number, campgrounds frequently fill by early afternoon in mid-summer. At such times, you may be directed to "overflow" campgrounds at which the only facilities provided are pit toilets. For complete campground listings and information about how to register at your campsite, refer to the Reference section, page 273-74.

Backcountry Camping

Backcountry camping is allowed at a multitude of campgrounds on trails in the Rocky Mountain parks. Most campgrounds are more than six km from the closest road. All overnight trips require a wilderness pass—obtainable for a fee from a park informa-

tion centre. Some trails have quotas which fill early on long weekends. But overcrowding in the Rockies' backcountry is generally not a problem—less than two percent of park visitors walk more than a kilometre from the roads. When you pick up your wilderness pass, you can also get the latest information on trail conditions and seasonal hazards.

Camp only in designated campgrounds, on the tent sites provided. Practice minimum impact camping. Most backcountry campsites are now equipped with bear poles for food storage, but be sure to carry enough rope with you to stow your food out of a bear's reach. Pack out all your garbage. Fires are prohibited in many areas—a lightweight campstove is essential. Groundwater and snowmelt are usually potable, but contamination with *Giardia lamblia* has been recorded.

Random camping is allowed only in specific areas or to mountaineers at the base of certain climbing routes. Backcountry travellers may take advantage of the voluntary registration system. It ensures that someone will come looking if you are overdue. This registration must be returned at the end of your trip. There are

Left: A hiker admires the alpine landscape

backcountry campsites in Mt. Assiniboine and Mt. Robson provincial parks, and BC Parks operates Naiset cabins at Mt. Assiniboine. Fees are charged.

Hiking and Backpacking

The Rocky mountain parks are a hiking and backpacking paradise, with over 4,000 km of trails. These include everything from short walks at roadside to wilderness routes nearly 200 km long. For the adventurous, trackless passes beckon to seldom-travelled side valleys, offering many opportunities for exploration.

Backpackers require a wilderness pass—available at a park information centre. They must be familiar with the dos and don'ts of minimum impact travel and camping, and with travelling in bear country. Snow lingers in the high country year-round. Lightweight, durable and waterproof equipment is essential, as is a campstove. Fires are prohibited in many areas. In general, camping is allowed only in designated campgrounds.

At time of publication, some of the parks still offered scheduled interpretive hikes. Private guides can also be hired for walking and hiking. Contact a park information centre.

Water Sports

Non-motorized boats are allowed on most lakes and rivers in the Rocky Mountain parks. Gasoline-powered boats may be launched only on Lake Minnewanka, Pyramid Lake, Yellowhead Lake, Moose Lake, Upper Waterton Lake and Middle Waterton Lake. Boats with electric motors and no on-

Backcountry hikers silhouetted against a stunning mountain backdrop near Lake O'Hara

board generator may be launched on any lake where non-motorized boats are permitted.

Canoe and boat rentals are available at many of the popular lakes: Louise, Moraine, Emerald, O'Hara, Pyramid, Maligne, Waterton and Cameron. Commercial boat tours operate on Lake Minnewanka, Maligne Lake and Upper Waterton Lake. Commercial rafting companies operate on the Athabasca, Maligne, Bow, Kootenay, Columbia, Fraser and Kicking Horse rivers.

Canoeists and kayakers will find a variety of calm water and whitewater on the major rivers in the Rockies. Reaches of the Bow, Kicking Horse and Athabasca rivers can be navigated in open boats most of the summer. There is challenging whitewater on the lower Kicking Horse, Yoho, Maligne, upper Bow, Fraser and Whirlpool rivers. There are usually two high-water levels—one in late spring, and the other at the peak of the glacial melt season in early August. Contact a

park information centre for information on routes and conditions.

The Waterton Lakes are the best location for boardsailing. Winds are sporadic at other locations. Some lakes are closed to this activity. Consult a park information centre for details.

Swimming

The water in lakes and rivers in the Rockies is cold. The most popular outdoor swimming holes are Annette Lake, Edith Lake and Horseshoe Lake in Jasper, and Johnson Lake, Cascade Ponds and Herbert Lake in Banff. There is an indoor pool at Jasper, and outdoor pools at Waterton Park and at Radium Hot Springs pools.

Fishing

A century ago, many lakes and rivers in the Rockies teemed with fish. However, the glacially fed waters are cold and low in nutrients. Fish grow slowly. Over-fishing has reduced both the quantity of fish and the average size of individual specimens. To com-

By the 1920s, the automobile had supplanted the pack horse and train as the principal means of transport in the Rockies

pensate, some lakes have been stocked. This practice satisfies anglers, but the introduction of non-native species has threatened the viability of some native fish stocks.

Various species of trout and char comprise most of the catch in the Rockies. The most popular roadside lakes for fishing are Minnewanka, Emerald, Wapta, Bow, Patricia, Pyramid, Maligne and Waterton. Consult a park information centre to determine open seasons for the waters you would like to fish, catch limits and other restrictions that may apply. A national park fishing licence is required. A provincial fishing licence is required in the provincial parks.

A successful day of fishing is not necessarily measured by the size of the catch. Fishing offers the chance to relax in spectacular surroundings with the opportunity to view birds and other wildlife. In acknowledgement of the dwindling fish populations in most lakes, many anglers now use barbless hooks and practise catch and release.

Trail Riding

Horseback travel has been a traditional means of access and transportation in the Rockies for more than a century. Horse use results in the degeneration of trail surfaces. In recent years, the mixture of horse traffic and foot traffic on some trails has led to much complaint from the hiking faction. Nonetheless, commercial outfitters offer day rides and pack trips at several locations in the Rockies. To alleviate conflicts, these concessions operate on specific trails. Horse-hiker separations have been installed in some areas where trails are shared. Sleigh rides are offered at several locations in winter. Public horse use is allowed on some trails. Contact a park information centre.

Cycling

Bicycle touring is very popular in the Rockies. Two short tours in particular are considered classics: the Golden Triangle, and the Icefields Parkway.

The Golden Triangle uses Highway 1, B.C. Highway 95 and the Kootenay Parkway to make a triangular circuit that crosses the continental divide twice. The triangle requires three days and has some good hills. It can be ridden clockwise or counter-clockwise, beginning at Banff, Castle Junction, Lake Louise, Golden or Radium.

Wide shoulders, spectacular scenery and many campgrounds and hostels combine to make the Icefields Parkway one of the best cycle touring roads in the world. Three to five days suffice for a one-way trip with some sightseeing. The hills are steeper but shorter if biked north to south. Arranging transportation at either end of the route will necessitate two vehicles, or bus travel. If you have the time, you can simplify logistics by biking the Icefields Parkway both ways.

Jasper and Banff townsites are well suited to exploration on bicycle. You can take an enjoyable day ride from Banff along the Bow Valley Parkway towards Lake Louise. Kananaskis Country also offers the combination of first-rate bicycling and fine scenery. Bike shops in Banff, Canmore, Lake Louise and Jasper will be glad to assist you in planning your cycling trip in the Rockies.

Mountain Biking

Mountain biking is permitted on specific trails only. These include many of the old fireroads. Most "no-biking" trails are now clearly posted, but check with a park information centre to ensure that biking is allowed before you go on your trip. Restrictions also apply in the provincial parks.

Table of Hikes

Walks	Half-Day Hikes	Full-Day Hikes	Overnight Hikes
BANFF	**BANFF**	**BANFF**	**BANFF**
Tunnel Mtn. Hoodoos	Johnston Canyon	Ink Pots	Skoki
Bankhead	Parker Ridge	C-Level Cirque	Egypt Lake
Fenland Trail	Bow Lake/Bow Glacier	Hillsdale Slide	**JASPER**
Bow Falls	Tunnel Mountain	Bourgeau Lake	Skyline Trail
Vermilion Lakes	Sundance Canyon	Plain of Six Glaciers	Brazeau Loop
Johnson Lake	Lake Agnes	Paradise Valley	Tonquin Valley
Moraine Lake Rockpile	Little Beehive	Boulder Pass	Fryatt Valley
Moraine Lake shoreline	Muleshoe	Boom Lake	**YOHO**
Lake Louise shoreline	Stony Squaw	Sunset Lookout	Yoho Valley
Bow Summit	Consolation Lakes	Glacier Lake	Little Yoho Valley
Stewart Canyon	**KOOTENAY**	Sarbach Lookout	**KOOTENAY**
The Marsh Trail	Stanley Glacier	**KOOTENAY**	The Rockwall
The Discovery Trail	Juniper Trail	Floe Lake	**MT. ROBSON**
Mistaya Canyon	Redstreak	Kindersley Pass	Berg Lake
Warden lake	Cobb Lake	**YOHO**	**MT. ASSINIBOINE**
KOOTENAY	Dog Lake	Hamilton Lake	All trails leading to
Marble Canyon	**YOHO**	Wapta Highline	Lake Magog
Paint Pots	Emerald Basin	Iceline	
Redstreak Loop	Emerald Lake shoreline	Twin Falls	
Sinclair Canyon	Sherbrooke Lake	Yoho Glacier	
Fireweed Trail	Paget Lookout	Mt. Hunter	
YOHO	Ross Lake	**JASPER**	
Emerald Lake shoreline	Leanchoil Hoodoos	Devona Lookout	
Hamilton Falls	Wapta Falls	Sulphur Skyline	
Centennial Trail	**JASPER**	The Palisade	
Walk-in-the-Past	Maligne Canyon: 5th	Maligne Canyon: 6th	
Spiral Tunnel	Bridge	Bridge	
The Great Divide	Cavell Meadows	The Whistlers	
Deerlodge	Whistler Summit	Wilcox Pass	
JASPER	Valley of the Five Lakes	Opal Hills	
Athbasca Glacier	Wabasso Lake	Bald Hills	
Miette Hot Springs	Buck and Osprey Lakes	Geraldine Lakes	
Sunwapta Falls	Old Fort Point	**ROBSON**	
Athabasca Falls	Stanley Falls	Kinney Lake	
Buck and Osprey Lakes	Geraldine Lookout		
Path of the Glacier			
Schäffer Viewpoint			
Maligne Canyon			
Annette Lake			
Moose Lake			
Mona and Lorraine Lakes			
Pocahontas			
Lac Beauvert			

Backpacking routes are described in *Classic Hikes in the Canadian Rockies, An Altitude SuperGuide* . There are more than 100 short walks and hikes in the Rockies that can be completed in less than a day. These are described in *Walks and Easy Hikes in the Canadian Rockies, An Altitude SuperGuide.*

Hikers relax on Wilcox Pass overlooking Athabasca Glacier

Climber on ridge of Mt. Victoria

When mountain biking, please stay on the trails, and be particularly alert for hikers, wildlife, fallen trees, washouts and other hazards. Carry a repair kit, extra clothing and food. Wearing a helmet is a good idea, too.

Mountaineering

Climbing mountains was the original recreational pursuit in the Rockies, and continues to be popular today. The variety of terrain and the scope of routes varies from walk-ups to demanding north faces in remote settings—the Rockies have it all. The benchmark elevation in the Rockies is 3,049 m. More than 700 peaks exceed this elevation.

Because most of the rock in the Rockies is sedimentary, it is crumbly—not a desired

characteristic for mountaineering. As a result, many mountaineering routes incorporate glaciers, snow and ice. Mountaineering in the vicinity of Lake Louise and Columbia Icefield focuses on snow and ice routes. Other high mountains that lure many climbers are Mt. Robson, Mt. Edith Cavell and Mt. Assiniboine.

Winter mountaineering is popular. Many mountains lend themselves to ski ascents and descents—particularly those on the Wapta, Waputik and Columbia icefields. The Alpine Club of Canada administers an icefield hut system that can be used for multi-day ski mountaineering tours. In winter, the abundance of frozen waterfalls makes the Rockies an international mecca for the pursuit of waterfall ice climbing.

Rock climbing on steep cliffs is popular on Yamnuska Mountain, Cascade Mountain, Mt. Rundle, Castle Mountain

and in the vicinity of Lake Louise. (Most rock climbers are not intent on reaching a summit, but in scaling difficulties encountered following a particular line to the top of a cliff.) Guidebooks to these areas are available. Check at Mountain Magic or Monod Sports in Banff, or Wilson Sports in Lake Louise for the latest news concerning the local crags.

What about the walk-ups? There are many mountains that have a rough trail leading to the summit. Most of these can be climbed by anyone who is reasonably fit and well prepared. Ask at a park information centre about trails suited to your experience and ability. The voluntary safety registration system is available to all climbers and mountaineers.

Professional mountain guides are available in Banff, Lake Louise, Field, Canmore, Jasper and Golden. These men and women can be hired by almost anyone determined to add the thrill of one of the Rockies' high alpine summits to their vacation memories. Call the Association of Canadian Mountain Guides, (403) 678-2885.

Horseback riding

Golfing at the Banff Springs Hotel Golf Course

Golf

There are public golf courses at the Banff Springs Hotel, Jasper Park Lodge, Waterton, Kananaskis Village, Canmore, Golden, Wintergreen, Radium and Fairmont. Contact the individual courses for details regarding tee times and green fees. The elevation in the Rockies will add distance to your drive.

Downhill Skiing

There are four downhill ski areas in the Rocky Mountain parks and two in Kananaskis Country. The oldest ski area is Sunshine Village on the continental divide southwest of Banff. Sunshine Village is reached by gondola, from which 12 lifts provide access to 61 marked runs. Sunshine's terrain is 20 per cent novice, 60 per cent intermediate, and 20 per cent expert. It is open the longest of any ski hill in Canada—early November to the May long weekend on average. On-hill accommodation is available.

Skiing at Banff Mt. Norquay originated in the 1920s. The steep mountainside has been used for ski jumping competitions and World Cup events. Norquay's

reputation as an expert ski hill changed with the addition of intermediate runs cleared in 1989. Night skiing is available three nights a week. Mt. Norquay hosts the first leg of the Banff Mountain Madness relay race during the annual winter carnival in late January.

The Lake Louise Ski Area is the largest in the Rockies, with three day lodges and 12 lifts servicing more than 40 marked runs on three mountainsides. Many runs feature snowmaking.

Shuttle service is available from most Banff and Lake Louise hotels to these ski areas. You can purchase ski vacation packages that include lift tickets, instruction, accommodation and local transportation.

The 52 marked runs at Marmot Basin in Jasper are serviced by six lifts. Terrain is divided equally between novice, intermediate and expert. Local hotels participate in ski packages, and transportation to Marmot is available from Jasper.

Nakiska at Mt. Allan in Kananaskis Country was the site of alpine skiing events during the 1988 Winter Olympic Games. Six lifts pro-

vide access to more than 20 runs. Seventy per cent of the terrain is intermediate. Accommodation and services are available nearby at Kananaskis Village.

Farther south in K-Country is Fortress Mountain. Seven lifts service terrain that is 20 per cent novice, 50 per cent intermediate and 30 per cent expert.

All these ski areas offer lessons, equipment rentals, sales and repairs. Equipment rentals are also available at many locations in Banff, Lake Louise and Jasper, including some of the major hotels.

Cross-country Skiing

The Rocky Mountain parks feature many cross-country ski trails that offer a refreshing way to experience winter. Most of the trails travel the major valley bottoms. In several areas, loop systems that are regularly groomed have been developed. These include Johnson Lake, Banff Springs Golf Course, Sundance Canyon, Lake Louise, Pipestone, Whitehorn, Emerald Lake, Pyramid Bench and Maligne Lake. Most skiers will find enough skiing to fill a

Snowboarding in the Canadian Rockies

You can rent cross-country ski equipment at most sports stores and at some of the major hotels. Dogs are not allowed on cross-country ski trails.

Other Activities

In some years, lakes in the Rockies freeze before the first significant snowfall and become huge skating rinks. The Vermilion Lakes, Lake Louise, Lake Minnewanka and Talbot Lake are the easiest to reach. You can also skate on the Bow River upstream from Banff. Chateau Lake Louise maintains rinks on Lake Louise until thaws impair the quality of the ice. Public indoor skating is available at arenas in Banff and Jasper.

In the national parks, vehicles must stay on designated roads. Dirt bikes, ATVs and

day at any one of these areas. Cross-country skiing is best between mid-December and late February.

Many of the summer hiking trails also serve as cross-country trails, but most involve travel in avalanche terrain.

Skiing these trails should not be attempted by inexperienced or unprepared parties, and even then, not without due regard for conditions. Obtain an avalanche forecast and other pertinent information from a park information centre.

What to Wear and Carry in the Rockies

Activity	Summer (May–September)	Winter (October–April)
Sightseeing by car	Raincoat, extra sweater, hat, gloves, sturdy shoes, sunglasses, food, water, first aid kit, map	Winter boots, winter coat, hat, gloves or mitts, scarf, extra sweater, sunglasses, extra food. Also carry in or on your vehicle: hot thermos, blankets, candle, winter tires, flashlight, booster cables, shovel, map, extra gasoline, matches
Day hikes	Hiking shoes or boots, full rain suit, sun hat, extra sweater, gloves or mitts, sunscreen, sunglasses, day pack, food, water, first aid kit, insect repellent, map	See cross-country skiing
Walks around town	Walking shoes, raincoat or umbrella, sunglasses, gloves	Winter boots, winter coat, hat, gloves or mitts, scarf, sunglasses
Cross-country skiing	Winter activity	Layered clothing, gloves or mitts, hat, scarf, sunglasses, food, hot thermos, first aid and repair kits, waxes, map

49

snowmobiles are not permitted.

The sports desks at many of the larger hotels provide contacts for seasonal activities not mentioned above. These include dog sledding and sleigh rides. Inquire at park information centres and at the Whyte Museum in Banff about special seasonal and historic interpretive events. These might involve a walk around town, along a trail or up a mountain.

One Climate, Lots of Weather

"Climate" describes the long-term averages of temperature, precipitation, wind, and humidity for a particular area. "Weather" describes the sunshine or storm you are experiencing at any given moment.

The Canadian Rockies lie in the path of a southwesterly airflow that brings moisture-laden weather systems inland from the Pacific Ocean. There are many mountain ranges between the Rockies and the Pacific coast. Being last in line for the precipitation released by these systems, the Rockies receive a good share, but less than you might expect.

Because of the Rockies' inland location, the humidity is usually low. The thin, dry air does not hold heat well. Nighttime temperatures often plummet. Altitude and glacial ice have a cooling effect on air masses passing over the range. At higher elevation the onset of autumn is hastened, and winter lingers. Above 2,000 m, most of the precipitation falls as snow.

The Rockies' climate in a nutshell: the air is cool and dry, summers are short, and annual precipitation is moderate. However, mountain ranges create local weather in many ways. Few are the days when the weather is consistent throughout the range. Many local weather effects can be traced to the influence of glaciers, large lakes or nearby high mountains.

What to Expect

There is no sure bet for timing a visit to the Rockies to coincide with good weather. However, the following summary may help.

Spring is usually underway throughout the Rockies by mid-May. Temperatures still reach below freezing at night, and valley-bottom daytime highs are in the 12 °C to 20 °C range. The May holiday weekend is statistically the best good-weather long weekend of the year, and is often part of a two- or three-week stretch of sunshine that brings green to the trees and the brown of spring runoff to the recently thawed rivers.

June is frequently a poor month, although it may begin well. As pioneer outfitter Fred Stephens commented, it can rain "seven days out of six." Temperatures are often cooler than in May. This pattern ends toward the beginning of July, when the weather improves greatly and summer arrives. A significant snowfall often occurs around July 15. After this, summer returns in earnest. Until the first week of August, daytime highs can reach to 30 °C and above. In recent years, thunderstorms have been increasingly common during this time.

Some years, a snowfall around August 12th to 17th breaks this pattern, and the remainder of the month sees a mixture of weather. In other years, the hot weather continues, although frost returns at night. In years of really poor weather, the summer months have been known to pass with barely a week of good weather between them.

The first week of September will often bring a heavy snowfall and a chill in the air, both night and day. Ten sopping centimetres of snow on the ground is not uncommon at

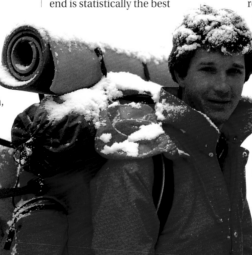

A hiker experiences unpredictable mountain weather

Lake Louise at this time. Unsettled weather continues until the arrival (usually!) of Indian summer. Beginning any time from mid-September to early October, this glorious stretch of weather features cloudless, warm days and cool, crisp nights, autumn colours, no bugs and no crowds. As a drawback, firesmoke from slash-burning on provincial forestry lands to the west sometimes obscures the views. In a good year, Indian summer may last for six weeks (it did in 1987 and in 1988). When it's over, there's no mistaking it, and the cheerless, dark cold of early winter begins.

Winter visitors to the Rockies should be prepared for harsh conditions. January daytime highs are commonly –15 °C, but there might be one or two cold snaps a winter that push the mercury to –40 °C day and night, for a week at a time. Wind chills in townsites and at ski hills can be severe. Heavy snowfalls are no longer as common as in the past. Twenty centimetres now qualifies as a good dump. Curiously, the heaviest snowfalls often descend from the thinnest clouds—with the sun visible through the gray.

The length of daylight is

Laser sailing on Lake Minnewanka

short from November to January—less than nine hours. For six months of the year, snow blocks access to many of the popular viewpoints. With all the lakes and rivers frozen, the landscape appears very different. Some say the Rockies are more beautiful in winter than at any other time.

In summary, to a traveller in the Canadian Rockies attempting to guess what weather lies ahead, the best advice is: "Be prepared for anything!" and "If you don't like the weather, come back in five minutes!"

As much as we may be accustomed to good weather elsewhere and looking forward

to seeing the Rockies for day after day under sunny skies, clouds, storms, changeability and low temperatures are characteristic of this range. The climate plays a key role in shaping the landscape and the environment. Were it not for the harsh climate, many of the wonders we have travelled to see would not exist.

Temperatures in the table below have been rounded to the nearest whole number. Precipitation includes the total rainfall and snowfall converted to its water equivalent (10 mm of snow equals 1 mm of rain). The month with the most hours of strong sunshine in the Rockies is July; the month with the least is January. Jasper townsite has the longest recorded frost-free period: 127 days. Lake Louise and Columbia Icefield have experienced years when there was no significant frost-free period. Banff has an average of 10 thunder days a year, while Jasper has seven thunder days a year. Comparative data for Waterton townsite is not available. ∆

Weather Data

Location	Mean Temp °C	Jan Low °C	July Hi °C	Precip mm	Snow cm	Frost Days	Fair Days
Calgary	3	–18	23	424	153	201	245
Banff	3	–17	22	471	251	221	216
Lake Louise	0	–22	21	684	418	271	236
Field	3	–15	24	557	323	no data	264
Columbia Icefield	–2	–19	15	882	643	no data	208
Jasper	3	–18	23	431	152	213	223
Edmonton	2	–22	22	467	138	212	230
Kootenay	2	–18	24	503	184	no data	201

Kananaskis Country

H ighway 1 (the Trans-Canada Highway) is Canada's principal east-west road, and is the longest paved highway in the world. Design and construction of the Rocky Mountain section of this road began in the mid-1950s. It was completed through the Rockies in 1958, and across

Rogers Pass in British Columbia's Selkirk Mountains, in 1962.

Highway 1 is not a superhighway of consistent standard from coast to coast, but an amalgamation of different roads under different jurisdictions. Nowhere is this more evident than in the section through the Rockies. The four-lane thoroughfare you follow to the mountains from Calgary dwindles to two lanes beyond Banff townsite.

For most of the year, Highway 1 can handle the traffic volume. But during peak hours in June, July and August it becomes very congested. More than 30 percent of the traffic is commercial trucks. The mix of commercial traffic and sightseers, on different schedules with different objec-

tives, is not a good one. You should make safe driving your priority. If something catches your eye, or if you want to check the *SuperGuide* for information, stop safely on the highway shoulder where permitted, or in a pull-out.

There is much to stop and admire. The 270 km drive through the Rockies from Calgary to Golden includes a succession of magnificent landscapes: the open vistas of the plains and foothills; the dramatic wall of peaks at the mountain front; the Bow Valley; the lofty, glacier-capped mountains near Lake Louise; the historic Kicking Horse Pass; and the Kicking Horse Canyon. All this tremendous scenery is subject to the ever-changing play of mountain light. Few sections of road in Canada combine such variety and visual appeal in so short a distance.

The Plains and Foothills

Calgary is at an elevation of 610 m and is often called the "Foothills City," although it lies on the interior plains. The foothills begin at Jumping-pound Creek, 38 km west of Calgary on Highway 1. The foothills are the easternmost

geological manifestation of the Rockies. They formed during the last phase of mountain building, between 85 million and 55 million years ago.

Most of the land adjacent to Highway 1 in the foothills is agricultural. The principal use is ranching. Oil and gas exploration and some logging also take place. From hills near the Cochrane turnoff (Highway 22 junction) and farther west, you obtain inspiring views to the front ranges of the Rockies. At 1,410 m, the crest of Scott Lake Hill west of the Cochrane turnoff is the second highest point on Highway 1 in Canada.

There are many glacial landforms at roadside in the foothills – kames, drumlins and eskers. These are mounds and ridges of moraine, left behind when ice age glaciers retreated from this area.

Chinook Country

The mountain front is typically a windy place. The Bow Valley funnels winds toward the foothills through a break known as The Gap, near Exshaw. This area is also frequented by a warm winter wind called a chinook (shih-NOOK).

Chinook means "snow eater." The wind can raise local

left: King Canyon

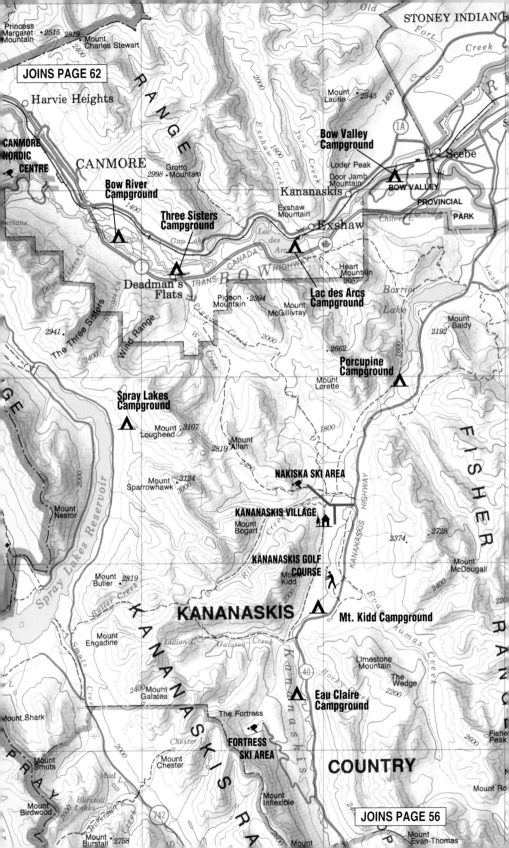

JOINS PAGE 62

STONEY INDIAN

Old

Fort

Creek

Princess
Margaret • 2515 2819
Mountain
Mount
Charles Stewart 2400

Harvie Heights

Mount • 2545
Laurie

1A

CANMORE
NORDIC
CENTRE

CANMORE

Grotto
Mountain 2998

1400

Bow River
Campground

Loder Peak

Seebe

Door Jamb
Mountain

Bow Valley
Campground

Kananaskis

BOW VALLEY

Three Sisters
Campground

Gap Lake

Exshaw
Mountain

Exshaw

PROVINCIAL

PARK

Chilver L.

Deadman's
Flats

Lac
des
Arcs

Heart
Mountain
2057

Lac des Arcs
Campground

Barrier

Lake

2941

The Three Sisters

2400

Wind Range

Pigeon
Mountain • 2394

Mount
McGillivray

2000

2662

Mount
Lorette

Mount
Baldy 2192

Porcupine
Campground

Spray Lakes
Campground

Mount
Lougheed 3107

Mount
Allan 2819

1800

FISHER

Mount
Nestor

Mount
Sparrowhawk 3124

NAKISKA SKI AREA

KANANASKIS VILLAGE

Mount
Bogart

2728

2374

Mount
McDougall

Mount
Buller 2819

KANANASKIS GOLF
COURSE

Mount
Kidd

Spray Lakes Reservoir

KANANASKIS

Butler Creek

Mount
Engadine

Lillian L.

Galatea Creek

Mt. Kidd Campground

2400

RANGE

2400 Mount
Galatea

40

Limestone
Mountain

The
Wedge 2200

Eau Claire
Campground

Mount Shark

The Fortress

SPRAY

Mount
Smuts

2000

Chester L.

Mount
Chester

FORTRESS
SKI AREA

Fisher
Peak

COUNTRY

742

Mud L.

Burstall
Lakes

Mount
Birdwood

Mount
Inflexible

Mount Ro

Mount
Burstall • 2758

Mount
Evan-Thomas

JOINS PAGE 56

Nakiska Village

temperatures as much as 40 °C in twenty minutes. A chinook results when warm air from a Pacific storm system breaks into the cold air of a high pressure mass situated over the foothills and plains. The storm system sheds its moisture west of the Rockies, and the dry air is compressed and heated as it descends rapidly to the ground on the eastern slopes. Chinooks are heralded by a cloud known as a chinook arch, which spans the length of the southern mountain front. At the same time, lenticular clouds often form over the mountains to the west.

In a typical winter, there will be 20 chinook days at the mountain front. The effects of chinooks that last several days will be felt as far east as Medicine Hat in southeastern Alberta. During a chinook, the weather in the mountains is often unsettled.

Lodgepole pine trees that grow in areas frequented by chinooks are subject to redbelt. The warm winds dry out the pine needles when the sap is flowing too slowly to replenish them. The foliage subsequently turns brown, but redbelt does not often kill the tree.

The combined effects of local windiness and chinooks keeps snow accumulation low at the mountain front. Elk, bighorn sheep and deer depend on grasslands here to survive the winter.

Kananaskis Country

Kananaskis Country is 4,000 square kilometres of provincial land that lies south of Highway 1 between Morley and Canmore. Unlike the nearby national parks, where resource extraction and most motorized recreation are prohibited, Kananaskis Country is a "multi-use" area. It incorporates three provincial parks, as well as natural areas, forestry reserves, grazing lands, mining and petroleum leaseholds, a resort and recreational developments. Kananaskis was a Cree native, reportedly struck by an axe but not killed.

Provincial funds have been lavished on Kananaskis Country. Outdoor enthusiasts will find a range of opportunities and well-equipped facilities. There are more than 3,000 auto-accessible campsites in approximately 20 campgrounds. Reservations can be made at many of these. The backcountry features more than 30 campgrounds for hikers and trail riders.

Bow Valley Provincial Park is on Highway 1X, just north of Highway 1. There are half a dozen short walking trails in the park, along with picnic areas and a campground. The impressive cliffs of Yamnuska Mountain loom to the north. *Yamnuska* is a Stoney word that means "flat-faced mountain."

The most popular destination in Kananaskis Country is the 500 square kilometre Peter Lougheed Provincial Park, at Kananaskis Lakes. The park visitor centre is on Highway 40, 56 km south of Highway 1. With its varied and accessible terrain, the park appeals to hikers, mountaineers, cyclists, mountain bikers, trail riders, skiers, boaters, campers and fishermen. There are facilities for the handicapped.

En route to Peter Lougheed Park, Highway 40 passes Kananaskis Village, a year-round resort that features three hotels, tennis courts, two 18-hole golf courses and an RV park. In winter, downhill skiers have two facilities to choose from: nearby Nakiska at Mount Allan (the site of alpine skiing events during the 1988 Winter Olympic Games), and Fortress Mountain.

Also in K-Country is the Canmore Nordic Centre, the site of nordic skiing events during the 1988 Winter Olympics. The centre is just south of Canmore on the Smith-Dorrien/ Spray Road. It features 56 km of cross country ski trails. In summer, you can use the trails for hiking, mountain biking and interpretive walks.

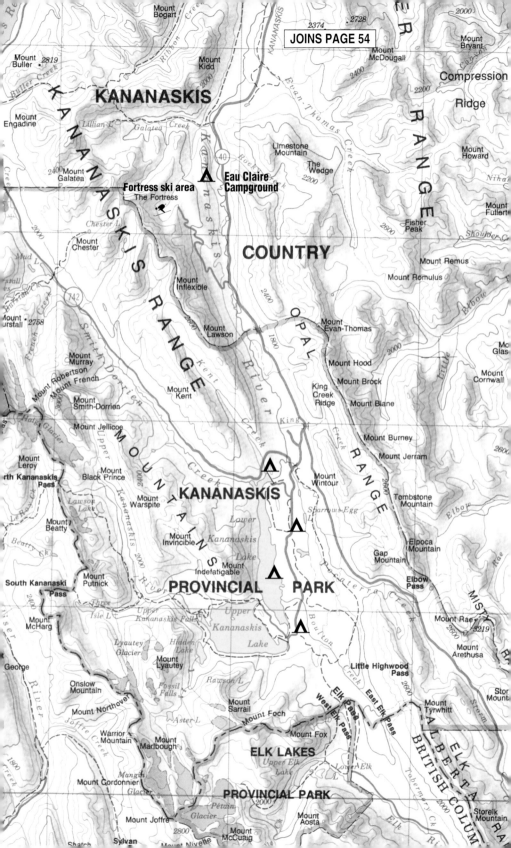

Continuing south from the Nordic Centre, the Smith-Dorrien/Spray Road climbs steeply between Chinaman's Peak and Mt. Rundle to the Spray Lakes Reservoir. This area was formerly within Banff National Park, but was removed in 1930 to allow a hydro-electric development that involved diverting and damming the headwaters of the Spray River. The Smith-Dorrien/Spray Road eventually leads to Peter Lougheed Provincial Park. En route there are many hiking trails.

More information on opportunities in Kananaskis Country is available from the Bow Valley Provincial Park headquarters, or by writing to the address provided in the Contacts section. For a complete guide to Kananaskis Country, see *Kananaskis, An Altitude SuperGuide* by Ward Cameron.

Lac des Arcs

Highway 1 makes an S-curve along the shore of Lac des Arcs. When William Cornelius

Mt. Kidd

Van Horne, general manager of the Canadian Pacific Railway (CPR), first saw Lac des Arcs in 1883, he was favourably impressed. He immediately suggested that the area be set aside as a park, and promised to "build a fine house on that island in the lake." The Department of the Interior complied, and surveyed the surroundings so that the CPR might proceed with the development of a resort.

The next time Van Horne passed the lake, he was more familiar with the merits of Banff as a potential CPR resort. A typical mountain-front windstorm was blowing at Lac des Arcs. The setting had lost

its appeal, and the issue was never raised again. It's just as well—a "fine house" the size of the Banff Springs Hotel would never have fit on the tiny island! Those in the know thereafter jokingly referred to the lake as "Van Horne's park."

Lac des Arcs was eventually protected in Banff National Park when the park reached its maximum size in 1902. However, in 1930, the Bow Valley east of Canmore was deleted from the park so that hydro-electric developments and mining could take place. Quarrying of limestone, cement operations and milling of magnesite continue near Lac des Arcs today. Tundra swans stop here on their spring and autumn migrations.

Lac des Arcs is French for "lake of the bows." Natives found Douglas fir saplings suitable for bow-making along the banks of the river. Thus, the Bow River and this lake were named. Δ

Eagle Flyway

In 1992, ornithologist Dr. Peter Sherrington discovered a major golden eagle flyway that crosses the Bow Valley near Canmore. The spring migration takes place between late March and mid-May, and the fall migration between late September and early November. During these migrations, Dr. Sherrington estimates that 6,000 eagles pass over the area. As many as 845 eagles have been counted on a single day. The eagles are travelling between wintering grounds in the tropics and summer nesting grounds in north-central Canada. Some of these birds may even be travelling across the Bering Strait to Siberia. The eagles travel at speeds of up to 120 km per hour. Fifteen other species of raptors have been seen using the flyway.

Canmore

Canmore with the Three Sisters in the background

As with many towns in the Canadian Rockies, the origin of Canmore is linked to the construction of the CPR, which reached here in 1883. But unlike some other railway towns that quickly came and went, outcrops of coal in the base of Mt. Rundle immediately guaranteed Canmore's future. The coal was mined to fire the railway's locomotives, and the town's population grew to 450 by 1888.

However, the discovery of oil in southern Alberta in 1914 largely sealed the fate of Canmore's coal industry. Most of the mines closed by 1922, but operations at one seam continued until 1979. Since then, Canmore has made the transformation from industrial town to residential community and visitor centre.

What has remained constant over this period of change, how-ever, is Canmore's pride in its signature landmark: The Three Sisters. Originally called The Three Nuns, these peaks are unofficially known by locals as Faith, Hope and Charity.

In 1988, Canmore was the site of the cross-country ski events of the Winter Olympic Games. The Canmore Nordic Centre was built for this momentous occasion, and has since hosted a number of international nordic skiing, dog sledding and mountain biking competitions. This facility is a veritable playground for competitive athletes and those who ski and bike for pleasure. Its 56 km of trails are frequented year round, and in winter, 2.5 km of track-set ski terrain is even lit in the evening.

Canmore is known for its thriving art community. A number of shops and galleries feature the ceramics, jewellry, paintings and sculpture of local artisans, many of whose works are displayed in booths at the Canmore Folk Festival.

Each year, Canmore hosts this event on the first weekend in August. Musicians, puppeteers and clowns perform throughout the long weekend for crowds that gather on blankets in front of the stages. Contributing to the appeal of this colourful atmosphere are the food vendors, whose appetizing menus feature the most tempting dishes from local restaurants.

During the September long weekend, the annual international Highland Games are held, when thousands of musicians, Scottish dancers and visitors gather in the highlands of the Canadian Rockies. Visitors can enjoy music during the battle of the bands,

Canmore

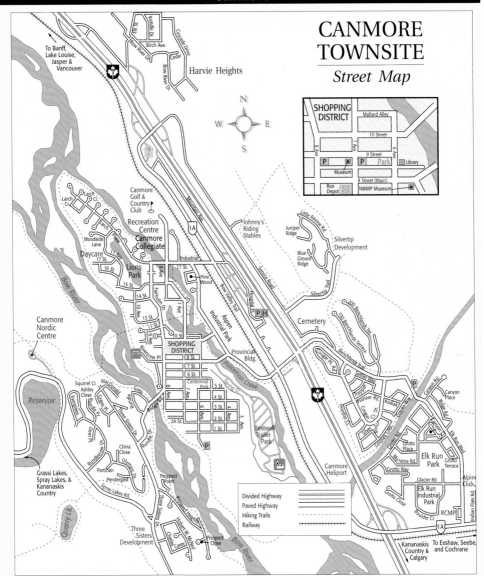

CANMORE TOWNSITE
Street Map

dance performances and traditional competitions such as caber tossing and the tug of war.

The Canmore Centennial Museum, established in 1984 and opened to the public in 1988, traces the history of Canmore's development since its days as a mining town. Its mining artifacts,

archival photographs and newspaper clippings were gathered from Canmore residents, and some items date back to the late 1800s. Also featured in this museum is a historical doll collection. Visitors will recognize toys from their past among the 1,300 dolls displayed here. The Olympic

Collection is frequented by those who are nostalgic for the exciting period that marked Canmore as an international tourist destination. The Olympic Collection is comprised of official '88 Olympics clothing, photographs signed by various athletes, medals, newspaper articles and memorabilia.

Banff National Park

T he first national park in Canada and the third created in the world (after Yellowstone in the U.S., and Royal in Australia) resulted from a dispute over hot springs discovered at what is now known as The Cave and Basin National Historic Site. These springs were well known to

natives and have been visited by at least two American prospectors in 1874, one of whom had wintered in a shack nearby. But it was the rediscovery of the springs on November 8, 1883 that set the national park ball rolling.

Three railway workers stumbled onto the springs while prospecting at the end of the construction season of the CPR. There was no plumbing in the Wild West, and hot water was a valuable com-

SuperGuide Recommendations

Sights/Attractions
- Mt. Rundle from Vermilion Lakes
- Cave and Basin
- Banff Springs Hotel
- Bow Falls
- Hoodoos Viewpoint
- Banff Information Centre
- Whyte Museum of the Canadian Rockies
- Luxton Museum of the Plains Indian
- Banff Centre Arts Festival
- Sulphur Mountain Gondola

Hikes/Activities
- Fenland Trail
- Tunnel Mountain Summit
- Marsh Trail & Sundance Canyon
- Trail at the Cave and Basin
- Bow River from downtown to the Banff Springs Hotel
- Golf at the Banff Springs Hotel
- Upper Hot Springs
- Horse carriage tour of Banff

modity. The trio's inept handling of the discovery, abetted by double-dealing and government bureaucracy, got them into legal hot water. Many others filed claims and counterclaims to "ownership" of the springs.

The Canadian government eventually convened a hearing to settle the dispute. Some parties that had claimed an interest in the springs were compensated for the expenditures they had made in "improvements," and on November 28, 1885, the springs and a surrounding area of 26 square kilometres were set aside as a federal reserve—the forerunner of Banff National Park.

In 1886, George Stewart, the surveyor appointed to identify the boundaries of the Banff Hot Springs Reservation, recommended that additional area should be added. His advice was quickly heeded, and in June of 1887, Rocky Mountains Park was established. Stewart served as its superintendent for eleven years. The area around Lake Louise was designated as a forest park reserve in 1892, and incorporated into Rocky Mountains Park in 1902 when the park reached its maximum size. The park officially became

Banff National Park in 1930.

The other reserves that later became national parks in the Rockies were: Yoho, established 1886; Waterton Lakes, established 1895; and Jasper, established 1907. Kootenay National Park was proclaimed in 1920. Today, Banff National Park includes 6641 square kilometres of land. It is part of the four mountain park block that covers 20,160 square kilometres. In 1985, the Rocky Mountain national parks were proclaimed a UNESCO World Heritage Site. The adjacent B.C. provincial parks of Mt. Assiniboine, Mt. Robson and Hamber were added to the designation in 1990. More than nine million people now enter Banff National Park each year. Almost half of these people stop in the park.

The impressive cliffs of Mt. Rundle form the western wall of the Bow Valley for 12 km between Canmore and Banff. These cliffs contain many cirques and avalanche paths, and are nearly 1.6 km high at one point. The cliffs comprise the sequence of sedimentary formations (Palliser limestone, Banff Shale, Rundle limestone) that also forms many other massive cliffs in the front ranges.

Mt. Rundle was named by

left: Banff Springs Hotel, Bow River

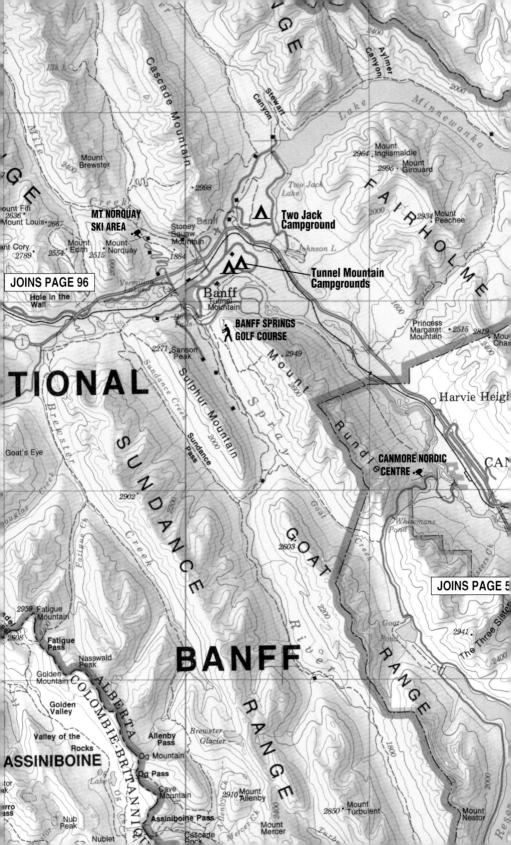

JOINS PAGE 96

JOINS PAGE 5

MT NORQUAY
SKI AREA

Two Jack
Campground

Tunnel Mountain
Campgrounds

BANFF SPRINGS
GOLF COURSE

CANMORE NORDIC
CENTRE

Cascade Mountain

Elk L.

Mile

Mount
Brewster

Mount Fifi
2636

Mount Louis • 2667

nt Cory
2789

Mount
Edith
2554

Mount
Norquay
2515

Stoney
Squaw
Mountain

1884

• 2998

Banff

Two Jack
Lake

Aylmer
Canyon

Stewart
Canyon

Lake

Minnewanka

Mount
Inglismaldie
2964

2995 Mount
Girouard

FAIRHOLME

2934 Mount
Peechee

Johnson L.

Princess
Margaret
Mountain • 2515 2819

Mou
Char

Harvie Heig

CAN

Vermilion

Banff
Tunnel
Mountain

Bow Falls

2271 Sanson
Peak

• 2949

Mount
Spray

Mount
Rundle

Whitemans
Pond

TIONAL

SUNDANCE

Sulphur Mountain

Sundance Creek

Sundance
Pass

2902

Goat's Eye

Brewster Creek

Douglas Creek

2959 Fatigue
Mountain

2608

Fatigue
Pass

Fatigue Ck

Nasswald
Peak

Golden
Mountain

Golden
Valley

ALBERTA

COLOMBIE-BRITANNIQ

ASSINIBOINE

Valley of the
Rocks

Og Lake

Allenby
Pass

Og Mountain

Og Pass

Cave
Mountain

Nub Peak

Nublet

Assiniboine Pass

Cascade
Rock

2910 Mount
Allenby

Brewster Glacier

Allenby Ck

Og Pass

BANFF

GOAT

2603

Goat

Creek

Goat
Pond

2941

The Three Sister

RANGE

RANGE

RANGE

Mount
Mercer

2850 Mount
Turbulent

Mount
Nestor

2000

2400

1800

2400

2200

2000

Hole in the
Wall

Banff To Do List

Sights
- Banff Springs Hotel
- Bankhead
- Bow Falls
- Bow Lake
- Bow Summit
- Cave and Basin National Historic Site 762-1566
- Fenland Trail
- Lake Minnewanka
- Sulphur Mountain Gondola 762-2523
- Sundance Canyon
- Tunnel Mountain
- Hoodoos

Entertainment
- Banff Park Museum 762-1558
- Banff Springs Bowling Centre 762-6892
- Interpretive Programs 762-1500, 522-3833
- Library 762-2661, 678-2468
- Luxton Museum of the Plains Indian 762-2388
- Movies: Lux Theatre 762-8595
- Music: Banff Centre 762-6300
- Natural History Museum 762-4747
- Theatre: Banff Centre 762-6300
- Whyte Museum of the Canadian Rockies 762-2291

Swimming
- Solace Spa, Banff Springs Hotel 762-2211
- Upper Hot Springs 762-2056
- Johnson Lake (in season)
- Cascade Ponds (in season)

Shopping
- Banff Avenue, Bear Street, Banff Springs Hotel, major hotel lobbies

Dining
- See reference section

For Other Activities
- See reference section

The east gate of Banff National Park

James Hector for Robert T. Rundle, Methodist missionary to the Stoneys of the Bow Valley in 1844 and 1847. Rundle did an excellent job teaching the Stoneys. More than a decade later, they still said grace at their meals and sang hymns in Cree, the only native tongue known to Rundle. Mt. Rundle was first climbed by surveyor J.J. McArthur in 1888. The highest of the seven summits (2,949 m) is the third summit south from Banff. The mountain's cliffs are popular with rock climbers in summer, and with waterfall ice climbers in winter.

Where's the River?

The Cascade hydro-electric plant is just east of the first turnoff to Banff. As you drive past the plant, the high banks on either side of the highway give the impression that you are following a river course. But if you look for the river, you won't see one.

Before the last advance of the Wisconsin Glaciation, the Bow River probably flowed here. Moraines deposited by the retreating ice blocked the river's course. The river formed a large lake west of Banff townsite and eventually eroded a new channel over Bow Falls between Tunnel Mountain and Mt. Rundle. The riverbed here was abandoned.

Many incomplete, pillar-like hoodoo formations have been eroded into the river banks here. On a terrace atop these hoodoos is a 690-year-old Douglas fir tree, the oldest known of its species in Alberta. The sparsely vegetated hoodoos have protected this tree and a few others almost as old from being consumed by fire. The coal mining town of Anthracite occupied this vicinity in the 1880s. Road cuts here expose steeply tilted rocks of the Kootenay, Fernie and Sulphur Mountain formations.

A Surveyor's Blunder

As you drive between Canmore and Banff, you can see why Tunnel Mountain was known to natives as Sleeping Bison Mountain—it looks like a bison lying down. The origi-

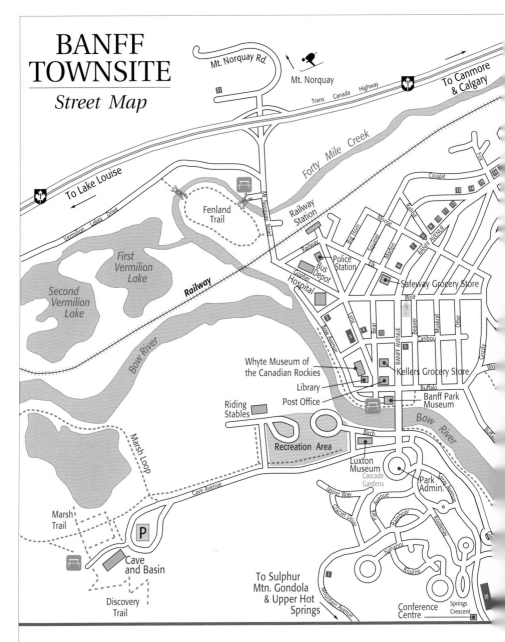

BANFF TOWNSITE
Street Map

ACCOMMODATIONS:

1 • Rimrock Resort Hotel	**6** • Banff International Hotel	**11** • Irwins Motor Inn	**16** • Dynasty Inn	**21** •
2 • Bow View Motor Lodge	**7** • Ptarmigan Inn	**12** • Banff Avenue Inn	**17** • Charlton's Cedar Court	**22** •
3 • Banff Park Lodge	**8** • Travellers Inn	**13** • Siding 29 Lodge	**18** • Banff Caribou Lodge	**23** •
4 • Homestead Inn	**9** • High Country Inn	**14** • Woodland Village Inn	**19** • Rundlestone Lodge	**24** •
5 • Mt. Royal	**10** • Red Carpet Inn	**15** • Charlton's Evergreen Court	**20** • Spruce Grove	**25** •

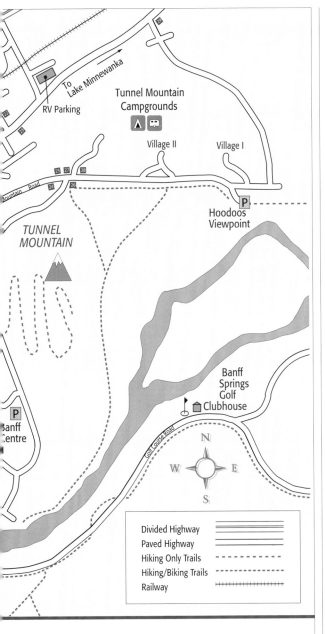

Divided Highway
Paved Highway
Hiking Only Trails
Hiking/Biking Trails
Railway

26 • Douglas Fir Resort & Indoor Waterslides   31 • Timberline Lodge
27 • Hidden Ridge Chalets   32 • Brewster Mountain Lodge
28 • Banff Rocky Mountain Resort
Lodge   29 • Banff International Hostel
s   30 • Banff Springs Hotel

nal CPR survey in this part of the Bow Valley must have been cursory at best; in 1882, the surveyor, Major Rogers, indicated that a 275 m tunnel would be required through the mountain. His superiors were skeptical. A followup investigation found ample room for the railway in the Bow Valley north of Tunnel Mountain, but the name has endured.

Banff—Siding 29

The first train stop near what is now Banff was called Siding 29. It was located in the meadows at the foot of Cascade Mountain. With development of the hot springs in 1886, executives of the CPR realized the potential for a resort nearby and sought a more appealing name for the community that was about to develop.

Banffshire was a Scottish county, now named Grampian. It was the birthplace of George Stephen, the CPR's first president, and Donald Smith, its vice-president. At a meeting held in Montreal to discuss the building of a hotel at the new Hot Springs Reservation, an underling suggested the name "Banff" to flatter the executive members who were present. The railway's general manager, William Cornelius Van Horne,

Rocky Mountain Parks: Developed Hot Springs	
Name	**Avg. Temp. °C**
Upper Hot Springs, Banff	47.3
Cave, Banff	32.8
Basin, Banff	34.5
Radium Hot Springs	47.7
Miette Hot Springs	53.9

The Cave and Basin National Historic Site

liked the name, and so Siding 29 became Banff. With completion of the Banff Springs Hotel in 1888, it soon became evident that the existing train station was too far away from the main attractions. The station was moved to its present site, and Siding 29 became a ghost town. Several of its buildings were moved to Banff.

Variations on the pronunciation of "Banff" are endless and comic: Ba-NIFF-…BARNFF…BAN-fuh-fuh… The correct pronunciation is BAMFF.

A Touch of the Tropics

The eight hot springs in the vicinity of Banff have a combined outflow of more than 3,800 litres per minute. Much of this hot water eventually drains into the wetlands west of Banff townsite, where it has a moderating effect on the local environment.

Wild orchids are common in the Rockies in damp locations, but do not normally occur in such abundance. Six species bloom here in spring. Three hundred other plant species can be found nearby. The hot springs water raises the temperature of the wetlands enough that they remain largely ice-free in winter. Migratory bird species,

including ducks, Canada geese and killdeer, sometimes take advantage of the open water, and save themselves the flight south or west by becoming year-round residents. Almost 100 species of birds have been recorded in the area.

There are two fish species that are native to these warm waters: Banff longnose dace and brook stickleback. The government added mosquitofish in 1924 in an attempt to cut down on mosquitoes near Banff. Aquarium buffs have also tampered with nature's balance, adding their favourite species to see if they would survive. Some of these introduced species have fared too well. Largely due to competition from the introduced species, the Banff longnose dace is now extinct. On the banks above the wetlands, you may see the non-poisonous wandering garter snake, a rarity in Banff.

Aerial view of the Cave and Basin

Banff Townsite

Banff townsite is situated in the Bow Valley at the confluence of the Spray River and the Bow River, on the lower slopes of Tunnel Mountain and Sulphur Mountain. The elevation is 1,371 m. The perma-

nent resident population is about 8,500. However, on a busy summer night, almost 30,000 people stay in the vicinity of the townsite. Banff is the only self-governing town in a Canadian national park. It achieved this status on January 1, 1990, when it became Alberta's 109th town.

The Cave and Basin National Historic Site— Birthplace of Banff

In 1874, Stoney natives told two American prospectors about the hot springs at Banff. The prospectors built a cabin on the Bow River and wintered

Norman Luxton—Mountain Entrepreneur

In a community whose history is noted for larger-than-life figures, one Banff resident assumes prominence—Norman Luxton. The son of a Winnipeg newspaper editor, Luxton was a man of adventure. He arrived in Banff in 1901 after several of his newspaper ventures in Vancouver had failed, and after he had helped paddle a dugout war canoe across the Pacific Ocean.

Luxton opened the "Sign of the Goat" trading store soon after his arrival. It specialized in animal heads and pelts, mounted and dressed by Luxton. He also established Banff's first consistent weekly newspaper, *The Crag and Canyon*, which he published until 1951. Using the *Crag's* presses, Luxton wrote and published guidebooks to Banff and vicinity. In 1906, Luxton was instrumental in Canada's purchase of a threatened bison herd from Montana. He helped in the roundup and transport of the animals to

Wainwright, Alberta. Descendants of these animals can be viewed today at Elk Island National Park.

Luxton changed the way Banff viewed itself as a resort when he rebuilt the King Edward Hotel following a fire in 1914. Until that time, tourist facilities had operated during summer only. At the hotel's re-opening, Luxton announced that the King Edward would never close. To illustrate the point, he threw the front

door key into the woods. Luxton organized the first Banff Winter Carnival in 1917 to help generate winter business.

Luxton is best remembered for his relationships with the Stoneys from Morley and Nordegg. For 47 years, he organized the Banff Indian Days. His forthright dealings and sincere interest in native culture earned him the trust and respect of the Stoneys. Luxton was always quick to assist on the reservations when he was needed.

In 1951, Luxton opened a museum of native culture in his Trading Post on the Bow River. Later, with the backing of Calgary's Glenbow-Alberta Institute, Luxton moved his record of 60 years' involvement with the Stoneys into an adjacent building. The Luxton Museum of the Plains Indian still operates today. Luxton died in 1962 at the age of 86. Stoneys in full traditional dress attended his funeral.

Elk or Wapiti

The montane ecoregion of the Bow Valley in Banff National Park is ideal habitat for elk. Half again as large as an adult deer, a bull elk is 1.5 m tall at the shoulder. The Shawnee name for elk is *wapiti* (WAH-pih-tee), which means "white rump." The tawny or white rump patch, with the short tail of matching colour, help identify the animal.

The elk prefers to feed on grasses and tender vegetation. Like other members of the deer family, elk ruminate: while resting, they chew cud—food regurgitated from their multi-chambered stomachs.

Female elk (cows) spend most of the year in the valley bottoms with the off-spring and immature males, sometimes forming herds of 50 or more animals. One or two calves are born in late May or early June. The cow will vigorously protect her young from human intruders. Mature bulls venture to higher elevations in late spring, and spend the summer there alone or in small groups before returning to the valleys in late August or early September.

The antlers of the male begin to grow in April. It is true that the number of "points" on each side of the antlers gives a rough indication of the animal's age. Six points, the usual maximum, indicates an animal older than four

years. Such an antler rack may reach 1.5 m in length, and 1.8 m in width. The antlers fall off in February or March.

The antlers play a major part in the annual courtship, the rut, which begins in late summer. Each mature bull attempts to gain a large harem of breeding-age females. Relative size of

antlers is a factor in establishing the dominant male, the one in any given herd who will build a harem. Less endowed bulls will usually yield the issue without a fight, but sparring and locking of antlers is sometimes used to settle the dispute. You can often see young bulls practising this behaviour in the spring and summer.

Usually, a bull is in his fourth or fifth year before he first succeeds in assembling a harem. He remains with them throughout the winter, leading the movements of the 15 to 30 animals. Elk are familiar winter residents of Banff, Jasper and Field townsites, and most townsfolk have learned to tolerate their presence

with caution and humour. This can be difficult, given that in their quest for food, elk do much damage to gardens.

During the rut, the bulls scrape the bark from trees with their antlers and mark the trees with musk from their antler glands. Both sexes bugle—a strange combination of sounds that includes grunts, and a resonant, whistle-like noise that ascends in pitch. This elaborate courtship often takes place on the main streets of Banff and Jasper townsites. Elk in rut or with young are very unpredictable and dangerous. Visitors are advised to keep at least 30 m away—sometimes a difficult thing to do.

Elk are native to the Canadian Rockies but were exterminated by hunting and a succession of severe winters in the southern part of the range during the late 19th century and early 20th century. The animals we see today are descended from five elk re-introduced from Manitoba in 1900, and some 300 brought from Yellowstone National Park between 1917 and 1920.

White elk signs warn you of areas frequented by elk. Please reduce your speed and be particularly observant along these sections of highway, especially at dawn and dusk.

left: Banff Avenue from Cascade Gardens

Cascade Mountain remains largely the same, but times have changed the look of Banff Avenue in the past century

in the area, trapping furs. One of the men, John Healy, intended to develop a claim at the springs, but lacked the means to hire a surveyor. The springs faded into obscurity.

On November 8, 1883, as construction of the CPR wound down for the winter, three workers came to Banff to look for minerals. They approached Sulphur Mountain and followed the smell of sulphur to the springs now known as The Basin. Further investigation revealed the entrance to The Cave spring.

On a subsequent trip, Frank McCabe and his brothers, William and Thomas

McCardell, used a limbed tree as a ladder and climbed down into The Cave for a dip. In those days, there was no plumbing in the Wild West. A hot bath was a rarity. The prospectors had found liquid gold. They built a crude fence around the springs, and a rough shack to establish their claim.

Banff Indian Days

The CPR's trains were noted for punctuality, but railway travellers on the mountain section of the line were sometimes confronted with unexpected and lengthy delays when the rails were inundated by flood or avalanche. In June of 1889, floodwaters of the Bow River washed out a section of railway line, stranding guests at the Banff Springs Hotel. It was apparent that the railway would be closed for 10 days. Desperate for ideas to entertain the idle guests, the hotel contacted outfitter Tom Wilson. He suggested

that Stoneys be brought from the reserve at Morley to exhibit their skills in games and contests.

Wilson went to Morley and returned with 250 willing Stoneys who raced and roped horses, danced and demonstrated their culture. The event was tremendously successful. It later became an annual celebration known as the Banff Indian Days.

The Banff Indian Days were more than a tourist attraction. For the Stoney, Kutenai, Shuswap and Sarcee peoples, the festival was a rendezvous with kin that

helped keep their cultures alive. However, changing native consciousness and unrecouped expenses incurred in staging the rodeo events led to the demise of Banff Indian Days in 1978.

In the late 1920s, the CPR staged another event that became an annual fixture at the Banff Springs Hotel—the Highland Gathering and Scottish Music Festival. The tradition of pipers continues today at special events at the hotel and at Chateau Lake Louise.

Present-day Banff Avenue

The trio's designs on the springs were confounded by their own bungling and by government red tape. The land around Banff was not surveyed, and the Ministry of Mines did not recognize hot water as a commodity on which a claim could be filed. Knowledge of the springs spread quickly. The scent of dollars was as strong as that of the sulphurous steam. The potential for quick profit attracted others, some of whom attempted to file their own claims. To thoroughly confuse the issue, McCabe conspired to sell the original trio's interest without consultation—to a federal Member of Parliament, no less!

Unknown to the prospectors, railway magnates Sandford Fleming and William Cornelius Van Horne were at this time suggesting that a federal reserve be established in the vicinity of Banff. They wanted the CPR to receive preferential treatment in matters relating to the reserve's development. The Canadian government realized the importance of having the railway pay its own way, and astutely saw the opportunity that a developed hot springs would present to all Canadians. Prime Minister John A. Macdonald quipped: "These springs will recuperate the patient and recoup the treasury." They would also become the cornerstone for Canada's first national park.

The Minister of Mines was instructed to draw up the necessary wording, and the 26 square kilometre Banff Hot Springs Reservation was established on November 28, 1885. At an inquiry held in 1886 to settle the outstanding claims to the springs, the claimants were dismissed for $1,775. By any standard, the forerunner of Canada's first national park

was an inexpensive purchase.

Although it is popular to mock the three young railway workers for their bungling and their greed, the truth is that the timing of their discovery and claim was critical in the founding of Canada's national park system. Had a few more years passed after the construction of the CPR and the area become more developed, it would have been very difficult for the federal government to expropriate the land and create a park.

Sundance Canyon

Sundance Canyon is located 3.8 km along a wheelchair-accessible, paved bike path from the Cave and Basin National Historic Site. En route to the canyon there are fine views along the Bow River, particularly of the dogtooth spire of Mt. Edith to the north. Hike clockwise on the 2.5 km canyon loop. Sundance

Canyon has been eroded into a bedrock fault at the mouth of a hanging valley. Two viewpoints overlooking the Bow Valley are featured in the descent. The canyon was named for the ritual sundance of Stoney natives, said to have been performed nearby.

Hot and Cold Running Water

There are 60 known hot springs in Canada. Since Roman times, healing properties have been attributed to hot spring water. Although many people are skeptical about those claims, there is no question that the presence of hot springs in the Rockies,

close to settlement and to transportation routes, was crucial to the initial popularity of the mountains with tourists.

The heated water that emerges at a hot spring does not originate underground. It was originally surface water, rain or snowmelt that filtered down through cracks in the bedrock. Rock within the

Dr. Brett's Sanitarium

Dr. R.G. Brett was medical supervisor for the CPR. In 1886, he set up practice in a box car at Siding 29. Brett knew a good thing when he saw one. Hot springs, a new railway, a new park and the Victorian fascination with "healing waters" all meant potential for business. Soon, Brett was installed as doctor to the park, and began construction of a private spa and hospital at Banff.

Brett's Sanitarium could accommodate 50 guests and 40 of the doctor's patients. Apparently, Brett managed this odd configuration in such a manner that "those as hotel guests [were] not aware that there [was] a hospital under the same roof." Hot spring water, advertised to cure every ill, was piped 2,400 m from the Upper Hot Springs to a variety of baths through a wooden pipeline insulated with moss.

For the privilege of using the water, Brett paid the government $15.00 per tub, per year. For the benefit of soaking, clients paid substantially more—$2.00 a day—and not all in Banff were happy with the developments: "The Sanitarium, that being under skilled medical supervision, enjoys a practical monopoly of those visiting the springs in search of health." Despite the complaints,

Brett's Sanitarium

many clients testified to the healing powers of the waters and Dr. Brett's treatments.

Brett also constructed the Grand View Villa in 1886 at the Upper Hot Springs. By its own advertisement, the Villa doubled as massage parlour and billiard hall. "Ice cold temperance drinks" were sold. When the Villa burned in 1901, the government didn't renew the lease, and took over subsequent development at the Upper Hot Springs.

As with many frontier businessmen, Brett diversified. He operated a transportation service, a drug store and an opera house. In 1910, he separated his hospital and hotel businesses. Brett bottled and sold "Banff Lithia Water." He

later served 13 years as a member of the Alberta Legislative Assembly, and became Lieutenant Governor of the province. Mt. Brett in the Massive Range west of Banff commemorates him.

The Sanitarium, subsequently named the Bretton Hall Hotel, burned in 1933. The site has been occupied by the Banff National Park administration building since 1936. The building's colourful and well-tended garden provides a picturesque foreground for the view along Banff Avenue to Cascade Mountain. The site of Brett's Mineral Springs Hospital eventually became Banff's first community hospital. Today, the old hospital building houses the YWCA.

James Brewster—From Buckskin to Buses

The history of exploration in the Rockies in the late 19th century and early 20th century is one of travel by packhorse over trails new and old. The outfitters and guides were responsible for equipping a party of city folk for weeks or months of travel in the wilds. They suggested and cleared the route, and dealt with the various disasters that could befall both experts and greenhorns on horseback in an unforgiving environment. Those attracted to the profession of outfitting and guiding were equal to the task, and left behind a legacy of more than tall tales. In one case, a transportation and tour business with packhorse origins at the turn of the century still thrives today.

Outfitting was a tough market to break into, but two young brothers from Banff, Bill and Jim Brewster, gained a foothold in 1902. That year, the CPR sent them to a sportsman's show in New York City to drum up business for the Rockies, and by agreement, for themselves. They were successful in both aims, and soon had the finances to begin outfitting large parties. In 1904, the Brewsters were granted the exclusive right to outfit clients at the Banff Springs Hotel, and the following year, the exclusive rights to horse-drawn taxi service at both the hotel and Banff railway station. In 1908, similar concessions were granted at Lake Louise and Field. With a monopoly on these services, business

thrived. About this time, two other brothers, Fred and Jack, established transportation and outfitting services in Jasper.

The Brewster Brothers expanded into other ventures—a boarding house, a bakery, an opera house and the ice harvest. From mid-January to mid-March, ice sheets from the Bow River were cut into blocks and packed into box cars. The ice was stored in ice houses and used by the CPR in its hotels and dining cars throughout western Canada the following summer.

The company came under the control of Jim Brewster in 1909, and the various interests were divided into two operations: Brewster Trading and Brewster Livery

(or transportation). In 1912, Jim bought the Banff Hotel and renamed it the Mt. Royal Hotel. This attractive building gave the company the opportunity to market complete vacation packages in the Rockies.

In 1915, regulations governing automobiles in the national parks were relaxed, and Jim became owner of the first automobile in Banff National Park. Impressed with its potential, he committed to the massive and expensive enterprise of turning a horse-oriented carriage and outfitting business into a motor-oriented tour company. The Brewster Transport Company, forerunner of today's Brewster Transportation, came into existence.

Jim Brewster's other ventures experienced mixed fortunes. A newspaper failed, but one of his greatest coups was his purchase of the lease to a CPR cabin in upper Healy Creek in 1936. Developments there led to creation of the Sunshine Ski Area.

Of Jim Brewster it was stated in 1913: "He has done more to put the town on the map...than all the other residents combined." Through his many enterprises and interests, Brewster continued to be a spokesman and emissary for tourism in Banff and the Canadian Rockies until his death in 1947.

Family ownership of Brewster Transportation ended in 1965 with its purchase by Greyhound Canada.

Banff Cemetery

Banff's cemetery is the final resting place for more than 2,000 of the town's residents. The earliest recorded burial dates to 1890.

To reach the cemetery, follow Buffalo Street east from town. You may enter through a pedestrian gate on your left as you approach the vehicle gate. Please close the gate behind you, and be respectful during your visit. Many of those interred featured prominently in the life and affairs of the town and the Rockies. A few are described briefly here.

Tom Wilson (1859-1933) was Banff's pioneer outfitter and trailguide. The copper plaque on the headstone was originally unveiled on a monument in the Yoho Valley in 1924. It was moved here after his death. (See page 109)

Mary Schäffer Warren (1861-1939) was a Quaker who hailed from Philadelphia. She readily traded the life of the eastern gentry for the western frontier. The Stoneys called her *Yahe-Weha*, which means "mountain woman." Her most celebrated packtrain journey was to Maligne Lake in 1908. Her second husband, Billy Warren, was the guide on that trip. He built a home for her in Banff near the cemetery, and is buried beside her. (See page 238)

Byron Harmon (1875-1942) was a photographer and businessman who arrived in Banff in 1903. He is best known for his mountaineering and landscape photography in what were then remote corners of the Rockies. (See page 84)

William McCardell was one of three railway workers who stumbled onto the Cave and Basin hot springs while prospecting for minerals in 1883. The "discovery" of the springs led to the establishment of Rocky Mountains (Banff) National Park. (See page 70)

Norman Luxton (1874-1962) was pre-eminent among Banff businessmen. He operated stores, hotels and a newspaper, founded the Banff Winter Carnival and organized the Banff Indian Days. In 1952, he opened the Luxton Museum of the Plains Indian. (See page 67)

James I. Brewster (1882-1947) was the most influential of the Brewster clan. He and his brother, Bill, started a guiding company in 1902. By the 1940s, Jim was at the helm of an empire that included a transportation company, hotels and a ski hill. The mausoleum, one of three in the cemetery, also houses the remains of Jim's parents. Bill Brewster is buried under the trees, a few plots to the north. (See page 73)

A.O. Wheeler (1860-1945) was a topographic surveyor and mountaineer, best known for founding the Alpine Club of Canada in 1906, and for surveying the Alberta-B.C. border from 1913-25. Wheeler named many features in the Rockies. His two wives are buried beside him. (See page 250)

R.G. Brett (1851-1929) came to Banff as the CPR's resident physician in 1886, setting up business in a railway boxcar. He saw the opportunity to diversify, and became one of Banff's most successful businessmen. Brett's Sanitarium, built in 1886, was for a while a curious mixture of hotel and hospital. (See page 72)

Ebenezer William (Bill) Peyto (1868-1943) began work with Tom Wilson and became one of the best trailguides in the Rockies. Peyto was a talented amateur geologist, and was also noted for his outrageous garb and off-beat sense of humour. He was a Lance Corporal in the Boer War, hence the military headstone. (See page 177)

Tom Wilson's headstone

The Banff Springs Hotel in the early 1900s

The Upper Hot Springs

earth's crust is hotter than on the surface. The temperature increases approximately 1°C for every 33 m descent, until at three km below the surface, the temperature is hot enough to boil water. Any groundwater that manages to filter down this far is pressurized, and naturally percolates back to the surface along other crack systems. With the eight hot springs at Banff, the return to the surface is along the Sulphur Mountain Thrust Fault. These springs have a combined outflow of more than five million litres per day. The Basin spring is the most copious, accounting for almost 20 per cent of the combined flow.

During its return to the earth's surface, hot spring water dissolves and absorbs minerals from the bedrock. As a result, some hot springs are slightly radioactive—formerly a desired healing property. The "rotten egg" smell at some springs is partly due to sulphur in the water, but more due to algae, which metabolize the sulphur and give off hydrogen sulphide as a by-product. The minerals and algae combine to give the waters their unique colours.

If the groundwater does not filter to a significant depth, or if it becomes mixed with cold water on its return to the surface, the discharge from a spring will not be hot. Such springs are called mineral springs. The Paint Pots in Kootenay and the Ink Pots in Banff are examples. There are also many cold water springs in the Rockies.

Mineral deposits of crumbly tufa (TOO-fah) mark active and inactive outlets of the hot springs at Banff. Tufa is calcite—crystallized deposits of calcium. The tufa deposits in the vicinity of the Cave and Basin are seven metres thick. This crumbly rock was a major factor contributing to the demise of the 1914 Cave and Basin structure, and to the closure of the swimming facility in 1994.

Developing the Feature Attraction

Developments at the Cave and Basin began the year after the reserve was proclaimed. In 1887, bathhouses were installed, and a tunnel was blasted to reach the Cave, as the sick could not climb down the ladder through its opening. Those who visited the Cave before and after this modification claimed that the tunnel decreased the temperature of the spring water. The pools were encased in concrete to deepen them, and to prevent the crumbly walls of tufa from collapsing. Whether seeking miracle cures, soaking tired joints, or just enjoying the high life, bathers paid ten cents a swim.

During a visit in 1911, J.B. Harkin, the first national parks commissioner, was impressed by the popularity of the hot springs. He also noticed that facilities could not meet the demands of heavy visitation. The following year, architect Walter Painter (who designed renovations at the Banff Springs Hotel and at Chateau Lake Louise), was employed to design a new swimming facility. Constructed between 1912 and 1914 at a cost of $200,000, the new Cave and Basin featured the largest swimming pool in Canada at the time. In its architecture and finishing, the building was hailed as a masterpiece.

When the deposits of tufa beneath the building settled, the walls cracked and the building became unsafe.

Ted Kissane

Few people promote tourism in Banff National Park as effectively as Ted Kissane. As Regional Vice President for Canadian Pacific Hotels and Resorts, Kissane supervises seven properties—Hotel MacDonald, the Chateau Lake Louise, the Banff Springs, Kananaskis, the Jasper Park Lodge, Chateau Airport and the Palliser. He's also General Manager of the Banff Springs, the most successful CP hotel in Canada with over 500,000 visitors per year.

In 1888, the creator of the Banff Springs Hotel, William Cornelius Van Horne, told visitors: "You shall see mighty rivers, vast forests, boundless plains, stupendous mountains and wonders innumerable; and you shall see it all in comfort. Nay, in luxury."

Kissane markets Banff in much the same way: "I tell visitors that they are coming to one of the most beautiful places in the entire world. The fact that Banff is in a national park is an added benefit because it is being preserved for future generations. It is an undisturbed environment that is unlike the developments you see in Europe."

"At the Banff Springs Hotel,

visitors experience the heritage of a company that helped build Canada. When Canadian Pacific built the railway back in 1887, it constructed these historic hotels to develop tourism for the railway. These hotels are living history. The Banff Springs Hotel and the Chateau Lake Louise are Canadian icons recognized worldwide—they are destinations in and of themselves."

Although this region is blessed with natural and historic grandeur, many guests are looking for something more. "Not everyone wants to go into the backcountry. The customer of to-day wants a choice of activities in the hotel and frontcountry. Our challenge has been to accommodate the tourist who says, 'Gee, if we come to the Banff Springs in the winter and we don't ski and it's cold outside, what do we do?'"

One response is the $12-million Solace Spa—2,600 square metres of luxury with three cascades of mineral water and eleven other pools including indoor and outdoor saltwater pools. The spa offers every therapeutic treatment imaginable: herbal wraps, Turkish scrubs, Hungarian Kur baths, aromatherapy mineral baths, algae body masks and Italian Fango mud facials. The Pine Herbal Bath may be as close as these tourists get to the forest.

Kissane believes the townsite has done a great job in providing a full range of services that customers want. "And if they don't want to be in a busy little mountain town, they can always go to Lake Louise or Jasper—or stay in overnight lodge accommodations in the backcountry. There are so many choices here, which is why we are one of the most successful tourist destinations in North America. "

Bow Falls

Public health regulations demanded chlorination of the hot pools, and it was found that the chlorine combined with minerals in the water to produce an unhealthy sediment. Looking every bit its age, the Cave and Basin was closed in 1976.

Amid proposals to turn the site into a commemorative garden in time for the national parks centennial in 1985, the "Save the Cave and Basin Swimming Pools Committee" was formed to garner public support for a restoration of the facility. More than 21,000 people signed a petition, providing the impetus for the grant of funding. Instead of building a garden, Parks Canada spent $12 million rebuilding the Cave and Basin as a replica of Walter Painter's 1912 design. A facsimile of the original 1886 bathhouse was also constructed. The Cave and Basin Centennial Centre was offi-

cially opened by the Duke of Edinburgh during a royal visit in 1985. Unfortunately, the problems of the site had not been rectified, and the swimming facilities were closed permanently in 1994. More than 600,000 people now visit the site annually.

Several walking trails originate from the Cave and Basin. The Discovery Trail leads to the upper entry of the Cave and Basin. Displays along the Marsh Trail illustrate how the hot spring water affects the local ecology. Another trail leads along the Bow River to Sundance Canyon. You must pay a fee to enter the Cave and Basin complex, but you may walk the trails free of charge.

Upper Hot Springs

"I threw away the crutches I had used for four years, after I had been here 10 days." During Banff's early days, there were many such testi-

monials to the healing powers of the hot springs water. Handrails on the stairway to Dr. Brett's Grand View Villa were reinforced with crutches no longer needed by patients—although it was reported that upon arrival, the doctor issued all patients with crutches, whether required or not! In 1901, the government cancelled Dr. Brett's lease and began development of a public facility at the Upper Hot Springs. The present structure was completed in 1935.

Perhaps because of their high elevation (1,584 m), these hot springs are the most temperamental of those near Banff. There have been occasions during droughts in spring and autumn when the flow has stopped completely. Following the 1964 Alaska earthquake, the spring water was discoloured with sediment for several days.

The view from the Banff Springs Hotel features the Bow River and the gap between Mt. Rundle & Tunnel Mountain

Banff Springs Hotel

The Canadian Pacific Railway (CPR) was completed through the Rockies in 1884. Although the primary objectives in building a transcontinental railway were to bind the young country together and to make new lands accessible for settlement, it was apparent that railway commerce alone would not be sufficient to turn the venture into a paying proposition.

The huge debt incurred in constructing the railway demanded a more immediate cash flow. With an eye on the splendid scenery of the Rockies and on the hot springs and new national parks, CPR vice president and general manager, William Cornelius Van Horne, had the answer: "Since we can't export the scenery, we'll have to import the tourists."

The CPR's chain of mountain hotels was initiated in 1886 with the construction of Mt. Stephen House at Field. Other hotels were built at Rogers Pass, Three Valley Gap and in the Fraser Canyon. For Banff, Van Horne envisioned a luxury resort, and chose a site at the confluence of the Bow and Spray rivers. Famed architect Bruce Price was commissioned to design the building. It would eventually cost $250,000. Construction of the Banff Springs Hotel began late in 1886.

In the summer of 1887, Van Horne visited the construction site and was shocked to see the building being constructed backwards. The kitchen overlooked the rivers, and the guest rooms faced the forest. He hastily sketched additions to correct the matter. Amid much national interest, the 250-room hotel, complete with sulphur water piped 2,100 m from the Upper Hot Springs, opened June 1, 1888. It was the largest hotel in the world at the time. Room rates started at $3.50 per day.

The Banff Springs Hotel immediately turned the tiny community of Banff into a destination resort for the gentry of the late Victorian era. More than 5,000 visitors arrived that first summer. By 1903, additions and renovations had increased the hotel's capacity to 500. In 1904, almost 10,000 guests registered, and many were turned away to sleep in railway cars at the train station—a privilege for which Van Horne charged $1.50 per night. The hotel's season was lengthened to accommodate business.

Plans were drawn in 1911 to completely overhaul the building. Initially, only one major expansion was undertaken—the two-million-dollar Painter Tower, designed and constructed by CPR architect

Today, the Fairmont Banff Springs Hotel can accommodate 1,700 guests in its 770 rooms

Walter Painter. The north wall of the nine-storey tower went out of plumb during construction. The error was not noticed until it was too late, so rather than tear the walls down, the bricklayers brought the wall back towards vertical as they worked higher. As a result, the tower wall bulges outwards at mid-height. "Rundle rock" from a quarry along the Spray River was used to face the tower, which was opened with great fanfare in 1914. One visitor dryly commented: "The building is high. There is only one thing higher in the attractive concern, that is the price of liquor."

The CPR completed its nine-million-dollar reconstruction program at the Banff Springs Hotel between 1925 and 1928, yielding the general outline of the building we see today. It has been described as having "corridors for the invalid, turrets for the

astronomer, and balconies for the lovers." During this construction, the only surviving wing of the 1888 hotel burned.

The CPR lavished a great deal of money on furnishing the pride of its hotel fleet. Talented craftsmen worked with the finest materials. Windows were imported from Europe, and fossil-bearing stone from Manitoba. The furniture and ornaments were painstakingly detailed to match period pieces. Upon its completion, for a short time, the new Banff Springs Hotel eclipsed the scenery as the principal tourist attraction in the Rockies.

During the past century, the Banff Springs Hotel has hosted many noted guests—movie stars, royalty, diplomats and heads of state. Banff's air strip was built by townsfolk when jazz musician Benny Goodman wanted to visit the hotel—by plane!

The golf course at the Banff Springs Hotel is considered one of the 10 most scenic in the world. The original course was completed using prisoner-of-war labour during the First World War. The course was completely redesigned by Stanley Thompson in 1927, to a length of 6,729 yards, and par 71. Nine more holes were added in 1988.

Over the last ten years, more than $175 million has been invested in the restoration and renovations of the Fairmont Banff Springs Hotel. Additions to the resort include a Conference Centre, the Solace Spa and specialty boutique shops.

Bow Falls and the Bow River

Banff residents and visitors are fortunate that the Bow River flows through town. The walk along the riverbank to Bow Falls offers escape from the busy streets nearby, and fea-

The town of Banff with Cascade Mountain in the background

Mt. Norquay

In 1894, businessman George Paris acquired the first pair of skis in Banff, and promptly broke one of them while schussing to town from the Upper Hot Springs. Interest in skiing built slowly. The activity became established when ski jumping was featured at the first Banff Winter Carnival in 1917. After the 1918 carnival, keen skiers formed the Banff Ski Club. Club members requested permission to clear trees from the slopes of Mt. Norquay (NOR-kway) so that they might develop some expert skiing terrain. The park superintendent granted permission with the stipulation that not every tree be cleared. So the Ski Club members left one tree on the first run cleared, the celebrated Lone Pine. The Mystic

Norquay chairlift

Ridge-Mt. Norquay ski area grew from these humble beginnings.

The six-kilometre road to the ski area climbs steeply from the

interchange on Highway 1. From the pulloff at kilometre five there is a grand overview of the Bow Valley. The meadow nearby is called "The Green Spot" and is home to Columbian ground squirrels. You may see bighorn sheep and mule deer on the road or in the forest nearby. The road is a popular training ground for Banff's athletic set. Keep an eye out for runners and cyclists. At road's end are the trailheads for hikes to Stoney Squaw, Cascade Amphitheatre, Elk Pass, Mystic Pass and Forty Mile Creek. Mt. Norquay (2,522 m) was named for John Norquay, a premier of Manitoba, who is said to have made the mountain's first ascent in 1887 or 1888.

A bighorn sheep tickles the fancy of a young admirer   *RCMP march in the Canada Day Parade on Banff Avenue*

tures tranquil views of this picturesque river. You can visit the Banff Park Museum in Central Park on your way to the falls. The 2.1 km trail, which is mostly paved and wheelchair accessible, begins at the boat house at the corner of Wolf Street and Banff Avenue.

The Bow River is the longest river in Banff National Park. From its headwaters at Bow Lake, 90 km to the north, it drains an area of 2,210 km2. After flowing through Banff, the Bow eventually joins the South Saskatchewan River in southern Alberta. The river's name comes from the Cree words *manachaban sipi*: "the place from which bows are taken." Natives made hunting bows from Douglas fir saplings found on its banks.

The Bow River has not always followed this course through Banff. Before the last advance of the Wisconsin Glaciation, the river may have flowed between Tunnel Mountain and Cascade Mountain. When the ice age glaciers receded, the river's course was blocked with moraines. A large lake formed west of the present townsite. Its waters eventually spilled through the gap between Tunnel Mountain and Mt. Rundle, at the present site of Bow Falls. The area west of Banff is still wetland—a legacy of the ancient lake. Ancient river terraces or levées, are scattered throughout the town.

The trail climbs to a viewpoint above Bow Falls, and then descends to river level. The 10 m high falls are being eroded into the contact between two rock formations. Looking upstream, the rocks of the west (left) bank are 245-million-years-old, and those of the east (right) bank are 320-million-years-old. The jagged formation of the west bank extends into the riverbed, creating the rapids. Slightly downstream from the falls, the Spray River enters the Bow River. From here, you may ascend to the Banff Springs Hotel, or return along the riverbank to your starting point.

Sulphur Mountain Gondola

The eight-minute gondola ride to the crest of Sulphur Mountain whisks you to an

Tunnel Mountain Drive

If you think traffic in Banff is bad today, consider the situation facing horse and buggy on the original Tunnel Mountain Drive. A series of tight switchbacks climbed the steepest section of the road, giving rise to the name Corkscrew Drive. When automobiles were allowed in the park in 1915, the switchbacks were removed.

Tunnel Mountain Drive is

Corkscrew Drive in the 1920s

Banff's back road, and is a good cycling route. Other good outings for cyclists are to Sundance Canyon, Lake Minnewanka and Johnson Lake.

elevation of 2285 m, and is the easiest way to a mountain top near Banff. The panoramic view from the gondola's upper terminal includes Banff townsite, the Bow Valley, Lake Minnewanka and the surrounding mountain ranges.

Sulphur Mountain is a favourite haunt of bighorn sheep. You may be surprised and alarmed at how tolerant these particular animals have become of humans. They are accustomed to being fed and now expect similar treatment from all visitors. Please refrain from feeding them.

Famous Visitors

It would be easier to answer the question: "Who hasn't visited Banff?" than to list all the famous people who have stopped for a night. For more than a century, the mix of luxury hotels and magnificent scenery has been an irresistible lure for travellers, both notable and nondescript. Referring to the diversity and distinction of visitors, one park superintendent commented that the guest register of the Banff Springs Hotel was "the most interesting reading in the world."

In the Banff Springs Hotel's guest registers you'll find, among others, the signatures of royalty: King George VI and Queen Elizabeth, the Duke and Duchess of Connaught, the King of Siam and Prince Rainier; of politicians: Winston Churchill, Teddy Roosevelt, William Lyon Mackenzie King, Robert Kennedy and Pierre Trudeau; of movie stars and popular personalities: Ginger Rogers, Marilyn Monroe, Gregory Peck, Henry Fonda, Burt Lancaster, Laurence Olivier, Jack Benny, Helen Keller and Glenda Jackson.

In 1886, **Prime Minister John A. Macdonald** and his wife, Lady Agnes, crossed Canada by train. Macdonald was a recluse for much of the trip. John Niblock, Western Superintendent of the CPR, was assigned the task of looking after Lady Agnes. During their return from the west coast, Niblock wired ahead for a bouquet of flowers to be presented to Lady Agnes on her arrival at Banff. Something went awry with either the transmission or the deciphering of the telegram, for when the Prime Minister's wife stepped off the train, a bewildered CPR employee presented her with a bag of flour. Lady Agnes was not put off, and returned to Banff annually in the late 1880s. During these visits she stayed at a cabin built for her on the grounds of the Banff Springs Hotel.

When **King George VI** and **Queen Elizabeth** visited Banff in 1939, Jim Brewster chauffeured them around town and led them on a walk up Tunnel Mountain. Legend has it that Jim stunned his wife Dell by dropping by their home for lunch in the midst of the tour, unannounced, with the King and Queen in tow.

When jazz musician **Benny Goodman** visited Banff in the 1930s, he insisted on travelling by airplane. This caused a problem, as Banff had no airstrip. The townsfolk rallied to the cause, and soon Banff had its airstrip and Benny Goodman had his visit to Banff.

Marilyn Monroe stayed at the Banff Springs during filming of River of No Return in 1953. While on a set, she fell down the bank of the Bow River and sprained an ankle. During the remainder of her stay, the bell staff drew straws each morning to see who would win the coveted assignment of pushing Marilyn in her wheelchair through the hotel.

Novelist **Arthur Hailey** was a guest at the Mt. Royal Hotel when it burned in 1967. When he left his room at the sound of the alarm, he hurriedly collected the unpublished manuscript, Airport.

Two of Banff's most famous guests are ones who have never left: ghosts reported to haunt the Banff Springs Hotel. One is a bride who tripped and fell to her death on the stairs near the Rob Roy Room. Those who know the room say there is a cold spot on its floor where she landed, and that during gatherings the bride's presence can be felt as she searches the room for her husband and the happiness taken from her.

The other ghost is said to make more spontaneous appearances. **Sam McAuley** was a Scots bell captain who vowed to haunt the hotel after his death. Guests have seen him hovering in the air, holding a lantern outside the ninth floor of the hotel. Two other guests, accidentally locked out of their room, telephoned for a bellman to let them in. When the bellman arrived, he found the guests in their room. They said that an elderly, white-haired man in an old uniform had let them in with a pass key. The bellman who had been summoned, quickly left, not wanting to share his duties with the spectre of Sam McAuley.

Norman Sanson, for whom the north peak of Sulphur Mountain is named, frequented this ridgetop for more than 30 years earlier this century. In his capacity as curator and meteo-rologist for the Banff Park Museum, Sanson was required to make trips to the mountain top observatory every other week to record weather data and calibrate equipment. Evidently, Sanson liked the job, or the exercise, or the view, for he doubled the required frequency of ascents of the mountain, eventually logging more than 1,000 trips. The last of these was in 1945 to record observations of a solar eclipse. The Vista Trail leads to the recently refurbished observatory.

The Banff Park Museum

The Victorian gentry who visited Banff at the turn of the century had a tremendous fascination with the animals of the "Wild West." Although many of these visitors didn't dare stray too far from the carriage roads and bridle paths, they still felt a need for close contact with wild animals to make their mountain experience complete.

The government of Canada obliged, and in 1895 it built a museum to display stuffed examples of the wildlife of western Canada. In 1903, the collections were moved into the Banff Park Museum, constructed at the considerable cost of $10,000. The "railway pagoda style" building was finished inside with Douglas fir, and designed to allow natural lighting. Until 1936, the building also served as the park superintendent's office.

From 1904 to 1937, the grounds between the museum and the Bow River were occupied by a zoo and aviary. Eventually, more than 60 species were represented. Not all were native to the Rockies—one of the most popular was a polar bear. Attitudes gradually changed, and it became evident that protection of animals in the wild was more consistent with the objectives of national parks than having them caged and on display. The zoo was closed in 1937, and the animals were shipped to other institutions. The polar bear went to the Calgary Zoo.

Although many of the exhibits in the museum today reflect the "trophy head" mentality that prevailed in the early 1900s, some demonstrate a perception decades ahead of its time—the portrayal of animals as integral parts of an ecosystem. This perception is evident in the handiwork of Norman Sanson, the museum's curator from 1896 to 1942. Sanson's work included the collection of specimens and the recording of weather data from an observatory atop Sulphur Mountain. In all, he made more than 1,000 trips to the observatory and hiked more than 32,000 km in the course of his work. Under Sanson's direction, the museum became known as "The University of the Hills." Today, it contains an excellent reading room and is highly recommended.

The Banff Park Museum was restored in 1985 as part of the national parks centennial. It has been designated a National Historic Site and is the oldest natural history museum in western Canada. An entry fee is charged.

The Banff Centre

The Banff Centre for the Arts had modest beginnings as a

Competing with Banff

During its heyday, Bankhead rivaled Banff as the most thriving community in the Rockies. Residents of Bankhead enjoyed many conveniences: rail service, a hotel, school, two dairies, skating rinks, court, churches, tennis courts and a library. Some homes had running water, sewers and electricity - before these amenities came to Banff.

The train station at Bankhead was a whistle stop. One night when the train carrying the CPR payroll passed through, a clerk threw the payroll bag in the general direction of the station. He missed. Concerned mine officials found the payroll the next day, in a snowbank 400 m from the station.

One aspect of civilization that Bankhead lacked was a cemetery. Most residents thought that bad luck would befall the family of the first person to be buried in a new cemetery, so burials were made in Banff—much to the consternation of park officials. When a Chinese labourer at Bankhead was murdered in 1921, it was thought that he had no family, so he was interred as the first, and only, burial at Bankhead's cemetery. When word of his death eventually reached his homeland, the labourer's family requested that his remains be shipped to China. This request was fulfilled in 1939 and Bankhead's cemetery was closed.

summer theatre school in 1933. The first campus on Tunnel Mountain was constructed in 1947. It was affiliated with the University of Calgary until 1978. The Banff Centre provides resources and instruction for advanced artistic development amid inspirational surroundings. Artists of many disciplines train here. Some live in residence on campus.

The Banff Festival of the Arts is held during the summer, and a school of manage-

ment stages several annual events, including the Banff Television Festival, the Banff Festival of Mountain Films and the Banff Mountain Book Festival. These attract international entries and attention.

The Eric Harvie and Margaret Greenham theatres are the venues for films, theatre, ballet, dance and concerts. Check the Centre's schedule for entertainment opportunities: 762-6300.

Whyte Museum of the Canadian Rockies

Artists Peter and Catharine Whyte had already made tremendous personal contributions to the artistic heritage of the Rockies when they decided to preserve the writings, artwork and memorabilia of other Rocky Mountain artists and pioneers. In the mid-1950s, they established the Whyte Foundation, and began collecting material. In

Byron Harmon

By the early 1900s, the CPR was doing a more than respectable job of "importing the tourists" to the Rockies. But no one had fully realized that if the physical scenery couldn't be exported, at least photographic images of it could. The Rockies were awaiting the first photographer who would take up the considerable challenge of bringing the mountains to everyone. Just such a person stepped off the train in Banff one day in 1903. Byron Harmon, an itinerant, energetic, imaginative photographer from Tacoma, Washington had found his niche.

Harmon quickly moved away from portraiture, the standard fare of the day, and took a photographic interest in the mountain landscape. He developed a love of hiking and mountaineering, and was among the founding members of the Alpine Club of Canada in 1906. He soon became the Club's official photographer. In this capacity, Harmon travelled to the annual summer mountaineering camps and broadened his familiarity with the

Rockies, Purcells and Selkirks. His direct involvement with those doing exploration gave his images an authenticity and impact that could not be matched. The public gobbled it up. Seeing more and more of the range each year further inspired Harmon in his professed goal to photograph every mountain and glacier in the Rockies twice.

Harmon also enjoyed success as a Banff businessman. He developed a popular series of post-

cards and calendars, featuring views "Along the Line of the CPR," and marketed them at home and abroad. His store on Banff Avenue expanded to include a curio shop, a photo studio, a theatre, a book store, a drug store, a tea shop, a library, a woollen store and a beauty parlour. His photographs were circulated widely in newspapers and mountaineering journals, and his movie footage was sought for international distribution. By 1920, Harmon's name was globally recognized as synonymous with the Rockies. *The Banff Crag and Canyon* wrote: "Byron Harmon is the best asset Banff has in the line of advertising the village to the outside world."

Harmon eventually rambled farther afield in the world on trips of personal exploration, but the Rockies remained his favourite landscape. He died in Banff in 1942.

A collection of more than 6,500 of Harmon's images is housed in the Whyte Museum of the Canadian Rockies.

Main Street, Bankhead

1968, this collection became available to the public when the Whyte Museum of the Canadian Rockies opened.

Housed in the museum is the Archives of the Canadian Rockies—the largest collection of artistic and historical materials related to these mountains, with some 4,000 volumes. Also included are manuscript collections, oral history tapes and extensive photographic collections. Featured are those of George Paris, Byron Harmon and the Vaux Family. The museum also houses the 2,075-volume Alpine Club of Canada library.

The museum was renovated and expanded in 1993. Its galleries are venues for displays of contemporary and historic art and photography, lectures, films, readings and concerts. The Whyte Foundation also has

in its care two heritage homes and four log cabins, built and formerly occupied by Banff area pioneers. Tours are available.

The Whyte Museum makes a good rainy-day diversion. It is open daily in the summer, and operates with reduced hours in the winter. The building is wheelchair accessible. Call 762-2291.

Cascade Mountain

The mountain that forms the northern backdrop for Banff was named by James Hector in 1858. Hector translated the Stoney name *Minihapa*: "mountain where the water falls." Cascade Mountain (2,998 m) was first climbed in 1887 by a party that included outfitter Tom Wilson. Although the mountain has a formidable appearance, an easy, if long, mountaineering

route lies along the left skyline. The frozen waterfall on the mountain's east slopes is a popular winter location for waterfall ice climbing.

Banff Train Station

Banff's original train station, Siding 29, was located in the meadows at the base of Cascade Mountain. The principal destinations for those getting off a train in Banff were the hot springs and the Banff Springs Hotel. It soon became obvious to the CPR that a station was required closer to these attractions.

When CPR general manager William Cornelius Van Horne visited Banff in 1887 to inspect the construction of the Banff Springs Hotel, he twice demonstrated his renowned reputation as a man of action. First, when he saw that the hotel was

Cascade Mountain from Mt. Rundle

The Rocky Mountaineer in the mountains

being built facing backwards, he sketched plans for a rotunda to salvage the view. Next, when asked about plans for the new railway station, he grabbed a piece of paper, fired off another quick sketch, and said: "Lots of good logs there. Cut them, peel them, and build your station."

The old station from Siding 29 was moved to Van Horne's site, and was incorporated into the new station. It was used until 1910, when the present stone and stucco structure was built. This building has been called the "most famous railway station in Canada."

Passenger train service between Vancouver and Calgary is provided by Rocky Mountaineer Railtours. This amazing trip takes visitors through the alpine heart of the Canadian west. Departure times are co-ordinated to mazimize the daylight hours in the most scenic spots. Reservations can be made by calling 1-800-665-7245.

Tunnel Mountain

With an elevation of 1,692 m, Tunnel Mountain is the lowest feature to which the name "mountain" is applied in the Rockies. Although it is a steep climb, the well-beaten 1.8 km path to the summit hardly qualifies as mountaineering. From trail's end, you enjoy unrestricted views over the Bow Valley. The trail begins at the parking area on the south side of St. Julien Road, 350 m south of Wolf Street. You can reach the trailhead easily by walking east from town on Wolf Street or Caribou Street.

In 1882, Major Rogers, a surveyor for the CPR, determined that Tunnel Mountain blocked the Bow Valley. He thought that a tunnel would be required for the rails to proceed. His superiors were skeptical. A follow-up investigation found ample room for the railway in the valley between Tunnel Mountain and Cascade Mountain. The tunnel was never built, but the mountain's name has endured.

Looking east from Tunnel Mountain's summit, the mountains of the Fairholme Range are prominent. These mountains extend along the east side of the Bow Valley, from Lake Minnewanka to Exshaw. Mt. Rundle (2,949 m) rises to the south. It was named for Methodist mission-

ary, Robert T. Rundle. In 1844 and 1847 he preached to Stoney natives near the present site of the Banff airstrip. To the north is Cascade Mountain (2,998 m), highest near Banff. To the west, beyond the rooftops of Banff townsite, are the Vermilion wetlands. On the western skyline are the peaks of the Massive Range.

Tunnel Mountain Hoodoos

The Tunnel Mountain Hoodoos are located 6 km east of town on Tunnel Mountain Road. The paved 500 m Hoodoos trail is wheelchair accessible, and leads along the bank of the Bow River to viewpoints that overlook the hoodoos and the Bow Valley. The trail also provides excellent views of Mt. Rundle and Tunnel Mountain.

The hoodoos are freestanding pillars that have been eroded by rain, snowmelt and wind, from debris-flow deposits. The debris-flows occurred at the end of the Wisconsin Glaciation, approximately 11,000 years ago, when surges of ice-dammed water entered the Bow Valley from

Mt. Rundle from Tunnel Mountain

Hoodoos with the Banff Springs Hotel in the background

side valleys. The deposits are 30 m deep. Each hoodoo was formerly protected by a capstone that prevented the material directly beneath from weathering away.

The word "hoodoo" is used throughout western North America to describe natural columns of rock. Stoney natives thought that the Tunnel Mountain Hoodoos were giants turned to stone, or teepees that housed "bad gods." There are other hoodoo formations nearby in the Bow Valley. You can see them from Highway 1 between Banff and Canmore.

Douglas fir and limber pine grow along the Hoodoos trail. Limber pine has long, curved needles in bundles of five. Its trunk and branches are frequently contorted. The tree is locally common on cliff edges and other windy locations in the montane ecoregion, south of Saskatchewan River Crossing.

Bankhead

In 1883, surveyor G.M. Dawson reported the existence of coal in the mountains east of Canmore and Banff. The Canadian Anthracite Company began mining this coal in 1886. The company entered into a supply agreement with the recently completed CPR, whose tracks passed conveniently nearby. Not wishing to depend on an outside supplier, the railway acquired the rights to other coal claims in the area, and in 1903, it created a subsidiary company to mine coal for its locomotives.

The CPR selected narrow seams in the base of Cascade Mountain for its mining operations. Rather than digging mine shafts down into the mountain as was common, miners reached these seams by burrowing upwards at a slight angle. The coal was then knocked down into mining cars which gravity assisted in returning to the mine portal. Three points of entry (A-, B- and C-level) gave access to the seams, and 55 km of mining tunnels were excavated. Production peaked in 1911, with 300 men employed below ground, 180 employed above, and 250,000 tonnes of coal mined.

A community developed near the mine. Named Bankhead after a Scottish town, it had every convenience of the day, including a hotel, skating rink, tennis courts, library and an electricity plant with sufficient output to supply power to Banff townsite as well. At the height of the mining operations, between 900 and 2,000 people, mostly immigrants, lived at Bankhead.

A sad aspect of life at Bankhead was that of the 60 Chinese labourers. These men had the dirtiest of jobs—sorting the different coal pieces by hand. They lived apart from the Europeans in an area known as Chinatown. The rhubarb they planted in their gardens still grows at Bankhead today.

Bankhead's semi-anthracite coal burned intensely, but was brittle. Much of the mining effort created coal dust. This dust was mixed with pitch and compressed into briquettes to make a transportable heating fuel—a costly operation. The Bankhead mine endured six strikes. The last of these, in 1922, spelled the end of the mine. Most of the buildings were soon removed or demolished. Many were transported

Beaver

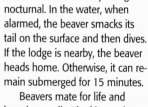

The beaver is the largest rodent in the Canadian Rockies, and the second largest rodent in the world. It is Canada's national animal, and its likeness appears on the nickel coin. The beaver's coat is reddish-brown. It has webbed rear feet, fingered hands and prominent incisor teeth. The beaver is a remarkable swimmer and has a large, flat tail that it uses as a rudder, as a source of propulsion and as a balancing prop when gnawing at tree trunks. (The tail is not used to scoop mud.) The ears and nostrils seal to keep water out, and the lips close behind the incisor teeth so that the beaver can chew underwater.

The beaver prefers to eat the inner bark of deciduous trees—especially trembling aspen and poplars. Shrubs, saplings and aquatic plants are also prominent in its diet. It cannot digest the fibrous matter completely and does not have a multichambered stomach, so the beaver excretes the food and eats it again.

The beaver creates wetlands to ensure that it can safely travel to and from its favourite food sources. It builds a dam on a slow-moving waterway, using trees, branches, rocks and mud. Trees are felled with the incisors, towed by mouth and put into place with the dexterous hands. Beavers have been known to fell trees 1.7 m in diameter, but prefer those 20 cm to 25 cm in diameter.

As the water level rises upstream from the dam, a pond forms. The pond must be deep enough not to freeze solidly in winter. The beaver selects an elevation on the pond bottom on which to build a large, dome-shaped house—the lodge. The industry required in creating and maintaining the dam, pond and lodge is a family effort. Three generations of beavers may occupy a lodge. Although the beaver remains in its lodge all winter, it does not hibernate. It feeds from a food supply cached underwater at the lodge entrance.

The beaver compensates for

its slowness on land by being nocturnal. In the water, when alarmed, the beaver smacks its tail on the surface and then dives. If the lodge is nearby, the beaver heads home. Otherwise, it can remain submerged for 15 minutes.

Beavers mate for life and breed annually. The kits are born in mid-spring and stay with the parents until the beginning of their third year. When the young adults move out, they may travel several hundred kilometres to find a suitable location for their own pond.

In creating a pond, the beaver does the other animals a great service. Moose, deer and elk also require wetland vegetation, and are given additional range. Fish inhabit the waters, and fish-eating birds such as osprey, bald eagle, belted kingfisher and great blue heron take up residence. But for the beaver, there comes a point of diminishing return for its incredible industry. The pond eventually begins to fill with sedges, and as its nearby food supply declines, the beaver is forced to relocate.

With the recent absence of major forest fires in the Rockies and the resulting lack of aspen growth, favourable new locations for this remarkable animal are becoming scarce. Its numbers are dwindling. The Fenland Trail and Vermilion Lakes are two of the best places in the Rockies to see beavers.

Fenland Trail

A fen is a lowland covered wholly or partially by water. The self-guiding Fenland Trail explores a shaded white spruce forest along the banks of Forty Mile Creek—an area typical of the wetlands west of Banff townsite. These wetlands are in varying stages of a natural process called succession, which will eventually see them transformed from open water into montane forest.

The self-guiding trail features ten interpretive stops:

1. The wetlands in the vicinity of Banff townsite were a natural barrier to fires that swept the Bow Valley after the construction of the Canadian Pacific Railway in the 1880s. This mature white spruce forest was spared by fire, and is ancient compared to most other forests in this valley.
2. Black bears are adept tree climbers. The scarred bark of trembling aspens reveals dark claw marks left by bears.
3. The view at this stop demonstrates how wetlands in the fen are shrinking, whereas the forest is becoming more extensive.
4. Many of the wetlands in Banff townsite have been created by the handiwork of beavers. The mound of sticks and mud is a lodge: home to a beaver family.
5. Beavers are aquatic rodents, and create canals in their shallow ponds. These deeper canals provide escape routes from predators such as coyote, wolf and bear.
6. Spring floodwaters undermine the banks of Forty Mile Creek, causing trees to topple.

Forty Mile Creek from the Fenland Trail

Highwater washes disturbed soil into the nearby fen. This soil creates more habitat for vegetation, accelerating the fen's succession into forest.
7. The Vermilion wetlands are among the best bird-watching locations in the Rocky Mountain parks. Bald eagle, osprey, American dipper, red-winged blackbird and a variety of waterfowl are common.
8. Forty Mile Creek provides a natural moat, making the interior of the fen unattractive to predators. Cow elk raise their young here in spring, and bulls herd their harems during the autumn rut.
9. The buds of willows, aspen and red osier dogwood are an important food source for elk, deer and moose.
10. As the stumps reveal, the white spruce of this area made attractive building timbers in Banff's early days. Hay crops were harvested from the nearby marshes until 1910. The level of the nearby First Vermilion Lake was controlled by a concrete dam until 1985. Impacts like these are no longer tolerated in the vicinity of the Fenland, as nature's balance is allowed to return.

The Fenland Trail is usually closed during the elk-calving season of late spring and early summer.

to Banff, Canmore and Calgary. The miners either took up a new way of life locally or moved to other coal mining areas in western North America.

You can walk an interpretive trail through the ruins of Bankhead's industrial section, reached from the Lake Minnewanka Road. Hikers can follow the C-Level Cirque trail onto the flanks of Cascade Mountain, passing the C-Level mine ventilation shafts en route. New mining claims have not been allowed in the Rocky Mountain parks since the National Parks Act was proclaimed in 1930. The last mining operation ceased in Yoho in 1952.

Lake Minnewanka

Lake Minnewanka is the largest body of water in Banff National Park, and is the only hydroelectric reservoir in a Canadian national park. The outlet of the original lake was first dammed in 1912 to generate electricity at the Bankhead mine. With the closure of the mine in 1922, a new facility was installed to supply power for Banff. In 1941, another dam was constructed under the War Measures Act, to greatly increase the output of the Cascade hydroelectric plant.

These dams have had a considerable effect on the landscape. They raised the water level by 25 m and lengthened the lake by 8 km, inundating large tracts of montane meadow and forest. The reservoir submerged a reach of the Cascade River and the village of Minnewanka Landing. In addition, the Ghost River at the east end of the lake was

Lake Minnewanka

dammed and diverted to flow west into the new reservoir. The lake is now 90 m deep.

One translation for Minnewanka yields "lake of the water spirit." Apparently, the spirit is not benign, for another translation is "Devil's Lake." A Stoney legend tells of a creature—half fish, half human—that can move the lake waters at will. The Stoneys would not canoe or swim in the lake. Apparently, such malevolent creatures formerly lived in other lakes in the Rockies. According to the Stoneys, many were killed by lightning.

Boating and fishing have been popular on Lake Minnewanka since the 1880s. A 15 kg lake trout was caught here in 1987. The motor launches *Daughter of the Peaks* and *The Aylmer* once plied the waters from the resort village of Minnewanka Landing. The village, complete with warden station, is now submerged. Scuba divers often explore the ruins. Lake Minnewanka is the only lake on which gas-powered motor boats may be launched in

Banff National Park. A commercial boat tour operates, with several departures daily.

The 1.7 km walk to Stewart Canyon along the north shore of the lake is suitable for families. The oldest native campsite near Banff is partly submerged in Lake Minnewanka near the mouth of the Cascade River. It dates back 11,500 years. On the south side of the outlet dam, there is a plaque that commemorates the Palliser Expedition. The parking area and dam are frequented by a bold flock of bighorn sheep. Please do not feed them.

Johnson Lake

This popular picnic area is accessed from the Lake Minnewanka Road. Turn right, 1.2 km north of the Highway 1 interchange. Follow the winding road as it climbs for 3.3 km to the Johnson Lake junction. Turn right and follow this side road 2.3 km to Johnson Lake, which has the added attraction of being Banff's local swimming hole. The 2.4-km loop trail around the lake features fine views of Cascade

Bighorn Sheep

The bighorn sheep is the symbol of Banff National Park, and is its second most common large mammal. Visitors often confuse bighorn sheep and mountain goats. To simplify identification, remember: sheep are tawny brown with brown horns and a white rump patch, whereas goats are white or cream-coloured with black horns.

The bighorn ram stands about one metre tall at the shoulder, and when mature, has a set of thick, brown horns that spiral forward. These horns are never shed. Together with the skull, they can account for 13 per cent of the animal's 125 kg weight. It is possible to estimate the age of a ram by counting the annuli, or rings, on one of its horns. Each annulus contains a dark and light band, together representing one year of growth. The female sheep (ewe) grows horns too; however, these are less spectacular, and curve backwards.

The rams flock together in high places during summer and early autumn. The dominant ram must constantly defend his place. Usually, this is done without battle in what is called the "present" (pree-zent)—when two rams turn their heads sideways to allow each to inspect the horns of the other. As the autumn rut approaches and the issue of who will breed with a harem of ewes becomes more cruicial, diplomacy wanes. The rams duel, charging headlong at each other and meeting with a mighty crash. Thick armour bones beneath the horns usually prevent serious injury. However, duels to

the death can take place. Although the position of the dominant male in the flock changes frequently, the dominant female, who dictates the summer movements of the ewes and lambs, may endure many years.

Grasses are the most important foods for bighorn sheep. The animal cannot tolerate a snow depth of more than about 30 cm, as this limits its travel and access to food. Hence, wind-scoured slopes in the front ranges offer the best winter habitat for bighorns. Grizzly bears, wolves and cougars are the animal's principal predators. They may achieve success by forcing sheep to run over a cliff. Deaths on the highway and railway are the major drain on the population of bighorn sheep. In some locations, the viability of individual herds is threatened. When driving in areas frequented by sheep,

please reduce your speed and be prepared to stop. Poaching of trophy rams is also a serious problem.

Bighorn sheep are generally accustomed to humans and will often allow us to approach closely. This puts both humans and sheep in peril. With their horns and sharp hooves, sheep are capable of inflicting serious injury. Accustomed to nutrition-poor handouts from people, sheep may not be able to endure a hard winter. If a sheep approaches you, scare it away by shouting and waving your arms.

Mountain and Mt. Rundle, and the opportunity to see elk, muskrat and deer.

Vermilion Lakes

The three Vermilion Lakes are reached from the Vermilion Lakes Drive, which begins just south of the Mt. Norquay interchange on Highway 1. Photographers will recognize the lakes as the setting for the postcard view of Mt. Rundle.

The extensive wetlands immediately west of Banff are probably the remainder of a large lake. Moraines deposited at the end of the Wisconsin Glaciation temporarily blocked the course of the Bow River, causing the lake to form. The lake's waters eventually found an outlet between

Mt. Rundle in winter from Vermilion Lakes

Tunnel Mountain and Mt. Rundle near the present site of Bow Falls. Today, the Vermilion Lakes are sustained by annual floods from the Bow River.

In order to preserve boating and fishing opportunities, the water level of the First Vermilion Lake was formerly controlled by a man-made dam. Since the controversial

Trembling Aspen

Trembling aspen is the most common tree in North America, and dominates the forest near Muleshoe viewpoint. It is a member of the willow family. In the Rockies, this deciduous tree prefers gravels at the base of mountainside streams. It regenerates principally by root suckering, hence the "clone" stands of uniformly aged trees.

It is easy to differentiate between aspens and other trees of the poplar family. Aspen leaves are pale green and heart-shaped with fine-toothed edges. Balsam poplar and cottonwood poplar leaves are larger, more elongated and dark, shiny green. In autumn, aspen leaves turn bright yellow, whereas poplar leaves turn more golden. The bark of mature aspens is white or greenish-white and smooth. Poplar bark is gray and furrowed.

You will notice that the bark of the aspens at Muleshoe is scarred to a uniform height. Elk and mule deer feed on the tree bark and underlying cambium layer in winter, producing the scarring. Aspen is the staple food of beavers, and the buds and shoots are also favourites of moose. On windy days, the origin of the name "trembling" is obvious. The leaves flutter easily because the plane of each leaf stem is at a right angle to the plane of the leaf. Native peoples called the aspen "noisy leaf." They reportedly used the dust from its bark as a sun-

screen, and chewed the cambium layer beneath the bark as a cure for headaches.

Mt. Rundle from Vermilion Lakes

removal of the dam, the lake level has dropped and the basin has begun to fill with aquatic vegetation—the first stage in the succession from montane wetland to flood-plain forest. In a few hundred years, the Vermilion Lakes may look like the forest along the nearby Fenland Trail. Water levels of the second and third lakes are controlled naturally by beaver dams. The maximum water depth is about five metres.

Osprey and bald eagles nest at the First Vermilion Lake. Beavers and muskrats can be seen at the Second Vermilion Lake. The Third Vermilion Lake, near the road's end, is partially fed by hot spring water. The moderating effect keeps part of this lake ice-free, and provides winter habitat for some birds that normally migrate.

The Vermilion Lakes are among of the best areas in Banff for bird-watching. They are also a good place to see coyotes, wolves and elk, especially in winter. The wetlands contrast with the dry slopes of Mt. Norquay on the opposite side of Highway 1, where a flock of bighorn sheep frequents the coniferous forest.

Vermilion Lakes Drive

This short drive makes an excellent evening excursion from Banff townsite and is particularly recommended to cyclists. Follow Mt. Norquay Road north from town. Turn left (west) onto the Vermilion Lakes Drive, just before the Highway 1 interchange. The Vermilion Lakes Drive follows the north shore of the extensive Vermilion wetlands for 4.7 km to a turnaround, with viewpoints en route. Δ

Banff to Lake Louise
The Bow Valley Parkway

The Bow Valley Parkway was completed in 1920 as the first road between Banff and Lake Louise. Today, it offers a less crowded, less hectic alternative to Highway 1. Information on this section of the Trans-Canada starts on page 102. The speed limit along the Bow Valley Parkway is 60 km per hour. Views are more varied and generally better than on Highway 1—particularly betweenBanff and Castle Junction. There are good chances to see wildlife: bighorn sheep, elk, mule deer, coyote, black bear and wolf. Use caution: the road is popular with cyclists. To reach the Bow Valley Parkway, follow Highway 1 for 5.6 km west from the Mt. Norquay interchange.

The First Visitors

The recorded human history of the Rockies spans less than 200 years, but for thousands of years preceding, native peoples traveled and lived here. When the ice of the Wisconsin Glaciation began to recede from the Bow Valley 11,000 years ago, natives ventured into the Rockies. More than 370 prehistoric sites have been discovered in Banff National Park. Some of the best examined are in the vicinity of Banff townsite. The oldest for which there is an accurate date is one near the Second Vermilion Lake. It is 10,800 years old. A campsite on the north shore of Lake Minnewanka may be 11,500 years old. Artifacts include arrowheads, animal bones and iron-stained mud called ochre. Examples of rock art exist at other locations in the Rockies.

Evidence of much more recent habitation has been found within Banff townsite. Pit houses used by Stoneys and possibly by Shuswaps have been found along Spray Avenue and at the Banff Springs Golf Course.

The prehistoric natives were hunter-gatherers, but not strictly nomadic. It appears that 10 per cent of the sites were occupied year round. The natives lived in small family groups. Their movements were largely dictated by those of their wildlife quarry. The Bow Valley was also part of a long-distance travel route. Natives would cross the Rockies east to west via the Ghost Valley, Lake Minnewanka, the Bow Valley, Healy Creek and Simpson Pass. From there, they descended to the Kootenay Valley and the Columbia Valley.

Locally, the natives encountered by the first Euro-Canadian explorers were a tribe of the Sioux Confederation. Elsewhere called the Assiniboine, Nakoda or Dakota peoples, they became known locally as the Stoneys. (Assiniboine means "those who cook by placing hot rocks in water.") The Stoneys hailed from the Lake of the Woods country in what is now northwestern Ontario. They fled west from Euro-Canadians and the scourge of smallpox. The Stoneys displaced the Kutenai people to the western slopes of the Rockies, and maintained an uneasy truce with the hostile tribes of the Blackfoot Confederacy to the south. It has been estimated that at the time of European contact, the Stoney population was only 250.

When Treaty #6 and Treaty #7 were signed in 1876 and 1877 respectively, the Stoneys were placed on reserves near Nordegg at Morley, and along the Highwood River southwest

JOINS PAGE 98

JOINS PAGE 152

JOIN PAGE

ROCHEUSES

SAWBACKES

CHEUSES RANGE

TAI

RANGE

PARC

NATION

MASSIVE RANGE

BALL RANGE

ATIONAL

Hawk Ridge

3235 Peak
Glacier

Flints Park

Cascade

Wildflower

Mount
Avens

Pulsatilla
Pass

Badger
Pass

Protection Mountain

Pulsatilla
Mountain

Block
Mountain

Sawback L

Johnston

Luellen
Lake

Stuart
Knob

Helena Ridge

Rockbound L

2728 Eisenhower
Peak

Castle Mountain

CANADIAN PACIFIC

Castle Mountain
Campground

Castle Junction

93

Altrude Creek

Smith
L

Johnston
Canyon

Johnston Canyon
Campground

RIVER

Vista Lake

Altrude

Storm
Mountain 3155

Twin
Lakes

Copper
Mountain 2795

Gibbon
Pass

Redearth

Mount
Ball
3307

Shadow Lake

Pilot
Mountain 2941

Massive
Mountain 2435

Mount
Brett
2984

Pharaoh Creek

East Horse Creek

Isabelle Peak
3094

Ball
Pass

Haiduk Ck

Haiduk
Lake

Black Rock L

Pharaoh Peaks
2711

Pharaoh L

Bourgeau L

Mount 2931
2400 Bourgeau

Haiduk
Peak
2920

Scarab

Mummy L

Egypt L

Healy
Pass

Whistling
Valley

Monarch
Ramparts

Redearth Pass

Simpson Pass

SUNSHINE
SKI AREA

Tale L

Tale Falls

Verdant
Creek

East Verdant

The
Monarch
2904

Eohippus

North Simpson

Grizzly
L

Rock Isle L

Larix L

Standish
Ridge

Quartz Hill

2580

Citadel
Pass
2608

93

Vermilion
Crossing

1400

RIVER

Mystic Lake

Mount
2850 Ishbel

Cockscomb
Mountain 2777

Ranger Canyon

Mount Fifi
2636
Mount Louis 2667

Mount Cory
2789

Mount
Brewste

Mount
Edith
2515

Mount
2554

MT NOR
SKI ARE

Hole in the
Wall

Mile

Elk L

Goat's Eye

Eagle
Mountain

Mount
Howard Douglas 2850

Lookout
Mountain

Fatigue Ck

Howard Creek

Douglas Creek

Brewster

Healy Creek

2959 Fatigue
Mountain

Hole-in-the-Wall overlooking the Bow Valley

Hole-in-the-Wall

of Calgary. The Stoneys' knowledge of the Rockies benefited many early European explorers. Some of the Stoneys from Morley and Nordegg became guides and advisors to Tom Wilson, Walter Wilcox, Samuel Allen, A.P. Coleman and Mary Schäffer.

Backswamp and Muleshoe

The reach of the Bow River just west of Banff townsite is extremely gentle, dropping only 13 cm in each kilometre. Across the Bow River from Backswamp viewpoint, Brewster Creek enters the main valley. Material deposited by this tributary has created an alluvial fan. The Bow River lacks the energy to cut through this obstacle, so it has been diverted to the near side of the valley.

Upstream from the fan, there was once a lake. The lake has now become the "Backswamp"—filled with sedges, rushes and a few young trees—the first stage in the succession from shallow pond to floodplain spruce forest. Backswamp contains peat deposits that are nine metres deep. Peat is decomposed vegetable matter that is partially carbonized on its way to be-

coming coal.

The wetland at Muleshoe was created by a different process. Bends in a river are known as meanders. As a river erodes more deeply into a valley bottom, it may abandon some meanders for a more direct course. The crescent-shaped pool left behind is called an oxbow lake. At Muleshoe, the bed of the Canadian Pacific Railway was built between the river and the oxbow lake, sealing the oxbow's fate. Instead of filling with sediment washed into its basin from the Bow River at high water, the stagnant Muleshoe is now filling with vegetation.

The vegetation in these wetlands is a favourite with moose. The small lakes and stagnating ponds are good habitat for beaver, muskrat, osprey, wolf, coyote and waterfowl.

Hole-in-the-Wall

If you look east from the Muleshoe viewpoint, you will see Hole-in-the-Wall—a solution cave, 600 m above the Bow Valley on Mt. Cory. The cave was eroded by meltwater from a glacier that almost filled this valley during the Great Glaciation. Although its

massive entrance hints at great things, Hole-in-the-Wall is only 30 m deep. There are many other small solution caves nearby.

Hillsdale Slide

The hilly terrain on the Bow Valley Parkway is the product of a landslide that occurred 8,000 years ago. When the ice of the Wisconsin Glaciation filled the valley, it undercut the surrounding mountainsides. After the ice receded, part of Mt. Ishbel on the east side of the valley broke away in one of the largest measured landslides in the Rockies. The Hillsdale Slide blocked Johnston Creek and diverted it west, where it is now eroding Johnston Canyon.

Johnston Canyon

Johnston Canyon is 23.6 km west of Banff. This is one of the best places in the Rockies to appreciate a limestone canyon. An ingenious suspended walkway allows you to walk within the cool depths of the canyon and obtain a close view of the effects of flowing water.

Johnston Canyon is being eroded into a fault system in the predominantly limestone bedrock. Seven waterfalls mark the locations of resistant

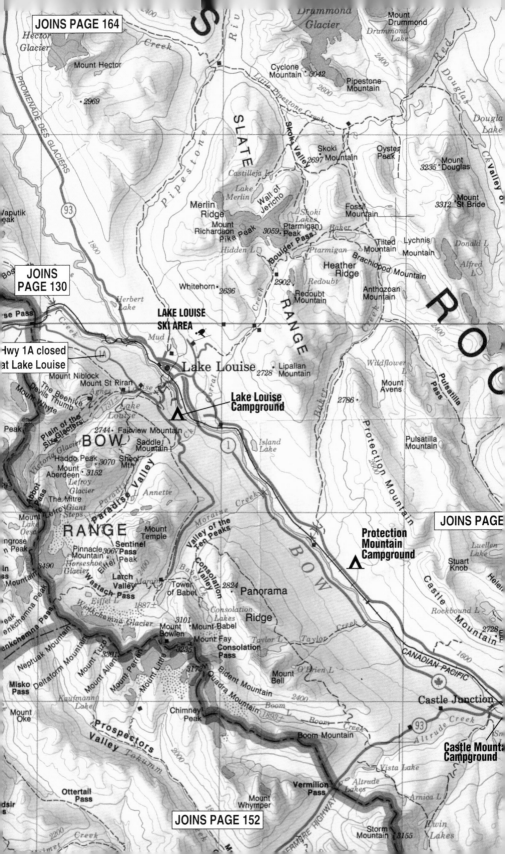

JOINS PAGE 164

JOINS PAGE 130

JOINS PAGE

JOINS PAGE 152

Drummond
Glacier

Mount
Drummond

Drummond
Lake

Mount Hector

Hector
Glacier

Cyclone
Mountain • 3042

Pipestone
Mountain

Douglas

Dougla
Lake

· 2969

Skoki
Valley

Skoki
2697

Skoki
Mountain

Oyster
Peak

Mount
3235 · Douglas

Waputik
eak

93

Castilleja L.

Lake
Merlin

Wall of
Jericho

Shoki
Lakes

Fossil
Mountain

Mount
3312 · St Bride

Donald L.

Alfred
L

Merlin
Ridge

Mount
Richardson

Pika Peak

Ptarmigan
Peak
3059 ·

Baker

Tilted
Mountain

Lychnis
Mountain

Hidden L.

Boulder Pass

Ptarmigan

Heather
Ridge

Brachidpod Mountain

Whitehorn · 2636

2902 ·

Redoubt

Anthozoan
Mountain

Bos

JOINS
PAGE 130

Herbert
Lake

Redoubt
Mountain

se Pass

LAKE LOUISE
SKI AREA

Mud L.

RANGE

Wildflower
L.

Pulsatilla
Pass

Hwy 1A closed
at Lake Louise

1A

Lake Louise

Lipalian
Mountain
2728 ·

Mount
Avens

Mount Niblock

Mount St Riran

Lake Louise
Campground

2786 ·

Pulsatilla
Mountain

The Beehive

Mount
Whyte

Devils
Thumb

Agnes

Lake
Louise

Island
Lake

Peak

Plain of the
Six Glaciers

2744 · Fairview Mountain

BOW

Saddle
Mountain

Sheol
Mtn

L. Annette

Abbot
Pass

Victoria
Glacier

Haddo Peak

Mount
Aberdeen · 3152

Lefroy
Glacier

· 3070

Paradise Valley

Mount
Temple

Protection
Mountain
Campground

JOINS PAGE

Luellen
Lake

Lake
Oesa

The Mitre

Giant
Steps

Moraine

Mount
Babel

Stuart
Knob

Helen

ngrose
n Peak

RANGE

Pinnacle
Mountain

Sentinel
Pass

3067
Eiffel
Peak

Valley of the
Ten Peaks

Consolation
Valley

2824

Panorama

Castle
Rockbound L.

2728
E

in
ss
Mountain

3490

Horseshoe
Glacier

Wastach Pass

Eiffel L.

Larch
Valley

1887±

Tower
of Babel

Ridge

Castle Mountain

Neptuak Mountain

Wastachemna Peak

enkchemna Peak

Wenkchemna Glacier

3101

Mount
Bowlen

Mount Babel

Mount Fay

Consolation
Lakes

Taylor L.

Taylor

CANADIAN PACIFIC

1600

Misko
Pass

Deltaform Mountain

Mount Tuzo · 3391

Mount Allen

Mount Perren

Mount Little

· 3235

3173

Bident Mountain

Mount
Bell

O'Brien L.

Castle Junction

Mount
Oke

Kaufmann
Lake

Chimney
Peak

Quadra Mountain

2400

93

Altrude
Creek

Sm

Prospectors

Valley

Takumm

Boom
L.

1883±

Boom

Creek

Castle Mounta
Campground

Ottertail
Pass

2000

Boom Mountain

Vista Lake

Altrude
Lakes

Arnica L.

dsir

Creek

Vermilion
Pass

Mount
Whymper

Storm
Mountain · 3155

Twin
Lakes

dolomite rock. The Lower Falls are 1.1 km from the trailhead and are 15 m high. The Upper Falls are 2.7 km from the trailhead and, with a height of 30 m, mark the deepest point in the canyon. Opposite the Upper Falls viewpoint is a travertine wall—a cliff coated with a combination of algae and calcium carbonate. You may see the American dipper in the fast-flowing water of the canyon. The canyon is one of two known nesting sites in Alberta for the black swift.

You may extend your walk from Johnston Canyon to the Ink Pots, mineral springs that are 5.7 km from the trailhead. Rain and meltwater that has filtered into cracks in the surrounding rock returns to the surface at the Ink Pots. Air carried in the spring water disturbs sediments in the springs. Two of the Ink Pots are rich with clay and appear milky. The bases of all contain quicksand.

The aquifer for these springs is only eight metres below the surface, so they are not hot springs. The temperature of 3.6 °C is close to the average annual air temperature for this elevation. The seven springs have a combined outflow of 2,100 litres per minute.

Johnston Creek campground is opposite the parking lot for Johnston Canyon.

Moose Meadows

Moose Meadows is a clearing alongside the Bow Valley Parkway, 2.5 km west of Johnston Canyon. The meadows were formerly on the floodplain of the Bow River. The river now flows on the other side of the valley, and the meadows have become vegetated with stunted white spruce, grasses and shrubs, including red osier dogwood.

You are not likely to see moose in Moose Meadows. A 1993 estimate gave a population of only four moose for the Bow Valley between Castle Junction and Banff. However, you will probably see Columbian ground squirrels, of which there are hundreds nearby. Gray wolves and coyotes also frequent the area.

Pilot Mountain (2,935 m) dominates the view southwest. Its name was chosen by surveyor G.M. Dawson in 1884 because the mountain is a prominent landmark in the Bow Valley. Pilot Mountain exhibits the characteristics of both a castellated mountain and a horn mountain. Its sedimentary formations lie in horizontal layers. Alternating resistant cliffs and recessive ledges give the castellated or layered appearance. Glaciers once cloaked the mountain and whittled its upper slopes into a horn shape. From this viewpoint, you can also see the Hillsdale Slide to the southeast.

Silver City

In 1883, the CPR's "end of steel" reached this part of the Bow Valley. When construction halted in December, the rails were at the entrance to Kicking Horse Pass. Three communities sprang up in the Bow Valley that year: Siding 29 near what is now Banff; Holt City at what would later become Lake Louise; and Silver City.

The Sawback Burn

Prescribed burn at Lake Minnewanka near Banff, 1988

The fire-scarred trees that you see between Backswamp and Johnston Canyon are the legacy of prescribed burns in 1991 and 1993 and a wildfire in 1998. These fires killed some ancient Douglas firs, the most fire-resistant tree species in the Rockies. Prescribed burns reintroduce fire into the ecosystem in a controlled manner. This helps create the mosaic of forest habitats required to support a diversity of species. Although the charred forest may appear ugly now, the longterm benefits will help ensure biodiversity in the Bow Valley.

There is some silver in the rocks of the Canadian Rockies, but not in a quantity sufficient to make mining worthwhile. Those who promoted Silver City sought to reap their windfall not from ore, but from the miners who came looking to get rich. Silver City went from boom to bust in less than two years, but at its peak in 1884, it was larger than Calgary, and 2000 people lived on these meadows.

When it became clear that Silver City was a fraud, the prospectors quickly moved on. Unfortunately, many of them went to Golden City, where the rumoured gold was as scarce as Silver City's silver. One of Silver City's six hotels was dismantled and floated down the Bow River to Banff, where it was rebuilt. The only person who stayed was Joe Smith, Silver City's third resident.

Park wardens turned a blind eye as he hunted, trapped and prospected in the area until his health failed in 1937.

Today, all that remains of Silver City are the stumps of trees felled when the site was cleared. Part of *The Alaskan* was filmed here, and the meadows were the scene of an internment camp during World War I.

Castle Mountain campground is on the east side of the Bow Valley Parkway, 500 m south of its junction with the Kootenay Parkway (Highway 93 South). There is a store, gas station, pay telephone, accommodation, warden station and hostel at the junction. The Rockbound Lake and Silverton Falls trailhead is 200 m south of the junction.

Castle Cliffs

Near Castle Junction, the Bow Valley Parkway crosses the fault that separates the front ranges to the east from the eastern main ranges to the west. North of Castle Junction, all the mountains are in the eastern main ranges. Castle Mountain (2,766 m) is the best example of an eastern main range mountain in the Rockies. From bottom to top, the cliffs demonstrate a common sequence of sedimentary formations: Cathedral limestone, Stephen shale and Eldon limestone. The shale has been eroded into a ledge, creating the "layer cake" or castellated appearance.

Castle Junction to Baker Creek

The Wisconsin Glaciation was an ice age that lasted from 75,000 years ago to 11,000 years ago. There were three distinct glacial advances and

Having twice staked his political fortunes on his "national dream"—the construction of a railway from ocean to ocean—Canadian prime minister John A. Macdonald was now inspecting the completed project firsthand. Weary from the years of political battles and desperate financial dealings that had made the Canadian Pacific Railway a reality, Macdonald retired to his private car for much of the trip. There, he apparently indulged in the bottled strength upon which he had become reliant. His wife, Lady Susan Agnes Macdonald, was more outgoing and quite taken with railroading. At the siding of Laggan, she stole the show.

Lady Agnes rode in the locomotive of the train from Calgary.

While pusher locomotives were engaged for the crossing of Kicking Horse Pass, she announced that she would ride on the pilot beam (cow catcher) of the lead locomotive "from summit to sea." The prime minister thought it a ridiculous idea,

but Lady Agnes is reported to have made good on her word. Cowcatcher-riding then became the rage, much as flagpole-sitting and wing-walking would in later generations.

Lady Agnes was party to another humorous incident in the Rockies. On the return trip from the west coast, CPR superintendent John Niblock was assigned to take care of her. He wired ahead to Banff for a bouquet of flowers to be presented to Lady Agnes when the train arrived in Banff. Apparently, something went wrong with either the transmission or the deciphering of the telegram, for when Lady Agnes stepped off the train, a bewildered CPR employee presented her with a bag of flour.

A veteran hiker explores Sunshine Meadows

Tree-in-the-Road

The Bow Valley Parkway divides at several places, offering eastbound and westbound travellers different views of the Bow Valley. In one place, it divides for but a few metres, to bypass what was formerly a large, white spruce tree.

Two stories tell why this tree was left standing in the middle of the road. The official story is that the park superintendent thought it was a magnificent specimen, and ordered it protected. The unofficial story relates that when crews were clearing the right-of-way for the road, an intimidating foreman took a nap under the tree. The workers did not want to invoke his wrath by waking him, so the tree was spared. In August of 1984, tree-in-the-road blew down in a violent thunderstorm that also toppled many other trees in Banff and Yoho national parks.

retreats in that time. The first two advances extended through the Bow Valley beyond Canmore. The last advance stopped near Castle Junction. Across the Bow Valley from Storm Mountain viewpoint, you can see many irregular-shaped elevations in the forest—piles of rubble called moraines, left behind by the retreating ice.

Storm Mountain (3,161 m) is just south of Vermilion Pass on the continental divide. Its name is indicative of the weather that frequently travels from west to east through the pass. The mountain was first climbed in 1889 by a surveying party that included outfitter Tom Wilson.

The Castle Lookout trailhead is 4.8 km northwest of Castle Junction. The trail climbs four kilometres to the site of an abandoned fire lookout on the slopes of Castle Mountain. Protection Mountain campground is 11.2 km northwest of Castle Junction. Accommodation and meals are available at Baker Creek Chalets, 14.3 km northwest of Castle Junction. There is also a picnic area here.

Doghair Forest

Most trees in this part of the Bow Valley are lodgepole pine. The lodgepole requires the heat of a forest fire to crack open its resin-sealed cones and allow effective seeding. Much of the Bow Valley burned in the decades immediately following the construction of the Canadian Pacific Railway. This created dense stands of lodgepole pine, known as doghair forest. At this elevation, lodgepole pines are usually replaced after about 130 years by a coniferous forest of Engelmann spruce and subalpine fir.

Morant's Curve

The viewpoint at Outlet Creek offers a spectacular panorama of the Wenkchemna Peaks, Mt. Temple and other summits of the Bow Range in the vicinity of Lake Louise. Mt. Temple (3,543 m) is the third highest mountain in Banff National Park. The Bow River and the CPR tracks are in the foreground. Nicholas Morant was a photographer for the CPR. He popularized this view on a postcard, and it has since been known as Morant's Curve.

There is a picnic area at Corral Creek, just before the northern end of the Bow Valley Parkway. Turn west (left) onto Whitehorn Road to reach Highway 1, Lake Louise, Moraine Lake and the Icefields Parkway. Turn east (right) to reach the Lake Louise Ski Area and the Skoki trailhead.

Banff to Lake Louise— Highway 1

Sunshine Meadows

Sunshine Meadows span an arc of 14 km along the continental divide southwest of Banff. They are part of an alpine meadow system that covers more than 40 square kilometres. The meadows are not accessible to the casual summer visitor, but for those with the energy, a six-kilometre hike along a steep gravel road grants access to the meadows and a trail system. The Sunshine turnoff is 8.3 km west of Banff. Follow the Sunshine Road nine kilometres to the parking lot at the trailhead.

Sunshine Meadows are at an average elevation of 2,225 m. The average annual temperature is –4 °C and more than seven metres of snow falls. Vegetation on the meadows has adapted to a growing season that lasts less than two months. Most of the plants are low in stature, with small flowers and leaves. The less surface area a plant offers to the moisture-robbing effects of cold, wind and harsh sunlight at this altitude, the more moisture and nutrients it retains for growth. You may recognize miniature versions of many plants common at lower elevations.

More than 340 species of plants grow at Sunshine Meadows—one third of the plant species in Banff and Jasper national parks. Some are rare in the Rockies, and many are at either the extreme northern or the extreme southern limit of their range. In a colourful celebration of nature's means of ensuring the survival of species, a multitude of beautiful wildflowers blooms in mid-summer.

The view south from some of the slopes above Sunshine Meadows includes Mt. Assiniboine (a-SINNI-boyne), the "Matterhorn of the Rockies." Hikers and climbers bound for this mountain sometimes use the Citadel

Mt. Assiniboine

The summit of the highest mountain in this part of the Rockies, Mt. Assiniboine (a-SINNI-boyne), is visible from places on Sunshine Meadows. The 3,618-m mountain was named by surveyor G.M. Dawson in 1884. The Assiniboine are members of the Sioux Confederation, and are also known as the Nakoda or Dakota peoples. Assiniboine means "those who cook by placing hot rocks in water." Locally, the Assiniboine are called Stoney.

The quest to become the first to ascend Mt. Assiniboine drew many expeditions in the 1890s, including several organized by American explorer Walter Wilcox. The first ascent was made in 1901 by James Outram (OOT-rum) and guides. Outram trooped directly to Assiniboine from a series of first ascents in Yoho, culminating a remarkable summer of mountaineering.

Mt. Assiniboine Provincial

Golden larch trees provide a foreground for Mt. Assiniboine

Park lies entirely within B.C., and was created in 1922. In 1973, the park was expanded to its present area of 386 square kilometres. Roughly triangular in shape, the park occupies an area between the boundaries of Banff and Kootenay national parks. In 1990, Mt. Assiniboine Provincial Park

was added to the Rocky Mountain Parks World Heritage Site. Apart from Mt. Assiniboine, the park's chief attractions are glacial lakes, wildlife and extensive alpine meadows. There is no motor vehicle access to the park, but six backpacking approaches can be made.

Pass trail that crosses Sunshine Meadows.

The Sunshine Ski Area

Between 1929 and 1932, several skiing parties from Banff journeyed to Sunshine Meadows. They were delighted with the skiing conditions. Jim Brewster, president of Brewster Transport, was one of these early skiers. In 1934, he obtained a winter lease on a cabin that the CPR had built in 1928 for its summer trail riding vacation business. In 1936, Brewster bought the cabin for $300. He hired mountain guides to teach skiing, and the popularity of the area grew rapidly.

The first permanent ski lift was installed in 1945. At that time, skiers reached the village by a hair-raising bus ride along Sunshine Creek. The gondola was installed in 1980 at a cost of $12 million. It greatly improved access to the ski hill. The gondola climbs 450 m in its 4.5 km ride to Sunshine

Village. There are 10 ski lifts and more than 60 marked runs within the ski area boundary. The village comprises a hotel constructed in 1965, and various dining facilities. The much-renovated original cabin is still in use.

Since the late 1970s, there has been a sequence of contentious proposals to develop additional facilities and terrain at Sunshine. Ski enthusiasts cite the area's abundant snowfall, and advocate more lifts and the clearing of new runs. Environmentalists argue that large-scale commercial operations like ski hills are incompatible with the prime objective of national parks: the preservation of ecological integrity. In the case of Sunshine, with its unique vegetation, this argument is especially poignant.

Remembered for their Contributions

The names of two mountains above the Sunshine Road commemorate two key people

in the history of Banff National Park—one an explorer, and the other an administrator.

Mt. Bourgeau (boor-ZJOWE) (2,930 m) on the north side of the road was named in 1858 by James Hector of the Palliser Expedition, for the Swiss-born expedition botanist Eugene Bourgeau. In the course of the three-year expedition, Bourgeau collected 460 species. Apparently, Bourgeau was not a good horseman. He spent most of his time in the Rockies camped in the Bow Valley while Hector and the others explored on horseback.

Mt. Howard Douglas (2,820 m), to the south of the road, was named for the second superintendent of Rocky Mountains Park (Banff), and later Dominion Commissioner of Parks. Howard Douglas was an enthusiastic supporter of enlarging the park in 1898. He realized that the province of Alberta would soon be established, and that land for an expanded national park would subsequently be very difficult to acquire. Chiefly through his recommendations, the park's area was increased in 1902 from 413 square kilometres to 7,000 square kilometres.

However, this was too much too soon, and the fledgling forestry branch of the Department of Interior was unable to administer so large an area. From then until 1930, the area of what is now Banff National Park went through a series of reductions to accommodate provincial demands for access to resources to satisfy mining, logging and hydroelectric interests. By advocating expansion of Banff National Park

Indian Paintbrush

Indian paintbrush is one of the most abundant and easily identified wildflowers in the Rockies. It is usually red, red-orange, yellow or crimson at roadside. Purple and cream-coloured varieties are found at higher elevations. The petals of Indian paintbrush are green. It is the bracts surrounding the petals that are coloured.

This flower is a parasite. It attaches its roots to those of nearby plants, so it can flourish in apparently desolate places—like the gravels at roadside. The colourful bracts attract the two

species of hummingbirds in the Rockies. Varieties of paintbrush occur throughout western North America.

Deer

White-tailed deer

Mule deer

The two species of deer in the Rockies are similar in size and appearance. Both have reddish-brown coats in summer, changing to gray in winter. The coats of the young are spotted. Adult males (bucks) stand about one metre tall at the shoulder. The more common mule deer has larger ears and eyes, and a narrow white tail with a black tip. The tail of the white-tailed deer is wider, matching the colour of the coat on top, and completely white underneath. Both have whitish rump patches.

The antlers of mule deer bucks are equally branched, while those of the white-tailed branch upwards from a forward-reaching main beam. White-tailed and mule deer are occasionally known to crossbreed in the Rockies, producing the mule-tail; it has the ears and eyes characteristic of the mule deer, and the tail and antlers of the white-tailed.

When alarmed, the white-tailed raises its tail and gallops away with the tail switching from side to side. The mule deer flees in hops and bounds. Both species initially bolt a short distance when surprised, often exhaling loudly through the nostrils. From a safe vantage, they will turn around to study their pursuer.

Because they lack upper incisors, deer tear vegetation away from the ground or from branches rather than cropping it the way a horse does. Wolf, coyote, cougar, wolverine, lynx and grizzly bear are the predators of deer. Healthy animals are not often caught, but the young and adults weakened by worms, parasites, or lack of food are frequently taken. Deaths due to road kills and collisions with trains account for three quarters of recorded mule deer mortalities in Banff and Jasper national parks. Please drive carefully.

Where are the Dropped Antlers?

With male elk and deer dropping antlers every year, why aren't we tripping over them when we go for a walk? You will occasionally find a dropped antler in the woods. However, most discarded antlers are quickly eaten by rodents that crave the minerals in the bony material. The remainder of the antlers decompose. Note that all natural objects in national parks are protected, and antler collecting is not permitted.

Castle Mountain

at a time when it was still possible, Howard Douglas ensured that a significant area would remain protected, and unknowingly guaranteed the future existence of the Rocky Mountain parks block.

Wild Bill's Place

Bill Peyto (PEE-toe) was a pioneer outfitter, guide, trapper, prospector and later, a park warden. In the late 19th century and early 20th century, he built a number of cabins in the backcountry of Banff and Kootenay national parks, to serve him on his winter traplines. While tracking a grizzly bear in August of 1993, park wardens discovered a previously unrecorded cabin near the Sunshine interchange. Historians recognized Peyto's craft in the logwork. The cabin could have been an early park warden cabin, or perhaps a secret getaway where Peyto escaped the bustle of nearby Banff.

Twinning of Highway 1

In 1996, Parks Canada twinned the section of Highway 1 between the Sunshine interchange and Castle Junction. The $32 million project increased the length of the four-lane, divided highway to a total of 47 km from Banff's east gate. Although the twinning may improve safety for motorists, and will reduce collisions with elk and deer, the environmental assessment for the project predicted an overall negative impact on the biodiversity of the Bow Valley. Of principal concern is habitat loss, and the highway fencing, which will obstruct wildlife travel routes. The highway design incorporated wildlife underpasses and two overpasses. The suitability of such overpasses for most species was unknown at the time of construction. This gamble on the part of park mangers is one of a myriad of development stresses on the ecosystem of the central Canadian Rockies.

Sawback Range

The Sawback Range forms the eastern flank of the Bow Valley between Banff and Castle Junction. These mountains are part of the front ranges. They feature vertically thrust limestone slabs whose crests have been eroded to create the serrated appearance. An interesting phenomenon is Hole-in-the-Wall, a solution cave high on the slopes of Mt. Cory (2,802 m). Farther north is a free-standing slab of limestone called The Finger. The most picturesque of the Sawback peaks is Mt. Ishbel (2,908 m), particularly in early evening or when dusted with snow. The charred forest on the slopes of the Sawback Range is from forest fires in 1991, 1993 and 1998.

Castle Mountain

Castle Mountain (2,766 m) dominates the east side of the Bow Valley, 30 km west of Banff. James Hector of the Palliser Expedition named the mountain in 1858. In 1946, the name was changed to Mt. Eisenhower to honour Dwight D. Eisenhower, World War II commander of Allied forces in Europe, and later U.S. President. The story goes that Eisenhower was supposed to attend a ceremony to proclaim the new name for the mountain. However, he failed to show up, detained by a golf match elsewhere. Locals took a sarcastic view of the name

change, and the grassy terrace on the south end of the mountain became known as "Eisenhower's green." (It is a good place to look with binoculars for bighorn sheep and mountain goats.) In 1979, the name Castle Mountain was re-associated with the main massif, and the southernmost tower was designated Eisenhower Peak.

Although impressive, Castle Mountain is not one of the high peaks in the Rockies. Several thousand mountains are higher. The highest of Castle's seven summits is not Eisenhower Peak, but the farthest one north. A.P. Coleman made the first ascent of Castle Mountain in 1884. He followed a "walk-up" route on its eastern slopes. The west-facing cliffs are popular with rock climbers.

Gray Jay and Clark's Nutcracker

Gray jay

Clark's nutcracker

The two most common birds on the Chateau Lake Louise grounds are the similar-looking gray jay and Clark's nutcracker, members of the crow family. While chipmunks and ground squirrels have been eyeing your picnic lunch or ice cream cone from ground level, these birds have undoubtedly taken an interest from the air. Initially endearing in their complete lack of fear of humans, these ever-present scavengers will temper your fascination if they depart on the wing with part of your lunch.

The gray jay is the slightly smaller of the two species, with grayish-white plumage, light-coloured face, dark neck and a blunt beak. Immature jays are dark gray. The Clark's nutcracker

is much more chunky in build, with gray plumage and black and white wings. Its long beak is designed for extracting the seeds from lodgepole pine and whitebark pine cones. The bird was named for William Clark of the Lewis and Clark Expedition.

The Clark's nutcracker is the noisier of the two birds. It makes guttural, crow-like sounds. The gray jay is a quieter neighbour, making cooing noises most of the time. Both birds stash food to tide them over during the colder months, although the Clark's nutcracker heads a short distance out of the mountains for most of the winter. While it is tempting to feed these birds, please refrain from doing so.

Mount Temple as seen from Highway 1

Bourgeau Thrust Fault

Highway 1 crosses the Bourgeau Thrust Fault just east of Castle Junction. This bedrock fracture separates the front ranges from the eastern main ranges. Castle Mountain is an eastern main range peak. Its rocks are colourful, and lie in horizontal layers. Mt. Ishbel, southeast of Castle Mountain, is a front range peak. Its rocks are drab, gray limestone that have been thrust vertically. North of Castle Mountain, the mountains you see are in the eastern main ranges.

Castle Junction to Lake Louise

Castle Junction is the intersection of Highway 1 and the Kootenay Parkway (Highway 93 South). The junction is 30 km west of Banff, and 28 km east of Lake Louise village. You may exit here to the Bow Valley Parkway.

From Castle Junction to Lake Louise, Highway 1 follows the Bow River through a doghair forest of lodgepole pine. Many of these trees naturally seeded following a fire that burned much of the Bow Valley between Banff and Lake Louise in 1896. You may see elk, mule deer and black bear here. Canada geese frequent backwaters of the Bow River and often nest near the shoulder of the road. There is a picnic area and toilet at the Taylor Lake trailhead, 8.2 km west of Castle Junction.

As you approach Lake Louise, the enormous shape of Mt. Temple (3,543 m) dominates the west side of the valley. The Lake Louise overflow campground is not a place where lake waters collect during high runoff. It is a gravel pit used as a campground when other campgrounds are full.

Mt. Hector

Between Castle Junction and Lake Louise, westbound travellers have fine views of Mt. Hector (3,394 m) with the Bow River in the foreground. Mt. Hector is one of 56 mountains in the Rockies that exceed 3,353 m. It was named for James Hector of the Palliser Expedition, and was first climbed in 1895. An alpine valley glacier is concealed from view on its north slopes.

Highway 1 crosses the Bow River and the Canadian Pacific Railway 2.9 km before the Lake Louise interchange. Exit if you would like to visit Lake Louise and Moraine Lake. Δ

Coyote and Gray Wolf

Coyote

Gray wolf

The coyote (KEYE-oat, or keye-OAT-eee) and gray wolf are the two most common wild dogs in the Rockies. At first glance, they appear similar. The coyote is smaller, less stocky and more fox-like in profile. Its coat is gray on top, brown on the sides and pale underneath. Usually seen alone or in twos, coyotes occasionally congregate to hunt larger game.

The coyote is a scavenger. Much of its diet comprises the carrion left at kills made by other animals. In campgrounds and towns, coyotes sometimes get into garbage and kill domestic pets. They also feed on rodents, snowshoe hares and some vegetation.

The coyote has few predators. Wolves and cougars might kill it to reduce competition for food, and bears will attack a coyote if it encroaches on a kill. During the hunt, coyotes are frequently trampled under the hooves of deer, elk and moose. Still more die on the highways and railway—between 30 and 50 each year in Banff National Park alone.

The coat of the gray wolf shows much more variation in colour than that of the coyote. Brown fur is common, but black and white animals also occur in the Rockies. The eyes are always yellow. In profile, the wolf is much more stocky than the coyote. Wolves usually travel in packs of up to a dozen animals. The "lone wolf" accounts for about 10 per cent of the population.

Wolves range over territories of several hundred kilometres. The movements of the pack coincide with those of the deer, elk, moose and caribou that comprise the bulk of the wolf diet. An adult wolf consumes an average of 4.5 kg of meat a day—the equivalent to 11-14 caribou, elk or deer a year. Moose, sheep, snowshoe hares and rodents are also hunted.

The wolf is the dominant carnivore in the Rockies. Grizzly bears will not attempt to displace a pack of wolves from a kill. When wolves hunt from a pack, they first single out a victim—usually the young, the old or the infirm. They chase their prey and harass it until it collapses—usually from wounds to the flanks, head and neck. This is dangerous business for the wolf. A wolf that is only five years old may have suffered half a dozen major bone fractures in the course of its hunting career.

Wolf packs have a dynamic and complex social order. The movements of the pack are controlled by the dominant (alpha) female, the only female to breed in the pack. She establishes a den towards the end of winter. It is thought that the size of the litter of pups, born in late April, varies with the availability of food. When conditions are good for the wolf, its litter naturally increases. If the local populations of elk, deer and caribou begin to decline, the wolf's fertility decreases to keep a balance of predator and prey.

The typical litter is half a dozen pups, born with black fur. Once the young are weaned, other pack members may help feed them. By late summer, the pack regroups because teamwork is required for successful winter hunts of large prey. At that time, the howling of wolves—part communication, part territorial claim, part celebration—echoes at night through the low valleys of the Rockies.

The wolf has twice been eradicated from Banff National Park. Its return in the 1980s re-established one of the most important predator-prey relationships. There are six wolf packs in Banff, totalling about 60 animals. However, their future is not secure. Many wolves are killed each year in collisions with trains and vehicles. Wildlife biologists refer to the railway in Banff as the wolf's biggest predator.

Tom Wilson—Trailblazer of the Rockies

"I knew you'd be back. You'll never leave these mountains again as long as you live. They've got you now." It was 1882. Major A.B. Rogers, surveyor of the line through the mountains for the CPR, was addressing outfitter Tom Wilson. Wilson had worked with Rogers the previous summer. The Major was a hard master, and Wilson vowed never to return to the Rockies. But Major Rogers was right. The lure of the unknown was too great for 22-year-old Wilson. He would be in the thick of exploration in the Rockies for the next 20 years.

Wilson was born near Toronto in 1859. He left home at age 16 and wandered through the American midwest. In 1880, he enlisted in the North-West Mounted Police (forerunner of today's RCMP), and served in the Cypress Hills of southern Alberta. The following year, he began his long association with the Rockies, packing supplies for the CPR survey in the Bow Valley.

Wilson had an uncanny ability for being in the right place at the right time during the heyday of exploration in the Rockies. He is credited with several firsts, any of which would have assured him fame: one of the earliest crossings of Kicking Horse Pass, a solitary crossing of Howse Pass and the discoveries of Lake Louise and Emerald Lake. Wilson also claimed many other discoveries, some disputed: the finding of ore on Mt. Stephen, the discovery of Marble Canyon, the first crossing of Wilcox Pass and the first journey in the Yoho Valley. His knack for being in the limelight is best

underscored in that most famous Canadian photograph: "The Last Spike." In the background you can see Wilson in a Stetson hat, eyes fixed on the camera at the historic moment the Canadian Pacific Railway was completed.

Wilson settled in the foothills at Morley in 1885. From there, he led hunting clients into the Rockies. The popularity of the new national park soon prompted a move to Banff. Wilson had learned much about the Rockies during the railway survey—knowledge now in demand. Mountaineers sought his services to better their chances of reaching summits. Tom quickly became Banff's premier outfitter and guide.

After 1898, the mountaineering interest shifted north to peaks near Lake Louise and Columbia Icefield. Wilson and his partner, Bob Campbell, astutely moved their operations to Lake Louise, Field and Emerald Lake. In the course of outfitting mountaineering expeditions of the Dominion Topographic Survey, Wilson topped several summits himself. Wilson hired many assistants.

Two went on to equal him in the lore of the Rockies—"Wild" Bill Peyto (PEE-toe) and Jimmy Simpson. The emergence of the Brewster Brothers as competition and Tom's apparent lack of business acumen rapidly undermined his monopoly on guiding by 1904. The need to find winter range for his large horse stock prompted him to build a ranch and trading house at Kootenay Plains on the North Saskatchewan River. The enterprise failed.

Wilson's influence in the Rockies was waning, but his contribution continued to be recognized. In 1906, he was asked to be a founding member of the Alpine Club of Canada. In 1924, a bronze plaque commemorating Wilson was unveiled at the initial outing of the Trail Riders of the Canadian Rockies in the Yoho Valley. The plaque was later moved to his grave in the Banff cemetery.

In 1920, disillusioned with the failure of his Kootenay Plains venture, Wilson left the Rockies. But Major Rogers' words rang true again, and Tom returned to Banff in 1927. During his last years, he became a fixture at the Banff Springs Hotel and at Chateau Lake Louise, encouraged by the CPR to recount tales of his glory days to enthralled guests. In the limelight again, Tom wasn't ashamed to blow his own horn.

Larger than life, with memories to match, Tom Wilson had returned to the Rockies for the last time. He died in Banff in 1933 after outliving many of his contemporaries. He is commemorated in Mt. Wilson, near Saskatchewan River Crossing.

Lake Louise and Moraine Lake

B y the summer of 1882, the route for the Canadian Pacific Railway had been staked through the Bow Valley to Kicking Horse Pass. Outfitter Tom Wilson was packing supplies for the survey. At camp near the confluence of the Bow River and Pipestone River, Wilson thought he

heard thunder booming through the valley. Stoney natives were camped nearby. Wilson asked them about the sound. They said it came from avalanches on "snow mountain above the lake of the little fishes." The following day, Wilson and his Stoney guide Edwin Hunter visited the lake.

Although Wilson would later ramble at great length about how he had never before gazed upon such a "matchless scene," his initial impression of Lake Louise was perfunctory. It was just another pretty lake in the mountains. (Walter Wilcox, a subsequent explorer, called it "a muskeg filled with mosquitoes and stumps.") Wilson

named it Emerald Lake. Two years later the name was changed to honour Princess Louise Caroline Alberta, the fourth daughter of Queen Victoria and the wife of the Governor General of Canada. The province of Alberta was later named for her.

Lake Louise is 2.4 km long, 500 m wide and 90 m deep. The elevation is 1,731 m— slightly more than a mile above sea level, and 200 m above the floor of the Bow Valley. The lake is fed by glacial meltwater. The maximum surface temperature of 9 °C is reached in August. The lake's surface is frozen from November until June. It's no wonder the fishes are little!

Lake Louise Train Station

The Lake Louise Train Station is one of the oldest buildings at Lake Louise, and dates back to the turn of the century. In 1990, it was proclaimed a National Historic Railway Building. After passenger rail service was discontinued in 1990, the station was redeveloped as a restaurant that includes several restored railway cars. "The Station" helps keep local railway history alive, and is recommended to train buffs.

Fairmont Chateau Lake Louise

Tom Wilson cut a trail to the shore of Lake Louise in 1888. The first building at the lake was a log cabin built that year by Dave White. In 1890, the CPR built its first log chalet. When explorers Samuel Allen and Walter Wilcox booked a visit in 1893, they were told to bring a tent. The chalet had burned. It was succeeded by a split-level, wooden structure that housed 12 guests. Two timbered wings were added in 1900, and the result was a bizarre yet attractive combination of Tudor and Victorian styles, with a capacity of 200 guests.

The 94-room Painter Wing, including the Victoria dining room, was completed in 1913, boosting the building's capacity to 400 guests. The Hillside staff residence was also built that year. A hydroelectric generator was built on Louise Creek in 1917, bringing modern comforts to the remote setting. The rustic Chalet had been transformed into Chateau Lake Louise. *Château* (shah-TOE) is a French word that means "mansion."

Whereas the CPR marketed the Banff Springs Hotel as an all-round resort in the lap of

left: Lake Louise

Hikes

Lake Louise Shoreline
This 1.9-km walkway is wheelchair accessible. In late afternoon, beavers can often be seen along the shoreline.

Plain of Six Glaciers
This hike is a continuation of the Shoreline walk. More challenging than many other hikes in this area, the trail to the Plain of Six Glaciers can also be travelled on horseback. From the teahouse at 2,165 m, you can see six glaciers.

Lake Agnes
The hike to Lake Agnes is popular for the view it offers and the cosy teahouse on the lake shore. On the way to Lake Agnes, you will pass the tiny and picturesque Mirror Lake.

Moraine Lake Rockpile
This easy, 250-m hike offers the area's best view of Moraine Lake and the Wenkchemna Peaks.

Lower Consolation Lake
This 2.9-km hike is a great place to see wildflowers in the summer months. The trail to Lower Consolation Lake is relatively flat, and makes for a leisurely outing.

Larch Valley
This 3.2-km hike is a steep trek that gains 352 m of elevation to a lovely view of the Wenkchemna Peaks.

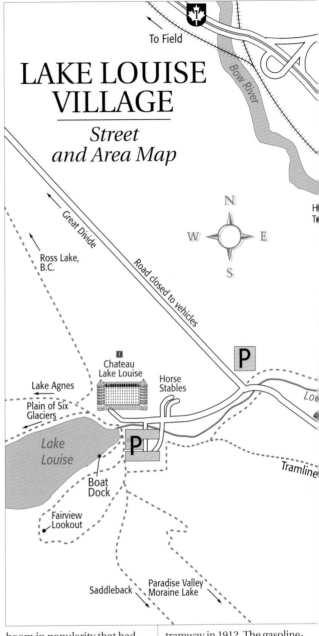

luxury, the Chateau was to appeal to those with an active interest in the outdoors. The sales pitch worked. Mountaineers, artists and trail riders flocked to Lake Louise. The Chateau experienced the boom in popularity that had befallen its sister hotel at Banff.

The alternately dusty and muddy carriage road from Lake Louise Station was a constant source of complaint. Tracks were laid for a narrow-gauge tramway in 1912. The gasoline-powered tram operated until 1930, making as many as 30 round trips from the station each day. Today, the abandoned tram grade is a popular trail for walking, biking and

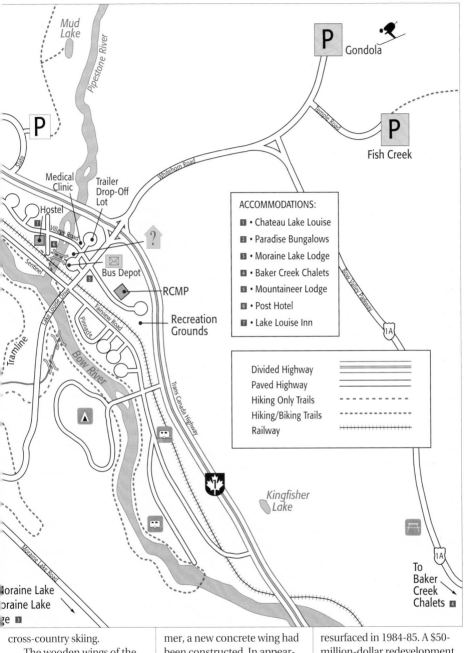

Mud Lake

Pipestone River

P

P Gondola

Temple Road

P

Fish Creek

State

Whitehorn Road

Medical Clinic

Trailer Drop-Off Lot

Hostel

Village Road

Bus Depot

Sentinel

Lake Louise Drive

RCMP

Fairview Road

Pinnacle

Recreation Grounds

Tramline

Bow River

Bow Valley Parkway

1A

Trans Canada Highway

ACCOMMODATIONS:
- 1 • Chateau Lake Louise
- 2 • Paradise Bungalows
- 3 • Moraine Lake Lodge
- 4 • Baker Creek Chalets
- 5 • Mountaineer Lodge
- 6 • Post Hotel
- 7 • Lake Louise Inn

Divided Highway	═══════
Paved Highway	───────
Hiking Only Trails	- - - - -
Hiking/Biking Trails	··········
Railway	+++++++++

Kingfisher Lake

Moraine Lake Road

Moraine Lake
oraine Lake
e 3

To Baker Creek Chalets 4

1A

cross-country skiing.

The wooden wings of the Chateau burned on July 3, 1924, but the hotel didn't miss a beat. Dinner was served that evening in the Victoria dining room. By the following sum-mer, a new concrete wing had been constructed. In appear-ance, the hotel changed little during the next 60 years. The Tom Wilson restaurant was added to the Painter Wing in 1983, and the exterior was resurfaced in 1984-85. A $50-million-dollar redevelopment began in 1986. The 150-room Glacier Wing was added, along with a 400-vehicle parkade, a new entrance, a lobby and a retail area.

The first Chalet

The Chalet in 1909

The capacity of the hotel is now 1,100 guests in 515 rooms. The Chateau has been open year-round since 1983. Some of the 650 summer staff are accommodated in six residences on the hill behind the Chateau.

The poppies that grow on the Chateau grounds are not native to the Rockies. The smaller variety is the Icelandic poppy, native to Siberia. The larger, reddish-orange variety is the Oriental poppy.

School Days

The first recorded mountaineering ascent from the line of the CPR was that of Castle Mountain, by A.P. Coleman in 1884. Surveyors of the Dominion Topographic Survey began routinely topping summits as part of their work in 1886. But recreational mountaineering did not begin in earnest until 1891, when Samuel Allen arrived. Allen's mother was a member of the Philadelphia aristocracy and had visited Lake Louise with the Vaux family in 1889. It was a custom of the Vauxes to give lantern slide presentations detailing their summer outings when back in Philadelphia. Samuel Allen, a

Yale student, attended one of these presentations and was introduced to the Rockies.

Allen made ascents of Mt. Burgess at Field and Devil's Thumb near Lake Louise in 1891. After climbing the Matterhorn in 1892, he returned in 1893, meeting Walter Wilcox, a school mate

from Yale. Their exuberance for tackling the "unconquered difficulties" near Lake Louise was matched only by their relative ignorance of the dangers involved. The pair made two attempts to climb Mt. Victoria and one attempt on Mt. Temple. With their scant mountaineering experience

The First Overnight Guest

During the survey and construction of the Canadian Pacific Railway, the present townsite of Lake Louise was known as "The Summit" because it was near the crest of Kicking Horse Pass. Two men with the last name of Holt were involved with the railway in this locality, and the siding then became optimistically known as Holt City. CPR executive Donald Smith changed the named to Laggan in 1883, recalling a similarity with a mountainous area in his Scottish homeland.

A.P. Coleman, a geology professor from the University of

Toronto, was the first tourist at Laggan. He arrived by construction train in 1884. His first experience with accommodation in the area marked an inauspicious beginning for a destination that would eventually rely solely on tourism, not railway building.

"When darkness fell I paid for my bed in advance, according to the cautious practice of the hostelry, and retired to the grey blankets of bunk No. 2, second tier, in the common guest chamber, trying to shut out sights and sounds from the barroom by turning my back. An hour or two later another man scrambled into the bunk,

The Chateau in the 1920s

The Chateau today

and primitive equipment, they were mere Davids taking on Goliaths of mountains. That they failed is not surprising.

The following summer Allen and Wilcox returned, teaming up with three other students to form the Yale Lake Louise Club. None of the newcomers had experience in

mountaineering. They survived the summer's exploits—although just barely. Three of the party made first ascents of

somewhat the worse for whisky, and tucked himself into the blankets beside me. It appeared that my half-dollar paid for only half the bed."

Undeterred, Coleman made other arrangements for the following evening. While exploring in the vicinity, he lamented the "heaps of foulness and scars of fire that marred the beauty of the valley." Coleman returned to the Rockies frequently during the next 45 years, and carried out important explorations.

As a stay at the lake was the principal reason for getting off the train at Laggan, the siding's name was changed to Lake Louise in 1913, to prevent confusion among the increasing number of visitors.

Mt. Temple and Mt. Aberdeen. Other travels included the first visits to Paradise Valley and to the Valley of the Ten Peaks.

Lake Louise pamphlet from the 1920s

Lake Louise: Twenty Questions

1. What gives the lake its colour?

Fine particles of glacial sediment called rock flour are suspended in the water. Their minute and uniform size allows them to reflect the blue and green wavelengths of light. The colour is affected by the season, the depth of water and the lighting. Mineral content of the water is not significant.

2. How many guests can stay in Chateau Lake Louise?

Up to 1,100.

3. How deep is Lake Louise?

90 m.

4. How long is Lake Louise?

2.4 km. It is 550 m wide.

5. How high is Mt. Victoria?

3,464 m.

6. How far away is Mt. Victoria?

It is 10 km to the cliff beneath Upper Victoria Glacier, and an additional kilometre to the mountain's summit.

7. Why do I keep hearing thunder?

Thunder is uncommon at Lake Louise. You are probably hearing the rumble of snow and ice avalanches from the Upper Victoria Glacier. Sound from these events takes 30 seconds to reach the Chateau, so you may hear the avalanche but miss seeing it.

8. What is that yellow scum on the water?

Yellow tree pollens collect on the water during late June and July.

9. What are the common birds?

There are two similar-looking birds that frequent the Chateau grounds—the Clark's nutcracker and the gray jay. Both have grayish-white plumage, with white and black markings. The Clark's nutcracker is the larger and sleeker looking of the two species, with a pointed beak. You may also see ravens and chickadees.

10. What is the Plain of Six Glaciers?

The Plain is the forefield of Lower Victoria Glacier, from which six glaciers are visible.

11. Who was Louise?

Princess Louise Caroline Alberta was the fourth daughter of Queen Victoria, and the wife of the Governor General of Canada in 1884.

12. Who was Agnes?

Officially, Lake Agnes was named for Lady Susan Agnes Macdonald, the wife of Canada's prime minister in the late 1880s.

13. Is that a California poppy?

The most common flower on the Chateau grounds is the Icelandic poppy, native to Siberia.

14. How cold is the water?

Cold! The annual high temperature of 9 °C is reached in early August.

15. Does the lake freeze?

Yes, from early November until early June.

16. How much snow falls here each year?

The average snowfall is 418 cm.

17. Can you walk around the lake?

A developed trail exists on the northwest shore only.

18. Where do the Chateau staff live?

Most of the staff live in six residences behind the Chateau. Some live in Lake Louise village.

19. Who lives in the house by the bridge?

The house was occupied by the Swiss guides until the 1940s. Since then, it has been the residence of the Chateau manager.

20. Is it safe to drink the water?

The Chateau takes its water from the lake, but it is treated before consumption. It would not be wise to drink the lake water near the shore.

The Chateau Lake Louise

Allen and Wilcox gave many names to features in the area. Most of the names chosen by Allen were of Stoney origin. Allen and Wilcox sometimes each chose a different name for the same feature, and a competitive element entered into their relationship. This culminated when both explorers sought to publicize accounts of their travels. Wilcox's large volume *Camping in the Canadian Rockies* eventually went through many best-selling editions. Later editions also chronicled his attempts on Mt. Assiniboine and his quest for the headwaters of the Athabasca River. His map of the Lake Louise area was remarkably accurate in comparison to Allen's privately published chart. Wilcox also published *Guide to the Lake Louise District,* which in the eyes of the public made him the authority on the area.

Wilcox continued to make annual visits to the Rockies until 1940, with photography being his chief interest. His photographs, taken with a huge plate camera nicknamed "Big Bertha," are a fine visual record. During his later visits, Wilcox took an active interest in what he saw as over-development of the national parks. He died in 1949.

Samuel Allen returned to the Rockies in 1895 but never completed his written work. His father refused to support his son's explorations, and thwarted publication of his map. Allen soon developed what was diagnosed as schizophrenia, and was confined to an institution until his death in 1945. Allen's native names have been adopted in the Lake O'Hara area, but have been largely supplanted near Moraine Lake. The mountain that he named Shappee—peak six of the Wenkchemna Peaks—is today known as Mt. Allen. Mt. Wilcox and Wilcox Pass near Columbia Icefield commemorate Walter Wilcox. The youthful zeal which characterized these adventurers' summer vacations carries into the present. Today, the Rockies are as much a mountaineer's playground as they were a century ago.

Georgia Englehard

Georgia Engelhard first visited Chateau Lake Louise as a 20-year-old in 1926. Swiss guide Edward Feuz Jr. led her to the summit of Pinnacle Mountain near Moraine Lake. Edward was impressed with her stamina, skill and zest for climbing. Georgia Engelhard had found her element, and in a few years would establish herself as a first-class alpinist almost without peer. One of the other Swiss guides commented: "When she goes uphill she goes like a rocket. What she needs is a mountain goat, not a guide."

In the summer of 1929, Georgia climbed nine mountains in nine days, including Hungabee Mountain—one of the most difficult in the region. In 1931, she made 38 ascents, including eight of Mt. Victoria. In 1933, she and Edward Feuz Jr. made the first traverse of Mt. Victoria from south to north (left to right). They took only six hours to travel from Abbot Pass Hut to the teahouse at the Plain of Six Glaciers.

In 1935, Engelhard met O.E. Cromwell in the Swiss Alps. They became inseparable, climbing in Europe and Canada without guides. Eventually, they married. Between them, they accomplished 86 first ascents in the Rockies and Selkirks, and Edward Feuz Jr. said of Georgia that she had been to the summits of more mountains in her 25 years of climbing than he had in his 50 as a guide.

The couple retired to Switzerland, close to the Feuz family's home. Georgia Engelhard died in 1985, and Cromwell followed her a few months later.

Mt. Victoria

More than one million people pause in front of Chateau Lake Louise each year and take more than one million photographs of the lake. Most photographers are attempting to capture the beauty of the water. However, the backdrop—Mt. Victoria—is an inseparable element of the scene and its symmetry. As a result, Mt. Victoria (3,464 m) is probably the most photographed mountain in the Rockies.

Mt. Victoria is also one of the most frequently climbed mountains in the Rockies. Today, most mountaineers reach the summit by following the sinuous and spectacular southeast ridge from Abbot Pass, as did the first ascent party of 1897. This ridge is to the left of the summit as viewed from the Chateau.

In the early 1900s, it was the mark of a successful alpine vacation to have climbed Mt. Victoria. Mt. Victoria North (3,388 m), the righthand peak, was first climbed in 1900. The first complete traverse of the mountain was accomplished in 1909, along the skyline ridge from north to south. The imposing northeast face directly below Mt. Victoria's summit was first climbed in 1922. In 1968, this route was climbed in winter by a group of Calgary mountaineers.

Although a relatively easy peak by contemporary standards when good weather and good conditions prevail, any ascent of Mt. Victoria involves hazards. Avalanches on the approach from Lake Louise are common. On the summit ridge, mountaineers must be extremely careful not to trip or stumble. In places, the icy ridge is less than a metre wide. In 1954, seven Mexican climbers perished in a fall on the mountain's northeast face. A memorial plaque was later taken to the summit—a grim reminder to mountaineers of the risks of their pursuit.

The Plain of Six Glaciers

Although a trip to the summit of Mt. Victoria is for mountaineers only, you don't have to

be a mountaineer to get close to the glaciers on the mountain's flanks. The Plain of Six Glaciers trail is recommended if you have a day available to explore this landscape. Wear sturdy hiking shoes and carry extra clothing and water.

The trail follows the north shore of Lake Louise and passes beneath 100-metre-high cliffs near the lake's far end.

The trail climbs through ancient forest and across avalanche slopes beside the glacial meltwater stream. This is a good place to see hoary marmots. Keep straight ahead at trail junctions. The trail emerges onto moraines on the north side of the forefield of

Lake Louise

Victoria Glacier. From it, six glaciers are visible: Upper Victoria, Lower Victoria, Lefroy and unnamed glaciers on Mt. Lefroy, Mt. Aberdeen and Popes Peak.

The Victoria Glacier was first studied by amateur scientists and photographers of the Vaux family in the 1890s. From their work, glaciologists know that Lower Victoria Glacier has receded 1.2 km in the last 160 years.

The trail follows a short terrace beneath a cliff, and climbs alongside moraines towards the Plain of Six Glaciers tea house. From the switchbacks just before the teahouse, you have a good view of Lower Victoria Glacier. Lower Victoria Glacier has been receding rapidly in recent years. Glaciologists suspect that if this trend continues, the toe of the glacier may become detached from the main body of ice, in which case it will soon waste away. Look for mountain goats near the trail just before the teahouse.

The Plain of Six Glaciers

teahouse was built by Swiss guides for the CPR in 1924. It operates during the summer months, serving lunches and refreshments. The teahouse is nestled in the upper subalpine forest, just out of harm's way beside a large avalanche path. Pikas and hoary marmots live in the boulders nearby.

Capable hikers may continue 750 m beyond the teahouse to a viewpoint overlooking Lower Victoria Glacier. Here, you are in the heart of a glacial landscape. Above, 500-metre-high cliffs glisten with ice and meltwater. Always, there is the unnerving sound of falling rock, as ice, water and wind erode the mountains.

Retrace your route to the trailhead. If you return late, you may see the beavers that live near the delta of Lake Louise. They often walk along the trail nibbling willows, oblivious to tourists.

Lake Agnes

When Tom Wilson visited Lake Louise in 1882, his Stoney guide told him of two other lakes high on a neighbouring mountainside. One of these was named "the goat's looking glass." According to legend, mountain goats combed their beards while gazing at their reflections in the still waters. This lake is now called Mirror Lake. The second lake, subsequently named Lake Agnes for the wife of Canada's first prime

The Swiss Guides

In August of 1896, a group from the Appalachian Mountain Club made an attempt on the yet unclimbed Mt. Lefroy near Lake Louise (3,423 m). It was a tragic and pivotal day in the history of mountaineering and tourism in the Rockies. Near the summit of the mountain, Phillip Abbot unroped from the others to explore a gully. He slipped and fell 500 m to his death. It was the first fatality in North American mountaineering.

Many in the Club questioned the purpose of mountaineering after this shocking event. But in the spirit of the day, Club member Charles Fay decided to avenge Abbot's death. In 1897, Fay and British mountaineer H.B. Dixon organized a group of the world's foremost mountaineers to attempt Mt. Lefroy.

To increase the chance of success, Dixon brought with him Peter Sarbach, a Swiss mountain guide with whom he had climbed in Europe. Without incident, Sarbach led nine climbers, including Fay and Scottish mountaineer John Norman Collie, to the summit, on the anniversary of Abbot's death.

Two things were clear to the CPR: Lake Louise was supplanting Banff as the departure point for mountaineering explorations, and the presence of mountain guides made the mountaineering safer, and more likely to be successful. Successful clients were happy clients who would return. In 1899 the CPR imported Swiss guides of its own, and mountaineering in the Rockies became a thriving business.

Members of Feuz (FOITS) family were the most celebrated Swiss guides. Edward Feuz and his sons Edward Jr., Ernest and Walter, and his nephew Gottfried, made a tremendous contribution to mountaineering in Canada. Between them they led 130 first ascents in the Rockies, Purcells and Selkirks. Most prolific was Edward Feuz Jr., who accounted for 78 of these first ascents between 1903 and his retirement in 1944.

When not exploring new ground, the guides routinely trooped experienced mountaineers and novices up and down the slopes of the most desired summits: Mt. Lefroy, Mt. Temple, Mt. Victoria, Mt. Stephen and Mt. Sir Donald, Their fee was $5.00 per day. In all the mountaineering outings undertaken by the guides during five decades, not a single client was seriously injured.

Five summits of Mt. Lyell (lie-ELL), west of Saskatchewan River Crossing, were named in honour of five of the Swiss guides in 1972. Most of the other guides had prominent mountains named for them earlier in the century. Edward Feuz Jr., the last of the original Swiss guides, died at Golden in 1981 at age 96.

Lake Agnes

Plain of Six Glaciers

minister, is an excellent example of a glacial tarn. Together, the lakes were called "the lakes in the clouds" by the CPR in its promotions at the turn of the century. Both lakes can be viewed from the Lake Agnes trail.

The hike to Lake Agnes is the most popular excursion in the Rockies. Most people are attracted by the teahouse on the lakeshore, but there are other attractions on this steep, 3.4-km hike. Take a leisurely pace and pause often to observe the interesting features of the landscape.

The Lake Agnes trail branches from the Lake Louise lakeshore trail just beyond the Chateau, and immediately begins its ascent through damp, lower subalpine forest. The dominant trees are Engelmann spruce and subalpine fir, with an undergrowth of feathermosses. From the first switchback at km 1.6, Lake Louise is visible directly below. The gravelly area at the end of the lake is a delta. You may see muddy sediment plumes dispersing into the water. Across the lake are the quartzite cliffs of Fairview Mountain (2,744 m). At this point, you are

slightly less than halfway to Lake Agnes.

As you continue the climb, notice the gradual transition to upper subalpine forest. The trail crosses a swath that formerly contained a wooden pipeline, used when Lake Agnes was the water source for the Chateau. A section of pipeline is still imbedded in the trail. At the horse-hiker barrier, turn left. In a few minutes, you reach "the goat's looking glass"—Mirror Lake. Big Beehive forms the backdrop for the lake. Goats don't frequent Mirror Lake anymore, but you may see them on distant mountainsides.

Climbing away from Mirror Lake, the trail enters an open area in the forest—the bottom of a kilometre-long avalanche path on Mt. St. Piran. Snow avalanches sweep the mountainside here in winter and spring, precluding the growth of mature trees. The jumble of dead trees and branches downslope from the trail testifies to the power of these avalanches.

Mt. St. Piran was named for the English birthplace of the first manager of Chalet Lake Louise—Willoughby Astley. He

supervised the clearing of many trails in the area, including this one. Higher on the mountainside, the trail enters stands of Lyall's larch. Mt. Aberdeen (3,151 m) and the glacier-capped summit of Mt. Temple (3,543 m) are visible to the south.

Bridal Veil Falls is 500 m from Mirror Lake. Immediately above the falls is the teahouse on the shore of Lake Agnes. Big Beehive flanks the south side of Lake Agnes. Directly across the lake is the pinnacle of Devil's Thumb (2,458 m), first climbed by Samuel Allen in 1891. The two high peaks to the west are Mt. Whyte (2,983 m) and Mt. Niblock (2,976 m). These mountains were named for a vice president and superintendent of the CPR, respectively. Apparently, Whyte and Niblock enjoyed the fishing in Lake Agnes. Their success may have been too great, for fish repopulate slowly in the cold, nutrient-deficient water and are scarce in the lake now. Fishing is no longer allowed. The surface of Lake Agnes is frozen from late October until June.

If you're feeling tired, it may be the effects of the climb. Since leaving the

Chateau, you have gained 387 m, roughly the equivalent of 130 flights of stairs. Lunch, refreshments and snacks are available in-season at the teahouse. The original teahouse was built in 1901 by the CPR. The present building is a privately owned reconstruction, completed in 1981. Just south of the lake's outlet is an interpretive display that describes the history of the teahouses.

You may see hoary marmots and pikas in the rocks along the lakeshore beyond the tea house. Red squirrels, least chipmunks, Columbian ground squirrels, golden-mantled ground squirrels, Clark's nutcrackers and gray jays compete for your attention

Sunrise on Lake Louise

nearby. Please refrain from feeding them.

If you have energy remaining, you may extend this hike to Little Beehive, Big Beehive, or the other teahouse at the Plain of Six Glaciers. Otherwise, it's all downhill back to the Chateau.

Coniferous, but Not Evergreen

One of the most popular trails near Moraine Lake leads to Larch Valley, located between Pinnacle Mountain and Mt. Temple. The valley is named for the species of tree called Lyall's larch, or subalpine larch. This tree is rare in Canada. It grows only in scattered mountainous areas of southwestern Alberta and southeastern B.C. It does not occur north of Bow Pass in the Rockies. The tree was named for David Lyall, a naturalist with the Franklin Expedition.

The branches of Lyall's larch are gnarled in appearance. They feature small, black knobs that bear clusters of bright green needles. The branches are often covered in a black, woolly down. Larch trees are deciduous conifers—they shed their needles annually. This shedding is an adaptation feature that conserves hard-to-obtain nutrients

in the winter. Before dropping off in early October, the needles turn yellow and gold. Then the tree becomes dormant with the buds for next year's growth already formed.

Because of the high elevation at which they are found, Lyall's larches are very slow-growing. They prefer rocky soil and are seldom consumed by fire. Large trees are often several hundred years old. The treeline larch forest is not dense, and flower-filled glades add to the attraction in summer. Under blue skies and with the Wenkchemna Peaks as

Larch forest

a backdrop, Larch Valley is a photographer's paradise in autumn, and in recent years has been a very popular destination.

Strong hikers can climb beyond Larch Valley to the crest of Sentinel Pass. At 2,611 m, the pass is the highest point reached by trail in the mountain national parks.

The Giant Steps in Paradise Valley

Lake Louise Ski Area

The Lake Louise Ski Area is the largest in Canada, with 12 lifts and 40 runs on three mountainsides. The ski area evolved from the enterprise of Sir Norman Watson, an eccentric Englishman who sought to build a system of ski chalets in the Rockies, modelled after those in Switzerland and Austria. Watson financed the expansion of Skoki Lodge in 1936 and the construction of Temple Lodge in 1938. The parks branch did not allow any other chalets to be constructed, and Watson turned his efforts to developing the first ski lifts and clearing runs on Whitehorn Mountain and Lipalian Mountain.

One chairlift at the Lake Louise Ski Area operates in the summer, taking passengers to Whitehorn Lodge. This vantage provides an excellent view of the Bow Valley and the mountains near Lake Louise.

Skoki Valley

The front range valleys northeast of Lake Louise include some of the most spectacular alpine terrain in Banff National Park. Within a day's hike of the trailhead are more than a dozen lakes, appealing subalpine and alpine meadows, and half a dozen valleys to explore. The area is known as Skoki (SKOWE-key).

In 1911, a group of American mountaineers climbed in the area, naming many of the features, including the Skoki Valley. *Skoki* is a native word that means "marsh." In 1931, local ski enthusiasts constructed one of the Rockies' first ski lodges in the valley. Today, Skoki Lodge is

Charles Fay

The mountain that Samuel Allen named Heejee (Peak One) is now known as Mt. Fay, in honour of Professor Charles Fay of Boston. Fay and his companions from the Appalachian Mountain Club made annual pilgrimages to the Rockies at the turn of the 20th century, and accomplished first ascents of many high mountains: Hector, Lefroy, Victoria, Goodsir South, Vaux, Chancellor and Balfour. Fay was also in the party that made the third ascent of Mt. Stephen near Field. The Club's journal, *Appalachia,* communicated the mountaineers' adventures, and greatly increased the popularity of the Rockies with climbers from the U.S. and Europe.

As well as being the founder of the Appalachian Mountain Club, Fay established the American Alpine Club in 1902.

He made twenty-five visits to the Rockies, including one at age 84 in 1930, the year of his death.

When Mt. Fay (3,234 m) was named in 1902, it was still unclimbed. Professor Fay came to the Rockies in 1904 to make its first ascent. Unfortunately, hijinks by two guides, the Kaufmann brothers, conspired to place English mountaineer Gertrude Benham on the summit on the same day that Fay made his unsuccessful attempt. Fay was incensed. He registered a complaint with the CPR, and the Kaufmanns were dispatched to Switzerland, never to return to Canada.

The glacier beneath Mt. Fay extended almost to Moraine Lake a century ago. The prominent ice bulge on the mountain's north face is now one of the most popular alpine climbs on the continent.

Moraine Lake from the Rockpile

operated by the Lake Louise Ski Area, and hosts hikers and skiers in a rustic atmosphere. It is reached by a 14-km hike or ski from the Fish Creek parking lot.

Paradise Valley

In 1894, members of the Yale Lake Louise Club made the first visit to Paradise Valley. As is often the case with exploration, the discovery was made in a roundabout fashion. Walter Wilcox, Samuel Allen and their companions entered the valley by a high mountain pass at its head instead of following the creek from the Bow Valley in the manner of today's trail.

On that day in 1894, the weather had been poor and the surroundings gloomy as the party toiled up the pass. But from its crest, through thinning clouds, came a glimpse of an idyllic, mead-owed valley to the south. Struck by the contrast, Allen

bestowed the name *Wastach*, which means "beautiful." Wilcox called it Paradise Valley.

Throwing caution to the wind, the party descended into the trackless new valley, not certain how they would get out of it and back to Chalet Lake Louise. At the conclusion of a very long day, two of the group were benighted; and their campfire, too pathetic to give much comfort when needed, later rekindled and set much of the valley ablaze.

Today, hikers and back-packers enter Paradise Valley from the trailhead at km 2.3 on the Moraine Lake Road. Features of the area include: Annette Lake, the north face of Mt. Temple, Horseshoe Glacier, stands of Lyall's larch and a series of slab waterfalls known as the Giant Steps. Hiking cir-cuits can be made to Lake Louise via Saddleback Pass, and to Moraine Lake via Sentinel

Pass. One of the most easily accessible backcountry camp-sites in Banff National Park is located in Paradise Valley.

Moraine Lake

Whereas Lake Louise is known for its symmetry and early morning calm, the vista at Moraine Lake is more austere. The forbidding cliffs of the Wenkchemna Peaks brood close at hand, dominating a stark landscape of rock, ice, water and sky.

Samuel Allen and Walter Wilcox first glimpsed Moraine Lake from the slopes of Mt. Temple in 1893. Allen called it Heejee Lake. A year later, Wilcox crossed Wastach Pass into the upper part of the Valley of the Ten Peaks. The stark nature of the valley was in marked con-trast to the lush green of Paradise Valley to the north. In response, Wilcox coined the name "Desolation Valley."

Tower of Babel and Mt. Babel

The upper valley floor is indeed desolate. The ice-mantled, shaded, north faces of the Wenkchemna Peaks are a sombre and imposing sight, towering more than 1,200 m above the Wenkchemna Glacier. The obvious, ice-filled couloir at the far end of the lake is often used by mountaineers as an approach to the routes above. Rockfall in the couloir is common. Not surprisingly, fatal accidents occur.

Walter Wilcox made the first visit to the shore of Moraine Lake in 1899. He later wrote: "No scene has given me an equal impression of inspiring solitude and rugged grandeur." Ignoring Allen's previous name for the lake, Wilcox named it on the assumption that the rockpile that dams its outlet is a glacial moraine. Although many other lakes in the Rockies are dammed by moraines, geologists think that Moraine Lake is dammed by rockslide debris. Some have suggested that the rockslide debris landed atop glacial ice and was deposited at the outlet when the ice receded. This would make the Rockpile both rockslide debris and moraine!

You are encouraged to walk the interpretive trail to the top of the Rockpile for the famous "twenty-dollar view." The Wenkchemna Peaks were featured on the Canadian twenty-dollar bill until 1989. The boulders in the Rockpile

Moraine Lake Rockpile

Walter Wilcox, the first visitor to Moraine Lake, was a keen and knowledgeable observer of the landscape. He named the lake on the assumption that its waters are dammed by a moraine deposited by the Wenkchemna Glacier—a manner in which many other lakes in the Rockies have been formed.

Wilcox was probably incorrect. It seems likely that the Moraine Lake Rockpile was deposited by a rockslide from the cliffs to the south. The boulder fields attest to the fact that the cliffs are in a continual process of tumbling down, and one can almost trace the path of this rockslide in the scarring on the hillside.

Another theory states that the Rockpile may have been a rockslide that landed on the glacier while the ice was still advancing. The boulders were transported to

The Tower of Babel as seen from the Rockpile trail

this point as surface moraine and deposited when the glacier receded. Yet another theory states that the rockslide came to rest on top of an existing moraine. Whether dammed by rockslide or moraine, the name Moraine Lake is still appropriate. Fine examples of moraines are visible at the far end of the lake, and part of the

Moraine Lake Road is built along the crest of the lateral moraine.

Moraine Lake is less than half the size of Lake Louise, and is relatively shallow. There is considerable seasonal variation in the volume of water it contains, and by autumn in some years, the level is so reduced that barely a trickle escapes at the outlet.

are Gog quartzite and silt-stone, rock formations that underlie the lower half of the Wenkchemna Peaks. Gog quartzite is one of the oldest and hardest rocks commonly visible in this part of the Rockies. Many of the boulders are covered with ancient, slow-growing rock lichens. Some feature fossils. Several slabs in the Rockpile display rippled surfaces—a permanent record of wave action on the ocean floor where the sediments were deposited 560 million years ago.

Hiking trails depart from the parking lot for Sentinel Pass, Larch Valley, Wenkchemna Pass, Paradise Valley, Lake Louise and Consolation Lakes. The Moraine Lake Road is not plowed in winter. During this time, the lake is the sole domain of cross-country skiers and a few mountaineers. Meals, accommodation and boat rentals are available in-season at Moraine Lake Lodge.

The Wenkchemna Peaks

Samuel Allen and Walter Wilcox first saw Moraine Lake and the surrounding mountains during their attempt on Mt. Temple in 1893. The following summer, Allen observed the mountains again from Sentinel Pass. He named them using the Stoney words for the numbers one to ten. *Wenkchemna* means "ten."

Allen's nomenclature was arbitrary, as there are more than ten peaks alongside the valley. Most of Allen's names have now been replaced with names of politicians and mountaineers, but peaks four,

Aerial view of Moraine Lake

nine and ten—Tonsa, Neptuak and Wenkchemna—retain their original names. Peak six is now called Mt. Allen. Other names bestowed by Samuel Allen are still in use in the Lake O'Hara area.

Popularly called "The Ten Peaks," the name "Wenkchemna Peaks" was officially adopted in 1979. The highest is Deltaform Mountain (Peak Eight), at 3,424 m.

Mt. Temple

Mt. Temple (3,543 m) dominates the northwest edge of the Valley of the Ten Peaks. Mt. Temple is one of the largest mountains in the Rockies, occupying 15 square kilometres. It is the eleventh

Pika

The tiny pika (PEE-kah or PIE-kah) is largely heard but not seen. It lives in the quartzite blocks and rubble of boulderfields and rockslides. With a minuscule tail, big, round ears and a gray coat, it looks like a tennis ball with ears. The pika's folk name is "rock rabbit." It is one of two members of the rabbit family in the Rockies. The other is the snowshoe hare.

The pika is active during the daytime. It gathers grasses, lichens, leaves and wildflowers and dries them on boulders. It then stashes the haul within the boulderfield. The pika does not hibernate. During the winter, it uses rocky corridors under the snow to reach its food caches. It also eats partially digested pel-

lets of its own dung. The pika has two sets of upper incisor teeth, one behind the other.

Large boulderfields may feature a colony of pikas, which take turns acting as lookouts. The characteristic shrill "eeeep" warns their fellows of approaching danger. Eagles and hawks can pick off the pika from above. More dangerous are martens, ermine and weasels, which hunt the pika through its bouldery home.

Lower Consolation Lake

highest in the range, and the third highest in Banff National Park. The mountain was named for Sir Richard Temple, patron leader of a scientific expedition that visited the Rockies in 1884. The summit glacier was named Macdonald Glacier after Canada's first prime minister.

Samuel Allen, Walter Wilcox and L.F. Frissell made the first ascent of Mt. Temple in 1894, the first time a summit exceeding 3,353 m had been reached in Canada. It was seven years until a higher mountain was climbed. Their climbing route, not visible from Moraine Lake, is the "regular route" on the mountain today.

In the 1960s, climbers began to pit their skills against the mile-high, glacier-capped north face of Mt. Temple that rises above Paradise Valley.

Eight routes have since been established. Some combine a high degree of difficulty and danger. The east ridge, climbed from the Moraine Lake Road, is also a popular route.

Consolation Valley

Suddenly a long stretch of water opened before us and disclosed a beautiful scene. Beyond the pretty banks of the stream, lined with birch and willow bushes, appeared in the distance an Alpine peak, fringed in a narrow border of ice near its tooth-like crest…Everything in these beautiful surroundings helped to make one of the most beautiful pictures I have ever seen in the Rockies.

Two days after his first visit to Moraine Lake Walter Wilcox explored the Consolation Valley. The new valley con-

trasted with the austere Desolation Valley beyond Moraine Lake, and gave rise to the quoted passage. Thus, Consolation Valley was named.

Today, you can follow Wilcox's path to Lower Consolation Lake and enjoy the same view. Along the way, you pass the Tower of Babel, the flat-topped peak immediately east of the Moraine Lake Rockpile. The "tooth-like crest" is Mt. Bident (3,084 m) and Quadra Mountain (3,173 m). A hanging glacier occupies the ledge beneath them. Upper Consolation Lake is concealed from view farther up the valley.

The Consolation Lakes are tarns—lakes that occupy glacially-scoured depressions. The valley floor is covered with boulders that have tumbled from the cliffs of Mt. Babel (3,101 m) and Mt. Fay (3,234 m) to the west. These boulders have dammed Lower Consolation Lake. The boulders are covered in rock lichens and are home to hoary marmots. Their shrill whistles of warning may be heard echoing in the valley.

The upper Consolation Valley is no less a chaos of moraine and rubble than exists in the Valley of the Ten Peaks. However, the larch-covered slopes of Panorama Ridge to the east are the consolation—a delight to the eye—especially in autumn, when the larch needles turn gold. ∆

Yoho National Park

T he junction of the Icefields Parkway is 2.7 km west of Lake Louise on Highway 1. This is the most troublesome intersection for tourists in the Rockies. Many people confuse directions to the town of Field with Columbia Icefield. They end up bewildered in Field, looking for

glaciers where there are none. Turn north (right) onto the Icefields Parkway (Highway 93 North) if you want to visit Columbia Icefield and Jasper. Keep straight ahead for Field, Yoho National Park and Golden.

Approach to Kicking Horse Pass

Just west of the Icefields Parkway junction, Highway 1 crosses the Bow River. From here to Kicking Horse Pass, the highway follows Bath Creek. The braided creek bed is a good place to see wildlife: coyote, wolf, moose, elk, black bear and grizzly bear. The forest here is a homogenous stand of lodgepole pine. The double tracks of the CPR are adjacent to the highway. The line that is higher on the embankment was completed in 1982 to

lessen the grade for westbound trains between Lake Louise and Kicking Horse Pass. The lower grade is steeper, and is generally used by eastbound trains, most of which are empty. Highway 1 curves sharply west, crosses Bath Creek and begins the short climb to Kicking Horse Pass.

Kicking Horse Pass

Highway 1 reaches the crest of Kicking Horse Pass, 9.7 km west of Lake Louise. This is the boundary between Banff National Park, Alberta, and Yoho National Park, B.C. The elevation just west of the pass is 1,646 m, the highest point on Highway 1 in Canada. Most people expect a time zone change here at the B.C.-Alberta border. However, the change from Mountain time to Pacific time takes place 120 km west on Highway 1, at Glacier National Park. Cathedral Mountain (3,189 m) is prominent in the view west. Cathedral Glacier covers its eastern slopes.

In July of 1871, the province of British Columbia entered Confederation. Eastern Canadians had been anxious that B.C. be included to prevent the resource-rich province from coming under U.S. control. Part of the deal

negotiated between Canada and its newest province called for a railway connection to the rest of the country, to be completed within a decade.

The construction of Prime Minister John A. Macdonald's "national dream" of railway steel from coast to coast was a saga that took 14 years to play out. The characters, intrigue and scandal involved are the stuff of Canadian legend. The financial cost was not one the fledgling country could bear, thus a syndicate of wealthy businessmen was formed— the Canadian Pacific Railway. These dedicated men eventually spirited the railway through crisis after crisis, and, mortgaged to the hilt, oversaw its construction between 1881 and 1885.

The difficult terrain on the west slope of Kicking Horse Pass made it a poor choice for the route of the railway. Yellowhead Pass and Howse Pass to the north each offered easier prospects for railway construction. The Yellowhead route had the backing of many surveyors, including the original engineer-in-chief of the CPR, Sandford Fleming. Of a journey over Kicking Horse Pass, Fleming wrote: "I do not think I can ever forget that terrible walk; it was the greatest

left: Mt. Stephen and the Yoho River

JOINS PAGE 98

Hwy 1A closed
at Lake Louise

President
Pass
3124
The Vice
President
3063
The
President
Emerald
Pass
Mount
rpole
President
Range
PRESIDENT
Mount
Carnarvon
2545
ATIONAL
RANGE
Emerald
Peak
Michael
Peak
Yoho Pass
Emerald
Lake
Wapta
Mountain
2788
PARK
Burgess
Pass
Mount
Burgess
Monarch Campground

⛺ Monarch Campground
⛺ Kicking Horse Campground

Daly Gla
Niles
Glacier
Mount
Niles
Mount
Waputik
Peak
Bath
Glacier
93
1900
Mount Bosworth
Lost
Lake
Herbert
Lake
JOINS PAGE 98
Mud
Mount Ogden
Paget
Peak
Sherbrooke
Lake
Kicking Horse Pass
Upper Canyon
Narao
Peak
1A
Mount Niblock
Mount St Riran
The Beehive
Devils Thumb
Mount Agnes
1731
Lake
Louise
Popes Peak
Plain of the
Six Glaciers
2744 Fairview Mo
BOW
Saddle
Mounta

Field
Mount
Stephen 3185
Cathedral
Crags
Vanguard
Peak
3185
Cathedral
Mountain
Haddo Peak
Mount
Aberdeen 3152
3070
Sheol
Mtn

Mount
Dennis
Dennis
Pass
Duchesnay
Pass
2400
Mount
Victoria
3459
Wiwaxy
Peaks
Mount
Huber
Lefroy
Glacier
The Mitre
Giant
Steps
RANGE
Paradise Valley
Mou
Temp

Boulder
Creek
CP
Natural
Bridge
1
Mount
Duchesnay
Odaray
Pass
Odaray
Mountain
Lake O'Hara
Mount
Lefroy
Mount
Oesa
Anne

McArthur
Pass
Lake
McArthur
Mount
Schaffer
Ringrose
Peak
Yukness Mountain
Pinnacle
Mountain
Horseshoe
Glacier
3067
Sentinel
Pass
Pinnacle
Peak
Larch
Valley
Wastach Pass
1887

NATIONAL
Park
Mountain
Mount
Owen
2800
Opabin
Pass
Hungabee Mountain
Biddle Pass
Mount Biddle
Curtis Peak
Wenkchemna Peak
3490
Wenkchemna Pass
Eiffel L
Eiffel Pk
Wastach Glacier

Mount
Hurd
Hurd
Pass
Misko
Mountain
Neptuak Mountain
Deltaform Mountain
Misko
Pass
Kaufmann
Lake
Mount Tuzo 3246
Mount Allen
Mount Perren
PROSPECTORS
VALLEY
Pekim

Allan Peak
Fulmen
Mountain
Ottertail Falls
Mount Vaux • 3307
Mount
Ennis
Hanbury
Peak
Mount
Oke
1800

Chancellor Peak
mpground

Hanbury
Glacier
OTTERTAIL
Silverstope Ck
McArthur Creek
Goodsir Creek
Goodsir
Pass
River
2200
Ottertail
Pass
Creek
Helmet

Hoodoo Ck
3277
Chancellor
Peak
⛺ Hoodoo Creek
Campground
Butwell
Peak
North
Tower 3520
Mount Goodsir
South
Tower 3581
Sentry Peak
Goodsir
Glacier
Sharp
Mountain
Sharp
Glacier
Helmet
Falls
Limestone Peak
West Washmawapta
Glacier
Washmawapta
Icefield

Aquila
Mountain
Wapta Falls
Zinc Creek
Helmet
Mountain
Zinc
Mountain
3154
1400

Clawson
Peak
Tatton Ck
1600
YOHO
OTTERTAIL RANGE
Manganese Mountain
Buttress
Peak
2941
Rockwall
Pass
Wolverine Pass

Coral
Mountain
CROZIER ROAD
Beaverfoot
Mount
Mollison
Striped
Mountain
2000
Mount Drysdale
Mount
Gray
2910
Tumbling
Glacier

trial I ever experienced."

However, the purpose of the railway was to help bind the young country together, and to introduce settlement onto the prairies. If the line was constructed through Yellowhead Pass, the prairie adjacent to the U.S. border would come under U.S. influence. Thus, the selection of Kicking Horse Pass in 1881 was a desperate political and economic one, and the difficulties presented by the surveyor's line would be dealt with later. On the Big Hill west of the pass, the CPR is still dealing with the costly consequences of this decision.

FIELD
Street Map

100 metres

Yoho National Park

The origin of Yoho National Park is connected with the construction of the railway. By December of 1883, the track had been laid to the crest of Kicking Horse Pass. The following year, the railway was completed through what is today the park. The community of Field developed to support railway operations. In 1886, the CPR built a dining room at Field to eliminate the need to haul heavy dining cars over the pass.

Passengers who stopped at Field were enthralled with the mountain scenery. William Cornelius Van Horne, the CPR general manager, decided to enlarge the dining room and add facilities for overnight accommodation. The new building was named Mt. Stephen House. It was the CPR's first hotel in the Rockies.

Soon, the town of Field became a destination for climbers, artists and scientists. At the prompting of the CPR, the government set aside an area of 16 square kilometres near the foot of Mt. Stephen. The Mount Stephen Reserve was the forerunner of Yoho,

Yoho National Park To Do List

Sights
- Burgess Shale 343-6783
- Emerald Lake
- The Great Divide
- Lake O'Hara 343-6433
- Leanchoil Hoodoos
- The Meeting of the Waters
- Natural Bridge
- Spiral Tunnels
- Takakkaw Falls
- Twin Falls
- Wapta Falls

Camping 250-343-6783
- Chancellor Peak
- Hoodoo Creek

- Kicking Horse
- Takakkaw Falls

Horseback Riding
- Emerald Stables, 100 m south of the Emerald Lake parking lot 343-6000

Boat Rentals
- Emerald Sports 343-6000

Hostels 403-762-4122
- Whiskey Jack

Entertainment
- Interpretive programs: 343-6783
- Libraries: 344-6516, 762-2661
- Movies: 344-5510, 762-8595

Where are the Icefields?

If you are looking for the "icefields" at Field, you missed the turnoff for the Icefields Parkway. Drive 25 km east from Field to the junction with Highway 93 North. Follow signs for Jasper and Columbia Icefield at this junction.

Canada's second national park.

In 1897, German explorer Jean Habel (AHH-bull) published an account of his explorations in the Yoho Valley. Habel's principal discovery was a lofty waterfall. Van Horne went to see the waterfall for himself and christened it *Takakkaw* (TAH-kuh-kah), Cree for "it is wonderful." Pressure mounted from the CPR, local outfitters and explorers to enlarge the Mt. Stephen Reserve to include the Yoho Valley. This was accomplished in 1901, with the founding of the Yoho Park Reserve. Yoho is a Cree expression of awe and wonder. National park status followed in 1911. Since 1930, Yoho has included 1,313 square kilometres. The first road from Lake Louise to Golden, called The Kicking Horse Trail, was completed in 1927. Highway 1 was completed through the park in 1958.

Lake O'Hara

Since the first accounts extolling the beauties of Lake O'Hara appeared at the end of the 19th century, the area has exerted an irresistible pull on mountain-lovers from all over the world. Lake O'Hara's chief attractions are more than two dozen lakes, rugged peaks and alpine meadows. Adding to the lure is motorized access. Bus transportation is available to a campground and lodge, central to a network of hiking trails.

Surveyor J.J. McArthur first saw Lake O'Hara in 1887. He mentioned it to a retired British colonel, Robert O'Hara, who subsequently made several visits. In the fashion of the day, it became known as "O'Hara's Lake." The Alpine

Club of Canada held one of its first annual camps near the lake in 1909, and the CPR built a bungalow camp on the shore in 1926. These cabins were the forerunner of today's privately owned Lake O'Hara Lodge.

Lake O'Hara is located directly across the continental divide from Lake Louise. Some of the mountains that form O'Hara's backdrop are familiar in name, if not in appearance, from this perspective. Many

The Great Divide

The junction with Highway 1A is 2.3 km west of Kicking Horse Pass. You can backtrack three km along Highway 1A to The Great Divide. Here, Divide Creek wanders onto the continental divide and branches. You can stand with the provincial boundary between your feet, and watch the parting of waters destined for two oceans, 4,500 km apart. The creek is usually dry by late summer.

The Great Divide is one of the few artificial tourist attractions in the Rocky Mountain parks. The bed of the creek has been lined with concrete and boulders to force the creek to divide. No doubt the creek originally divided naturally. But such a feature is bound to be short-lived. One branch of the creek would eventually erode a deep-

er channel and capture all the flow. The initial creekbed engineering was the work of the CPR. Curiously, no one has since thought it appropriate to remove it.

The Great Divide is a good viewpoint for train enthusiasts. The tracks of the CPR pass close by. A cairn commemorates explorer James Hector, who made the first crossing of Kicking Horse Pass in 1858. Another cairn and plaque describe the work of the Interprovincial Boundary Survey from 1913 to 1925. Interpretive displays contrast the eastern slopes and western slopes of the Rockies. The Ross Lake trailhead is on Highway 1A, two kilometres east of the junction with Highway 1. It is a 1.2 km walk to the peaceful lake.

Lake O'Hara

Highway Passes in the Rockies

Pass	Elevation	Corridor	First Recorded Crossing
Kicking Horse	1,625 m	Highway 1, CPR	Hector, 1858
Vermilion	1,651 m	Kootenay Parkway	Hector, 1858
Yellowhead	1,125 m	Yellowhead Highway, CNR	Unknown, ca. 1820
Bow	2,069 m	Icefields Parkway	Hector, 1858
Sunwapta	2,035 m	Icefields Parkway	Wilcox, 1896
Highwood	2,210 m	Highway 40, Kananaskis	unknown
White Man (Canmore)	1,677 m	Smith-Dorrien/Spray Road South of Canmore	unknown

names in the area are Stoney in origin, and were given by mountaineer Samuel Allen between 1893 and 1895.

The number of visitors to the Lake O'Hara area is controlled in an attempt to reduce impacts on the fragile alpine vegetation. Visitors must make reservations in advance to stay overnight in the campground, cabins or lodge, and to ride the bus. The access road is not open to public vehicles or bicycles. You may choose to hike to Lake O'Hara, but you will still require a reservation to stay overnight. Call Yoho National Park well in advance for details: 250-343-6783.

Where Waters Divide

Just west of the Highway 1A junction there are rock cuts at roadside. Look for mountain goats here in early summer. For decades, bighorn sheep were thought to be absent from Yoho. However, in the early 1990s, sheep were seen at the mineral lick near these rock cuts. They now probably range on Mt. Bosworth, directly north.

A navigable break that leads across a mountain range is known as a mountain pass. In the Rockies, if a mountain pass separates rivers that flow to different oceans, the pass is on the continental divide. Kicking Horse Pass is on the continental divide. There are hundreds of passes in the Rockies, but most are rugged and remote, and today, only three on the continental divide are crossed by roads in the Rocky Mountain parks.

The major passes in the Rockies were scoured by ice ages during the last 2.4 million years. The lakes found near these passes formed after the Wisconsin Glaciation—the most recent ice age. Lobes of ice detached atop the passes as the Wisconsin glaciers receded. The ice melted and slumped into hollows, creating lakes called kettle ponds. Wapta Lake is an example of a kettle pond. During construction of Highway 1 in 1956, permafrost was uncovered in a road cut near the lake—evidence of the last ice age. The marsh at the east end of Wapta Lake is ideal habitat for beaver and water-fowl. You can see several large beaver lodges from the highway.

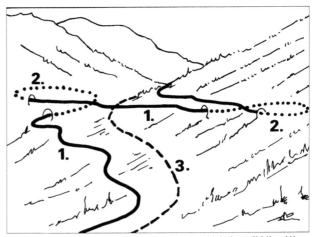

Diagramatic view of the Spiral Tunnels in which the solid line (1) represents the exposed track, the dotted line (2) represents the tunnelled part of the railway track, and the dashed line (3) indicates the Trans-Canada Highway

Western Slopes Rivers

West of Wapta Lake, the Kicking Horse River begins its steep descent from the continental divide. Because they have less distance to travel to reach sea level, rivers on the western slopes of the Rockies have steeper gradients than those on the eastern slopes. With more energy, they carve deeper, V-shaped valleys. You can see the V-shape clearly in the upper Kicking Horse Valley west of Wapta Lake.

The Big Hill

From Wapta Lake to the river flats east of Field, the Kicking Horse Valley descends almost 300 m in six kilometres. The terms of the CPR's agreement with the government required that the grade of the railway line could not exceed 2.2 per cent. The Kicking Horse Valley dictated a grade twice as steep.

To comply with the terms of the agreement would have meant the construction of tun-nels. The work would have required at least an extra year. The CPR needed to be in

A Hero Remembered

There are three railway sidings on The Big Hill. One of these commemorates engineer Seth Partridge. One night in August of 1925, Partridge was manning a pusher locomotive above the Upper Spiral Tunnel. He heard an avalanche of mud, water and rocks sweeping the mountainside above.

Partridge knew that the Yoho siding house was directly below. He stopped his locomotive and raced down the mountainside to warn the men sleeping in the siding house of the danger. When he reached the house, he was too breathless to yell, but managed to get everyone outside before the slide hit, demolishing the building. For his brave and heroic act, Partridge was awarded $1000 by the American magazine *Liberty*.

A train weaves its way through the Spiral Tunnel in this 1940s photograph

business as soon as possible, to begin paying off its incredible construction debt. General manager William Cornelius Van Horne decided to adopt a "temporary solution." The CPR would run its rails straight down the hill, and rectify the problem when it could afford to. Thus was created The Big Hill—a notorious section of track that would be the bane of both railway workers and railway executives for the next 25 years.

Runaway trains can occur on grades that exceed one per cent. The first construction train that attempted to descend The Big Hill ran away and plunged into the canyon, killing three workers. Three manual safety switches were installed and manned around the clock. The switches were set to divert runaway trains onto spur lines, where as one worker remarked: "Wrecks could take place without hindering traffic on the main line." A series of whistle blasts from an approaching train meant that the engineer had the train under control. If all looked right to the switch man, he would open the switch, granting access to the main line.

Brakemen got off and walked beside descending trains, watching for overheating brakes and locked wheels. Speed was limited to 13 km per hour for passenger trains and 10 km per hour for freights. Train size was limited to 17 cars. Sand was applied to the rails to increase friction. The Big Hill was hard on workers and equipment. Delays and breakdowns were common. Fortunately, there was never a derailment or runaway involving a passenger train.

One engineer, finding a runaway on his hands and not wanting to face a certain wreck on a spur line, signalled all the switchmen to let him through and proclaimed to his mortified brakeman: "Here goes for Field!" The train survived the descent and the engineer briefly basked in the glory of being the only one to pilot a runaway the entire length of The Big Hill. A few minutes later, he was unceremoniously fired. The message was delivered in a telegram marked "Rush."

Uphill trains had their

problems too. The steep grade required four locomotives to haul a 15-car train, and additional "pusher" locomotives were sometimes dispatched to help trains stalled on The Big Hill. It took an hour for trains to climb from Field to Wapta Lake. With all the wear and tear on equipment, the CPR built a roundhouse and yard at Field in 1898 to service locomotives and rolling stock.

The large number of steam engines working near Field had a pronounced effect on the community. A thick deposit of coal soot collected on everything. The town of Field was drab and dirty, and residents neither bothered to paint or decorate their homes, nor hang out their laundry! Diesel locomotives replaced steam power by 1956. You may still see coal cinders at railside today.

The steepness of the track isn't the only problem that confronts the CPR on The Big Hill. The railway line passes through avalanche paths on Mt. Bosworth, Cathedral Mountain and Mt. Stephen. Winter snow and ice avalanches frequently bury the tracks and derail unfortunate trains in their path. This happened as recently as 1986, finally prompting the CPR to construct the concrete snow shed visible at the bottom of The Big Hill. Mud slides, rockfalls and flash floods also occur along this section of the line, and sometimes cover Highway 1 as well—most recently in August of 1994.

The Spiral Tunnels

William Cornelius Van Horne's "temporary solution" to the problems posed by the grade of

The Big Hill was finally rectified in 1909 with the completion of the Spiral Tunnels. These two ingenious tunnels combine to create a figure eight deep within Mt. Ogden and Cathedral Mountain. This doubles the length of the line on The Big Hill and reduces the overall grade to 2.2 per cent.

The Lower Spiral Tunnel in Mt. Ogden is 891 m long, has a curvature of 226° and an elevation change of 17 m. The upper tunnel in Cathedral Mountain is 992 m long, has a curvature of 288° and an ele-vation change of 15 m. One thousand men were employed for almost two years in the construction of the tunnels. Each tunnel had two headings that were excavated towards each other. The error in alignment where the tunnel headings met was less than 5 cm (2 inches). The tunnels cost $1.5 million and consumed 700,000 kg of dynamite.

Although a tremendous improvement, the tunnels have not been without their problems. During the days of steam engines, condensation caused icicles to form on the tunnel roof and walls. In an attempt to alleviate this problem, manually-operated doors were installed on the Upper Spiral Tunnel to keep cold air out. The doors have now been removed. Between 1954 and 1962, the interior of the tunnels was lined with concrete and steel arches to prevent rocks falling onto the tracks. Ice build-up from seeping water is still a problem in the tunnels during winter. The tunnels were enlarged in 1992 to allow the passage of double-

"Hell's Bells" Rogers

"Every man present had learned, in three days, to hate the Major with real hatred. He had no mercy on horses or men—he had none on himself. The labourers hated him for the way he drove them and the packers for... the way he abused the horses—never gave their needs a thought."

Outfitter Tom Wilson was describing Major A.B. "Hell's Bells" Rogers, the man in charge of surveying the route through the Rockies and the Columbia Mountains for the CPR. Obstinate and seemingly indestructible, Major Rogers was noted for his profanity, the amazing length of his moustache and his diet of chewing tobacco and raw beans. Despite these shortcomings, he was a competent railway surveyor, having proven himself in the U.S.

In July of 1881, surveying parties organized by Rogers converged on Kicking Horse Pass. From a camp in the Bow Valley, Rogers sought a volunteer to accompany him to the pass. None except Wilson dared for fear of

being starved to death or lost in the woods." Rogers' real motivation was uncertainty over the whereabouts of his nephew, Albert. Rogers had dispatched Albert to find a way over Kicking Horse Pass from the west—something that hadn't been done since 1858.

On horseback, Rogers and Wilson came to the edge of a torrential glacial stream just below Kicking Horse Pass. Although he had only been in the Rockies one summer, Wilson knew that the power of such streams was not to be underestimated. He suggested they camp on the near bank and cross in the morning, when the stream's volume would have dropped.

"Afraid of it are you? Want the old man to show you how to ford it?" And with that, the Major and his steed plunged into the icy waters. The water bowled the horse over in an instant, and Wilson was obliged to rescue the Major, whose temper had understandably cooled. The horse made its own way out of the creek, fortunately on the near bank.

And so Bath Creek was named. Thereafter, whenever Bath Creek was in spate, surveyors and railway workers would sardonically remark: "The old man's taking another bath." Albert Rogers was located several days later by Wilson on the west side of the pass, exhausted from the rigours of his journey in the valley of the Kicking Horse.

Major Rogers' claim to fame was the discovery in 1882 of the pass across the Selkirk Range which now bears his name.

Cathedral Crags

ing from one portal while the last cars of the train are still entering the tunnel at the other portal. On average, 30 trains travel through the tunnels each day.

The Spiral Tunnel viewpoint is the most heavily visited roadside pull-off in any Canadian national park. The intersections are dangerous. Observe the posted speed limit and lane markings, and signal your intention to turn well in advance. You can see the Upper Spiral Tunnel in Cathedral Mountain from a viewpoint on the Yoho Valley Road.

height container cars.

From the viewpoint on Highway 1, you can see the Lower Spiral Tunnel in Mt. Ogden. Locomotives on long freight trains will be seen exit-

Climbers and Controversy

In 1896, Jean Habel (AHH-bull), a German professor and mountaineer, rode the railway west to Field. On The Big Hill, a pyramid-shaped mountain to the north caught his eye. (It was the mountain you see from the Spiral Tunnel viewpoint.) He called the peak Hidden Mountain, and resolved to return the following year and climb it.

Habel's party journeyed from Emerald Lake across Yoho Pass to the Yoho Valley opposite Takakkaw Falls. They followed the Yoho Valley north to Twin Falls and ascended onto Yoho Glacier. The party ran out of supplies before they could locate and attempt to climb Hidden Mountain. On his return to Germany, Habel wrote an account of his exploration. It was widely read and brought attention to both the professor and the Yoho Valley.

Outfitter Tom Wilson vehemently insisted that he had first

explored the Yoho Valley in 1894 while prospecting for minerals. He claimed to have suggested and organized Habel's journey for him. In return, Habel was to publish a description of the scenery for public consumption. Some feel that in claiming another "first" in the area, Wilson was jealously guarding his domain. But there may be truth in his version of the events.

Wilson did outfit Habel's party

in 1897, and the guide on the trip, Ralph Edwards, stated it was Habel's intention to climb Mt. Balfour, not Hidden Mountain. Nonetheless, Habel's published account succeeded in attracting public attention to the new valley, and was instrumental in the subsequent expansion of the Mt. Stephen Reserve. The argument of who first explored the Yoho Valley is moot anyway. Prehistoric native campsites have been found along the Yoho Valley Road.

Jean Habel explored the upper reaches of the Athabasca River in 1901. He died shortly after. Mountaineer John Norman Collie renamed "Hidden Mountain" Mt. Habel. But anti-German sentiment prevailed after World War I, and the name was changed to Mont des Poilus (day-pwah-LOO), to commemorate French foot soldiers. In 1986, Jean Habel finally got his due in the Yoho Valley when a peak at the head of Yoho Glacier was named for him.

The Monarch Mine

At the bottom of The Big Hill, you can see mine portals in the cliffs of Mt. Stephen south of the highway, and on Mt. Field to the north. Tom Wilson found ore at the base of Mt. Stephen in 1882. He sent a sample off for analysis and was informed that the ore was valuable, but would require expensive refining. Wilson staked a claim, but being without the finances to mine it, turned it over to others. The claim was resold, and was registered as the Monarch Mine in 1892.

For sixty years, various companies worked the mine for lead, zinc, silver and traces of iron, silica, sulphur and gold. A refining mill was built at the base of The Big Hill. The operation was powered by hydroelectricity generated from nearby Monarch Creek. Ore was brought down from Mt. Stephen by a 160-m tramway.

The Kicking Horse Mine opened on Mt. Field in 1910. It too used a tramway to bring down the ore, which was then trucked to the Monarch mill. The mines operated intermittently until 1952 and employed as many as 120 workers. More than 930,000 tonnes of ore were extracted. Production peaked in the mid-1940s. The mine entrances are now sealed.

Yoho Valley Road

The Yoho Valley Road intersection is at the base of The Big Hill, 22.3 km west of Lake Louise, 3.7 km east of Field. Turn north for Kicking Horse campground, Takakkaw Falls, Takakkaw Falls walk-in campground, Whiskey Jack hostel and trailheads for Yoho Pass and the Yoho Valley. The 14-km-long road is narrow and cannot be safely negotiated by large recreational vehicles, nor by cars pulling trailers. Park these in the first parking lot on the right. The road is not plowed between October and June.

Historic Railway Sites

You can see two sites connected with the CPR near the bottom of The Big Hill. Drive in to Kicking Horse campground and park at the Walk in the Past trailhead. Nearby is the Old Bake Oven, a Dutch oven used in 1884 when this site was occupied by a railway construction camp. You can also pick up an interpretive pamphlet and follow the Walk in the Past trail. At trail's end, you will see an abandoned narrow-gauge locomotive, used in the construction of the Spiral Tunnels.

Upper Spiral Tunnel Viewpoint

From this viewpoint at km 2.1 on the Yoho Valley Road, you can see the Upper Spiral Tunnel in Cathedral Mountain. Note the three levels of track. This viewpoint is at the interface of the montane and subalpine ecoregions. The surrounding forest includes: Douglas fir, white spruce, lodgepole pine, cottonwood poplar, Engelmann spruce and subalpine fir. The view south to Mt. Stephen (3,199 m) is superb.

Meeting of the Waters

Meeting of the Waters is where the Kicking Horse River receives a major tributary: the Yoho River. (The Yoho is the larger of the two rivers at this point.) The Yoho River is thick with glacial sediment. The waters of the Kicking Horse River are much more clear. Both rivers are glacially fed. However, lakes upstream on the Kicking Horse River act as settling ponds.

Viewpoint sign near Takakkaw Falls

Takakkaw Falls

West of the Yoho Valley Road, there are extensive avalanche paths on Wapta Mountain. Avalanches here sometimes deposit snow 10 m deep on the road. In some years, this delays the road's opening until late June. The avalanche paths are a good place to look for elk, moose, grizzly bear and black bear. You may see hoary marmots at roadside. Please do not feed them.

Takakkaw Falls

Whiskey Jack hostel and the Yoho Pass-Iceline trailhead are at km 13. It's another kilometre to road's end at a parking lot near the base of Takakkaw (TAH-kuh-kah) Falls. *Takakkaw* is Cree for "it is wonderful!" Looking at these falls, it is easy to understand that sentiment, and how Yoho came by its motto: "rockwalls and waterfalls." The falls are best lit from late morning until early evening in summer.

Surveyors argue about how to measure the height of waterfalls. Some think that only the biggest cascade should be included in the height. Others feel that all the cascades should be included. If you count all of Takakkaw's cascades, it is 380 m high and second highest in Canada, after Della Falls on Vancouver Island. If you count only the largest cascade, Takakkaw is 254 m high and probably fourth highest in Canada. Helmet Falls (352 m), and Hunlen Falls (259 m) are higher. However, the ranking doesn't matter: Takakkaw is the most impressive waterfall in the Rockies.

Takakkaw Falls are fed by the meltwaters of Daly Glacier,

Most of the sediment drops from the river's flow onto the lake bottoms.

Switchbacks

At km 5.5, the Yoho Valley Road makes a zigzag climb to bypass a canyon on the Yoho River. Vehicles longer than seven metres cannot negotiate the middle bend, and are forced to reverse along one length of the switchback. Use caution here, and yield the right of way to any vehicle negotiating the middle bend. You may see mountain goats nearby.

Cathedral Crags

The pinnacled summits of Cathedral Crags (3,073 m) are featured in the view south from the Yoho Valley Road. The ice of Cathedral Glacier can be seen in the notch to the left of Cathedral Crags. A lake that forms beneath the ice occasionally discharges through the notch, creating debris flows that inundate the railway and highway below. This phenomenon is known as *a jökulhlaup* (YOWE-kull-up)—Icelandic for "glacier flood." The CPR installed a pumping station on the glacier after the last such event in 1984, in an attempt to keep the lake from reaching the critical level.

which flows from the Waputik Icefield. The amount of water in the falls varies with the time of year and the time of day, and will be at maximum on a hot afternoon in July or August. You may hear boulders carried in the stream as they tumble down the cliff. *Waputik* (WAH-poo-tick) is Stoney for "white goat." Mountain goats are often seen at the base of the falls.

In January of 1974, four local climbers succeeded in climbing the frozen Takakkaw Falls, the most difficult waterfall ice route completed to that date. This event heralded the arrival of waterfall ice climbing as a significant winter activity in the Rockies.

Yoho Valley

Although the Takakkaw Falls parking lot is the ultimate destination on the Yoho Valley Road for those seeing the Rockies by vehicle, it marks a prominent departure point for hikers. With its waterfalls, lakes and relatively quick access to upper subalpine and alpine landscapes, the Yoho Valley is one of the most popular backpacking areas in the Rockies.

For strong hikers with a full day to spend, Yoho Lake, The Iceline, Twin Falls, the Whaleback and Yoho Glacier are each recommended hikes. For those with more time, multi-day loop hikes can be created using the backcountry campsites in the area.

The summits adjacent to the Yoho Valley have been popular with mountaineers since 1901, when James Outram teamed up with the conqueror of the Matterhorn, Edward Whymper, to make first ascents of most of the major peaks.

Kicking Horse River, Highway 1

At the base of The Big Hill, Highway 1 crosses the Kicking Horse River and descends to the Kicking Horse flats. The Kicking Horse River is fed by melting snow and ice from glaciers along the continental divide. Glacial meltwater transports rubble and sediment. At the bottom of The Big Hill, most of the larger particles carried by the river drop out of

William Cornelius Van Horne

The Van Horne Range west of Field commemorates William Cornelius Van Horne. He was appointed general manager of the CPR in 1881, and later was its president and chairman of the board. Much to the chagrin of the Canadian press, Van Horne was an American directing a Canadian venture. His career was the ultimate success story. In twenty years, he had worked his way from a telegraph operator for the Illinois Central Railroad to become chief of one of the largest of railway undertakings, the Canadian Pacific. At the age of 38, he was touted as "one of the greatest railway generals in the world." He needed to be. He was about to oversee construction of a railway committed to crossing two mountain passes that had not been surveyed.

Van Horne was a bear of a man, with a remarkable memory and no apparent requirement for sleep. In his meteoric rise to the top he took no rest either from learning about his profession, preferring to acquaint himself with other railway jobs by working them on his days off. As a result, he knew every aspect of railroading, from yardwork, to

scheduling, to operating locomotives. In all matters, Van Horne paid tenacious attention to detail, saving pennies here and minutes there, making railroads pay.

Van Horne's crowning achievement with the CPR was the creation of a hotel business, and the establishment of working relationships with an array of mountaineers, artists and scientists who visited the Rockies. These travellers publicized their exploits, thus repaying the CPR by generating more tourist business.

Van Horne was forthright in his support of proposals to establish Banff and Yoho national parks. Although his motivation was primarily commerce, we can be thankful to this dynamic man for the direct role he played in helping create Canada's national park system.

Town of Field with Mt. Dennis in the background

the flow, creating the gravelly outwash plain. This outwash plain, one of several in Yoho, is seven kilometres long. The wildflower, yellow mountain avens, thrives on the gravels. Its twisted, dandelion-like seed pods appear in midsummer.

Daily and seasonal variations in glacial melt affect the river's volume and produce an ever-changing braided stream on the flats. The peak flow of the Kicking Horse River occurs in August. Most other rivers in the Rockies peak in June and July.

The Kicking Horse Valley is the largest in Yoho. In summer, you may see white-tailed deer, mule deer and black bear. In other seasons, elk and coyotes are common. Wolves and moose are seen by fortunate visitors. The portion of the Kicking Horse River within Yoho National Park was designated a Canadian Heritage River in 1989. The commemorative plaque is at riverside near the park information centre in Field.

Mt. Stephen

Looking at Mt. Stephen (3,199 m) from the town of Field, you might think that it is one of the highest mountains in the Rockies. Although it is not, the vertical relief from base to summit is 1940 m, a figure matched by few other mountains so close to the road.

The sequence of rock formations that comprises the cliffs of Mt. Stephen is the same resistant "castle-building" sequence that you saw in Castle Mountain. It was in the shales of the Stephen Formation, near mid-height on the mountain, that railway workers discovered fossils in 1886. The Stephen Fossil Bed and its trilobites subsequently became world famous.

Home Ownership in the National Parks

Residence in the national parks is restricted to those who have a "need to reside"–employees of the parks and essential services. All land in national parks is owned by the Crown. Homeowners, businesses and hotels lease their land from Parks Canada and pay annual land taxes. They own the buildings, but not the land. Parks Canada does not regulate non-resident home ownership. This results in many cases where homeowners do not reside or work in the parks. This severely limits the accommodation available to those with a need to reside.

Banff, Jasper, Waterton Park and Field are officially called "townsites," and private homes are allowed. The number of available lots is limited. Lake Louise is officially a "visitor centre," and private homes are not permitted. All accommodation there is government- or business-owned, and allotted solely for occupancy by essential staff.

Dominion Land Surveyor J.J. McArthur and his assistant made the first ascent of Mt. Stephen in 1887—the first time a summit over 3,049 m had been climbed in Canada. In his surveying work, McArthur became an accomplished mountaineer. He made first ascents of many prominent mountains in the central Rockies.

In the early 1900s, Mt. Stephen, along with Mt. Lefroy and Mt. Victoria at Lake Louise, and Mt. Sir Donald at Rogers Pass, were "must" ascents for any mountaineer visiting western Canada. The CPR stationed Swiss guides at Mt. Stephen House in Field to lead aspiring alpinists to Mt. Stephen's summit. The mountain was named for George Stephen, first president of the CPR. When Stephen was later knighted, he chose to name himself after the mountain: Lord Mount Stephen.

In the Shadow of Mt. Stephen

The community of Field developed from a railway construction camp in 1884. It was named for Cyrus Field, promoter of the first trans-Atlantic communications cable, who visited the railway "end of steel" that year. Originally, Field occupied both sides of the Kicking Horse River. Some buildings on the north side of the river were destroyed by an avalanche from Mt. Burgess in 1909—a good incentive for relocation!

Field's heyday occurred at the turn of the 20th century, when scientists, artists, climbers, railway workers, miners and outfitters rubbed

Glen Brook

Glen Brook with the sign he carved at Marble Canyon Warden Station in 1953

Field Resident and Retired Park Warden Glen Brook said: "I wanted to go to the mountains bad. I didn't have a clue what they looked like, but I knew I wanted to go there. I was milking cows on the farm when a girl came up and said 'There's a phone call for you.' [A friend, working at Deer Lodge in Lake Louise, was calling about a job at Marble Canyon bungalow camp.] So, on my 19th birthday, I took a bus to Banff."

That was 1935. Glen Brook has called the mountains home ever since. He spent five years as a chore boy at Marble Canyon before serving with the Calgary Highlanders in World War II. On his return in 1944, he fell into his dream job—park warden posted at Marble Canyon. His territory was northern Kootenay National Park. Glen patrolled the trails on foot, snowshoe and horseback. The telephone at his station was his only link to the outside world—when it worked.

"In those days, the wardens were all trappers. They just pinned a badge on them and called them 'warden.' In fact, that's how I got the job. The previous warden was fired for poaching."

At that time, Glen's closest neighbours were the wardens at Castle Mountain, 17 km east, and at Kootenay Crossing, 44 km west. To escape his own company, Glen would ski to the CPR tracks at Castle Junction, stick his skis in a snowbank, flag down a passenger train and head to Banff or Calgary. Other times he would ski west to hand off his monthly report at Simpson Monument, occasionally taking a ride from there to Radium.

With their sons Sid and Alex, Glen and Irene moved to Yoho in 1955, taking residence in the warden station at Hector, near Wapta Lake. "I wasn't there a day or two when I decided to have a look over the ridge. I told Irene—about 11 o'clock in the morning as I was putting on my snowshoes—I'm going to see what's up that valley, I may be late for lunch. I was late for supper, too. I ended up at Lake O'Hara."

Two years later, the family moved down the hill to Field and Glen took the job of Chief Park Warden.

"Field was a little town then. It's not quite the same now. People didn't shift around like they do now. Everybody knew everybody. I've been in every house in this town."

elbows while using the town as a base for their ventures. Mount Stephen House, the CPR's first mountain hotel, was constructed in 1886, and drew visitors from around the world. In the summer of 1912, it registered almost 8,500 guests. It was at Mt. Stephen House that the formation of the Alpine Club of Canada was proposed in 1906. The club held its first annual camp at Yoho Pass that summer.

With the rising popularity of the automobile in the 1920s, the CPR shifted its hotel interests to "bungalow camps." Mt. Stephen House was sold to the YMCA in 1918. It was operated as a hostel until its demolition in 1953.

As with most settlements in the Rockies, Field is located on an alluvial fan where a tributary stream enters a main valley. The elevation is 1,250 m. The forest near the townsite includes tree species of both the montane and subalpine ecoregions. Bird-watchers may see pileated woodpecker,

Natural Bridge

ruby-crowned kinglet, Brewer's blackbird, common raven, black-billed magpie, Bohemian waxwing, evening grosbeak, Townsend's warbler, common flicker, American robin, chickadee, violet-green swallow, cliff swallow, dark-eyed junco, rufous hummingbird, and B.C.'s provincial bird—the Steller's jay.

Field's climate is often belittled by residents of other Rocky Mountain communities. Annual precipitation here is about 20 per cent more than in Banff. It rains one day in three in summer. The town spends much of the winter in the icy shade of Mt. Stephen and Mt. Dennis. Winter inversions frequently trap the valley in chill-

ing cloud, and a vicious northeast wind called the Yoho Blow sometimes howls in winter across the Kicking Horse flats, sending the snow flying and the wind chill plunging.

Still, some 300 people make Field their home. The community is the administrative centre for Yoho National Park. Most of its residents find employment with the park, and the hotels and visitor services in the area. The tourist facilities are the park information centre, store, hotel and approved accommodations. The closest campground is Kicking Horse, 4.7 km east.

Emerald Lake Road

At the intersection west of Field, turn north for the Emerald Lake Road. This eight-kilometre-long road was first cleared in 1904, and was known as "Snow Peak Avenue." The road leads to Emerald Lake. Looking north and south from the road, you can see several "snow peaks" that are visible: The President, The Vice President, Mt. Carnarvon and Mt. Goodsir North. Tall, white bog orchids line the northbound ditch in early summer.

The Natural Bridge is at km 1.4. In this vicinity, the Kicking Horse River is eroding a canyon through weak shales. However, at the Natural Bridge, the river encounters a rock formation where the sedimentary layers have been folded into a U-shape. This offers more resistance to the

All in a Summer's Work

The year 1882 was momentous for Tom Wilson. In his work with the CPR survey, he discovered Lake Louise, crossed Bow Pass and Howse Pass, and found ore on the slopes of Mt. Stephen. At the end of the summer he topped it off by discovering Emerald Lake.

Wilson had left horses in a pasture near the present town of Field. The horses went look-

ing for better feed, and Wilson tracked them across the Natural Bridge to Emerald Lake.

"Emerald" is an obvious name for the lake, but was not bestowed by Wilson. He had already used that name for the lake now known as Lake Louise. But when the name of Lake Louise was made official in 1884, the name Emerald was reassigned to this lake, Wilson's other gem of a discovery.

Emerald Lake Lodge

flowing water. At one time, there was a small waterfall here. The river has succeeded in eroding a channel through the lip of resistant rock and undercutting it, just upstream from its edge, creating the crooked bridge. At high water, the river flows over the surrounding rock, and sometimes covers this natural phenomenon.

In terms of geological time, the Natural Bridge will be a temporary feature. Eventually, the Kicking Horse River will completely undermine it, causing it to collapse. Then a new waterfall may form upstream. Downstream from the Bridge, you can see resistant rock formations in the riverbed where this process took place in the past.

You can see examples of ripple rock in the base of the sign at the Natural Bridge. The rocks are siltstone, brought by the sign builders from a quarry in the eastern main ranges.

Emerald Lake

Emerald Lake is the largest of Yoho's 61 lakes and ponds. As with many lakes in the Rockies, its waters are glacially fed and dammed by a glacial moraine. The lake's remarkable colour is caused by fine particles of glacial sediment called rock flour that are suspended in the water. These particles reflect the blue and green wavelengths of light.

The 4.8-km circuit around Emerald Lake is one of the finest nature walks in the Rockies. The lake occupies a basin surrounded by high mountains. This basin traps storms, resulting in frequent rain in summer and heavy snows in winter. Coupled with the low elevation of the lake, the moisture supports trees more typical of B.C.'s wet interior forests: western red cedar, western yew, western hemlock and western white pine. The alluvial fan on the northeast shore of the lake is decorated with wildflowers in late June and early July. Among the most attractive are orchid species, including yellow lady's slipper. The Emerald Lake parking lot is also the starting point for trails to Hamilton Lake, Emerald Basin, Yoho Pass and Burgess Pass.

The original Emerald Lake Chalet was constructed by the CPR in 1902. The present lodge and cabins were completed in 1986. The main lodge building incorporates logwork from the original. The mountain south of the lodge is Mt. Burgess (2,599 m). It was featured on the Canadian ten-dollar bill from 1954 to 1971.

Sport fishing, trail riding and canoeing are popular activities at Emerald Lake. Canoe rentals are available. Along with moose and the occasional black bear, wildlife you may see includes American marten, swallows, bats, osprey, waterfowl and Common loon.

Emerald Lake

Muskeg Summit, Highway 1

West of the Emerald Lake intersection, Highway 1 crosses the Kicking Horse River and climbs a short grade. In the early days of the Canadian Pacific Railway, this troublesome hill was known as Muskeg Summit. Pusher locomotives from Field were sometimes needed to assist trains over the rise. Muskeg Summit was eliminated from the grade in 1902 when the tracks were diverted through a rock cut to follow the Kicking Horse River. As you descend the long hill west from Muskeg Summit, you may see sections

American Marten

The American marten is the most abundant carnivore in the Rockies. This member of the weasel family has a reddish-brown coat, a buff-coloured throat patch, pointed ears and a bushy tail. Martens live in the old-growth of subalpine forests, where they hunt small rodents and birds. They are nocturnal and not often seen, but you may be fortunate and see one in the old-growth spruce forest just north of the Emerald Lake parking lot. The martens that live here have the habit of clinging to tree trunks about four metres

off the ground, and inspecting hikers as they go past. These old trees are also excellent habitat for Downy woodpeckers and Hairy woodpeckers.

of the abandoned line in the trees at roadside.

Highest Mountains in Yoho

Highway 1 crosses the Ottertail River 8.5 km west of Field. To the north is the President Group—the mountains that surround Emerald Lake. To the south, concealed from view at the head of the Ottertail River, are the twin peaks of Mt. Goodsir—the highest mountains in Yoho. The Goodsirs are notable exceptions to the generally lower and more gentle topography of the western main ranges. With an elevation of 3,562 m, South Goodsir is the ninth highest summit in the Rockies. Charles Fay participated in the first ascent in 1903. North Goodsir, only 37 m lower, was first climbed in 1909. James Hector of the Palliser Expedition named the mountains for the Goodsir brothers, medical doctors in Scotland. Hector studied

The twin peaks of the Goodsirs

under John Goodsir at Edinburgh University.

Mt. Goodsir is part of the Ottertail Range. These mountains are home to many of Yoho's estimated population of 400 mountain goats. Mt. Hurd, the northern outlier of the Ottertail Range, is adjacent to Highway 1. Its slopes contain spar trees—evidence of a 1971 forest fire started by lightning. The Ottertail Valley trailhead is just east of the highway bridge.

Ottertail River to Hoodoo Creek

For the next 14.1 km, Highway 1 follows the Kicking Horse River through southwestern Yoho National Park. Westbound travellers can stop at the Ottertail Viewpoint. Beneath the viewpoint, the confluence of the Ottertail River and Kicking Horse River is marked by wet meadows, meanders and oxbow lakes. This is an excellent place to look for moose, wolf, coyote

Hector's Close Call

The Palliser Expedition of 1857 to 1860 was sent to central and western Canada by the British government to appraise the region for future settlement, resource wealth and transportation routes. It was a daunting undertaking in an unknown land. Captain John Palliser was fortunate that one of his charges, James Hector, a 23-year-old Scots doctor and geologist, was up to the task. Many of the expedition's findings regarding the topography of the Rockies were the result of Hector's ambitious travels.

In 1858, Hector sought a route across the Rockies to the Columbia River. From the Bow Valley he crossed Vermilion Pass, but instead of following the Vermilion and Kootenay rivers on a certain route to the Columbia River, his native guide led him west over the Beaverfoot Divide to the Kicking Horse Valley. It was there, near Wapta Falls, that Hector was kicked in the chest by his horse. The blow knocked him unconscious. His men assumed him dead and were preparing to bury him when, to their astonishment (and his!), Hector revived. Two days later, Hector noted that his men now called the river the

"Kicking Horse."

Hector's party followed the Kicking Horse River east from Wapta Falls and made an arduous crossing of Kicking Horse Pass. Undeterred, Hector kept going: north over Bow Pass, west to Howse Pass and east to Fort Edmonton. There, he took a few months rest before embarking in the dead of winter for Athabasca Pass.

Hector was a keen observer of nature and the Rockies' first name-dropper. Many of the place names we use today are the result of his experiences, imagination and observations.

and osprey. Farther west, the highway passes through a rock cut that bisects potholes that were eroded into the rock by meltwater at the end of the last ice age. At the bottom of the potholes, you can see the water-worn boulders that drilled these vertical shafts. There are attractive riverside picnic areas at Finn Creek and Faeder Lake. Elk are common at roadside.

Deerlodge

Hoodoo Creek campground is 22.6 km west of Field. There are two trailheads in the campground. The Deerlodge trail leads to Deerlodge cabin, the first park patrol cabin in Yoho. It was built in 1904 and restored in 1996. Warden John Tocher lived here from 1920 to 1926, when the railway was the only connection to the outside world. He brought the cook-stove to the cabin from nearby Leanchoil railway siding by slinging it between two horses and crossing the Kicking Horse River at low water in autumn.

The building stands in a montane forest that features large, black cottonwood poplar trees. There are eight functioning patrol cabins in Yoho today, but Deerlodge has been vacant for many years. It is usually locked but may be open for inspection during the summer. When the boardwalk is not submerged, hikers can enjoy a nearby nature trail that circles a montane wetland created by beavers.

Leanchoil Hoodoos

The Leanchoil (lee-ANN-coil)

The Burgess Shale

Charles Walcott of the Smithsonian Institution discovered another outcrop of the fossil-rich Stephen Formation in 1909 on the ridge connecting Wapta Mountain and Mt. Field. These sites, and others discovered more recently, are commonly referred to as The Burgess Shale, an old name for the Stephen Formation.

The creatures fossilized at the Wapta Mountain locality of The Burgess Shale are remarkably preserved. They lived in shallow water atop a cliff, and were annihilated by mudslides that swept them over the cliff. Entombed in thick silts, devoid of oxygen, they were not scavenged and never decayed. The cliff is known as the Cathedral Escarpment, and marks the shoreline of an ancient sea that covered the area 530 million years ago. Geologists call this period the Cambrian. By comparison, the dinosaurs disappeared 66 million years ago.

Walcott made repeated visits to his fossil quarries until 1917, and took a total of 65,000 fossil specimens back to the Smithsonian in Washington D.C. His administrative duties there precluded a comprehensive evaluation of all he had found. In the descriptions Walcott did record of his samples, he attempted to fit all of the fossil species into categories already known from the fossil record elsewhere in the world.

New research on Walcott's findings began in the 1970s and continues today. This research has revealed that The Burgess Shale fossils contain some species unknown from other sites. These unique species may indicate that 515 million years ago, there was a greater variety of life at the "body-plan" level than there is today. A reduction in the variety of lifeforms is contrary to the concept of an increase in diversity associated with evolutionary theory. These findings have led some scientists to radically revise their views on evolution.

The Burgess Shale sites have been designated special preservation areas. Access is only permitted on guided hikes (fee charged), or by permission of the park superintendent. Arrangements change yearly, so call the park well in advance for details (250-343-6783). You can see displays that portray some of the fossil species at the park information centre in Field.

Burgess Shale World Heritage Site

In 1981, the Burgess Shale fossil site on Mt. Field was added to the UNESCO list of World Heritage Sites. There is a plaque on the north side of the Yoho Valley Road, 800 m from Highway 1, and displays at the Field Information Centre.

Hoodoos trail also departs from Hoodoo Creek campground. It is one of the shortest and steepest trails in the Rockies. It climbs 450 m in only 1.6 km to a group of impressive natural pillars on the bank of Hoodoo Creek. These hoodoos were created by the same process as those near Banff townsite. (See p. 86.) Most of the Leanchoil Hoodoos still retain their capstones. This indicates that they are relatively recent in origin. Some geologists have referred to the Leanchoil Hoodoos as the best examples of till hoodoos in the world.

Leanchoil is another Scottish name associated with the CPR. The mother of CPR stockholder Donald Smith lived in a manor named Lethna-Coyle in Scotland. The name was conferred on the railway siding just west of here.

Wapta Falls— Yoho's Niagara

Just beyond Hoodoo Creek Campground, Highway 1 curves west and crosses the Kicking Horse River. Bighorn sheep were often seen at roadside here in 1994—the first recorded sheep sightings in western Yoho in many years.

The Wapta Falls turnoff is 24.7 km west of Field. The 2.4-km walk to the falls is highly recommended. The marsh adjacent to the abandoned access road is home to beaver, muskrat, great blue heron, belted kingfishers and moose.

You may see black bears and wolves here too. Gray wolves began to frequent this area in the early 1990s.

The 30-m drop of Wapta Falls is minuscule compared to other waterfalls in Yoho. However, what the falls lack in height, they make up in breadth. Most of the surface runoff and glacial meltwater in the park passes over the brink of this cataract, with a peak summer flow of 255 cubic metres a second.

Unlike most waterfalls in the Rockies, which are associated with canyons or hanging valleys, Wapta Falls is an erosion-resistant cliff of the Ottertail Formation. The confluence of the Beaverfoot River and Kicking Horse River is just

Porcupine

The porcupine is one of the largest rodents in the Rockies. Nature has provided it with a peculiar but highly effective means of protection. So slow moving that it cannot outrun any predator, the porcupine compensates by wearing a cloak of quilled armour that deters all but the most serious and agile would-be attackers—with the possible exception of the unwary family dog.

The 30,000 yellow and black quills are in reality hairs, and cover all but the porcupine's face, feet and underside. The quills are hollow and barbed, and cannot be shot at an attacker. The quills detach easily on contact, barbed end first, and work their way quickly into the skin.

Any animal hoping to kill a porcupine must first succeed in flipping it over and inflicting a fatal wound to its belly before porky's tail can inflict damage of its own. Wolf, lynx, fisher, wolverine and cougar are the only predators up to the task, but many don't survive an attempt. A face and throat full of quills can lead to blindness or starvation.

Most of the porcupine's diet comprises cambium, the tender layer beneath tree bark. Coniferous trees girdled of their bark indicate the presence of porcupines. The injury is often fatal to the tree. Recently, the porcupine has become accustomed to artificial additives in its diet. Delicacies include: plywood and chemically treated woods; salt-stained boots and backpacks; antifreeze; and tires, trim and brake lines on parked vehicles. Each spring, park maintenance crews inventory the damage to buildings and signs in the high country.

The average camper's experience of the porcupine will be a loss of sleep. Porcupines are nocturnal and vocal and have a bizarre repertoire that includes some sounds that are nearly human in character.

Porcupines do not hibernate but nestle in boulderfields or undergrowth. You are advised to wear shoes at all times when in porcupine habitat, and to keep dogs leashed and under strict control.

Wapta Falls

upstream from Wapta Falls. It was near here that James Hector was kicked by his horse in 1858—an incident that gave the Kicking Horse River its name. *Wapta* is a Stoney word that means "river," and was the original name of the Kicking Horse River. The Mt. Hunter trailhead is across Highway 1 from the Wapta Falls parking area.

The Yoho Blowdown

A violent windstorm in November of 1993 blew down many trees in Yoho. The biggest concentration was at the Yoho Blowdown (200 ha), adjacent to Highway 1 west of Wapta Falls. A blowdown is a natural process that topples weakened trees and opens large areas of forest to allow a natural succession of vegetation. The open areas become good habitat for many mammals.

Unfortunately, most commercial foresters view blowdowns as "wasted wood," and consider the downed timber to be a fire hazard. Soon after the Yoho Blowdown, forestry interests from Golden were pressing for permission to "salvage log" the area. This, despite the fact that commercial logging is illegal in national parks. Fortunately, the law was upheld. But the difference in attitudes toward the Yoho Blowdown underscores the resource-related pressures affecting the Rocky Mountain parks.

Kicking Horse Canyon

Beyond the west boundary of Yoho, Highway 1 follows the Kicking Horse River for 27 km to its junction with the Columbia River at Golden. The valley is V-shaped, and the river has eroded a spectacular canyon through the weak shales and limestones. In places, the road snakes along ledges carved from the mountainside above the canyon. The driving requires great attention and care. Slow down. The mountains on the south side of the valley are part of the western ranges, the oldest mountains in the Rockies. Look for deer, bighorn sheep, mountain goats and coyotes along this section of highway. ∆

Western Wood Lily

The western wood lily blooms during early summer in the lodgepole pine forest of the montane ecoregion. The stem of this plant may be 50 cm tall and the flower as much as 10 cm across. The orange petals of the flower are speckled inside with black dots on a yellow background. (The "tiger lily" is a different plant.)

The western wood lily suffers the fate of many attractive wildflowers. When the flower is picked, the plant usually dies. It is becoming

scarce in many areas. Please remember: it is illegal to pick wildflowers in a national park. The western wood lily is the provincial floral emblem of Saskatchewan.

Kootenay National Park

T he Kootenay Parkway (Highway 93 South) begins at Castle Mountain Village on the Bow Valley Parkway, and runs 106 km west and south through Kootenay National Park to B.C. Highway 95. Most people access the Kootenay Parkway at Castle Junction on Highway 1,

30 km west of Banff, 28 km east of Lake Louise.

The idea for a road across Vermilion Pass to connect Banff with the Columbia Valley originated in 1910. Robert Bruce, a businessman from Invermere, B.C., wanted a highway connection so he could transport fruit from an orchard industry he hoped to establish in the Columbia Valley. His overtures to the Canadian government to construct a highway eventually led to the establishment of Kootenay, Canada's tenth national park.

Bruce promoted his idea to the CPR, and a deal was made whereby the federal Department of the Interior would build the portion of the road between Banff and Vermilion Pass. The province

of B.C. and the CPR would construct the remainder.

Construction began in 1911 and soon went over budget. By November of 1914, Banff and Vermilion Pass were connected, but only two difficult stretches had been completed in B.C., totalling less than 30 km. With the outbreak of World War I, the project was suspended.

Bruce continued his efforts. In 1916, he suggested that the National Parks Branch complete the road. In return, B.C. could donate adjacent lands as a national park. The necessary federal-provincial agreement was reached in 1919. A strip of land eight kilometres wide on either side of the new highway was conveyed. With an area of 1,406 square kilometres, Kootenay National Park was officially established on this land in 1920. The Kootenay Parkway opened in June of 1923.

Four thousand five hundred vehicles travelled the route in the first year. The automobile had arrived to stay in the mountain national parks. The Kootenay Parkway is now open year round, and is travelled by 2.5 million vehicles per year. It is the only through-road in Kootenay National Park.

Kootenay is a park of tremendous diversity, incorporating Rocky Mountain and Columbia Valley climates, three distinct mountain topographies, 256 animal species and 993 species of plants. It is the only park in Canada that is home to both cactus and glacier. *Kootenay* is a native word that means "people from beyond the hills." Anthropologists now refer to these natives using the spelling Kutenai. The Kutenai lived in the Columbia Valley when the first Euro-Canadians arrived in 1800.

Castle Junction to Vista Lake

From Highway 1, the Kootenay Parkway climbs steadily up the west slope of the Bow Valley towards Vermilion Pass. The Boom Lake trailhead and picnic area are six kilometres from Castle Junction. This area is close to the continental divide and receives heavy precipitation. The picnic area is surrounded by ancient Engelmann spruce and subalpine fir trees—the climax vegetation of the subalpine forest.

The Vista Lake viewpoint is 7.2 km from Castle Junction. Puzzling features of topography often give insights into the

---

SuperGuide Recommendations

Sights/Attractions
- Radium Hot Springs Pools
- Marble Canyon
- Kootenay Valley viewpoint

Hikes/Activities
- Paint Pots and Ochre Beds
- Marble Canyon
- Fireweed Trail at Continental Divide

---

left: Marble Canyon

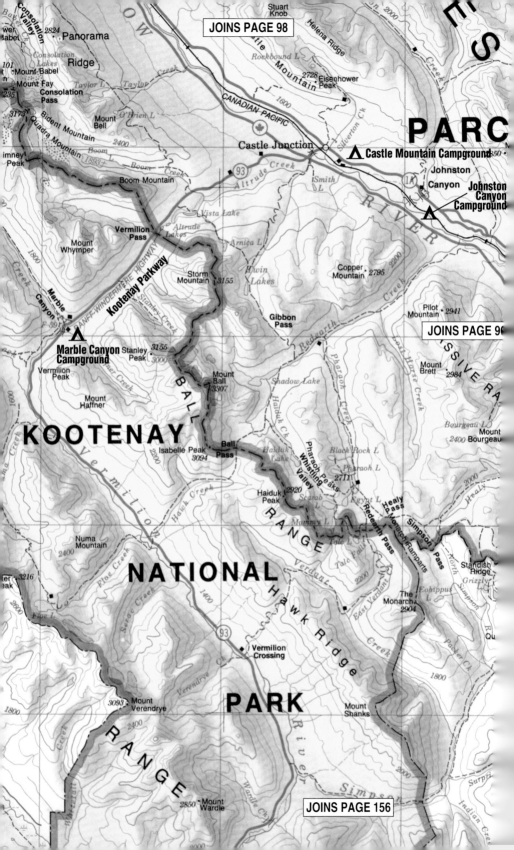

JOINS PAGE 98
JOINS PAGE 9
JOINS PAGE 156

PARC

Consolation
Valley
Panorama
2824
Consolation
Ridge
Mount Babel
Mount Fay
Consolation
Pass
3175
Bident Mountain
Quadra Mountain
imney
Peak
Taylor L.
Taylor
Consolation
Lakes
101
235

Stuart Knob
Helena Ridge
Rockbound L.
Eisenhower
Peak
2728
Castle Mountain
CANADIAN PACIFIC
1800
Silverton Ck
RIVER

Mount Bell
O'Brien L.
2400
Boom L.
Boom Creek
Boom Mountain

Castle Junction
93
Altrude Creek
Smith
L.

Castle Mountain Campground
1K
Johnston
Canyon
Johnston
Canyon
Campground

Mount Whymper
1800
Creek
Vermilion
Pass
Altrude
Lakes
Vista Lake
Arnica L.
Twin
Lakes
3155

Copper
Mountain
2795

Pilot
Mountain 2941

Marble
Canyon
F.391
Marble Canyon
Campground
Vermilion
Peak
Stanley
Peak
3155
3000
Stanley
Creek
Storm
Mountain 3155
Kootenay Parkway
THE WINDERMERE HIGHWAY
BANFF

Gibbon
Pass
Redearth
Creek

Pharaoh
Creek

Mount
Brett
2984

JOINS PAGE 9

SSIVER RA

Mount
Haffner

BALL
Mount
Ball
3307

Shadow Lake

Isabelle Peak
3094
Ball
Pass
Haiduk Ck
Haiduk
Lake
Pharaoh Peaks
Whistling
Valley
Black Rock L.
Pharaoh L.
2711
Bourgeau L.
2400
Mount
Bourgeau

KOOTENAY
2200
2400
Vermilion
Haiduk
Peak
2920
Scarab
L.
Egypt L.
Mummy L.
Healy
Pass
Redearth Pass
Monarch Ramparts
Simpson
Pass
Standish
Ridge
Grizzly

Numa
Mountain
2400
Floe Creek
Scarab Creek
1400
Hawk Ridge
Talc L.
Talc Peak
Verdant
Creek
2200
East Verdant
Redearth
Creek
North
Simpson
Eohtppus
Packer Ck

NATIONAL
3216
eak
2500
Floe L.
Sage Creek
Verendrye Ck
93
Vermilion
Crossing
1400
The
Monarch
2904
Mount
Shanks
1800

PARK
1800
3093
Mount
Verendrye
RANGE
2850 Mount
Wardle
River
Simpson
Surpri
Indian Creek

RANGE
2400
2000

Continental Divide

natural history of a landscape. Vista Lake lies in the deep valley of Altrude Creek, which drops steeply from the continental divide. How could this valley have been eroded so deeply in such a short distance, with so little water flowing through it?

At the end of the Wisconsin Glaciation, a lobe of glacial ice retreated to near the crest of Vermilion Pass. This ice rapidly melted as the earth's climate warmed. The tremendous discharge of water

eroded the valley of Altrude Creek through the rubble deposited in earlier ice ages. The meltwater also eroded the basins that now contain Vista Lake and the Altrude Lakes.

The Altrude Valley was originally known as the Little Vermilion. In 1939, a change of name was sought. A surveying party working at the pass combined the Latin words for "high" *(altus)* with "beautiful" *(pulchritude)*, to come up with the odd but appropriate name. The Altrude Lakes are on the south side of the Kootenay Parkway, close to Vermilion Pass.

Looking back toward the Bow Valley, Castle Mountain is prominent. It looks very different from this vantage—a six km-long cliff, the crest of which is never less than 2,650 m. The highest point on the mountain (2,744 m) is the summit farthest north.

The Bungalow Camps

Storm Mountain Lodge was built by the CPR in 1922. Restrictions on automobiles in Rocky Mountains Park had

been lifted in 1915. By the 1920s, it was clear that automobiles, not trains, were the preferred means of travel for tourists. The CPR began to construct and promote "auto bungalow camps" at a number of scenic locations in the Rockies: Johnston Canyon, Castle Mountain, Storm Mountain, the Vermilion Valley, Radium, Moraine Lake, the Yoho Valley, Wapta Lake, Lake O'Hara and Emerald Lake. The Dominion Parks Branch also built roadside campgrounds in the parks.

The CPR had sold most of its bungalow camps by the late 1940s. Many of the facilities evolved into the commercial accommodations still present at these locations. Storm Mountain Lodge is an example.

Continental Divide

The crest of Vermilion Pass (1,640 m) marks the continental divide and the boundary between Banff National Park, Alberta and Kootenay National Park, B.C. From here, waters flow east to Hudson Bay and the Atlantic Ocean via the Bow, Saskatchewan and Nelson river systems, and west to the Pacific Ocean via the Vermilion, Kootenay and Columbia rivers. There is no time zone change here.

Vermilion Pass is oriented parallel to the prevailing southwest winds. As a result, poor weather is often funnelled through the pass—a fact acknowledged in the name of nearby Storm Mountain (3,161 m).

Vermilion Pass Burn

The summer of 1968 was hot

Kootenay To Do List

Rafting
• Kootenay River Runners, 347-9210

Swimming
• Radium Hot Springs Pools, 347-9485

Entertainment
• Movies, 342-9518
• Library, 342-6416
• Park interpretive programs, 347-9505

Camping 347-9505
• Marble Canyon
• McLeod Meadows
• Redstreak

and dry across most of western Canada. On the afternoon of July 8, the temperature in Banff and Kootenay reached 30 °C, and winds were strong. At 4:30 p.m., a bolt of lightning struck the slopes of Mt. Whymper just west of Vermilion Pass. Fanned by the winds, the lightning spark kindled quickly. In three minutes, the mountainside was in flame. The Vermilion Pass Burn had begun.

Sixty-five firefighters were on the fireline within six hours. Nonetheless, the forest fire burned out of control for three days. On July 12, the weather cooled. The following day, rain came to the firefighters' aid. By July 18, the fire was out. The Vermilion Pass Burn consumed 26.3 square kilometres of subalpine forest, forced closure of the Kootenay Parkway and cost $160,000 to fight. It sounds like a disaster, but the burn was part of a natural and essential process of succession—the regeneration of the forest.

Most forests in the Rockies burn at least once every 180 years. Although it appears to destroy life, fire ultimately revitalizes the forest. It kills diseased tree stands, reduces competition for moisture and sunlight, creates stable seed beds by burning off loose soil layers, triggers the mass release of seeds, returns minerals to the soil and creates habitat for wildlife.

The Vermilion Pass Burn consumed a mature forest of Engelmann spruce and subalpine fir, with scattered lodgepole pine. The resin-sealed cones of the pines were cracked open by the blaze,

resulting in a mass seeding of this tree species. The lodgepole saplings quickly outgrew the less densely seeded spruce and fir to become the most common tree in the first stage of the fire-succession forest.

Studies of the Vermilion Pass Burn have yielded some interesting facts that illustrate the beneficial effects of forest fires. Within four years of the burn, there were nearly twice as many species of vegetation within the burned area as in the adjacent unburned area. The number of bird and wildlife species using the burned area also increased. You may see moose, deer and grizzly bear here. You can explore the Vermilion Pass Burn from the Fireweed Trail at the continental divide.

Aggressive fire suppression has prevented large forest fires in the Rocky Mountain parks during the last 55 years. This has altered the natural succession of forest habitats, and tipped the balance towards homogenous doghair forests of lodgepole pine. This type of forest offers poor range for many species of wildlife and birds. It has also turned large areas such as the Bow Valley and Kootenay Valley into tinder boxes. These valleys await a conflagration such as the one that occurred in Yellowstone National Park in 1988. To reverse this trend, and to attempt to create a mosaic of forest habitats, park wardens now use prescribed burns to re-introduce fire into the ecosystem in a controlled manner.

Peaks and Publicity

The Stanley Glacier trail is 3.2 km west of the continental divide. This half-day hike explores a steeply walled glacial valley. Stanley Peak (3,155 m), at the head of the

Common Fireweed

Common fireweed grows in dense thickets on recently burned areas and gravelly, disturbed ground. Numerous pink flowers grow atop a stem that may reach two metres in height. The low flowers on the stem open first. In late summer, it is common for flowers, buds and purple seed pods to be present on the same plant. Fireweed sheds a thick, yellow pollen in midsummer. It is the territorial emblem of the Yukon. Mountain fireweed (river beauty) is a smaller plant, with larger flowers. It grows at higher elevations and along glacial melt streams.

The charred trunks of the Vermilion Pass Burn

valley, was first climbed by Edward Whymper and guides in 1901. Whymper, who took part in the tragic first ascent of the Matterhorn in 1865, was considered the finest climber of Europe's "Golden Age" of mountaineering. Although 62 years old and past his mountaineering prime, he had convinced the CPR to sponsor him and an entourage of Swiss guides. In return, Whymper was to publicize the Rockies through magazine articles, and to help plan hiking trails and developments. It was hoped that Whymper would conquer Mt. Assiniboine, the "Canadian Matterhorn," as well.

The arrangement was repeated in two subsequent seasons, but the railway became unhappy with Whymper's lack of productivity. He didn't attempt to climb Mt. Assiniboine. The outfitters who travelled with Whymper could not handle his dour and apparently alcoholic temperament. The CPR dumped Whymper, but he made two more trips to the Rockies on his own. The last was in 1909. The CPR did receive some benefit from Whymper's scheme. He described the Rockies in one of his articles as "fifty Switzerlands in one"—a slogan that the railway put to good use in its advertising campaigns.

Marble Canyon

Marble Canyon is seven kilometres west of the continental divide. Here, the glacially fed waters of Tokumm Creek are eroding through the lip of a hanging valley to create a canyon in the dolomite bedrock.

It has taken Tokumm Creek 8,000 years to erode the canyon, which is 600 m long and has a maximum depth of 39 m. An interpretive trail leads along the canyon edge, and crosses seven bridges above its depths. You can also see a natural bridge. Please keep on the trail to spare the fragile canyon vegetation, and to avoid the risk of a slip into the chasm.

True marble is a metamorphic rock—limestone or dolomite that has been altered by extreme heat and pressure. The Cathedral limestone and dolomite in Marble Canyon is not metamorphic rock, but it has been polished smooth by the silt-laden waters of Tokumm Creek to create the marble-like finish. *Tokumm* is a Stoney word for "red fox." There is a campground on the opposite side of the Kootenay Parkway.

Paint Pots and Ochre Beds

These attractions are 2.5 km west of Marble Canyon. The walk to the Paint Pots and Ochre Beds leads to colourful deposits of clay and the outlets of three mineral springs. On the way, you are treated to a suspension bridge crossing of the Vermilion River. The area is good habitat for wildlife: wolf, coyote, deer, elk, moose, American marten, grizzly bear and black bear. Look for their tracks.

The clay at the Ochre Beds was created from sediments

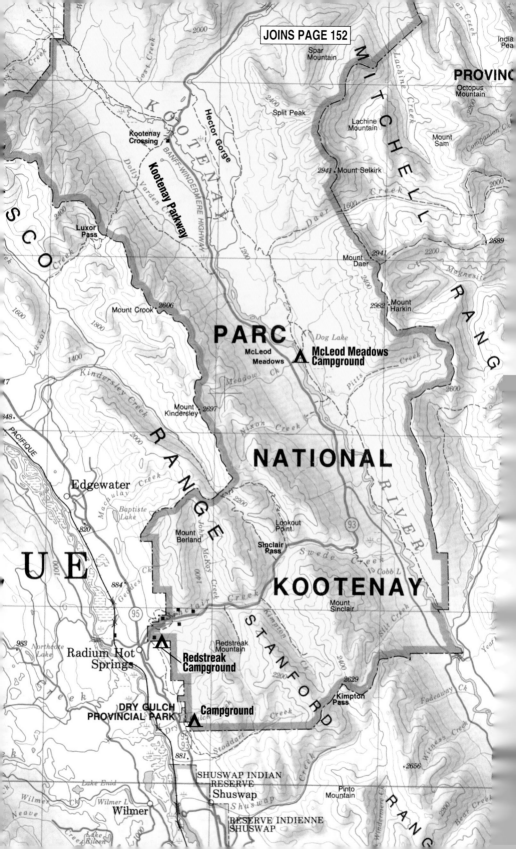

PROVINC

India
Pea

Octopus
Mountain

MITCHELL

Spar
Mountain

Lachine
Mountain

Mount
Sam

Split Peak

2941 · Mount Selkirk

KOOTENAY

Lost Creek

Kootenay
Crossing

Hector Gorge

Kootenay Parkway

BANFF-WINDERMERE HIGHWAY

Dolly Varden

Mount
Daer

2941

Mount
Harkin

2889

RANG

Luxor
Pass

ISCO

Mount Crook 2606

PARC

McLeod
Meadows

Dog Lake

McLeod Meadows
Campground

NATIONAL

Kindersley Creek

Mount
Kindersley 2697

Edgewater

MacKulay Creek

Baptiste
Lake

820

Mount
Berland

Lookout
Point

Sinclair
Pass

RANGE

John McKay Creek

RIVER

93

Swede Creek

Cobb L

UE

KOOTENAY

Mount
Sinclair

884

95

Sinclair Creek

STANFORD

Kimpton Creek

Radium Hot
Springs

983

Northcote
Lake

Redstreak
Campground

Redstreak
Mountain

Mount
Sinclair

2629

Kimpton
Pass

2400

DRY GULCH
PROVINCIAL PARK

Campground

881

SHUSWAP INDIAN
RESERVE
Shuswap

Pinto
Mountain

2656

Wilmer

RESERVE INDIENNE
SHUSWAP

The Paint Pots near Marble Canyon

deposited on the bottom of an ancient glacial lake. The remarkable colours result from saturation of the clay with iron-rich water. This water percolates to the surface nearby at the outlets of three mineral springs—the Paint Pots. The iron compounds in the water have also stained rocks and vegetation in the Vermilion River, suggesting its name.

The Ochre Beds were known to Kutenais from the interior of B.C. as "the place where the red earth spirit is taken." The Kutenais gathered the colourful clay, formed it into cakes and baked it in fire. The resulting compound was ground into powder and mixed with animal fat or fish grease to create a body paint, used in rituals.

The Kutenais discovered that the "red earth" was a valuable trading commodity. Once or twice a year, they would cross the Rockies to hunt bison and trade with the Stoneys at Kootenay Plains on the North Saskatchewan River.

In the early 1900s, commercial interests developed the Ochre Beds as a source of pigment for paint. The clay was excavated and hauled overland to Castle Junction to be shipped to Calgary by train. Partly because of the difficulty and cost in transporting the clay, the enterprise soon failed. Equipment remains at the Ochre Beds, rusting beside mounds of clay heaped for a harvest that was never completed.

Please do not to walk in the ochre deposits or remove any of the material. The clay will stain clothing and shoes. Disturbances of this soil may take many years to disappear.

The Rockwall

The Rockwall and Floe Lake

Beyond the Paint Pots, the Kootenay Parkway curves south along the Vermilion River. You can take a short walk to the river at the Numa Creek and Floe Lake trailheads. The river separates the eastern main ranges to the east from the western main ranges to the west. The western main ranges here contain one of the most remarkable geological features in the Rockies: The Rockwall. This cliff of Ottertail limestone is more than 900 m high in places. It extends 53 km through Kootenay and Yoho national parks.

The Rockwall Trail, a popular backpacking route, parallels the base of the cliff for much of its length. Highlights of the trail are: Floe Lake, expansive alpine meadows, larch forests, glaciated peaks and Helmet Falls—one of Canada's highest waterfalls.

Mt. Verendrye

Mt. Verendrye (vurr-EN-dree) (3,086 m) is one of the most impressive mountains along the Kootenay Parkway. It stands at the southern end of The Rockwall and is visible from near Vermilion Crossing.

Mt. Verendrye was named by surveyor G.M. Dawson for a French-Canadian explorer who attempted to journey overland to the Pacific in the early 1700s. The mountain was first climbed in 1922. The area between Mt. Verendrye and Mt. Wardle to the west contains prime mountain-goat habitat, and has been designated a special preservation area. A new park information centre opened at Kootenay Park Lodge in 1997.

Simpson Monument to Kootenay Valley

At Simpson Monument, the Kootenay Parkway curves southwest, following the Vermilion River as it flows through a break between the Vermilion and Mitchell ranges. The slopes of Mt. Wardle, north of the Kootenay Parkway, are home to approximately 70 mountain goats. The mountain goat is the symbol of Kootenay National Park. B.C. supports 56,000 mountain goats—the largest population in the world. After elk, goats are the second most common large mammal in Kootenay. The current population estimate enough for the park is 300 goats.

The Mt. Wardle goats sometimes descend to roadside to lick mineral-rich banks of glacial sediment. In doing so, they forsake their customary haven of cliffs and ledges. This is the only montane habitat in the Rockies used by goats in winter. Please do not approach the goats if you are fortunate to see them here.

Hector Gorge has been eroded by the Vermilion River, just upstream from where it joins the Kootenay River. The Kootenay Parkway bypasses

Kootenay Valley

the gorge by climbing over the south end of the Vermilion Range before descending to the Kootenay River. On the way, it passes Kootenay Pond, a kettle lake formed at the end of the Wisconsin Glaciation by the melting of a block of glacial ice. Look for claw marks left by bears in the bark of aspen trees nearby.

Kootenay Valley

The 30-km length of the Kootenay Valley between here and Sinclair Pass lies in the montane ecoregion. The mixed forest is home to healthy populations of red squirrels and ruffed grouse. The trees are interspersed with shrub thickets that support elk, moose, black bear and deer. The open grasslands feature colonies of Columbian ground squirrels. Wolves and coyotes range through the valley. Please drive carefully. Road kills of animals are common here.

On the west side of the valley rise the western ranges— the oldest mountains in the Rockies. The rocks in western range mountains have been severely faulted and folded.

These mountains were relatively unglaciated during the last ice age.

There are three picnic areas in the Kootenay Valley: Dolly Varden, McLeod Meadows and Kootenay River; and there is a campground at McLeod Meadows. Just south of Kootenay Crossing, a display details the construction and opening of the Kootenay Parkway.

Viewpoint

Eight kilometres south of McLeod Meadows campground, the Kootenay Parkway climbs from the floor of the Kootenay Valley toward the entrance to Sinclair Pass. The expansive vista from the viewpoint at the top of the hill reveals the grand scale of the Kootenay Valley, of which an 80-km length is visible. You can see the mix of forest habitats: aspen and poplar stands interspersed with grasslands on the valley floor; lodgepole pine on the lower mountainsides; and spruce and fir at higher elevations. Some of the pine trees have reddish-brown foliage caused by infestations of mountain pine beetles.

The Redwall

A few western larch trees grow near this viewpoint. This coniferous tree is not ever-green—its needles turn gold and drop off in the autumn. In Canada, western larch is found only in southeastern B.C. and at a few sites in southwestern Alberta. It is a desired tree for dimensional lumber. Kootenay is the only Rocky Mountain park in which it is found.

Sinclair Pass

Leaving the Kootenay Valley viewpoint, the Kootenay Parkway curves sharply west and crosses Sinclair Pass before descending into the Sinclair Valley. The V shape of the Sinclair Valley indicates that it has been eroded princi-pally by water. The Sinclair Valley escaped glaciation in the most recent ice age. The V-shaped valley we see is the product of tens of thousands of years of primarily water ero-sion—an oddity in the Canadian Rockies.

Sinclair Pass, Sinclair Creek and Sinclair Canyon were named for James Sinclair. In 1841, Sinclair led a group of 120 settlers from Manitoba across the Rockies by this route. Sinclair's group was sponsored by the Hudson's Bay Company. Their destina-tion was Oregon, which they intended to colonize to sup-port a claim by Britain. They eventually reached Oregon, but were ultimately unsuc-cessful in their aim. Sinclair's solitary visit to the hot springs in the lower canyon was the second recorded by a European. Sir George Simpson had been there earlier that summer.

Six hiking trails depart from the Kootenay Parkway in Sinclair Canyon. They offer the opportunity to explore the var-ied vegetation of this unique area in the Rockies. Olive Lake picnic area is at the crest of Sinclair Pass.

The Kootenay Parkway descends steeply for 9.3 km west of Sinclair Pass. At the bottom of this hill is the Iron Gates tunnel. When the Kootenay Parkway was upgraded in 1964, this tunnel was excavated so that the road surface would not have to be extended into Sinclair Creek. The "gates" of the tunnel are the iron-stained cliffs of the Redwall, through which the tunnel passes.

The grassy slopes beneath the Redwall are a favourite spot for bighorn sheep. As many as 100 sheep frequent this area in early summer. Please drive slowly and carefully.

Sinclair Canyon

Sinclair Canyon is a narrow cleft in the rock step at the mouth of Sinclair Creek. Although natives frequented the hot springs nearby—as evidenced by the pictographs that could then be seen in the area—James Sinclair had been advised by a Cree guide to avoid the canyon. Sinclair's party used a native trail that bypassed the canyon by climbing over the shoulder of Mt. Berland to the west, prob-ably much the same way the Juniper Trail does today.

The section of road con-structed in the canyon before World War I was soon washed away by high water. To solve the problem, engineers paved the canyon floor and redirected the creek underground. Today, you can travel in the depths of the canyon—an intimidating place where, for centuries, no one dared venture.

The hanging valley of Sinclair Creek empties into the Columbia Valley at the south end of Sinclair Canyon. The Juniper Trail departs from roadside. It features tremen-dous diversity, descending into cedar forest along Sinclair Creek, and climbing above Sinclair Canyon onto dry slopes frequented by bighorn sheep.

The park information cen-tre is on the east side of the Kootenay Parkway at the park

159

Radium Hot Springs

Hot spring water is rain and snowmelt that has percolated into the earth's crust through crack systems in the bedrock. Heated and pressurized, the water returns to the earth's surface along other crack systems. At Radium Hot Springs, the Redwall Fault provides a convenient vertical channel for the resurfacing water, the maximum recorded temperature of which is 47.7°C.

As hot springs go in the Rockies, those at Radium are fairly hot but relatively lacking in mineral content and are virtually odourless.

However, Radium Hot Springs are noted for their radioactive content. The waters contain traces of radium—an element that was formerly thought to have healing and restorative powers. In the Victorian era, it was fashionable for the elite to take their vacations at hot springs.

There is little record of Radium Hot Springs between 1841 and 1890, when Roland Stuart, a British aristocrat, purchased a lease on the land. He also acquired rights to market the waters from the springs—all for $160. Stuart did little to develop his lease during the next 21 years. For most of this time, a simple tent was the only facility provided for bathers.

Stuart was an associate of businessman Robert Bruce, who in 1910 proposed the road that would link Banff and the Columbia Valley. There were easier routes this road could have taken to the Columbia Valley, but the presence of the hot springs, owned by a friend, prompted Bruce to advocate a route across Sinclair Pass.

Radium Hot Springs

The development of Radium Hot Springs began in 1890

Stuart had trouble financing the development of the springs. In 1911, he was able to convince John Harmsworth (of Perrier fame), a paralysed multi-millionaire from France, to test the waters. After four months soaking in the springs, Harmsworth regained movement in his feet, and Stuart received backing for development.

Being a man accustomed to the high life, Stuart squandered most of the money. He built only a concrete pool and a bath house. Meanwhile, the B.C. section of the highway project had gone bankrupt. Robert Bruce began lobbying the Canadian government with his idea for a national park. In 1920, Kootenay National Park was established. The government could not condone a private lease on national park land, and expropriated Stuart's holding in 1922. Two years later, the Kootenay Parkway was completed. Stuart eventually received $40,000 through a compensation hearing at which some witnesses appraised the hot springs at half a million dollars.

To accommodate the increasing number of visitors, the hot pool was expanded in 1927. This facility burned in 1948 and was rebuilt in 1951. Additional renovations took place in 1968.

Sinclair Canyon looks much the same today as it did in the 1920s

boundary. From here, it is one kilometre to the town of Radium and the junction with B.C. Highway 95. Turn south for Redstreak Campground, Invermere and Cranbrook. Turn north for Golden.

Rocky Mountain Trench

As it descends into the Columbia Valley, the Kootenay Parkway leaves the Rocky Mountains and enters the Rocky Mountain Trench. The Rocky Mountain Trench is a rift in the earth's crust that parallels the western slope of the Rockies for their entire length. Here, it marks the division between the Rocky Mountains and the Purcell Range of the older Columbia Mountains to the west. The Rocky Mountain Trench was created by the stretching of the earth's crust. The Columbia River now flows through this rift.

The Rocky Mountain Trench is in the montane ecoregion. The benchlands and mountainsides are semi-arid. Coniferous forest dominated by Douglas fir prevails. The Columbia River Wetlands, which occupy much of the valley bottom, are the longest continuous series of wetlands remaining in North America. These provide important resting and breeding sites for migratory birds—more than 200 species have been recorded. The overall climate is much warmer and drier than in the Rockies. Radium, Invermere and Windermere are midwinter (sometimes even midsummer!) meccas for Rocky Mountain locals who are fed up with chill winds, snow and cloudy skies.

The steep, south-facing slopes in the Columbia Valley are important winter range for bighorn sheep and mule deer, and are frequented by predators such as cougar, lynx and coyote. Kootenay is the only national park in which Rocky Mountain Trench vegetation is represented. Some areas in the extreme south end of the park have been designated special preservation areas. These are home to prickly-pear cactus and the northernmost stand of ponderosa pine in the Columbia Valley.

The Columbia River

The 2044-km-long Columbia River is one of the major rivers of North America. It drains an area of 155,000 square kilometres in B.C. and the northwestern U.S. With such a large watershed, the Columbia has several distinct sources. Its most southerly source is Columbia Lake, 45 km south of Radium. From Columbia Lake, the Columbia River flows north for 250 km. It then makes a hairpin turn south and flows past Revelstoke, through the Arrow Lakes and across the U.S. border. Eventually, it reaches the Pacific Ocean beyond Portland, Oregon.

The Columbia River Treaty of 1961 forever changed this river. Three dams were constructed on the Canadian reach of the river. Including those in place before the treaty, 11 dams were constructed on the Columbia River in the U.S. Eighteen dams were also constructed on primary tributaries of the Columbia River: the Kootenay, the Snake, the Spokane, the Clearwater and the Flathead. The benefits of the dams are that they stabilize water flows and minimize the risk of flooding on the lower Columbia and they allow hydroelectric generation. The disadvantages: they killed one of the world's greatest salmon runs and submerged vast areas of pristine forest in B.C.

The salmon run was eliminated from the upper Columbia River with construction of the Grand Coulee Dam in Washington in 1939. Attempts to reintroduce salmon to the upper river—using fish ladders and barges—were unsuccessful. The construction of the additional dams on the upper river sealed the fate of the salmon run. △

Icefields Parkway South

"Through dense primeval forests, muskeg, burnt and fallen timber and along rough and steeply sloping hillsides, a constant flow of travel will demand a broad, well-ballasted motor road... this wondertrail will be world renowned."
                                                                            A.O. Wheeler, 1920

The Wonder Road

The Icefields Parkway (Highway 93 North) connects Lake Louise and Jasper, and provides access to Columbia Icefield, Bow Summit, Athabasca Falls and dozens of other points of interest. Experienced travellers are unanimous in their praise for the scenery along the Icefields Parkway. Many consider the drive from Lake Louise to Jasper the most spectacular in the world.

The Icefields Parkway follows the Bow, Mistaya, North Saskatchewan, Sunwapta and Athabasca valleys. These valleys are flanked by 12 icefields, five of which are visible from the road or nearby viewpoints. One traveller has counted more than 600 glaciers on the trip from Lake Louise to Jasper. Many of the popular viewpoints are best viewed before midmorning.

SuperGuide Recommendations

Sights/Attractions
- Crowfoot Glacier viewpoint
- Peyto Lake (Bow Summit) viewpoint
- Bow Lake

Hikes/Activities
- Bow Summit viewpoint trail
- Parker Ridge trail

Before the Icefields Parkway was built, there were easier routes leading north from Lake Louise. Swamps in the upper Bow Valley, coupled with many fallen timbers caused by forest fires in the late 19th century, made travel from Lake Louise to Bow Pass arduous. Natives and early explorers preferred to follow the Pipestone Valley northeast from Lake Louise. The Pipestone Valley connects with other front range valleys to reach the Sunwapta Valley north of Columbia Icefield.

One of the first parties to use the Bow Valley instead of the Pipestone Valley included American explorer Walter Wilcox and guide Bill Peyto (PEE-toe) in 1896. Other mountaineers subsequently followed this route in their quests to ascend the high peaks north of Lake Louise. The Pipestone Valley route fell into disuse and the route of today's Icefields Parkway became established.

The first complete journey from Banff to Jasper along this route was in 1904 by a party led by outfitter Jim Brewster. Three years later, explorer A.P. Coleman made a similar trip. From his experiences on this journey, Coleman became a strong proponent of a devel-

oped road between Lake Louise and Jasper, along a route he called "The Wonder Trail."

Construction of the forerunner of the Icefields Parkway began in 1931 as a Great Depression make-work project. Crews worked toward each other from Jasper and Lake Louise. When in full swing, the construction involved 625 men. Very few pieces of heavy machinery were used in overcoming the obstacles presented by the difficult terrain.

The crews met on the hill at the Big Bend just south of Columbia Icefield in 1939. Their finished product was a 6.5-m-wide gravelled road, 230 km in length, that in no place exceeded eight per cent in grade. The Icefields Parkway opened in June of 1940. The landscape it revealed was heralded in *The Banff Crag and Canyon* as "twenty Switzerlands in one."

When the Icefields Parkway was resurfaced in 1961, most of the grading was retained—a tribute to the original construction. Sections of road bed that were abandoned are being allowed to revegetate naturally. You can see them at various locations. The Icefields Parkway celebrated

left: Mt. Balfour at the head of Hector Lake   **163**

JOINS PAGE 176

JOINS PAGE 130

JOINS PA

BANFF

MONTAGNE

Conical Peak

Isabella Lake

Mount Kentigern

Martin Creek

Martin

Mount Harris

unt Weed

Mount Willingdon

Silverhorn Mountain

3094

3356

2500

3013

Clearwater Mountain

3000

3373

Marmot Mountain

Observation Peak

Bow Pass

Bow T

Clearwater Pass

Devon Lakes

Devon Mountain

Lake Alice

3002

Pipestone Pass

Fish Lakes

Cirque Peak

Dolomite Pass
Lake Katherine

Helen Lake

2200

Mount Jimmy Simpson

Helen Ck

Dolomite Peak

Mount Thompson

2972

2400

Portal Peak

Bow Lake

2000

Bow Glacier

St Nicholas Peak

Crowfoot Mountain

Crowfoot Glacier

Bow Peak

2868

Mosquito Creek campground

Molar Glacier

Molar Mountain

2002

Icefield

2941

Mount Olive

2200

2400

Mount Gordon

Balfour Pass

Hector Glacier

Molar Creek

Diableret Falls

Diableret Glacier

Balfour Glacier

Lake Margaret

Hector Lake

Mount Hector

Yoho Peak

Trolltinder Glacier

3246

Mount Balfour

Turquoise Lake

Pulpit Peak

2969

Icefield Parkway

PROMENADE DES GLACIERS

Trolltinder Mountain

Fairy L.

Lilliput Mountain

WAPUTIK

1800

Whaleback Mountain

Fairy Glacier

Waputik

Waputik Glacier

2400

RANGE

Icefield

Daly Glacier

Mount Daly

Bath

Waputik Peak

The Vice President

Takakkaw Falls campground

3063

Niles Glacier

Glacier

93

The President

Emerald Glacier

Takakkau Falls

Mount Niles

Pipesto

Michael Peak

Niles Ck

Lost Lake

1800

ONAL

ENT

RANGE

Yoho Pass

Sherbrooke

Bath

Mount Bosworth

Herbert Lake

Whi

Emerald Lake

River Valley

Mount Ogden

Paget Peak

Kicking Horse Pass

Mud

JOINS PAGE 130

Wapta Mountain

2788

Wapta Lake

1A

L

Mount Field

Upper Canyon

Ross L.

Mount Burgess

Narao Peak

Mount Niblock

Mount St Piran

ARK

The Beehive

Devils Thumb

Herbert Lake

its 50th year in 1990. Parks Canada held a reunion at Jasper Park Lodge for those who had worked on the road.

Services are few between Lake Louise and Jasper, particularly in winter when you should carry survival equipment, food and extra gasoline. The Icefields Parkway is popular with cyclists in summer. Please do not drive on the paved shoulders. Park only where permitted, and camp only at campgrounds.

Herbert Lake

There are hundreds of glacially formed lakes in the Rockies. Depressions scoured in the bedrock by glacial ice became natural places for water to collect when the ice receded. Moraines deposited by the retreating ice then impounded the meltwater. Lakes formed in this manner are called tarns. Herbert Lake is a fine example. It has no surface outlet.

When calm, Herbert Lake offers perfect reflections of Mt. Temple and other mountains near Lake Louise. It provides an appealing early morning or late evening haunt for photographers. Locals use the lake as a swimming hole for a few weeks in summer when its waters are (barely!) warm enough.

The forest around Herbert Lake is a homogenous stand of lodgepole pine—the product of a forest fire in the early 20th century. The canopy of the lodgepole pine forest is lighter in colour than that of older stands of spruce and fir that escaped the forest fire. There is a picnic area at Herbert Lake. There is no record of who "Herbert" was, but he was probably connected with the construction of the Icefields Parkway.

Mt. Hector

Mt. Hector (3,394 m) dominates the east side of the Icefields Parkway just north of Lake Louise. It is the 40th highest mountain in the Rockies, and was first climbed in 1895 by three members of the Appalachian Mountain Club of Boston. This mountaineering party helped pioneer the Bow Valley route north from Lake Louise. In doing so, they enjoyed as their reward one of the finest views in the Rockies from Mt. Hector's lofty summit.

Mt. Hector was named in 1884 for James Hector, who explored the Rockies during the Palliser Expedition of 1857-60. An alpine valley glacier flows down its northern slope. This glacier is the usual route of ascent for mountaineers. You can see the glacier from Bow Lake, farther north along the Icefields Parkway.

Hector Lake

The Hector Lake viewpoint is 16.5 km north of Highway 1. Hector Lake is approximately five kilometres long and is the second largest lake in Banff National Park. The lake has been impounded by a glacial moraine. The glaciers you see on the mountains above Hector Lake are part of the Wapta Icefield and the Waputik Icefield. *Waputik* (WAH-poo-tick) is a Stoney word that means "white goat." A rough trail to Hector Lake and a backcountry campground departs from roadside, one kilometre north of the viewpoint.

Mt. Balfour

If you look west from just

north of the Hector Lake view-point, you will see the icy summit of Mt. Balfour (3,272 m) rising above glaciers of the Waputik Icefield. During the first ascents of Mt. Stephen, Mt. Hector, Mt. Lefroy and Mt. Victoria, surveyors and climbers noticed an impressive mountain on the continental divide about 20 km north of Lake Louise. This peak, which James Hector had named Mt. Balfour, was scarcely visible from the valleys. Only from other summits could it be fully appreciated. It drew the collective attention of the mountaineering elite. Four attempts to climb it in 1897 and 1898 greatly increased knowledge of the area between Lake Louise and Bow Pass.

A party from the Appalachian Mountain Club succeeded in reaching Mt. Balfour's summit in August of 1898. Mt. Balfour retains an air of inaccessibility today. Its ascent is a favourite challenge in winter and spring for ski mountaineers.

Bow Peak

Bow Peak (2,868 m) is the mountain west of the Icefields Parkway near Mosquito Creek. Although several thousand mountains in the Rockies are higher than Bow Peak, few can match the panoramic view from its isolated summit. Bow Peak was first climbed by Walter Wilcox in 1896. It was later occupied as a camera station by the Interprovincial Boundary Survey, which mapped the boundary between Alberta and B.C. between 1913 and 1925. The colourful upper cliffs of the mountain are Gog quartzite.

This 1917 photograph shows the bottom toe of Crowfoot Glacier

The darker, lower cliffs contain slates and gritstones of the Miette group of formations.

There is a hostel and campground at Mosquito Creek. The Mosquito Creek trail provides hiking access to Molar Meadows, Molar Pass, Fish Lakes and the upper Pipestone Valley.

Dolomite Peak

The castellated towers of Dolomite Peak (2,998 m) are prominent on the east side of the Icefields Parkway, just north of Mosquito Creek. The mountain was named for its

likeness to peaks in the Dolomites of the Italian Alps. Dolomite rock forms when water seeps into limestone sediments before they have lithified. Calcium in the limestone is replaced with magnesium. The magnesium-enriched rock is usually tougher than limestone, and more colourful too. The cliffs in Dolomite Peak contain a mixture of limestone and dolomite. Although they appear inaccessible, most of the towers on Dolomite Peak pose little challenge to mountaineers. Many were first

The Miette Formations

The purple, brown and orange-coloured rocks at the junction of the Icefields Parkway and Highway 1 are slates of the Miette (mee-YETT) group of formations. Slate is formed from fine sedimentary particles that settled on ancient sea floors as clay. Under pressure, the clay lithified into shale. Under greater pressure and resulting heat, the shale was transformed into thin layers of slate.

The formations of the Miette

Group are the oldest visible in this part of the Rockies—570 million years old to 730 million years old. These formations accumulated to a maximum thickness of nine kilometres, making the Miette the thickest deposit underlying the Rockies.

Miette slate is also visible west of Jasper in the Miette Valley (which gave the formation its name). Miette gritstone is common in the Athabasca Valley south of Jasper.

Over 80 years later, Crowfoot Glacier's bottom section has completely receded

climbed in the 1930s by crews involved in the construction of the Icefields Parkway.

Crowfoot Glacier

Crowfoot Glacier is the first of a series of spectacular glaciers that you see between Lake Louise and Jasper. Crowfoot Glacier is known as a catchment glacier. Looking at the glacier, one can easily understand how it formed. The massive upper cliff of Crowfoot Mountain is a natural snowfence that traps windblown snow beneath. In the shade of the mountain, little of the accumulated snow melts. Over time, it becomes glacial ice. Under the influence of gravity, the ice flows downhill towards the cliff edge.

Recent glacial retreat has been dramatic at Crowfoot Glacier. Photographs taken earlier this century show that the ice formerly reached the moraines at the base of the mountain. Crowfoot Glacier was originally known as Trident Glacier, because it had three lobes shaped like the tines of a fishing spear. The modern name likens the glacier's appearance to the foot of the American crow, which has three splayed toes. The most southerly "toe" fell off in the 1920s, making the analogy obscure today. North of Crowfoot Glacier are two fine examples of cirque glaciers and terminal moraines. The Dolomite Pass trailhead is across the Icefields Parkway from the Crowfoot Glacier viewpoint.

Bow Lake

When Bow Glacier retreated from the Bow Valley at the end of the Wisconsin Glaciation, it left behind deposits of glacial rubble. Among these were moraines that impounded the Bow River, creating Bow Lake. Moraine-dammed lakes are common in the Rockies, but few are as large as Bow Lake. It is the third largest lake in Banff National Park. Almost all of the water in Bow Lake is glacial in origin. The principal inlet of the lake is just three kilometres from Bow Glacier.

There is a picnic area at the south end of Bow Lake. Sport fishing for various species of trout is popular. The swampy area at the lake's outlet is a good place to see moose.

Bow Glacier

Bow Glacier is the tip of an alpine iceberg. This tongue of ice is one of eight outlet valley glaciers that flow from the 40-square-kilometre Wapta Icefield on the continental divide. As with most other glaciers in the Rockies, Bow Glacier has receded during the last 100 years. In the early 20th century, the ice cascaded over the lower cliff to the valley floor.

You can view Bow Glacier from the parking area on the

Cirques

Many of the bowl-shaped depressions on mountainsides in the Rockies were created by cirque glaciers that eroded rearwards and downwards into the rock. In many instances, the glacial ice responsible has now melted, and all that remains is the shape that contained it—the cirque.

Cirques and cirque glaciers are prominent on north and east aspects of many mountains along the Icefields Parkway. These slopes are the most shaded and hence the most prone to glaciation. The Waputik Range south of Hector Lake features a number of cirques, some of which still contain vestiges of ice. Small cirque glaciers like these are known as pocket glaciers.

When two or more cirque glaciers erode different aspects of a summit, they create the horn mountain shape. Mt. Chephren, The White Pyramid, Mt. Athabasca and Mt. Fryatt are good examples along the Icefields Parkway.

Grizzly Bear

The grizzly bear is the most celebrated mammal in the Rockies. However, most of what people "know" about grizzly bears is inaccurate. In the Rockies, these animals are not marauding hunters. Their diet is 90 per cent vegetarian. Much of the meat a grizzly does eat is carrion, or kills strong-armed from other animals. There are far fewer grizzly bears in the Rocky Mountain parks than most people imagine; only 150 to 200. Of these, 40 to 60 are in Banff National Park. The grizzly bear is listed as a vulnerable species because of its dwindling numbers, low fertility rate and habitat loss. Despite the fact that the grizzly bear has no natural enemies, some wildlife biologists think that the species may become extirpated (locally extinct) in the Rockies within 30 years.

The section of the Icefields Parkway between Hector Creek and Bow Pass is where you are most likely to see a grizzly bear at roadside in the Rockies. The upper Bow Valley provides vegetation favoured by the grizzly in early summer and late summer. Side valleys to the east offer it quick access to favourite mid-summer habitat above treeline.

The grizzly bear spends almost every waking moment in a quest for food to tide it through its winter dormancy. At the peak of its feeding in August, an adult grizzly may feed for 18 hours each day, and consume 36 kg of food, representing 40,000 calories. Berries, roots, horsetail, herbs and the occasional rodent comprise the bulk of its diet.

The grizzly bear passes most of the winter in a state of dormancy. It digs a den into a steep hillside on a north or east facing slope where deep snow provides insulation. It does not cache food in the den. Instead, the grizzly lives off its reserves of fat. Most grizzly bears emerge from their dens in April.

Female (sow) grizzly bears mate every two or three years. Breeding commences at age five to seven years. The litter in the Rockies is usually a single cub. This represents the lowest reproduction rate among large North American land mammals. Mortality rate for cubs is 10 to 40 per cent in the first 18 months. The offspring of grizzly bears enjoy a lengthy apprenticeship with their mother: two summers, sometimes three.

The only natural threat to the young is the father (boar), who might try to kill them when they first emerge from the den. It is common for the siblings to remain together for a brief time after leaving the sow. Otherwise, grizzlies are solitary. Life expectancy is 20 years. The largest grizzly bear recorded in Banff National Park weighed 336 kg.

Black Bear

The montane forest near Rampart Creek campground is one of the best places in the Rockies to see black bears. It was formerly thought that the Rocky Mountain parks supported a large population of these animals. However, park wardens now think there are only 50 to 60 black bears in Banff National Park. Unlike the grizzly bear, which ranges through a variety of habitats from valley bottom to mountain top, the black bear prefers montane valley bottoms. There is very little of this habitat available, so the number of black bears is limited.

The black bear eats berries, leaves, insects and carrion—75 per cent of its diet is vegetarian. It is solitary except when with cubs. It spends most of each winter in dormancy, denning in natural shelters on lower mountainsides—caves, overhangs, fallen trees. The black bear is a more adept tree climber than the griz-

zly bear, and will use this tactic to avoid danger. Although its coat is generally black in colour with a white patch on the chest, cinnamon-coloured bears occur in the Rockies, especially in Waterton Lakes National Park.

Because it prefers valley bottoms frequented by people, black bears are more often involved in encounters with visitors than are grizzly bears. The black bear readily comes to associate humans with easily obtainable food. Once fed, a bear loses its innate fear of people and may begin to seek unnatural food sources. This is the kind of bear that breaks into vehicles or raids picnic tables in campgrounds. These bears are trapped and relocated by park wardens. Unfortunately, habituated bears usually return to where the pickings are easiest. If a bear is caught three times, it is destroyed. Between 1975 and 1985, 141 black bears were

destroyed in Jasper National Park.

Black bears also suffer tremendous mortality on the highways and railways in the Rockies. Twelve black bears were killed by vehicles in Jasper in 1993. Black bears reproduce more frequently than grizzly bears in the Rockies, but the replacement rate cannot keep pace with this kind of population drain. Some wildlife biologists think that the black bear may be on the verge of extirpation—local extinction in the Rockies—despite the fact that it is protected.

What can you do to help? Stay in your vehicle when you see a bear. Take photographs with a telephoto lens. Do not approach or feed a bear. Do not leave food or packs unattended. Store your camping food in the locked trunk of your vehicle or in the storage facilities provided.

Icefields Parkway, or you can follow the Num-ti-Jah Lodge access road and park closer to the lake. From here, you can hike to Bow Glacier along the trail that begins in front of lodge. The trail follows the lake's north shore to the delta at its principal inlet. It then follows a winding stream to a canyon that features a chockstone lodged across the chasm. The trail climbs above the canyon and brings you to a viewpoint overlooking the forefield of Bow Glacier and the waterfalls on the cliffs below the ice. These waterfalls are a popular location for waterfall ice climbing in winter.

Mt. Thompson

The prominent peak to the north of Bow Glacier is Mt. Thompson (3,065 m), named for American mountaineer Charles Thompson. Thompson was in the first party to set foot on the Wapta Icefield in 1897. During this party's ascent of Mt. Gordon, Thompson slipped into a crevasse near the summit. Roped to other members of the party, he was eventually rescued when John Norman Collie was lowered into the icy depths to lend assistance. Recalling the event, Collie named the mountain for his friend when he accomplished the first ascent the following year.

Jimmy Simpson

Jimmy Simpson began work in the Rockies in 1897 as camp cook for expeditions outfitted by Tom Wilson. Simpson took to trail life well, and went on to become one of the Rockies' most accomplished and celebrated trail guides.

Simpson was known to natives as *Nashan-essen,* which means "wolverine go quickly"—a reference to his legendary ability to travel in the mountains. He was a great hunter. He claimed to dream about the locations of game. When he went to that place the next day, he would find the animals. He is credited with taking a world record bighorn ram in 1920. He poached the animal, killing it three days after the end of hunting season.

Simpson cultivated an elite and wealthy clientele of hunters from the eastern U.S. He brought noted wildlife artist Carl Rungius to the Rockies in 1910. Rungius was so taken by the scenery, by the wildlife and by his host that he returned regularly, trading artwork for outfitting. Simpson eventually built a studio for Rungius in Banff, and amassed a valuable collection of his work. With references given by Rungius, other wildlife artists and big game hunters sought Simpson's services, and his business grew.

Simpson's wife, Billie, was an accomplished figure skater. Their two daughters followed in their mother's footsteps, achieving international renown in the 1930s. Jimmy cleared practice skating rinks on Bow Lake in winter, and levelled a section of Bow Glacier in summer.

Simpson died in 1972. The mountain immediately north of Num-ti-Jah Lodge was

Jimmy Simpson

named in his honour the following year. In doing so, the Canadian Committee on Geographical Names chose to break one of its new rules— that personal names could not be given to geographical features. The mountain was officially dedicated at a ceremony in August 1974, on what would have been Jimmy Simpson's 97th birthday.

Bow Summit

Between the turnoff for Bow Lake and Bow Pass, the Icefields Parkway travels beside upper subalpine wet meadows. Most of the low-lying vegetation here is willows and sedges. Nighttime temperature inversions trap cold air in the valley bottom, shortening the growing season. These wet meadows are frequented by grizzly bear, mule deer and moose. Observation Peak (3,174 m) is the prominent mountain on the east side of the highway.

Bow Lake

Bow Glacier

Bow Pass (2,069 m) is the highest point on the Icefields Parkway, and the highest point crossed by a highway in Canada that is open year-round. Follow the sideroad west to the Bow Summit trailhead. This short interpretive trail leads you through open upper subalpine forest to a viewpoint that overlooks Peyto Lake.

Here, just below treeline,

and under the chilling influence of the nearby Wapta Icefield, the average temperature is –4 °C. Snowfall is heavy and winds are harsh. Stands of Engelmann spruce and subalpine fir trees are interspersed with damp meadows that are home to a variety of wildflowers and small rodents. Higher on the slope to the south, you can see the krummholz trees that mark treeline.

Species of anemone (an-EMM-owe-nee) and the glacier lily are the first flowers to emerge from the melting snow at Bow Summit in June. Appropriately, anemone means "wind flower." By the third week of July, a full complement of upper subalpine and alpine flowers is in bloom. The snow lingers at Bow Summit until midsummer. The thin soils and sparse ground cover are easily damaged. Please remain on the paved pathway to the Peyto Lake viewpoint. You may also walk the Timberline Trail, a loop that explores the meadows to the south. Dress warmly for either walk.

Bow Pass

Bow Pass (2,069 m) separates waters that flow south into the Bow River and the South Saskatchewan River system, from those that flow north into the Mistaya River and the North Saskatchewan River system. The North Saskatchewan and South Saskatchewan rivers merge in the province of Saskatchewan. The water they carry eventually flows into Hudson Bay.

After crossing Bow Pass, the Icefields Parkway drops abruptly: 270 m in 5.5 kilometres to the floor of the Mistaya Valley. The road passes through colourful quartzite boulders of rockslide debris. To the south you can see Peyto Glacier and the Wapta Icefield.

Snowbird Glacier

Mt. Patterson (3,197 m) dominates the west side of the Mistaya Valley north of Bow Pass. The northeast face of the mountain sports one of the finest glaciers in the Rockies-Snowbird Glacier. Snow that falls on the southwest slopes of Mt. Patterson is scoured by winds and deposited in the indentations on the northeast face. As the bonding power of the ice and snow gives way to the relentless pull of gravity, avalanches sweep the mountainside. At the base of the glacier is a horseshoe-shaped terminal moraine that was created during the Little Ice Age advance.

A formidable and dangerous test piece for mountaineers, Snowbird Glacier was first climbed in 1967. The glacier is sunlit in early morning only. Mt. Patterson was named for a president of the Alpine Club of Canada.

Silverhorn Creek is 3.8 km north of Snowbird Glacier. The overflow campground here will be open when campgrounds at Waterfowl Lakes and Mosquito Creek are full. Woodland (mountain) caribou

Snowbird Glacier

The Red Roof at the Blue Lake

Num-ti-Jah Lodge

Around the turn of the 20th century, Jimmy Simpson spent many winters hunting and trapping between Lake Louise and Columbia Icefield. He came to know the area better than anyone else. In 1900, he established a camp on the shore of his favourite place—Bow Lake. In 1920, he obtained a lease to build his first cabin there, completed in 1923. This building still stands northwest of the Num-ti-Jah (numm-TAH-zjah) Lodge. Simpson's lease required that he spend $5000 adding improvements. He couldn't find enough large logs nearby to build a rectangular

building of that cost, so he built an octagonal one. He skidded the logs by horse team from Hector Lake. In his later years, the cabin became Jimmy's home and was known as "The Ram Pasture."

When work on the Icefields Parkway began in the 1930s, Simpson realized he had an opportunity to expand his business at Bow Lake. Num-ti-Jah Lodge was completed in 1937 on Jimmy's 60th birthday. The lodge has been enlarged since. *Num-ti-Jah* is a Stoney expression for the American marten, a weasel that lives in the subalpine forest.

Howse Peak

are sometimes seen on the highway here in late spring. Mt. Weed (3,080 m) is on the east side of the Icefields Parkway. John Norman Collie named the mountain in 1902 for George Weed, an American mountaineer who climbed in the Rockies in the 1890s and early 1900s.

Howse Peak Viewpoint

The ice-clad ramparts of the continental divide dominate the view west from Howse Peak viewpoint. The ridge in view is nine kilometres long and is never less than 2,750 m high. It contains seven mountains, and culminates in the 3,290-m summit of Howse Peak.

As the prevailing southwest winds rise to clear the continental divide, precipitation falls. This creates a rain shadow here in the Mistaya

Valley. The continental divide swings west from Howse Peak, and does not approach roadside again until Yellowhead Pass, nearly 150 km to the northwest.

Howse Peak was named for Joseph Howse, who worked for the Hudson's Bay Company from 1795 to 1815. In 1810, he crossed a pass just west of Howse Peak that was subsequently also named for him. The names Howse Peak and Howse Pass have been in use since 1814 and are two of the oldest English place names in the Canadian Rockies. At least one historian has ventured that Joseph Howse and Jasper Hawse (see p. 244) were the same person. Hawse ran a fur trade outpost in the Athabasca Valley in the early 1800s. Howse Peak was first climbed in 1898 via a glacier concealed from view on its west slopes. The northeast face of the

mountain, visible from the Icefields Parkway, sports some of the most difficult mountaineering routes in the Rockies.

You can walk downhill from the viewpoint to the marshy shore of Upper Waterfowl Lake—crossing the abandoned road bed of the original Icefields Parkway en route. The lake's shallow waters permit abundant growth of aquatic vegetation preferred by moose. You may see this animal here in the early morning and evening.

Waterfowl Lakes

There is a campground at Lower Waterfowl Lake. The Cirque Lake and Chephren Lake trailheads are located in the campground, at the footbridge across the Mistaya River. At this point, the river is narrow and is not confined in a canyon. Why have the waters of Upper Waterfowl Lake been

Little Critters

You will probably see four species of small rodents at Bow Summit. The smallest of the two common, striped rodents in the Rockies is the **Least chipmunk**—the smallest of the 16 chipmunk species in North America. Four gray stripes with black borders that extend from nose to tail differentiate it from the larger **Golden-mantled ground squirrel,** which has two white stripes with black borders that begin behind the ears. These rodents are a favourite food of many larger predators. They move constantly to avoid becoming easy prey. These critters eat seeds, insects, tender flowers and shoots, and spend the summer stockpiling dry foods in and around their burrows. They are dormant for six months of the year.

Least chipmunk

Golden-mantled ground squirrel

The **Columbian ground squirrel** is one of the most common mammals in the Rockies. You will probably see it standing upright at its burrow entrance, emitting an irritating "yeeek." The burrow is one of many in a colony. When alarmed, these rodents dive for cover, chattering loudly. However, they are curious, and will poke their heads above ground a short time later.

The coat is gray on the back and reddish-orange on the underside and feet. The Columbian ground squirrel eats incessantly: berries, roots, leaves, insects, seeds, flowers and carrion. What it doesn't eat immediately, it stores in its burrow to snack upon during the eight months of the year spent in quasi-dormancy. The Columbian

Columbian ground squirrel

Red squirrel

ground squirrel is a favourite food of hawks, coyotes and grizzly bears. At the end of their first summer, the young must seek their own territory. Many are killed by predators during this migration.

The red squirrel is a vociferous resident of the subalpine forest, and is probably the most frequently heard and seen mammal in the Rockies. Its coat is a dark, reddish-brown, with a white underside and white around the eyes. The bushy tail is tipped with black. Unlike the ground squirrels and chipmunks, the red squirrel is not approachable, and will often greet an intruder with a long-winded array of staccato chattering—a ruckus out of proportion to its small size.

The red squirrel prefers to eat the seeds from spruce and fir cones. Although it is commonly seen leaping from branch to branch gathering cones, it spends much of its time on the forest floor. It lives there in a midden—a pile of scales discarded from cones during feeding. Tree bark, berries, plant seeds, insects, fungi and unattended nestlings comprise the remainder of its diet.

Martens and hawks hunt the red squirrel in the trees, and lynx and coyote attack its midden. Other animals raid its food stockpiles, which can lead to the red squirrel's starvation during winter. Although it spends much of the winter in its midden, the red squirrel does not hibernate. It ventures above the snow on warmer days to search for food.

Bow Summit

Peyto Lake

From the viewpoint at Bow Summit, you obtain a spectacular overview of the Mistaya Valley and Peyto Lake—the fifth largest lake in Banff National Park. The lake is fed by meltwater from Peyto Glacier to your left. The meltwater stream from the glacier carries rubble and sediment. Where the stream enters the lake, the velocity of the water flow decreases and the rubble drops out. Over time, the rubble has built the large delta that now encroaches on the lake. The meltwater stream braids into many channels across the delta. You may see sediment plumes, where the stream deposits finer glacial sediments in the lake.

Extremely fine particles of glacial sediment are known as rock flour. This substance is responsible for the remarkable colour of Peyto Lake. Shortly after the ice melts from the lake's surface in June, the waters will be largely free of sediment. They appear dark blue, much the same as any other lake viewed from above. As the glacier melt season progresses and the content of rock flour in the water increases, the colour of the lake changes to its famous blue-green hue.

This happens because the rock flour particles reflect the blue and green spectra of light. The resulting colour at any given time will vary according to the uniformity of particle size, water depth and turbulence, the stage of the glacier melt season and the amount of sunlight. Viewing from above enhances the effect. Mineral content of the water is not a significant factor in producing the colour.

Peyto Lake in winter

The Mistaya (miss-TAY-yah) Valley fills the view north from the viewpoint. It has been eroded through the crest of an anticline, an arch-shaped fold in the bedrock. If you look at the mountains on either side of the valley, you will see that their rock layers angle upwards towards the valley's centre, indicating where the crest of the arch used to be. *Mistaya* is a Stoney word for grizzly bear. Explorer Mary Schäffer called the river "Bear Creek." The name was changed to avoid duplication.

JOINS PAGE 184

Mountain

Pinto Lake

Sunset Pass

2800

Waterfalls Creek

Shoe Leather Creek

Ely Creek

WHITEGOAT PEAKS

Purple Mountain

Lake of the Falls

Landslide Lake

Michele Lakes

Mount Cline

Resolute Mountain

93

2600

SKATCHEWAN

Rampart Creek campground

Rampart Creek

Wilson Icefield

3000

Mount Wilson *3261*

2400

Owen Creek

RIVIERE   SASKAT

Creek Lakes

ICEFIELDS PARKWAY

RIVER

11

Saskatchewan Crossing

Murchison Creek

Corona Creek

Corona Ridge

Spreading Creek

SI

2600

2200

Survey Peak

Mistaya Canyon

Mount Murchison *3337*

Glacier Lake

Mount Sarbach *3154*

Kaufmann L.

Totem Tower

Totem Creek

Mount Outram *3246*

Sir James Glacier

KAUFMANN PEAKS

Epaulette L.

2400

Howse River

Epaulette Mountain

Mistaya

1800

Noyes Creek

Waterfowl Lakes campground

bes agle Peak

David Lake

Lagoon L.

Mount David

Mount Chephren *3307*

White Pyramid

Chephren Lake

Waterfowl Lakes

2886

2600

Mount Noyes *3094*

WAPUTIK

2200

3290

Howse Peak

Aiguille Peak

Mount Synge

Cirque Lake

Silverton Creek campground

Silverhor

Mistaya Lake

es Creek

Coronation Mountain *3185*

Freshfield Creek

Conway Ck.

Howse Pass

Midway Peak

Stairway Peak

Aries Peak

Mount Weed

ville

Mount Strahan

Conway Glacier

Ebon Peak

JOINS PAGE 164

Silverho Mounta

BA

Mount Skene
Mount Bergne

2400

Ebon Creek

Breaker Mountain *3068*

Capricorn Glacier

Solitaire Mountain

CONWAY

Mount Conway

Barbette Glacier *3185*

Mount Patterson

2600

Parapet Glacier

Mt. Chephren

map as the "Duck Lakes." You may still see geese and ducks here. Look for moose too.

Mt. Chephren

Mt. Chephren (KEFF-ren) (3,307 m) rises majestically from the west shore of Lower Waterfowl Lake. Glaciers erode rearwards and downwards into mountainsides, producing bowl-shaped depressions called cirques. When cirques form on two or more sides of a mountain, they create a horn mountain. Mt. Chephren is one of the best examples in the Rockies.

The horizontal banding in the flanks of Mt. Chephren records different episodes of deposition, when the sediments that comprise the mountain's rocks were laid down on ancient sea floors. Horizontal orientation of rock layers is typical of eastern main range mountains, and renders their rocks more resistant to erosion than layers that have been tipped on edge.

Chephren was the son of Cheops, builder of the Great Pyramid in Egypt. Mt. Chephren was originally called Pyramid Mountain by explorer Mary Schäffer. It was subsequently known as the Black Pyramid. (The peak immediately west is still called the White Pyramid.) The name was changed in 1918 to avoid confusion with Pyramid Mountain near Jasper. Mt. Chephren is visible along a great length of the Icefields Parkway, from Bow Pass to the top of the Big Bend Hill. The mountain was first climbed in 1913.

Mt. Murchison

The Mt. Wilson viewpoint is 10 km north of Lower Waterfowl

constricted here, only to expand into another large lake just downstream?

Lower Waterfowl Lake is a tarn. It occupies a glacially sculpted basin. Upstream on the Mistaya River, Noyes Creek empties into the Mistaya valley from the east. The creek carries a large amount of rubble and debris. Where the creek enters the valley, the angle of the streambed and velocity of water flow decrease, causing this material to be deposited. Over time, this has created a landform called an alluvial fan. In this case, the fan has spread almost entirely across the valley floor, nearly damming the

Mistaya River, and creating Upper Waterfowl Lake. The Waterfowl Lake campground is built on the alluvial fan.

Geologists think that most material in alluvial fans in the Rockies was deposited between 6,000 years ago and 7,000 years ago, in a surge of meltwater when the last vestiges of Wisconsin Glaciation ice melted from the high peaks. Aerial views of Upper Waterfowl Lake show that about half of the lake's original area has been filled with sediment and aquatic vegetation.

The Waterfowl Lakes appeared on mountaineer John Norman Collie's 1903

Bill Peyto

Peyto Lake was named for Bill Peyto (PEE-toe), pioneer guide and outfitter, and later a park warden. During Walter Wilcox's 1896 expedition which camped at Bow Lake, Peyto disappeared one evening to sleep in solitude near this place. Later, upon seeing the lake for himself, Wilcox christened it "Peyto's Lake." The turreted peak across the lake from the viewpoint, with the prominent snow couloir descending from its summit, is also named for Peyto.

Lake. Just south of the viewpoint, the Icefields Parkway passes through a rock cut. The rock here has been polished by glacial ice. You can see striations—scratches caused by rocks imbedded in the underside of the moving ice. Looking north, Mt. Wilson (3,260 m) rises above the North Saskatchewan Valley. You can see the margin of the Wilson Icefield along the eastern skyline of the mountain.

Mt. Murchison (3,333 m) is on the east side of the Icefields Parkway between this viewpoint and Saskatchewan River Crossing. In 1858, James Hector of the Palliser Expedition travelled through the Mistaya Valley. He reported that natives considered Mt. Murchison to be the highest mountain in the Rockies. This is understandable. Mt. Murchison rises 1,920 m above the North Saskatchewan Valley—more than a vertical mile. This statistic notwithstanding, Mt. Murchison's principal peak doesn't even place among the 50 highest Rocky Mountain summits. However, the mountain is one of the highest along the Kutenai Trail, the native travel route that linked the Columbia River with the North Saskatchewan Valley.

If not the highest, Mt. Murchison certainly is one of the largest mountains. Its 10 summits are spread over 30 square kilometres. The first ascent of one of the two principal summits was claimed in 1902 by a party that included Scottish mountaineer John Norman Collie. However, recent evidence indicates that the highest summit was prob-

ably not reached until 1985.

Hector named the mountain for Rodney Murchison, an eminent geologist and the man who had recommended Hector to the Palliser Expedition. Mt. Murchison is prominent in a landscape that owes much of its appearance to ice-age glaciations. Ironically, Rodney Murchison adamantly refused to accept the theory of ice ages, first proposed by

Swiss naturalist Louis Agassiz in 1837. His intolerance caused heated disputes among European geologists of the day, and contributed to a scientific rift on the Continent that has still not healed.

The west side of the Mistaya Valley in this vicinity features one of the most spectacular mountain walls in the Rockies. It includes Mt. Chephren (3,266 m), the White

James Monroe Thorington

James Monroe "Roy" Thorington was an opthamologist from Philadelphia who made his first trip to the Rockies in 1914. It was the beginning of a life-long love affair with "The Glittering Mountains of Canada," as he titled a book in 1925. Thorington was a mountaineering scholar. No oth-

This photograph shows Thorington with guide Conrad Kain (left), atop Trapper Peak on the Wapta Icefield in 1933

er climber or author made such an extensive analysis of the history of mountaineering in the Rockies. His contribution was not strictly literary. Thorington wrote a great deal of the history with his own climbs: He tallied 52 first ascents in the Rockies.

Thorington led the "second wave" of mountaineering in the Rockies, arriving on the scene two decades after Collie, Fay, Outram and company. In the interim, many of the areas that had attracted those mountaineers had plunged into obscurity. Prominent mountains in

plain view from the trails were still unclimbed, as were many mountains more remote.

In a five-day period in 1923, Thorington, W.S. Ladd and guide Conrad Kain stormed the peaks in the vicinity of Columbia Icefield. They made the first ascent of North Twin (third highest in the Rockies), the first ascent of Mt. Saskatchewan, and the second ascent of Mt. Columbia—123 km of travel in an area that had scarcely seen footprints in 20 years. A few days later, they made the third ascent of Mt. Athabasca.

Thorington's book is one of the classics of Rockies' history. He later edited journals and guidebooks of the American Alpine Club. In the 1940s, he was the club president. Thorington outlived every mountaineer, guide and packer of his day. He died in 1989 in Philadelphia, at age 97.

Mt. Murchison

Pyramid (3,275 m), an unnamed peak (3,090 m), Epaulette Mountain (3,095 m), the Kaufmann Peaks (3,110 m, 3,095 m) and Mt. Sarbach (3,155 m). The mountainsides are riddled with cirques and niche glaciers. The cliffs feature the same sequence of rock formations that you see in Castle Mountain: Cathedral limestone, Stephen shale and Eldon limestone.

Mistaya Canyon

At the end of the Wisconsin Glaciation, the mouth of the Mistaya Valley was left hanging above the floor of the North Saskatchewan Valley. The silt-laden waters of the Mistaya River are now carving a canyon through the Eldon limestone at the mouth of the valley. You can follow a short trail to a footbridge over the canyon to inspect the deep slot that the river has eroded into the limestone, along with potholes and a natural bridge.

Rather than attempting to cross the Mistaya River where it was wider, Stoneys would cross it here on fallen trees. Mt. Sarbach (3,155 m) is south of Mistaya Canyon. The mountain commemorates Peter Sarbach, the first Swiss mountain guide to visit Canada. He led the mountain's first ascent in 1897. The trail beyond Mistaya Canyon leads to two destinations: Sarbach Lookout and Howse Pass.

A Mountain Crossroads

The steady descent from Bow Pass concludes at the bridge across the North Saskatchewan River. There is a warden station and telephone just south of the bridge. The North Saskatchewan River is 1,216 km long. More than 80 per cent of its water originates in the glacial melt and runoff in the Rockies. The river was proclaimed a Canadian Heritage River in 1989. *Saskatchewan* is a Cree word that means "swift current."

During your descent from Bow Pass to the North Saskatchewan Valley, you have probably noticed a change in the vegetation at roadside. Since you left Bow Pass, the Icefields Parkway has lost more than 700 m of elevation, and taken you from the upper subalpine ecoregion to the montane ecoregion. Saskatchewan River Crossing is the lowest point on the Icefields Parkway south of Columbia Icefield, and has an elevation similar to Banff townsite.

The North Saskatchewan Valley is one of only half a dozen valleys that cut across the grain of the Rockies, leading northeastward to the foothills and plains. The valley is in a rain shadow caused by higher mountains to the west. High winds and low precipitation keep the area relatively snow-free, making it favourite winter range for members of the deer family, bighorn sheep and mountain goats.

The North Saskatchewan Valley connects with the Mistaya Valley and the Howse Valley to provide a major artery along which animals travel into the mountains. On the river flats, you may see the tracks of most of the larger mammals, including grizzly bear, black bear, coyote and wolf.

Saskatchewan Crossing to Columbia Icefield
"The Crossing"

There were many hazards to travel by horse along the Wonder Trail, but none was greater than the crossing of the North Saskatchewan River at high water. Historical accounts elaborately describe the danger, the techniques involved and the disasters that often resulted. Many an expedition was cut short because of supplies lost or ruined when pack horses became submerged. No human fatalities were recorded, but many times, both outfitter and client went for an involuntary swim.

When construction of the Icefields Parkway was underway in the late 1930s, the crossing of the North Saskatchewan River again posed an immense problem. More than nine kilometres of riverbank were inspected before the site for the highway bridge was chosen. Racing against freeze-up, crews poured the bridge footings with difficulty.

Many travellers today cross the bridge over the North Saskatchewan River unaware of the drama that unfolded in the past at "The Crossing." If you park at the warden station and walk down to the riverbank, you can fully appreciate the daunting prospect that confronted early travellers. The braided nature of the river here indicates its glacial sources.

Howse Valley Viewpoint

The Howse Valley viewpoint is 1.3 km north of the bridge over the North Saskatchewan River. It is set in a stand of lodgepole pine that grew after the Survey Peak burn in July of 1940. This 40-square-kilometre forest fire was the last major wildfire in Banff National Park. It forced closure of the Icefields Parkway, which had just opened that summer.

Mt. Murchison (3,333 m) broods over the North

Mistaya Canyon

Saskatchewan Valley to the east. To the south, glaciers plaster the east faces of the peaks above the Mistaya River. On the western skyline, you can see the summit of Mt. Forbes (3,612 m), the second highest mountain in Banff National Park. The Mons Icefield is just north of Mt. Forbes. You can inspect the plaque that was unveiled when the North Saskatchewan River was proclaimed a Canadian Heritage River in 1989.

The valley floor immediately to the west is known as a hummock and hollow landscape. Huge blocks of glacial ice detached here at the end of the last ice age. As the ice blocks melted, they caused slumps in the underlying moraine. Some of these hol-

lows became lakes.

The Howse Valley extends to the distant southwest. It leads toward the Freshfield Icefield, one of the largest icefields in the Rockies. James Hector made the first visit to this icefield in 1859. John Norman Collie named it in 1897 for the eminent British scientist, explorer and mountaineer, Sir Douglas Freshfield. The Freshfield Icefield occupies 70 square kilometres and connects with other icefields and glaciers to form a massive system of ice. It is ringed by 16 summits higher than 3,050 m.

The David Thompson Highway

The Icefields Parkway reaches the junction with Highway 11,

Mt. Wilson and the North Saskatchewan River

75.2 km north of Highway 1. Bighorn sheep frequent the junction. Please do not feed them. In the autumn of 1940, five enthusiastic trailblazers drove two trucks west from Red Deer to the new Icefields Parkway. *The Banff Crag and Canyon* suggested that this route be called the David Thompson Highway, foreshadowing by decades the construction of the road that now bears that name.

The David Thompson Highway connects the Icefields Parkway with the city of Red Deer, 256 km east. The road soon takes you out of Banff National Park as it follows the North Saskatchewan River through the front ranges and foothills to the plains. Much of the area between Banff National Park and Rocky Mountain House is provincial forest. There are excellent campgrounds. The hike to Siffleur Falls is recommended.

Services are available in summer at the David Thompson Resort near Abraham Lake, at Nordegg and at Rocky Mountain House. The Kootenay Plains Ecological Reserve, downstream from the Big Horn Dam, is prime habitat for deer, moose, elk and sheep. Along the road, you can see two tree species uncommon in the Rockies: tamarack and black spruce. The needles of the tamaracks turn gold in September.

Rocky Mountain House National Historic Site details the history of the fur trade in this area between 1799 and 1875. Motorists travelling into Banff National Park along the David Thompson Highway require a park pass.

Saskatchewan River Crossing resort is immediately north of the Highway 11 junction on the Icefields Parkway. It provides meals, accommodation and gasoline, in season.

Mt. Wilson

Mt. Wilson (3,621 m) towers to the north of Saskatchewan River Crossing. The impressive yellowish cliffs high on the mountain contain quartz-rich sediments that were deposited on a seabed more than 400 million years ago. The sediments lithified into sandstone. Subsequent heat and addi-

tional pressure transformed the sandstone into quartzite, a metamorphic or "changed" rock.

Many of the quartzite cliffs on Mt. Wilson are vertical or overhanging. The dark streaks are water and rock lichens. In summer, you may see mountain goats on the grassy ledges at mid-height on the mountain. Bighorn sheep range there in the winter.

John Norman Collie named the mountain in 1898 for Tom Wilson—trail blazer and outfitter. In character and experience, Tom Wilson was every bit as tough as the rock in Mt. Wilson's cliffs. In longevity too—he outlived all his contemporaries.

The Crossing to The Weeping Wall

North of Saskatchewan River Crossing, the Icefields Parkway travels through a mixed montane forest of trembling aspen, balsam poplar, white spruce, lodgepole pine and Douglas fir. On the slopes of Mt. Wilson and Mt. Coleman, the aspens and poplars grow in fan-shaped groves on the gravels of seasonal and underground stream beds. These slopes are a colourful sight in September, when the trees' leaves turn yellow. Several flash-flood stream courses cross the Icefields Parkway in this area.

The Glacier Lake trailhead is 1.2 km north of the Highway 11 junction. This backcountry trail leads to the fourth largest lake in Banff National Park. On the west side of the valley, you can see the castellated summits of Mt. Amery (3,329 m) and its neighbouring mountains. Rampart Creek campground and hostel are 11.8 km north of the junction with Highway 11. The wet meadows nearby are frequented by moose and waterfowl. There is a fine view of Mt. Saskatchewan (3,341 m) from the highway, one kilometre north of the campground.

Graveyard Flats

Five kilometres north of Rampart Creek, the Icefields Parkway descends to Graveyard Flats. The flats are an extensive gravel outwash plain near the confluence of the Alexandra River and North Saskatchewan River. The Graveyard Flats allowed easy travel on horseback, and were a welcome relief to early travellers after the exasperating trail over Bow Pass and through the Mistaya Valley. The name "Graveyard" does not refer to the skeletal appearance of the abundant driftwood. When Mary Schäffer camped here in 1907, she found animal skeletons that had been left by native hunters. The Alexandra River was named in 1902 by mountaineer John Norman Collie for Queen Alexandra, wife of King Edward VII.

The Sunset Pass trailhead is on the east side of the Icefields Parkway. It leads out of Banff National Park to Pinto Lake and the Cline River in Alberta's White Goat Wilderness Area.

The Weeping Wall

There is a picnic area at Coleman Creek, seven kilometres north of Graveyard Flats. The North Saskatchewan Valley is much more confined here than farther south. Tremendous limestone cliffs sweep 600 m skyward on the east side of the valley, blocking the sun until mid morning. These cliffs sport many waterfalls. The greatest concentration is at the Weeping Wall.

These waterfalls are the products of melting snow and small seeps high on Cirrus Mountain (3,270 m). They are most profuse on hot days in late spring and early summer. In winter, the Weeping Wall is draped in pillars and curtains of ice. This creates a playground for the specialized pursuit of waterfall ice climbing.

The Big Bend

Much to the frustration of cyclists, the Icefields Parkway now gains 120 m of elevation and then promptly loses most of it, just before beginning the 420-m climb to Sunwapta Pass. Between these two climbs is the Big Bend. If the Big Bend seems an unusual feature to incorporate into a road, consider the dilemma facing the road builders. At this point, the North Saskatchewan Valley swings west to Columbia Icefield. In order for the road to continue north, the builders had to find a line with acceptable grade while contouring around the east end of Parker Ridge, and staying above the intimidating canyon of Nigel Creek. Not an easy task! The Big Bend helps lessen the steepness of the grade by taking the lower part of the climb along Parker Ridge as a sideslope.

In 1896, Walter Wilcox made a foray west through the small canyon opposite the middle of the Big Bend. It proved to be a wrong turn, but his party was the first to see Saskatchewan Glacier just beyond. The waterfall south of

Mountain Avens

Mountain avens is an evergreen plant that forms dense mats on river gravels, glacial deposits and disturbed land. There are two species: yellow—found in the montane and lower subalpine; and white—found in the upper subalpine, alpine and glacial areas. The Latin genus name for mountain avens is *Dryas*. Botanists refer to these gravels as dryas flats.

Mountain avens have short stems and leaves that are dark green and leathery above, and pale and felt-like beneath. The flowers of white mountain avens open like miniature roses. (Mountain avens is in the rose family.) The nodding flower of yellow mountain avens rarely opens fully. When gone to seed,

the flower pod of avens releases a dandelion-like fluff.

Mountain avens is one of the first plants to colonize riverbeds, stabilizing the soil and permitting larger plants to take hold. Graveyard Flats is carpeted with yellow mountain avens.

Weeping Wall

the Big Bend is fed by glacier melt from the north face of Mt. Saskatchewan. Halfway down the cascade, the water jogs eastward. Locals call it "Sideways Falls."

Road crews from Jasper and Lake Louise met and completed the Icefields Parkway on the Big Bend Hill in 1939. You may see bighorn sheep at roadside here, and mountain goats on the cliffs of Parker Ridge to the north.

Cirrus Mountain Viewpoint

There are two pulloffs near the top of the Big Bend Hill. The first of these provides an excellent view over the North Saskatchewan Valley. You can clearly see the U-shape of the valley, and ponder the thickness of glacial ice that carved it. The steep, slabby slopes south of the Big Bend were undercut by glacial ice during the last ice age. Rockslides are triggered when sheets of rock split away along weakened layers.

Cirrus Mountain (3,270 m) is on the east side of the valley. During mountain building, the rock formations in the mountain were bowed downwards into a U-shaped fold called a syncline. This particular syncline is part of the Castle Mountain Syncline, which extends 260 km from Castle Mountain in Banff to Mt. Kerkeslin in Jasper. If you think there's something not quite symmetrical about the U-shape of this syncline, you're right. Cirrus Mountain also contains a normal fault. After mountain building, the formations beneath the right-hand summit fractured and slipped downwards, relative to

Ice Climbing

Climbing ice has long been one of the most demanding facets of mountaineering. In the late 1950s, Scottish mountaineers began to attempt icy routes in the most difficult gullies in their homeland in winter, and the pursuit of waterfall ice climbing was born.

Most waterfalls in the Rockies are frozen for five to six months each year. Seeps that are mere trickles in summer create huge sheets and pillars of ice in winter. In the early 1970s, Canadian mountaineers began to attempt frozen waterfalls in the central Rockies. Equipment lagged behind determination and

courage, and the early ascents of long routes on the Weeping Wall, Takakkaw Falls and Snow Dome were tremendous achievements.

Typical of many pursuits, equipment and skill have quickly advanced to the point where routes formerly considered extreme or impossible are now climbed solo by unroped climbers in a fraction of the time required for the first ascent. Vertical and overhanging ice is routinely ascended. In pushing the limits of their sport, some ice climbers have established routes that combine a high degree of difficulty and danger in remote settings.

The Canadian Rockies are the ice climbing mecca of the world. If you are visiting in winter, look for climbers on the waterfalls along the Icefields Parkway and near the town of Field.

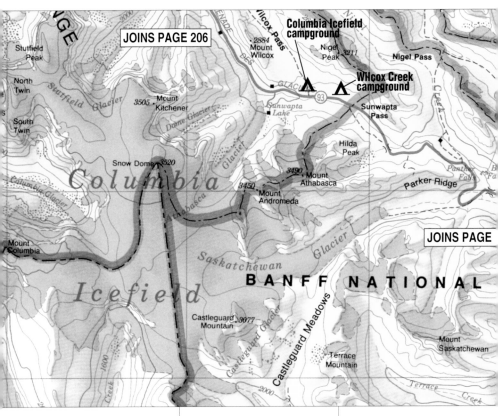

Map labels: JOINS PAGE 206 · Columbia Icefield campground · 2884 Mount Wilcox · Nigel Peak · 3211 · Nigel Pass · Stutfield Peak · WIlcox Creek campground · North Twin · 93 · Sunwapta Pass · Statfield Glacier · 3505 Mount Kitchener · Sunwapta Lake · Dome Glacier · South Twin · Hilda Peak · Snow Dome 3520 · 3490 Mount Athabasca · Parker Ridge · Panther Falls · Columbia Glacier · Glacier · 3450 · Mount Andromeda · JOINS PAGE · Columbia · Athabasca · Glacier · Mount Columbia · Saskatchewan · BANFF NATIONAL · Icefield · Castleguard Mountain 3077 · Castleguard Glacier · Castleguard Meadows · Terrace Mountain · Mount Saskatchewan · 1600 · 2000 · Terrace Creek · Creek

those beneath the lefthand summit.

From the second pulloff, you can see Bridal Veil Falls. A rough trail descends from the parking area to the canyon of Nigel Creek and a view of Panther Falls.

Coleman's Country

Natives knew better than to tackle the difficult terrain of the Bow, Mistaya and North Saskatchewan valleys when travelling from south to north in the Rockies. They followed trails through valleys in the front ranges to the east.

In 1892 and 1893, A.P. Coleman, a geology professor from Toronto, used these front range valleys in his search for the fabled giant peaks of the Rockies: Mt. Hooker and Mt. Brown. Coleman obtained information on the route from Chief Jonas of the Stoney tribe. He named a pass and creek in the high country northeast of here in honour of the chief. Coleman made repeated visits to the Rockies, and published accounts of his travels in *The Canadian Rockies, New and Old Trails.* Unfortunately for other early explorers, this book and its wealth of information did not appear until 1911.

Today, the Nigel Creek trail grants backpackers quick access to Coleman's front range valleys in southeastern Jasper National Park. These contain some of the most exquisite alpine and subalpine scenery in the Rockies.

The long climb to Sunwapta Pass continues beyond the Nigel Creek trailhead. Parker Ridge is on the west side of the Icefields Parkway. Avalanches from the ridge sweep across the road in winter and spring. Downed trees are piled at roadside. The Icefields Parkway curves west, revealing a tremendous view of Mt. Athabasca (3,491 m). From this perspective, it bears the unmistakable horn mountain shape. The Hilda Creek hostel is just north of the Parker Ridge trailhead.

Sunwapta Pass

At 2,023 m, Sunwapta Pass is the second highest point on the Icefields Parkway. Between here and Jasper townsite, you

Looking south from the top of the Big Bend Hill

By the time the Icefields Parkway was completed in 1939, Athabasca Glacier had receded enough that the road could easily pass through on the floor of the Sunwapta Valley. However, extensive rock cuts were still necessary to bypass the Sunwapta Canyon. If Athabasca Glacier re-advances, the present-day route of the Icefields Parkway will be in jeopardy.

lose 1,000 m of elevation in 110 km.

Sunwapta Pass marks the boundary between Banff National Park and Jasper National Park, and the watershed divide between the North Saskatchewan River, which drains to Lake Winnipeg, Hudson Bay, and the Atlantic Ocean; and the Sunwapta River, which eventually drains to the Arctic Ocean.

The boundaries of the two parks have not always met here. Immediately after it was established in 1907, the southern boundary of Jasper National Park was on the North Saskatchewan River, 40 km south. The area protected in Banff and Jasper underwent continual adjustment until the National Parks Act was proclaimed in 1930. Since then, only a few minor changes to the park boundaries have been made.

Sunwapta is Stoney for "turbulent river." A.P. Coleman named the river in 1892. The name is also applied to four other features along the Icefields Parkway. West of the pass, you can see a rock glacier on Mt. Athabasca. On the Jasper side of Sunwapta Pass, the Icefields Parkway crosses a gully. This gully is the course of a perennial springtime mud and slush avalanche that sometimes forces closure of the Icefields Parkway. A subalpine wet meadow covers the valley bottom northwest of the pass.

Road Blocks

When Walter Wilcox crossed Sunwapta Pass in 1896, Athabasca Glacier blocked the Sunwapta Valley ahead. To detour around the ice, Wilcox's party climbed north over the pass that now bears his name, and dropped down a rough track beside Tangle Creek to re-enter the Sunwapta Valley. This detour also bypassed the constriction of Sunwapta Canyon and the terrific jumble of the Mt. Kitchener Slide just north of Athabasca Glacier.

You can hike the Wilcox Pass trail today just as the explorers did. The trail begins at Wilcox Creek Campground and traverses alpine tundra—the haunt of bighorn sheep and grizzly bear. It offers excellent views of Athabasca Glacier and the surrounding mountains.

You have now reached Columbia Icefield. Camping options nearby are: Wilcox Creek Campground and Columbia Icefield Campground (no RVs), 1.9 km and 3.2 km north of Sunwapta Pass, respectively. The Columbia Icefield Information Centre and Snocoach terminal are 4.9 km north of Sunwapta Pass. Δ

Parker Ridge—A Walk on the Wild Side

If you are going to get out of your vehicle only once along the Icefields Parkway to go for a walk, Parker Ridge is the best place to do it. The Parker Ridge trail is a short and steep excursion to a mountain ridge that provides a splendid panorama of Saskatchewan Glacier and the southeast fringe of Columbia Icefield.

Since leaving the Weeping Wall, the Icefields Parkway has gained 450 m of elevation. This fact alone will produce a temperature some 3 °C lower at the Parker Ridge trailhead. However, the chilling mass of nearby Columbia Icefield may lower the temperature as much as 10 °C from what you experienced on the floor of the North Saskatchewan Valley a short while ago. Parker Ridge is a windy place, so bundle up. Take extra clothing, a snack and some water with you on your hike. Allow two to four hours for the round trip.

The Parker Ridge trailhead is located in a treeline forest. Here, vegetation growth is hindered by: high elevation, cold glacial air, near-constant winds, poor soils, avalanches and a northeast aspect. Leaving the parking lot, the trail crosses a subalpine meadow—a frost hollow, typical of areas adjacent to glaciers. Cold air from Hilda Glacier collects here, creating a local growing season so short that mature trees cannot develop.

The horn mountain shapes of Mt. Athabasca (3,491 m) and its outlier, Hilda Peak (3,060 m), are prominent to the west. The summits of these mountains protrud-

ed above the kilometre-thick ice sheets of the Great Glaciation. Since the retreat of the ice sheets, alpine glaciation has continued to whittle away at the upper mountainsides, creating the horn mountain shapes.

The trail enters a small but ancient forest. At one point, you squeeze between two massive Engelmann spruce trees that are probably at least 400 years old. However, most of the vegetation here is in stunted, krummholz form. (*Krummholz* is a German word that means "crooked wood.") The gnarled, dense, evergreen mats with silvery bark are subalpine fir trees. Taller Engelmann spruce grow from within the mats. Although they appear to be saplings, these are mature trees, possibly hundreds of years old.

The treeless areas on the northeast slope of Parker Ridge are either avalanche-swept rock or tundra comprised of sedges, white mountain avens, mountain heather, snow willow, arctic willow, woolly everlasting and purple saxifrage. The name saxifrage is derived from Latin words that mean "rock breaker." Purple saxifrage is one of the pioneering alpine plants whose roots help break apart rock and create primitive soil. Vegetation here is low in stature to reduce wind exposure, and to enable the plants to absorb heat from the dark soils. Thick, waxy leaves help retain moisture.

More than six metres of snow falls annually at Parker Ridge. Because of the shaded, northeast aspect and cold temperatures resulting from the elevation and proximity to Columbia Icefield, this snow takes a long time to melt. A few of the drifts are perennial features. Needless to say, the slopes of Parker Ridge are popular with skiers in winter and spring. However, don't be surprised if you see some diehards carving turns on a Parker Ridge snowpatch in midsummer—to the possible detriment of underlying vegetation.

The trail gains the open ridge at an elevation of 2,271 m. From here, follow the beaten path southeast (left) for 500 m to a vantage overlooking Saskatchewan Glacier. With a length of nine kilometres, this outlet valley glacier of the 325-square-kilometre Columbia Icefield is one of the longest in the Rockies. It

White-tailed ptarmigan

Parker Ridge—A Walk on the Wild Side

Saskatchewan Glacier

Krummholz

descends 750 m in elevation from the icefield rim to terminate in a marginal lake, the principal headwaters of the North Saskatchewan River.

Immediately south (left) of the head of the Saskatchewan Glacier is Castleguard Mountain (3,070 m). South of this mountain is the entrance to Castleguard Cave, one of the largest cave systems in Canada, and the third deepest in Canada and the U.S. More than 18 km of pas-

sages have been explored. Some of these follow ancient drainages beneath Columbia Icefield, and terminate in deadends that are choked with glacial ice. If the day is clear, the view beyond Castleguard Mountain will include the lofty summit of Mt. Bryce (3,487 m), 19 km distant.

If you look uphill along the crest of Parker Ridge, you will notice how the outlying ridge is rounded in appearance, becoming much more rugged toward

Mt. Athabasca. The rounded parts of the ridge were completely covered by moving ice during the Great Glaciation, whereas the jagged areas probably were not. If you choose to explore along the ridge to the cairn at the high point (2,350 m), please stay on the beaten path. The ridge crest features krummholz forms of whitebark pine, a common tree in windy locations, and coral-like fossils called Syringopora. Please do not remove the fossils.

Mountain goat, white-tailed ptarmigan, gray jay, Clark's nutcracker, pika and common raven are among frequently observed wildlife on Parker Ridge. Grizzly bear, wolverine and golden eagle may also be seen by fortunate visitors. The ridge was probably named for Herschel Parker, a mountaineer who made several first ascents of mountains near Lake Louise at the turn of the century.

The Columbia Icefield

With an area of 325 square kilometres, Columbia Icefield is the largest icefield in the Rockies. Thanks to the Icefields Parkway, it is also the most accessible. From the turnoff just south of the Icefield Information Centre, you can drive to within a few hundred metres of the toe of Athabasca Glacier and walk the remaining distance to the edge of the ice.

Columbia Icefield provides us with a window on the earth's icy past. Conditions on the icefield are much the same as during the last ice age—the Wisconsin—that held most of Canada and the northern U.S. in its chilling grasp between 75,000 years ago and 11,000 years ago. By getting to know Columbia Icefield, you can better appreciate the natural history of the Rockies, and of Canada.

The Ice Factory

Glaciers form in areas where more snow accumulates in winter than melts in summer. In the Rockies, this is usually at high elevations where the average temperature is below the freezing point, and the snowfall is heavy. Glaciers can also form on shaded aspects of steep mountainsides at lower elevations.

The average elevation on Columbia Icefield is 3,000 m. More than 10 m of snow falls on the icefield each year. The gentle terrain of the icefield prevents the loss of this snow to avalanches. The only significant losses are through wind, sublimation and summer melting.

By the end of summer, the surviving fallen snowflakes have been transformed into granular snow called firn. A new layer of firn snow forms each year. As the firn accumulates, underlying layers become compacted and the air is gradually squeezed out. This process is helped by saturation of the firn with meltwater that trickles down from the surface in summer. When a thickness of 30 m of firn has accumulated, the lower layers are so compressed that they have become glacial ice. Once a mass of glacial ice has developed, it must flow in order to be considered a glacier (GLAY-seer). Because it is heavy, glacial ice naturally flows downhill.

Athabasca Glacier: A River of Ice

Athabasca Glacier is the best-known glacier that flows from Columbia Icefield. It is an outlet valley glacier, and has many features common to glaciers everywhere. By studying its surface in detail, you can better understand how a glacier moves and what it does to the landscape.

From the icefield rim (on the skyline) to its terminus or ending point, Athabasca Glacier descends 600 m in 5.3 km. The steepest drop occurs about one kilometre from the icefield rim, and is marked by a prominent icefall where the glacier attempts to conform to a cliff in the bedrock. The surface of the glacier is moving faster and is under less pressure than the ice in contact with the bedrock. Consequently, the surface ice accelerates over the cliff and becomes heavily fissured. These fissures are known as crevasses (creh-VASS-ezz).

There are several varieties of crevasses: transverse, which run from side to side; marginal, which form at the sides and are parallel to the glacier's flow; and radial, where the ice splays out near the terminus. It has been estimated that there are more than 30,000 crevasses on Athabasca Glacier.

One common crevasse feature missing on Athabasca

SuperGuide Recommendations

Sights/Attractions
- Athabasca Glacier
- Columbia Icefield Information Centre

Hikes/Activities
- Guided Icewalk on the glacier
- Walk to toe of Athabasca Glacier
- Brewster Snocoach Tour

left: Mt. Athabasca

An unnamed lake provides the foreground for Mt. Athabasca (above left)...

Glacier is a bergshrund (BAIRG-schroond.) Bergschrunds form where the upper reaches of a glacier pull away from a mountainside. Bergschrunds are easy to spot on the north faces of many peaks in the vicinity of Columbia Icefield. Negotiating a way past these obstacles can be a difficult challenge to mountaineers.

Towers of ice that form in icefalls or on the edges of hanging glaciers are called seracs (sair-RACKS). There is a wall of seracs on the east face of Snow Dome, just to the right of the upper icefall of Athabasca Glacier. Avalanches of ice from this cliff frequently crash to the glacier surface. If you think you hear thunder on a clear day, look at this serac wall and you might see the end of an avalanche.

In August, look for the annual snowline in the vicinity of the uppermost icefall. Snow towards the icefield rim from that point is in the accumulation zone of the glacier, and will endure the summer to become glacial ice. Between the annual snowline and the terminus is the ablation zone, where the mass of the glacier is melting and its surface is

The Source of Three Great Rivers

Meltwaters from Columbia Icefield feed three of Canada's largest river systems, and eventually three oceans: the Pacific Ocean via the Columbia River; the Arctic Ocean via the Athabasca River and Mackenzie River; and the Atlantic Ocean via the North Saskatchewan River, Saskatchewan River, Nelson River and Hudson Bay. The summit of Snow Dome on Columbia Icefield is the apex of this tri-oceanic watershed. There is only one other such watershed in the world, in Siberia.

What Is an Icefield?

An icefield is a body of ice from which glaciers flow outwards in more than one direction. Columbia Icefield is part of the chain of icefields that cloak the continental divide between Kicking Horse Pass and Athabasca Pass. In addition to Columbia Icefield, there are 16 glacial features in the Rockies that are officially called icefields. Many other unnamed glacial features also meet the definition of an icefield.

The icefields of the Rockies did not form in recent times. They are remnants of the massive ice sheets that covered all but the highest peaks of the Rockies during the Wisconsin Glaciation. Some glaciologists think that these icefields may have almost completely disappeared during a warm period in the earth's climate, between 8,700 years ago and 5,200 years ago. They subsequently became re-established but are now waning again.

...as well as Mt. Andromeda and Athabasca Glacier

free of snow.

To the left of the lowest icefall, several glaciers tumble from the steep slopes of Mt. Andromeda, and avalanche their ice onto the surface of Athabasca Glacier. Like streams entering a river, these are called tributary glaciers.

Athabasca Glacier occupies a U-shaped valley, scoured when the glacier was larger. Because of the U-shape of its path, Athabasca Glacier is deeper along its midline than at its sides. The deepest point is 300 m, just below the upper icefall. As the glacier approaches the Sunwapta Valley, it leaves its confined side valley and widens. This, along with the melting in the ablation zone, makes the ice thinner near the terminus. The fastest-moving ice on the glacier is on the surface in the centre. It moves about 125 m a year at the icefalls, 80 m a year at the halfway point and 15 m a year at the terminus.

There are many meltwater streams on the surface of Athabasca Glacier. The water sculpts runnels in the ice and sometimes disappears into crevasses or chutes. The chutes are called moulin (moo-LANN) or millwells. The disappearing water emerges from the terminus after flowing within or beneath the ice. It is thought that this meltwater helps lubricate the base of the glacier, allowing the ice to flow more easily. A major subsurface stream network of Athabasca Glacier empties to the right of the terminus. From year to year, this point is marked by an ice cave of varying dimensions.

The colour of glacial ice is affected by its purity. Air and other impurities tend to reflect all wavelengths of light, causing ice to appear white or gray. The uniform and minute ice crystals deep within a glacier have had most of the air squeezed out of them, and reflect only the blue spectrum of light. The colour is not caused

Good Stew, Nigel!

Nigel Vavasour was a cook on John Norman Collie's 1898 expedition that made the first ascent of Mt. Athabasca and discovered Columbia Icefield. On the way north from Lake Louise, the party had lost many supplies when its testy pack horses plunged into the North Saskatchewan River. The larder was almost empty with serious climbing having just begun. While Collie and Woolley claimed glory on the heights of Mt. Athabasca, Stutfield and guide Bill Peyto undertook a more mundane pursuit. They hunted bighorn sheep near Nigel Pass in an area they called "Wild Sheep Hills." The hunt was successful, and the sheep stew that became the party's staple for the next two weeks must have been a success too, for the cook's name was applied to a number of features in the area: Nigel Pass, Nigel Creek and Nigel Peak.

Glacier Features

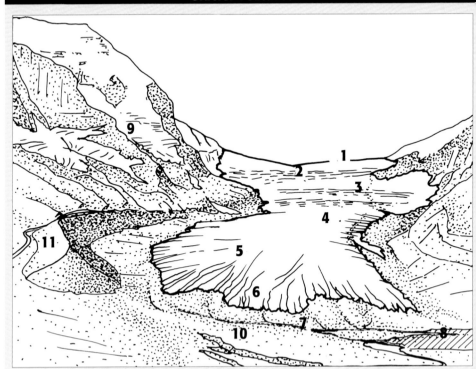

Above: This drawing of Athabasca Glacier shows the following glacier features: 1. The Columbia Icefield, 2. icefalls, 3. transverse crevasse, 4. marginal crevasse, 5. terminal crevasse, 6. the "toe" of the glacier, 7. meltwater stream, 8. meltwater lake (Sunwapta), 9. tributary glacier, 10. terminal moraine, and 11. lateral moraine.

Right: This cross-section diagram of a glacier shows: 1. the accumulation zone, where new snow is converted into glacial ice and 2. ablation zone, where glacial ice melts into water. Other features include: 3. crevasses, 4. new ice, 5. the movement of glacial ice, 6. the underlying bedrock, 7. a lateral moraine, and 8. the toe of the glacier.

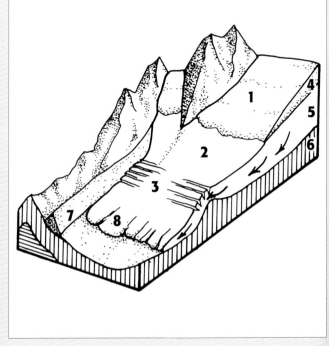

Mt. Athabasca (left) and Athabasca Glacier from Mt. Wilcox

Icefields of the Canadian Rockies

Name	Area in km²	Visible from Road	Location or Where Visible
Brazeau	25	✗	10 km southeast of Maligne Lake
Campbell	10	✗	West of Freshfield Icefield
Chaba	20	✗	West of Columbia Icefield
Clemenceau	200	✗	West of Columbia Icefield
Columbia	325	✔	Parker Ridge crest to Sunwapta Falls
Freshfield	60	✗	Southwest of Saskatchewan Crossing
Hooker	60	✗	East side of Athabasca Pass
Lloyd George	70	✗	600 km northwest of Jasper
Lyell	35	✔	North of Sask. Crossing
Mt. Brown	8	✗	West side of Athabasca Pass
Mons	16	✔	20 km west of Howse River viewpoint
Reef	25	✗	15 km east of Mt. Robson
Resthaven	40	✗	35 km northwest of Mt. Robson
Wapta	40	✔	Hector Lake, Bow Lake, Bow Summit
Waputik	32	✔	Hector Lake viewpoint
Washmawapta	6	✗	The Rockwall, west of Marble Canyon
Wilson	20	✔	Mt. Wilson viewpoint

by the mineral content of the ice.

The last significant surface feature of Athabasca Glacier is a rift along the glacier's edge, where the ice is in contact with rock. Solar heat absorbed by the rock melts the ice and creates a moat known as a randkluft. These moats usually fill with debris that topples down from the adjacent moraines.

The Rubble-Strewn Path

Glaciers created the blueprint of the Rockies, scouring the troughs of the major valleys, eroding deep cirques into mountainsides, gouging the basins of lakes and sharpening mountain summits into horns. Glaciers have also created many landforms with the rubble bulldozed and deposited in the process. Glaciologists call this rubble till. Till can be pushed by the ice, carried on or within the ice, or transported by glacial meltwater.

Moraines are the most common landforms created from till. Ground moraine is till that blanketed the surface or underside of a glacier. It was left in place when the glacier receded. Ground moraine covers most of the valley bottoms in the Rockies. Thus till, not bedrock, is the most common element in riverbeds and streambanks. The upper Sunwapta Valley, west of the Icefield Information Centre, is covered in ground moraine.

The most easily recognized moraine type is an end moraine, which forms where till is deposited at the terminus of a glacier. End moraines include terminal moraines, which are deposited at the maximum extent of a glacial advance, and annual moraines or recessional moraines, which show positions of the terminus during glacial re-

treat. The road to Athabasca Glacier cuts through a series of recessional moraines. Signs indicate the years in which they were formed. The most recent terminal moraine of Athabasca Glacier abutted the slopes of Mt. Wilcox behind the Icefield Information Centre. It is hard to distinguish. You can see terminal moraines more easily at Mt. Edith Cavell,

What Is an Ice Age?

The term "ice age" was first used by Swiss naturalist Louis Agassiz in 1837. Puzzled by the presence of strange boulders and by sets of parallel scratches in the bedrock of the Swiss Alps, Agassiz proposed that these were evidence of a large advance of glaciers during a period of global cooling—an ice age. Agassiz was ridiculed by many, but he persevered. It was the 1870s, before the theory of ice ages gained wide acceptance. The science of glaciology was officially established during the International Geophysical Year, 1956.

During an ice age, existing glaciers become much larger and new glaciers form. They link together into ice sheets more than a kilometre thick that flow from polar regions and high mountain ranges, inundating the landscape. At the height of the last ice age— the Wisconsin Glaciation, 18,000 years ago—the ice sheets covered all of Canada and the northern U.S. Glaciologists estimate that there have been 20 to 30 ice ages during the last 2.4 million years. The most pronounced of these was the Great Glaciation between 240,000 years ago and 128,000 years ago.

The evidence of ice ages is in-

disputable: horn mountains, U-shaped valleys, hanging valleys, moraine landforms, erratic boulders, bedrock striations. But the question of what causes an ice age has been debated for more than a century.

Today, the average global temperature is about 16 °C. An ice age like the Wisconsin Glaciation would have required a drop in the average temperature to about 6 °C. The theories proposed that could explain such a drop are:

1. Atmospheric dust clouds caused by volcanic eruptions or by the earth passing through meteor belts. The dust clouds would diffuse sunlight, cooling the earth's surface.
2. Fluctuations in the output of the sun, possibly linked to sunspot cycles.
3. A wobble in the earth's orbit on its own axis, coupled with the effects of the earth's elliptical orbit around the sun. This results in periods when winters in the northern hemisphere are longer and colder by virtue of the earth being farther from the sun, and the northern hemisphere being tipped farther away from the sun. The interaction of orbital factors creates a

cycle of seasonal variations that repeats every 22,000 years.
4. Changes in the shape of the earth's orbit around the sun from elliptical (as at present) to circular.
5. Changes in oceanic currents, such as a cooling or abatement of the Gulf Stream.
6. A succession of harsh winters.
7. Changes in the earth's cloud cover. Clouds reflect solar energy. Cloudier skies mean less sunshine reaches the earth, creating cooler temperatures.
8. Plate tectonics—the latitudes of continents have been different in the past.

No single theory has universal backing among glaciologists. In all likelihood, a combination of several factors probably creates an ice age. However, the fact that many now-extinct mammals, such as the woolly mammoth, were entombed in ice indicates that the onset of the last ice age may have been instantaneous. Study of pollens in glacial sediments from Greenland indicates that it may have ended just as abruptly, with the earth's temperature rebounding from ice age to "normal" in less than a decade.

Athabasca Glacier in the winter

many places, terminal and lateral moraines now act as the natural dams that impound many of the Rockies' best-known lakes, including: Lake Louise, Emerald Lake, Bow Lake and Peyto Lake.

An unusual feature that can result from surface moraine is the glacier table. This is a rock whose large size prevents the melting of the ice directly beneath, leaving it balanced on the resulting pedestal.

Large boulders of surface moraine were sometimes transported great distances from their places of origin by glaciers in past ice ages. Known as glacial erratics, these rocks help glaciologists understand the history of glaciation in the Rockies. There is a prominent "bear-shaped" erratic opposite the Icefield Information Centre.

Sometimes, ice that is covered in surface moraine will become detached from a glacier as it retreats. This creates a dead-ice moraine. These features can take centuries to melt, leaving behind a terrain of small hills and depressions known as a hummock-and-hollow landscape. The depressions become lakes known as kettle ponds. You can see this kind of landscape in the view west from the Howse Valley Viewpoint on the Icefields Parkway.

The cold environment on steep mountainsides permits the formation of a peculiar feature that is halfway between a moraine and a glacier. The rock glacier is an accumulation of rubble that contains just enough ice to allow the whole mass to creep downhill.

Snowbird Glacier, Victoria Glacier and Crowfoot Glacier.

The most impressive moraine near Athabasca Glacier is the lateral moraine on your left. A lateral moraine is composed of till pushed aside by the glacier. In 1994, this lateral moraine towered 120 m above the ice surface at the terminus. The snocoach ride onto Athabasca Glacier takes you down the steep slope of this moraine. Other good examples of lateral moraines can be seen nearby at Dome Glacier, and elsewhere at Cavell, Peyto, Victoria and Wenkchemna glaciers.

When tributary glaciers meet, parts of their adjacent lateral moraines combine and are carried on the ice surface "downstream" as a strip of rubble called a medial moraine. There is an excellent example on Saskatchewan Glacier, visible from Parker Ridge. There is another on Peyto Glacier.

Oval-shaped mounds called "drumlins" were created where a glacier re-advanced over a thick accumulation of ground moraine. Sinuous ridges called eskers mark the locations of streams that flowed beneath glaciers. In

An Ancient Forest

The Little Ice Age advance of the Athabasca Glacier reached its maximum in 1714. During this advance, the glacier encroached into upper subalpine forest. The terminal moraine of this advance is situated against the lower slopes of Mount Wilcox. This moraine also marks the trimline: trees between the moraine and the glacier were destroyed by the ice, whereas those outside the moraine survived.

In 1982, glaciologists cored an Engelmann spruce tree in the grove just outside the moraine. The core sample showed 680 rings. As each ring records a year's growth, this tree is now more than 690 years old–the oldest known tree in Jasper National Park, and possibly the oldest Engelmann spruce in North America. The "inception period" of the tree–a time when tree rings are not created–may add 20 to 50 years to this age.

You can see a rock glacier on the lower slopes of Mt. Athabasca at Sunwapta Pass.

The last in this list of glacial deposition features is the one that will make the greatest impression on those who stray from the trail to the terminus of Athabasca Glacier. A thick, black mud known as glacier goo claims many a running shoe here every summer. The goo is difficult to spot until you've taken one step too many, so it's a good idea to keep to the beaten path.

Glacial Advance and Glacial Retreat

The flow of glacial ice is controlled by gravity. Although the speed of the flow changes—generally faster in summer and slower in winter—the ice never stops moving. Any rock on a glacier's surface will eventually be carried to the terminus on the moving ice.

To explain glacial advance and glacial retreat, glaciologists frequently make an analogy to banking. In years when more ice forms in the accumulation zone than melts in the ablation zone, a glacier posts a profit and advances. The terminus of the glacier will move ahead relative to a fixed point off the glacier's surface. The height and width of the glacier may also increase. In years when more ice melts in the ablation zone than forms in the accumulation zone, the glacier takes a loss. Its terminus recedes relative to a fixed point off the surface of the ice. In some years, the losses and gains of winter and summer offset each other: the glacier breaks even and neither advances or retreats.

The earth's climate has been warming since the Little Ice Age ended in the late 1800s. Although some glaciers in the Rockies have experienced periods of minor advance since that time, the current state of glacial affairs is one of overall retreat. A few consecutive dry winters and unusually hot summers in the Rockies can greatly influence the state of its glaciers.

Space Age Meets Ice Age

Vehicle rides on Athabasca Glacier began in 1952, when Bill Ruddy amassed a fleet of 14 snowmobiles. Brewster Transportation acquired Ruddy's operation in 1969 and replaced the snowmobiles with various hybrid vehicles, culminating in the snocoach, a 56-passenger, all-terrain vehicle that has been in use since 1981.

Today, Brewster operates a fleet of Snocoaches, built by Canadian Foremost Ltd. of Calgary—a specialist in transportation for the oil industry. Each Snocoach weighs 19,700 kg, is 13 m long and is powered by a 210-horsepower Detroit diesel engine. Top speed is 42 km per hour, although this is never approached during the Snocoach tours. Fully loaded, a Snocoach is capable of climbing a 32 degree slope—equivalent to a double-black-diamond ski run.

You may book Snocoach rides at the Columbia Icefield In-

formation Centre. A shuttle bus provides transportation along a restricted access road to the Snocoach loading area on the east lateral moraine of Athabasca Glacier. From there, the Snocoach descends steeply to the glacier and travels one kilometre along the ice toward the lower icefall. At the turnaround point, you may disembark (at your own risk) to walk around on the ice. The round-trip takes less than 90 minutes. There may be a short wait for an available tour. The Snocoach Tours begin operation in May and continue until late September.

At the Columbia Icefield Information Centre, displays and audio-visual presentations explain the human and natural history of Columbia Icefield. You may also book a guided icewalk on Athabasca Glacier.

Sunwapta Lake

Sunwapta Lake is the lake near the terminus of Athabasca Glacier. It is a glacial tarn whose days are numbered. The lake began to form in 1938, when the retreating glacier uncovered a depression in the bedrock. The lake reached maximum size in 1966. It is now decreasing in size and depth as four tributary streams build four gravelly deltas into its waters. The streams deposit 570 tonnes of mud, gravel and rock into the lake on each hot day in summer.

Eventually, the depression that holds Sunwapta Lake will either be completely filled, or it will be buried by the ice of a re-advancing Athabasca Glacier. A similar fate awaits many other lakes in the Rockies.

A Frozen New World

Natives knew the location of Columbia Icefield; however, it was not glimpsed by Euro-Canadians until 1892. In that year, the party of A.P. Coleman saw the mantle of permanent ice and snow from high peaks to the east. The first close view and the claimed "discovery" of Columbia Icefield occurred in 1898. The mountaineers who made the discovery had been lured in quest of the two fabled mountains of the Rockies—Mt. Hooker and Mt. Brown—thought to be the highest in North America.

In 1827, Scottish botanist David Douglas crossed Athabasca Pass. En route, he paused long enough to climb a mountain west of the pass, which he named Mt. Brown. This was the earliest recorded mountaineering ascent in the Rockies. Douglas assigned elevations to Mt. Brown and to another peak that he named Mt. Hooker, of almost 4,900 m.

The Glacier Trail

Mountaineering parties in the early 1900s that were intent on ascending peaks at the southern edge of Columbia Icefield followed the Alexandra River to a base camp in Castleguard Meadows. If they wished to continue farther north, they were obliged to return along the Alexandra River to the North Saskatchewan River, and then cross Sunwapta Pass—a journey of approximately three days. This backtracking frustrated outfitter Jimmy Simpson and his clients. The supplies used descending the Alexandra could be put to better use exploring new ground. On the 1923 expedition of mountaineer James Monroe Thorington, Simpson decided to take a one-day shortcut from Castleguard Meadows to Sunwapta Pass—he led the packtrain down the Saskatchewan Glacier and over Parker Ridge.

Apparently, the horses took to the ice with little fuss. The ploy was repeated on the Smithsonian Institution Columbia Icefield Expedition of 1924, when Byron Harmon took this photograph. The crossing of Saskatchewan Glacier with horses soon became standard fare. In the late 1920s, outfitter Jack Brewster incorporated a visit to Castleguard Meadows via Saskatchewan Glacier into his pack trips from Jasper to Lake Louise—an outing known appropriately as "The Glacier Trail."

Natural Refrigeration

Glaciers and icefields are natural refrigerators that chill the air above them. Cold air is more dense than warm air, and stays closer to the earth's surface. It flows downhill off glacial ice into adjoining valleys as a catabatic wind. This wind will be present every day, hot or cold. It can reduce the temperature in the forefield of Athabasca Glacier by as much as 10 °C from areas nearby. Catabatic winds shorten the already short growing season close to glaciers, and create wind chills that effectively lengthen winter. These winds are one of the chief reasons why it is so difficult for vegetation to grow near glaciers.

The Columbia Icefield

Common Questions

Here are answers to some of the most commonly asked questions about Columbia Icefield.

How big is Columbia Icefield?
325 square kilometres. This is three times the area of the city of Toronto, and one quarter of the size of Yoho National Park. Columbia Icefield accounts for more than 30 per cent of the glaciated area in Jasper National Park.

How many glaciers are there in North America?
More than 200,000. Glacial ice covers more than 50,000 square kilometres in B.C.–0.5 per cent of the province's land area.

Why is Columbia Icefield the largest icefield in the Rockies?
It occupies a large alpine area ringed by many high mountains. There is a major valley southwest of the icefield. This valley channels the moisture-laden prevailing winds through a vertical rise of 2,200 m directly into the heart of the icefield. This elevation change creates heavy snowfall. Because of the high elevation at which it falls, little of the snow melts.

How much does it snow here each year?
At roadside, the average annual snowfall is 6.4 m. On the icefield itself, it is more than 10 m. Ten centimetres of snowfall is equivalent to one centimetre of rain.

What is the average elevation of Columbia Icefield?
Approximately 3,000 m above sea level.

What is the highest point on Columbia Icefield?
The 3,747 m summit of Mt. Columbia. Mt. Columbia is on the continental divide and is the second highest mountain in the Canadian Rockies. By the most direct feasible line of travel to mountaineers, its summit is 23 km from the Icefields Parkway. The mountain is not visible from nearby. The highest summit entirely within both Alberta and Jasper National Park is also found on Columbia Icefield: North Twin, 3,684 m high. It, too, is concealed from the road.

How thick is the ice?
The maximum known thickness on Columbia Icefield is 365 m. The ice cliffs visible on Snow Dome are more than 100 m thick. Athabasca Glacier is about 100 m thick at the upper icefall, and 300 m thick just below the lower icefall.

Why is some of the ice blue?
Air and other impurities of non-uniform size tend to reflect all wavelengths of light, making ice appear white or gray. Ice that has had most of the air squeezed out of it reflects the blue wavelengths. Ice on the surface of the glacier is therefore gray or white, whereas that within is often blue.

How big is Athabasca Glacier?
It is 5.3 km long from the icefield rim to the terminus. It descends 600 m in that distance. The average width is one kilometre. Its volume is 640 million cubic metres. It accounts for two per cent of the area of Columbia Icefield.

Is Athabasca Glacier the longest glacier in the Rockies?
Long, but not the longest. Saskatchewan Glacier is nine kilometres long. Other glaciers in the Rockies are slightly longer. The longest glacier in North America is the Bering Glacier in Alaska: 203 km.

Crevasse

How fast do glaciers move?
On average in the Rockies, about 15 m a year. Faster at icefalls, (125 m a year on Athabasca Glacier), and faster in the centre on the surface than at the sides or the base.

How long does it take for ice to flow from the Columbia Icefield rim to the terminus of Athabasca Glacier?
The "circulation time" is approximately 150 years. Some of the ice melting at the terminus may have formed on the icefield more than 800 years ago.

How deep are crevasses?
Large crevasses can be more than 30 m deep.

How far has the Athabasca Glacier retreated since the Little Ice Age ended?
About 1.6 km since 1870.

What has been the average annual rate of retreat during that time?
13 m, but in recent years, this

Common Questions

Columbia Icefield Information Centre

Exploring the toe of Athabasca Glacier

Glacier ice inside an ice cave

has dropped to one to three metres. Global warming may increase this amount.

Watermelon Snow

If you are visiting the Rockies in midsummer, you have probably noticed that many of the lingering snowbanks are tinged with pink. This is called watermelon snow, and is caused by an algae with a red eye spot. The algae provide food for species of tiny snow worms, so it is not recommended that you attempt to verify the watermelon flavour. However, take a sniff. Some people claim the snow smells like watermelons.

How many glaciers flow from Columbia Icefield?
There are eight named outlet valley glaciers: Athabasca, Dome, Kitchener and Stutfield (all visible from the Icefields Parkway); Columbia, Castleguard and Bryce (hidden from view on the south and west sides of Columbia Icefield); and Saskatchewan (visible from Parker Ridge). There are dozens of other valley, cirque and niche glaciers in the vicinity of Columbia Icefield.

Is it safe to drink glacier meltwater?
Perhaps. Although it shouldn't contain significant organic material, glacier melt is cold and full of sediments. Guzzled on a hot summer day, it may produce stomach upset. Glacial ice that formed in the 1950s contains ra-

dioactive fallout from atmospheric testing of nuclear weapons in the western U.S.

Will Athabasca Glacier disappear?
If conditions favouring glacial retreat persist, yes. If a colder climate that favours glacial advance returns, no. The current trend of global warming may contribute toward a period of accelerated glacial retreat.

How high is Mt. Athabasca?
Its summit is 3,491 m above sea level—nearly a vertical mile above the Icefield Information Centre. Of the 33 highest peaks in the Rockies (all more than 3,353 m), 13 adjoin Columbia Icefield.

How much does a Snocoach weigh?
19,700 kg empty; 23,600 kg with 56 passengers and driver.

199

He reported that these mountains towered some 1,800 m above Athabasca Pass.

Mountaineers knew that the peaks around Lake Louise also rose some 1,800 m above the valley floor, but only to 3,500 m. Mt. Hooker and Mt. Brown must truly be giants, higher even than Mont Blanc in the European Alps. The race was on to be the first to climb them.

A.P. Coleman, a geology professor from Toronto, made three attempts to find the mountains between 1888 and 1893. On the last trip, Coleman's party reached Athabasca Pass and ascended Mt. Brown. It turned out to be a peak of less than average stature for the Rockies. Coleman gruffly stated "We had been humbugged." He let the mountaineering world know that Douglas' famed peaks were frauds.

Coleman's announcement was not universally accepted. Some thought that he had climbed the wrong mountain from the wrong pass. Others wondered how Douglas, a first rate scholar, could have made such a blunder when he assigned the elevations to Mt. Hooker and Mt. Brown. In 1896, Walter Wilcox entered the fray. Forging the route now followed by the Icefields Parkway, Wilcox got close enough to Athabasca Pass to take a measurement of Mt. Brown's height, but his observations were inconclusive. Wilcox twice glimpsed the fringe of Columbia Icefield—at Saskatchewan Glacier and from Wilcox Pass—but the claim for its "discovery" was not to be his.

Enter John Norman Collie. In 1897, while returning from a climbing expedition to the vicinity of Saskatchewan River Crossing, Collie became intrigued with the view of the high, snowy mountains to the north. Surely the real Mt.

John Norman Collie

John Norman Collie was an erudite man: a professor of chemistry, the discoverer of neon gas, a talented artist, a pioneer in the fields of colour and X-ray photography and one of Britain's best mountaineers in the late 1800s. He had climbed in his native Scotland, in Norway and in the Himalayas.

Collie's first visit to the Rockies was at the invitation of American mountaineer Charles Fay in 1897. Collie participated in the first ascents of Mt. Lefroy and Mt. Victoria at Lake Louise, and the first attempt on Mt. Balfour. Later in the summer, Collie explored near Mt. Forbes and the Freshfield Icefield. The following year he made first ascents of Mt. Athabasca, Snow Dome and Diadem Peak, and claimed the discovery of Columbia Icefield.

Collie returned to the Rockies in 1902 with companions Hugh Stutfield and Hermann Woolley. They had an ambitious moun-

taineering plan that included an attempt on Mt. Columbia, second highest in the range. James Outram (OOT-rum) had similar designs, and contacted Collie to suggest a combined attempt. Collie, protective of his discovery of Columbia Icefield, reluctantly agreed. He considered Outram an "interloper." Collie may have been jealous of Outram's burgeoning list of Rockies' first as-

cents, which included Mt. Assiniboine and Collie's namesake peak on the Wapta Icefield.

The label proved correct. Outram climbed Mt. Columbia and Mt. Lyell (LIE-ell) before meeting Collie at the prearranged place. Collie's contempt for Outram's actions was barely concealed during the following 11 days, when the combined party made the first ascents of Mt. Freshfield and Mt. Forbes. After Outram departed, Collie added Howse Peak, Mt. Murchison, and Mt. Noyes to the expedition's tally.

Collie and Stutfield recorded their exploits in *Climbs and Explorations in the Canadian Rockies,* published in 1903. The book included Collie's map of the Rockies, a document that was relied on heavily by explorers for the next 20 years. On this map, the names of many features along the Icefields Parkway appeared for the first time. Collie died in Scotland in 1942, at age 83.

Hooker and Mt. Brown dwelled there yet? In 1898, he returned and followed Wilcox's route to Sunwapta Pass, from which he and Herman Woolley climbed Mt. Athabasca and "discovered" Columbia Icefield.

Collie was adept at deciphering topography, and correctly surmised that the high mountains in view on Columbia Icefield did not match those described by Douglas. Upon his return to England, Collie set out to solve the mystery of Mt. Hooker and Mt. Brown. For the first time, he looked up the original account of David Douglas (which had not been available to Coleman or Wilcox), and in an instant he had the solution. Douglas had thought the elevation of Athabasca Pass was 3,350 m, and had based his estimate of the height of Mt. Brown on that number. The true height of the pass is 1,748 m. Mt. Brown is 2,799 m, and the shoulder of Mt. Hooker above the pass is 2,600 m.

Douglas had obtained his elevations from a map made by David Thompson. In his work as a fur trade scout for the North West Company, Thompson had single-handedly mapped a vast area of western Canada. His maps were generally accurate and detailed. But in the matter of the height of Athabasca Pass, Thompson made one of his greatest contributions to exploration by way of an uncharacteristic blunder. Those who had come in search of the two elusive mountains had reopened travel in areas that had been unvisited since the decline of the fur trade. The published accounts of their journeys kindled an interest in the wild peaks and valleys of the Rockies that was global.

Mountaineering

To the general public, the motivation, equipment and know-how involved in mountaineer-

Sharon Wood

Mountain climbing is by its very nature a goal-oriented and highly disciplined activity. Yet few climbers attain those qualities as thoroughly as Sharon Wood, the first North American woman to reach the summit of Mount Everest.

"Rock climbing and mountaineering take me up into those high places where I've always dreamed of being. I love the intensity of the sport. It is the one thing in my life that I have to do perfectly. The consequences are severe, so it demands a perfect performance."

Introduced to the mountains by her father, Wood started technical rock climbing at sixteen, then got into mountaineering, and as a winter sport, she started climbing frozen waterfalls.

More often than not, climbing means persevering in less-than-ideal conditions. "Once I was soloing in Peru, and rocks started falling and one hit my shoulder. I

had to keep climbing with partial mobility, but it turned into a fascinating journey. What I love about that sport is the opportunity to explore our potential and how we are equipped to transcend pain and do what needs to be done."

The first woman to become a Canadian Climbing Guide and to gain recognition in the Interna-

tional Association of Mountain Guides, Wood has climbed the highest peaks in what are considered the most beautiful ranges in the world—the Himalaya, the Cordillera Blanca in the Andes, and further south into Argentina and Patagonia—yet she prefers the Canadian Rockies.

"This is the most beautiful mountain range in the world because the mountains are so new and rugged. The alpine terrain is absolutely spectacular because our treeline is lower. And the subalpine world is magical."

After twenty years of experience as an elite, professional mountaineer, Wood now travels the corporate lecture circuit where she has 40 speaking engagements a year in North America, linking the powerful metaphor of Mount Everest to the challenges faced by individuals and teams striving for excellence in their own endeavors.

ing are veiled in mystique. Mountaineers are assumed to be danger-seekers. Although there are routes to summits that involve difficulty and danger in the extreme, there are many routes to summits in the Rockies that involve very little difficulty and danger.

In a nutshell, climbing mountains is a pursuit in which the natural hazards are weighed against the rewards. Mountaineers chose to climb a particular mountain for the view it offers, for the technical experience it offers (snow, rock, ice), or for the challenge. High-tech equipment is not necessary for all routes, and when used, does not guarantee safe passage unless experience, sound judgement and preparedness govern its use.

In the Rockies, as with most northern mountains, the climbing routes on the north faces offer the greatest challenge and risk. The north faces you can see on Mt. Athabasca and Mt. Andromeda offer moderately difficult climbs by today's standards. However, the north faces of North Twin, Mt. Alberta, Mt. Columbia and Mt. Kitchener are among the test pieces of the mountaineering world. In addition, some of the winter waterfall ice climbing routes in alpine settings on Snow Dome, Mt. Patterson and the White Pyramid are extreme routes to which not many climbers in the world aspire.

Mt. Athabasca sports many routes to its summit, and is one of the most frequently ascended peaks over 3,353 m in the Rockies. The ascent and descent of one of these routes will take a competent party 10 to 15 hours in good weather and with good climbing conditions.

The remote peaks of Columbia Icefield—North Twin, South Twin and Mt. Columbia—are best approached on skis in spring. The effort necessitates a form of mountaineering that verges on the mini-expedition. Usually, it requires a day to approach within striking range, a day to ski or climb the peak and return to camp, and a day to ski out.

So with all that can go wrong and cause danger and discomfort, why bother? The mountains of the Rockies are unforgiving, and care not the least for the passing of human feet. However, when conditions relent, the summit view or the alpenglow of a high alpine sunrise or sunset is well

The Silver Ice Axe

Mt. Alberta (3619 m) is the fifth highest summit in the Rockies and is considered by many mountaineers to be the most difficult peak in the range to climb. The first climbing guidebook to the Rockies featured a photograph of the mountain in 1921. This brought Mt. Alberta to the attention of mountaineers throughout the world. In 1925, a large mountaineering party from Japan succeeded in making the first ascent. It was rumoured that they left a silver ice axe on the summit.

The rumour inspired attempts, but so difficult is Mt. Alberta that it was 23 years before the second ascent was made. There was an ice axe on the summit, but it was of the ordinary variety, with a steel head and wooden shaft. Much to the chagrin of Canadian mountaineers, it was taken by the second summit party. It is now in the Jasper Museum and Archives.

The High Mountains near Columbia Icefield

Mountain	Height in metres	Rank in Rockies	Visible from
Columbia	3,747	2	Athabasca Valley Viewpoint
North Twin	3,684	3	Tangle Creek trail
Alberta	3,619	5	Tangle Creek trail
Twins Tower	3,597	8	not visible from road
South Twin	3,580	10	not visible from road
Bryce	3,507	16	Parker Ridge
Athabasca	3,491	17	Icefield Information Centre
King Edward	3,490	18	not visible from road
Kitchener	3,480	19	Icefields Parkway at Tangle Creek
Snow Dome	3,451	22	Icefield Information Centre
Stutfield West	3,450	23	Tangle Creek trail
Andromeda	3,442	24	Icefields Parkway at Sunwapta Canyon
Stutfield East	3,390	33	Icefields Parkway at Tangle Creek

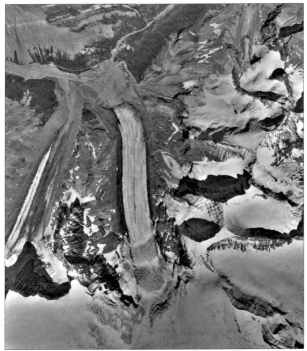

This aerial view shows Athabasca Glacier and Dome Glacier (left) as they extend toward the Icefields Parkway near the top of the photo

worth the price of admission. Being in the heart of wild and remote places at those special times is a big part of what mountaineering is all about.

The Frozen Wellspring

Glaciers cover 11 percent of the earth's surface. Including the glacial ice of polar regions, glaciers store more than 75 per cent of the world's fresh water in frozen form. Some of this ice is tens of thousands of years old and predates industrial pollution. When melted, it provides the purest water on earth.

The presence or absence of fresh water largely influences the distribution of life. Since the industrial age began, supplies of fresh water throughout the world have become polluted and scarce. The removal

of covering vegetation to allow agriculture has greatly decreased the ability of land to store water. Also, natural lakes have been drained and underground aquifers depleted to bring water to large cities. This process of desertification seriously threatens the future of agriculture and our ability to feed ourselves. Unless we develop a truly effective and economical means of de-salinating ocean water, our future hinges critically on the continued existence of locally available fresh water.

The glaciers of the Canadian Rockies give rise to most of the major rivers in western Canada. As glaciers in the Rockies dwindle, fresh water supplies are threatened. In the past, researchers studied the behaviour of glaciers as a cu-

riosity. Today, that curiosity has changed to concern for the future viability of agriculture, industry and settlement in western North America.

The recession of major glaciers in the Rockies has been plotted during the last century. Although we marvel at the horizontal distances the glaciers have retreated during this time, what is more alarming is the loss in mass of ice. Some glaciers are 200 m thinner at the terminus than 90 years ago. Athabasca Glacier decreased 57 per cent in area and 32 per cent in volume between 1870 and 1971. Earlier this century, it was estimated that Columbia Glacier, on the west side of Columbia Icefield, was shrinking at the rate of 13 million cubic metres a year.

Most glaciers in the Rockies are currently in retreat. If we choose to believe that the earth's climate is warming, and that greenhouse gases and ozone depletion are accelerating this trend, then the rapid retreat of glaciers makes the cause-and-effect relationship between hydrocarbon use and global warming very clear for us. By eliminating waste, reducing our use of fossil fuels and choosing products and lifestyles that do not contribute to global warming, we can help stave off the retreat of glaciers in the Rockies and elsewhere. Δ

Icefields Parkway North

North of the Columbia Icefield Information Centre, the Icefields Parkway follows the Sunwapta River. This river originates in Sunwapta Lake near the toe of Athabasca Glacier. The riverbed contains glacial sediment and rubble, and is carpeted with mountain avens. Across the Sunwapta Valley, Dome Glacier cascades from the rim of Columbia Icefield between Snow Dome and Mt. Kitchener. On the valley floor, the glacier's surface is covered in moraine and is hard to distinguish from the surrounding rock. Between Athabasca Glacier and Dome Glacier is a triangular-shaped patch of forest that escaped glaciation during the Little Ice Age advance. This forest contains some of the oldest trees in Jasper National Park.

Mt. Wilcox (2,884 m) is on the east side of the Icefields Parkway. Notice the massive scree slope that descends to roadside. The surrounding cliffs are a good place to see mountain goats.

Four kilomtres north of the Columbia Icefield Information Centre, the Icefields Parkway climbs away from the floor of the Sunwapta Valley to bypass a canyon on the Sunwapta River. This is the Tangle Creek Hill. A road sign warns: "Watch for sheep on road." More often than not, you will see members of the local flock of bighorn sheep standing in the middle of the road. Reduce your speed to 60 km per hour. If you would like to spend some time in the company of the sheep, pull safely off the road into one of the paved viewpoints.

The Mt. Kitchener Slide

It is 220 m from the viewpoints atop the Tangle Creek Hill to the Sunwapta River below. The river foams through a narrow canyon. What caused the change in character of the river from when you last saw it, farther south?

Some time after the last ice age, a rockslide from Mt. Kitchener blocked the Sunwapta River at this point, with debris piled 50 m deep. The Mt. Kitchener Slide is one of the largest measured rockslides in this part of the Rockies. You can see where the slide originated on the slopes above. Geologists think that the Mt. Kitchener Slide at one time dammed the Sunwapta River and caused a lake to form on the extensive flats that

you saw just north of the Columbia Icefield Centre. The river has since eroded a canyon through the rockslide debris, releasing the impounded waters.

If you look south from the viewpoint, there is a fine view of Mt. Athabasca (3,491 m) and its neighbour, Mt. Andromeda (3,450 m). Mt. Andromeda was originally called "Cirque Mountain." The bowl-shaped depression in its northern flank is a classic glacial cirque. Andromeda was the wife of Perseus in Greek mythology. It is also the name of the closest galaxy to the Milky Way, and of a northern constellation.

Tangle Falls

Mary Schäffer's 1907 expedition to the upper Athabasca Valley used Wilcox Pass to detour around Athabasca Glacier and the Mt. Kitchener Slide. The steep descent from the pass was made on a rough trail alongside Tangle Creek. Outfitters refer to untracked bush as "shin tangle." Thus, the creek and picturesque falls were named. You may see bighorn sheep here. The Tangle Creek trail to Wilcox Pass departs from the south side of the creek.

The ice-capped north face

left: Tangle Falls

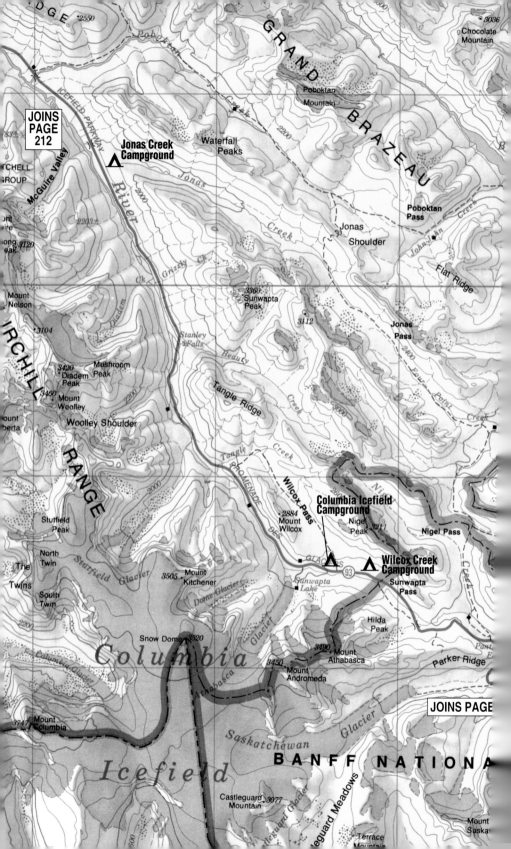

JOINS PAGE 212

RIDGE · 2550

GRAND BRAZEAU

Chocolate Mountain · 3036

Poboktan Mountain

· 3200

Poboktan Pass

ICEFIELD PARKWAY

Jonas Creek Campground

Waterfall Peaks

McGuire Valley

MITCHELL GROUP

River

Jonas

Creek

Jonas Shoulder

John-John Creek

· 2203

MITCHELL GROUP

Mount Nelson

· 3104

Grizzly Ck

Ck

· 3360 Sunwapta Peak

· 3112

Jonas Pass

Flat Ridge

Four Point Creek

FAIRCHILL RANGE

Diadem

Stanley Falls

Beauty

Creek

· 3420 Diadem Peak

Mushroom Peak

Creek

· 3460

Mount Woolley

Tangle Ridge

Mount Alberta

Woolley Shoulder

Tangle

Creek

PROMENADE

2000

Wilcox Pass

Columbia Icefield Campground

Nigel

Peak · 3211

Nigel Pass

Stutfield Peak

· 2884 Mount Wilcox

Nigel Pass

The Twins

North Twin

Stutfield Glacier

GLACIER

93

Wilcox Creek Campground

South Twin

· 3505 Mount Kitchener

Dome Glacier

Sunwapta Lake

Sunwapta Pass

Hilda Peak

Parker Ridge

Snow Dome · 3520

Columbia

Glacier

· 3490 Mount Athabasca

Columbia Glacier

Athabasca

· 3450 Mount Andromeda

· 3747 Mount Columbia

Icefield

Saskatchewan

Glacier

BANFF NATIONAL

JOINS PAGE

Castleguard Mountain · 3077

Castleguard Meadows

Castleguard Glacier

Terrace Mountain

Mount Saska

Stutfield Glacier

of Mt. Kitchener (3,480 m) looms across the Sunwapta Valley. This face sports two of the most difficult mountaineering routes in the Rockies, and is a complete contrast to the gentle, glaciated south slopes of the mountain, which are routinely ascended by ski mountaineers.

Stutfield Glacier

The Stutfield Glacier viewpoint is 8.5 km north of the Columbia Icefield Information Centre. The 1,100 m cliff between Mt. Kitchener (on the left) and the Stutfield Peaks is the backdrop for an age-old battle—the erosion of rock by glacial ice. Stutfield Glacier is one of eight outlet valley glaciers of Columbia Icefield. The icefalls here are among the most contorted and spectacular seen from the Icefields Parkway. Unfortunately, Stutfield Glacier is one of the most difficult scenes to photograph. The northeast aspect and resultant shading preclude good lighting except shortly after sunrise in mid-summer.

Hugh Stutfield was a companion of John Norman Collie during mountaineering expeditions in 1898 and 1902. In 1903, Stutfield and Collie co-authored one of the standard works of Rockies history, *Climbs and Explorations in the Canadian Rockies,* now a collector's item. Collie named a mountain just north of here for the other mountaineer on the 1898 trip, Hermann Woolley.

David Thompson

The National Historic Site plaque at the Whirlpool Valley viewpoint commemorates David Thompson, Canada's greatest explorer and map maker. Born in England in 1770, Thompson began work with the Hudson's Bay Company at age 14. During the next 28 years, he made many exploratory journeys in western Canada, trapping furs and establishing travel routes. He studied surveying and map making while recovering from a broken leg in 1790.

In the late 1700s, Thompson switched to the rival North West Company. In 1799 he built its outpost, Rocky Mountain House, on the North Saskatchewan River. In the winter of 1810-11, Thompson crossed Athabasca Pass and established the route of choice for the fur trade. He continued to the Pacific coast, making the first detailed map of the Columbia River basin.

Thompson created his exceptional maps as a sideline to his work, without the surveyor's standard tools. He used only astronomical data and a pocket watch to determine positions. Despite his contributions to the exploration of Canada and the industry of the fur trade, David Thompson died impoverished in Montreal in 1857.

Common Raven

The common raven is one of nature's most adaptable creatures. It is found throughout North America, Africa and Eurasia, and is equally at home in deserts, in cities and on mountain tops. The raven's diet is the key to its adaptability. These birds are opportunistic scavengers, and eat virtually anything.

Ravens are normally seen alone or in pairs, picking over the gravel at roadside or rummaging through garbage. Carrion is a favourite part of the raven's diet. A congregation of ravens usually indicates that an unfortunate animal has met its end. Some wildlife biologists think that ravens may be able to communicate to their fellows the whereabouts of such a feast. When a good feeding opportunity exists, large numbers of these birds quickly descend on the scene. Through behaviour and calls, ravens may also indicate the presence of potential prey—animals weakened by disease or hunger—to wolves and coyotes. The ravens will later benefit from a successful kill by being on hand to pick over the carcass.

Throughout history, we have regarded ravens as evil and unintelligent. However they occupy a prominent niche in the ecology, and with their keen eyesight, their inquisitive nature, their varied vocabulary and their structured social order, we should reconsider our impressions. Natives revere these birds. The raven is an important character in creation legends.

The raven remains in the Rockies year-round. Its smaller, look-alike cousin, the American crow, migrates a short distance south in winter. In flight, you can easily distinguish between the two: the raven has a wedge-shaped tail, whereas the crow's tail is squarish.

Woodland (Mountain) Caribou

You will be extremely fortunate to see caribou at roadside in the Rockies, but your best chance is near Beauty Creek. The caribou is a deer family member and has a brown coat with lighter patches on the neck, rump, belly and lower legs. The neck is fringed on its underside.

Both male and female caribou grow antlers that feature a forward-reaching "shovel." In summer, it is usually the females that carry antlers. Their "rack" is smaller than that of mature males. When they run, caribou carry their heads high and tilted back, and lift their legs in a distinctive prance. If you are close enough, you will hear the clacking made by tendons in the animal's legs. The caribou's large hooves help support it in deep snow, and leave a track that is more rounded than that of other deer family members. The wolf is the principal predator.

Jasper's caribou migrate between the high alpine in summer and low-elevation forests in winter. Their staple foods are ground lichens and rock lichens. Caribou "crater" through the snow to obtain these in winter. Because of their seasonal migration, Jasper's caribou have earned the unofficial designation "mountain caribou." In the northern part of Jasper, the caribous' migration takes them out of the park onto provincial lands, where they are

not protected.

Between 1960 and 1990, Alberta's caribou population decreased from 9,000 to 3,000. Population estimates for Banff and Jasper national parks suggest 350 to 400 animals, grouped into six herds. The herd that frequents Jonas Pass, just east of Beauty Creek, is thought to number 40 to 65 animals.

Endless Chain Ridge

Exit from the Icefield

After the confined and harsh landscape in the immediate vicinity of Columbia Icefield, the flats of the Sunwapta River are a welcome relief. For the next 14 km, the Icefields Parkway travels beside one of the largest glacial outwash plains in the Rockies. The old road bed is visible at many places along the east side of the valley. The 2.5-km trail to Stanley Falls follows part of this road. There is a hostel at Beauty Creek.

The backwaters of the Sunwapta River near the hostel give wonderful reflections of Mt. Kitchener to the south. The ice cliffs on Mt. Kitchener's summit are the fringe of Columbia Icefield. The Earl of Kitchener was a First World War hero. The backwaters are excellent habitat for moose and waterfowl. The river flats are coloured by the purple blooms of mountain fireweed in July.

Jonas Slide

For the next 30 km, the Icefields Parkway follows the Sunwapta River through spectacular scenery. The Jonas Creek campground is 25.9 km north of Columbia Icefield Information Centre. Two kilometres farther north, the Icefields Parkway passes through the debris of the Jonas Slide.

When the ice of the ancestral Athabasca Glacier scoured the Sunwapta Valley, it undercut the steeply tilted rock formations in the adjoining mountains. After the ice receded, some of these formations split away along weaknesses and tumbled to the valley floor in rockslides. There have been two major rockslides here; the more northerly slide swept a path almost four kilometres long. If you look at the slope to the east, you can see where this slide originated.

The colourful blocks are Gog quartzite, one of the oldest, hardest and most common rocks in the Rockies.

There is a warden station just north of Poboktan Creek,
30.9 km north of the Columbia Icefield Information Centre. The trailhead here gives access to Poboktan Pass and Maligne Pass, two of the alpine highlights of Jasper's backcountry. *Poboktan* is a Stoney word for "owl." The name was conferred by A.P. Coleman in 1892.

Endless Chain Ridge

The crustal forces that thrust the Rockies skyward created steeply tilted rock formations in the mountains of the front ranges. The resulting mountain shape is a "writing desk peak," or overthrust mountain. This mountain type has a uniformly inclined southwest-facing slope and a sheer northeast-facing cliff. Endless Chain Ridge is one of the best examples of an overthrust mountain in the Rockies. Overthrust mountains are common near Banff townsite (Mt. Rundle) and along the Yellowhead Highway east of Jasper.

Mary Schäffer named Endless Chain Ridge during her exploration of 1907. Although not endless, the ridge would have been in the view of explorers on horseback for several days. It is a prominent feature for some 20 km along the Icefields Parkway north of Poboktan Creek.

Bubbling Springs

Bubbling Springs is the outlet for a cold water spring. Groundwater filters downward through fissures in rock layers on the slopes above and is channelled laterally to the surface here. The silt in the water contains fine grains of quartz eroded from the rock of Endless Chain Ridge. A fire-succession forest of lodgepole pine surrounds the adjacent picnic area.

Sunwapta Falls

The Sunwapta Falls junction is 47.7 km north of the Columbia

Icefield Information Centre. The falls are one kilometre west along a sideroad. At Sunwapta Falls, the Sunwapta River has been diverted from its northwesterly course by a moraine. The river makes a 90° dogleg turn to the southwest

before flowing northwest again to join the Athabasca River. The river has taken advantage of a crack system in the Cathedral limestone bedrock to create the straight, steeply walled canyon immediately downstream from the

Mountain Goat

Many visitors to the Rockies have trouble distinguishing mountain goats from bighorn sheep. Remember: Goats are white or cream-coloured and have black horns; sheep are tawny brown with a light rump patch, and have brown horns. Mt. Kerkeslin is home to about 60 mountain goats. When they are moulting in late spring, these animals visit the mineral lick at Goats and Glaciers viewpoint. It is thought that the minerals they obtain here help restore their coats.

Mountain goats live in small groups on upper mountainsides. Grasses comprise 75 per cent of their diet. Grassy ledges and slopes that offer quick escape to cliffs are their favourite habitat. Not a true goat, the mountain goat is more closely related to mountain antelopes of Asia.

The horns of bighorn sheep provide an easy clue for distinguishing between males and females, but this is not true with mountain goats. To a casual observer, the horns of both sexes appear the same. The best way to tell if a goat is a female (nanny) is if a young kid is tagging along. The kid, born in June, stays with the mother for a year. Solitary goats seen in summer are usually males (billies).

The mountain goat is master of alpine ridge, cliff edge and

mountain top. Nature has equipped this animal with remarkable hooves, tendons and muscles. The split hoof is comprised of a soft pad surrounded by a hard, bony shell. The soft pad grips like a suction cup on steep slabs, and the bony exterior can be used to lever upwards on minuscule ledges. The strong muscles and tendons allow the goat to leap from ledge to ledge, and cushion the shock upon landing. The mountain goat is able to turn around on narrow ledges by standing on its front legs and walking its rear legs around on the cliff above.

Because of the fact that goats are so well equipped and spend

so much time in hazardous areas, they seem nonchalant about certain dangers. The author has seen a goat bedded down on a snow cornice overhanging a 1,000 m cliff. Avalanches, rockfall and starvation in severe winters account for most of the natural mortalities. Cougar and golden eagles are the principal predators, occasionally achieving success in attacks from above. You may see a nanny goat standing over her kid to protect against this threat.

The mountain goat population estimates available for the Rocky Mountain parks are: Banff, 800 to 900; Yoho, 400; and Kootenay, 300.

Sunwapta Falls

night nearby. Endless Chain Ridge is in view across the lake. There is a large boulder of Gog quartzite on the lakeshore in the Honeymoon Lake campground. Mt. Edith Cavell is the high mountain visible to the north of this vicinity.

Athabasca Valley

From the Honeymoon Lake Campground turnoff, the Ice-fields Parkway descends to the floor of the Athabasca Valley. The Athabasca is the longest and widest valley in the Rocky Mountain parks. The valley's breadth gives you an idea of how massive the glaciers of the Great Glaciation were when they filled it, nearly to the brim.

South from here, the Athabasca Valley extends into a heartland of glacial ice along the continental divide. Mt. Quincy (3,150 m) is prominent in the view. A.P. Coleman named the peak in 1892 for his brother, Lucius Quincy Cole-man. From here to the east boundary of Jasper National Park, the floor of the Athabasca Valley is in the montane ecoregion. It pro-vides excellent habitat for black bear, grizzly bear, elk and deer.

Mt. Fryatt

For the next 10 km, the Ice-fields Parkway passes close to the Athabasca River. *Athabasca* is a Cree word that means "place where there are reeds." It refers to the delta at the river's mouth in Lake Athabasca in northwestern Alberta. The Athabasca River is 1,231 km long. The 168-km reach in Jasper National Park

principal waterfall.

You can explore this canyon by following a two-kilometre trail along the north bank of the river. The trail that crosses the footbridge near the falls is the beginning of a day-long backpacker's route to Fortress Lake in Hamber Provincial Park, B.C. Meals, accommodation and gasoline are available in season at the Sunwapta Falls Lodge on the Icefields Parkway. Elk are often seen near the junction.

A Glacial Junction

Just north of Sunwapta Falls, the Icefields Parkway enters the Athabasca Valley. The ice age glaciers that filled the Athabasca Valley and Sun-wapta Valley merged here, leaving behind a complex of moraines. Blocks of ice slumped into hollows, creating kettle lakes. Honeymoon Lake, Buck Lake and Osprey Lake are examples.

Honeymoon Lake was named when a Jasper warden and his new wife spent the

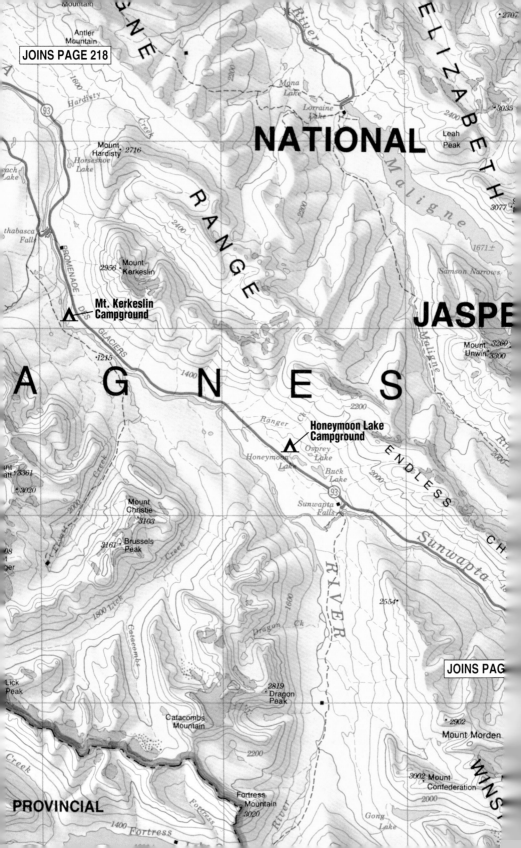

JOINS PAGE 218

JASPE

NATIONAL

ELIZABETH

Antler
Mountain

Mona
Lake

Lorraine
Lake

Leah
Peak

Mount
Hardisty 2716

Horseshoe
Lake

Hardisty

Creek

Maligne

3035

3077

1671±

Samson Narrows

Mount
Kerkeslin 2956

Mount
Unwin 3260
3300

Mt. Kerkeslin
Campground

RANGE

1215

GLACIERS

PROMENADE DES

AGNES

Ranger
Ck

Honeymoon Lake
Campground

Honeymoon
Lake

Osprey
Lake

Buck
Lake

ENDLESS

CH.

Mount
Christie
3103

Brussels
Peak

3361

3020

3161

Sunwapta
Falls

2554

Sunwapta

RIVER

Catacombs
Creek

Dragon Ck

Lick
Peak

Catacombs
Mountain

1800 Lick

JOINS PAG

2902

Mount Morden

2819
Dragon
Peak

Fortress
Mountain
3020

3002 Mount
Confederation

WINS

Gong
Lake

PROVINCIAL

Fortress

Creek

River

Athabasca Falls and Mt. Kerkeslin

that height. Many of the trees show black claw marks left when bears climbed them.

Goats and Glaciers Viewpoint

Although there are few glaciers visible, the prospect from Goats and Glaciers viewpoint, 16.9 km north of Sunwapta Falls, gives an impressive panorama of the Athabasca Valley. It is also one of the best places in the Rockies to see mountain goats at close range. The riverbanks beneath the viewpoint contain glacial sediment called till. This sediment is rich in sulphur-bearing minerals that lure mountain goats from the slopes of Mt. Kerkeslin.

The Athabasca River flows directly beneath the viewpoint. On a hot summer day, it will have the milky colour characteristic of glacially fed rivers. The Athabasca and its tributaries drain more than 75 per cent of Jasper National Park. The forest here is a homogenous stand of lodgepole pine—legacy of a large fire that swept the Athabasca Valley in 1889. The canopy of the pine forest is light green. In places, you can see stands of darker coloured spruce and fir trees that escaped the fire.

The unmistakable turreted form of Brussels Peak (3,161 m) is prominent in the view south. The difficult first ascent of this seldom-climbed mountain was not accomplished until 1948, after at least three previous attempts had failed.

The Mt. Kerkeslin campground is 2.3 km north of the viewpoint. There is a warden station and a hostel 2.7 km north of the campground.

was proclaimed a Canadian Heritage River in 1989.

The horn shape of Mt. Fryatt (3,361 m) is prominent on the west side of the Athabasca Valley. Captain Fryatt evacuated Allied troops from France in his boat *The Brussels* during World War I. He was captured and executed by the Germans in 1916. Mt. Fryatt is the second lowest of the 56 summits in the Rockies that exceed 3,353 m. It was first climbed in 1926. The name of Fryatt's boat is celebrated in the striking, turreted form of nearby Brussels Peak, visible farther north along the Icefields Parkway.

There are stands of trembling aspen near the Mt. Christie picnic area. The trunks of these trees have two types of scars caused by animals. When elk and deer cannot find grass to feed on in late winter, they strip the bark from aspens. These animals can only reach about 1.5 m from the ground, so mature trees are uniformly scarred to

Athabasca Falls

At the junction with the Athabasca Parkway (Highway 93A), turn west for Athabasca Falls. Whereas many waterfalls in the Rockies cascade from the mouths of hanging valleys, the 23-metre-high cascade of Athabasca Falls exists for a different reason.

When glaciers advance through a valley, they undulate. The ice is forced upwards by resistant rock formations, and then plunges downwards once it has flowed past them. At the site of Athabasca Falls, the ancestral Athabasca Glacier encountered a resistant outcrop of Gog quartzite. The glacier skipped over the outcrop and eroded a deep hollow downstream. It is over this glacial rock step that Athabasca Falls now cascades.

The Athabasca River carries the greatest amount of water of any river in the Rocky Mountain parks. Rain or shine, don't miss the incredible sensory experience of the thundering water, the mist and the spray from the viewpoints at the water's edge.

The spray from the falls keeps the area nearby moist and cool, and sustains a canyon forest of lodgepole pine, subalpine fir and white spruce. Feathermosses and lichens thrive in this area, along with shade-tolerant shrubs and wildflowers. There is a stand of moisture-loving black spruce just north of the junction on the Icefields Parkway. This tree is uncommon in the Rockies.

Looking east from Athabasca Falls, you can see the U-shaped fold of the Castle Mountain Syncline in Mt.

Goats and Glaciers viewpoint

Kerkeslin (2,956 m.) The mountain was named by James Hector in 1859. *Kerkeslin* is Stoney for "wolverine." Horseshoe Lake is 3.4 km north of Athabasca Falls on the Icefields Parkway. This deep lake occupies a depression in rockslide debris, and is a popular swimming hole for those who can brave its frigid waters.

Whirlpool Valley Viewpoint

The Whirlpool Valley viewpoint is 5.7 km north of Athabasca Falls. From its confluence with the Athabasca River to Athabasca Pass, the Whirlpool Valley is almost 60 km long. David Thompson of the North West Company was the first Euro-Canadian to travel this valley, in the winter of 1810-11. Athabasca Pass subsequently became part of the fur trade route across the Rockies, plied twice a year by the voyageurs until the 1840s. In autumn, the voyageurs would head west with supplies and mail. They would winter at various outposts along the Columbia

River, and return in spring return with furs. They crossed the Athabasca River near here: by fording it on horseback, by clinging to makeshift rafts, or by swimming.

It may seem confusing that the Whirlpool River, not the Athabasca River, leads to Athabasca Pass. James Hector bestowed the name in 1859 for descriptive reasons. Undoubtedly, the voyageurs had other names for this river. Today, the Whirlpool Valley is a wilderness enclave that is seldom visited.

Wabasso Lake

The Athabasca Valley south of Jasper townsite contains many lakes. These occupy hollows carved from the Miette gritstone bedrock by glacial ice. Trails lead to Wabasso Lake and the Valley of the Five Lakes. The surrounding forest is dominated by lodgepole pine, with an understory of twinflower, juniper and buffaloberry. The red and amber fruits of buffaloberry are a favourite food of black bears and grizzly bears. You may see

Mt. Kerkeslin and Horseshoe Lake

these animals here.

The Wabasso Lake trail passes through a montane meadow known as *Prairie de la Vache*—French for "cow prairie." Fur trader Gabriel Franchère saw bison here when he crossed Athabasca Pass in 1820. The meadow was used by the fur traders as a wintering range for horses. *Wabasso* is a Cree word for "rabbit"—probably referring to the snowshoe hare, the only true bunny in the Rockies.

Valley of the Five Lakes

The 4.6-km loop trail to Valley of the Five Lakes crosses a beaver pond and climbs over gritstone ridges covered with stands of Douglas fir and trembling aspen. Moose, beaver, muskrat, common loon and great blue heron are among the wildlife you may see.

The Maligne Range flanks the east side of this part of the Athabasca Valley. The most northerly peak is Mt. Tekarra (2,694 m). James Hector named the mountain for his Iroquois guide in 1859.

Athabasca River

The Icefields Parkway crosses the Athabasca River near Jasper, 8.4 km south of the junction with the Yellowhead Highway. Slightly downstream from this bridge, the Athabasca River begins to cut across the southeast/northwest grain of the Rockies, flowing to the foothills and plains to the east. It is thought that the river is as old as the Rockies, and was able to erode downwards through them as they were being uplifted, hence taking this unlikely course. The unmistakable shape of Pyramid Mountain (2,763 m) forms the backdrop for the townsite of Jasper in the view north.

Approach to Jasper Townsite

The junction with the Athabasca Parkway (Highway 93A) is 1.2 km beyond the Athabasca River bridge. Turnoffs for Wapiti Campground and Whistlers Campground follow. These are the only two camping options

close to Jasper townsite. *Wapiti* is a Shawnee word that means "white rump," and is an alternate name for elk. The trunks of aspen trees near Wapiti Campground show the characteristic black scarring caused when elk and deer eat the bark during winter. The Whistlers Tramway and a hostel are on the Whistlers Campground road. Elk and deer frequent this section of the Icefields Parkway. Drive with care.

The final noteworthy feature on the Icefields Parkway is the Miette River. This river flows from Yellowhead Pass, 26 km to the west. The Miette is an unusual river for the Rockies. Virtually none of its water is glacial in origin. It takes a meandering course to its confluence with the Athabasca River nearby. The quiet reaches and backwaters of the Miette River are excellent habitat for waterfowl, osprey, beaver, great blue heron and moose. The surrounding woods of white spruce, lodgepole pine, trembling aspen, Douglas fir and balsam poplar are among the best bird-watching locations in the Rockies.

The Icefields Parkway ends at the junction with the Yellowhead Highway (Highway 16), and the only stop light in Jasper National Park. Keep straight ahead for Jasper townsite. Turn west for Mt. Robson, Valemount, McBride and Prince George. Turn east for Hinton, Edson and Edmonton. Δ

Jasper National Park

It was the proposal to build a second transcontinental railway in Canada that led to the founding of Jasper, Canada's seventh national park. In 1902, the Grand Trunk Railway approached the federal government to form a partnership and build a line to link New Brunswick and B.C.—the Grand

Trunk Pacific Railway. The GTPR would cross the Rockies at Yellowhead Pass.

Boom times had come to Banff and Yoho national parks with the completion of the Canadian Pacific Railway in 1885. However, in 1902, the Athabasca and Miette valleys were still the domain of trappers, outfitters, mountaineers and a few settlers, virtually unchanged since the CPR had abandoned the Yellowhead Pass route in 1881. From its experience with the other "railway national parks"— Banff, Yoho and Glacier—the Canadian government recognized that a new railway across the Rockies offered another opportunity to capitalize economically on the scenery. It established Jasper Forest Park in September of 1907.

Jasper is the largest of the Rocky Mountain parks—larger than Banff, Yoho and Kootenay combined. It includes 10,878 square kilometres of the foothills, the front ranges and the eastern main ranges. Jasper is the third most visited national park in Canada, after Banff and Kootenay. Approximately 1,300,000 people enter the park each year.

The town of Jasper originated in 1911 as a railway settlement named Fitzhugh (FITS-hue), after the vice president of the Grand Trunk Pacific Railway. The GTPR rails reached Fitzhugh in August that year, and were at "Summit City" on Yellowhead Pass by November. The line was completed to Prince Rupert on the Pacific Ocean in 1914. The town's name was soon changed to match that of the surrounding national park. The park had been named for Jasper Hawse, who oversaw a fur trade outpost in the Athabasca Valley in 1817.

A second railway was constructed through Yellowhead Pass in 1913. The Canadian Northern Railway carried its first traffic in October 1915. Its mountain operations were based at Lucerne, just across Yellowhead Pass in B.C. The lines of the two railways were only metres apart in places. The redundancy was soon obvious to all. Beginning in 1916, the tracks west of Edmonton were consolidated. The new railway alignment through Jasper used the most favourable grades of each railway. The redundant rails were shipped to Europe for use in World War I. In 1922, the two railways amalgamated under government ownership as the Canadian National Railway. Rail operations at Lucerne were relocated to Jasper in 1924, doubling the town's population.

Some of the abandoned railway grades were eventually used for roadbeds. The Jasper-Edmonton Road opened in 1931 and was paved 20 years later. Although vehicles were driven across Yellowhead Pass as early as 1922, with the drivers building bridges as they went, it wasn't until 1968 that paving of the Yellowhead Highway was completed between Edmonton and Prince Rupert.

Jasper Townsite

Jasper townsite occupies an open setting with an expansive view on the west bank of the Athabasca River, just downstream from its confluence with the Miette River. The

left: Patricia Lake and Pyramid Mountain

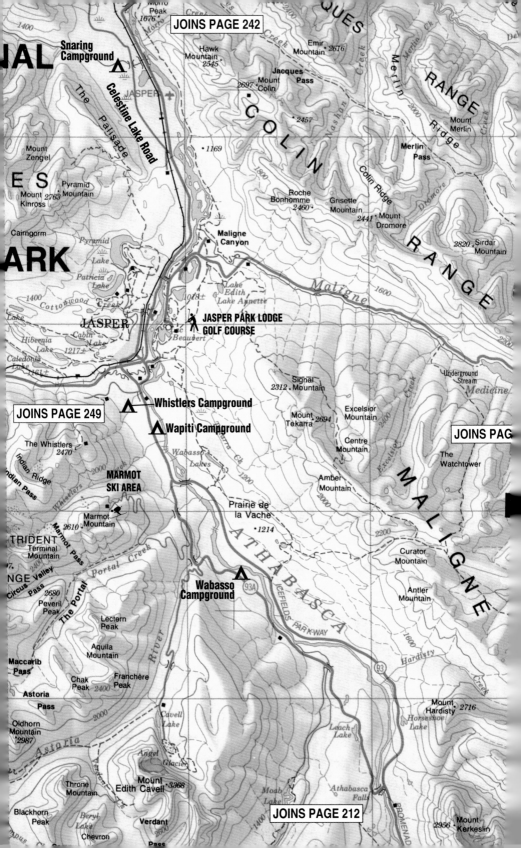

JOINS PAGE 242

Snaring Campground

Celestine Lake Road

The Palisade

Morro Peak 1676

Hawk Mountain 2545

Emir Mountain 2676

JACQUES

RANGE

Jacques Pass

Mount Colin 2697

Mount Merlin

Merlin Ridge

Merlin Pass

JASPER

Mount Zengel

COLIN

Pyramid Mountain

Mount Kinross 2763

1169

2457

Nashan Creek

Colin Ridge

Grisette Mountain 2441

Mount Dromore

2820 Sirdar Mountain

Cairngorm

Pyramid Lake

Roche Bonhomme 2460

Patricia Lake

RANGE

Maligne Canyon

Dromore Creek

1400

Cottonwood Creek

1018±

Lake Edith Lake Annette

Maligne

1600

JASPER

Cabin Lake

Hibernia Lake

1217±

Beauvert

JASPER PARK LODGE GOLF COURSE

Signal Mountain 2312

Excelsior Mountain

Underground Stream

Medicine

Caledonia Lake 1161±

JOINS PAGE 249

Whistlers Campground

Wapiti Campground

Mount Tekarra 2694

Centre Mountain

Excelsior Creek

JOINS PAG

The Whistlers 2470

Indian Ridge

Wabasso Lakes

Tekarra Ck

1200

Amber Mountain

2000

MALIGNE

The Watchtower

MARMOT SKI AREA

Indian Pass

Whistlers Creek

Marmot Mountain 2610

Marmot Pass

Prairie de la Vache

1214

2200

Curator Mountain

TRIDENT

Terminal Mountain

Circus Valley

NGE

Peveril Peak 2680

The Portal

Portal Creek

ATHABASCA

Antler Mountain

Wabasso Campground

93A

ICEFIELDS PARKWAY

Maccarib Pass

Lectern Peak

River

93

1600

Hardisty Creek

Astoria Pass

Chak Peak 2400

Aquila Mountain

Franchère Peak

Oldhorn Mountain 2987

2000

Cavell Lake

Mount Hardisty 2716

Horseshoe Lake

Astoria

Throne Mountain

Mount Edith Cavell 3368

Angel Glacier

Leach Lake

Blackhorn Peak

Beryl Lake

Verdant Chevron

Moab Lake

Athabasca Falls

2956 Mount Kerkeslin

PROMENADE

JOINS PAGE 212

Connaught Avenue in downtown Jasper

Lac Beauvert, Jasper and The Whistlers

elevation is 1,054 m. Although a thriving community of 4,500, Jasper has less bustle and more of a small-town feel than Banff. Most businesses and services are located on Connaught Drive and Patricia Street. The lawn in front of the park administration building on Connaught Drive is a favourite relaxing spot for visitors. The bus depot and train station are across the street. The environs of Jasper townsite, particularly the Pyramid Bench, are well suited to exploration by foot and by bicycle.

The campgrounds close to Jasper are Whistlers and Wapiti, respectively 3.8 and 5.5 km south from town centre on the Icefields Parkway. There are hostels on Whistlers Road and at Maligne Canyon.

Fairmont Jasper Park Lodge

To reach Jasper Park Lodge follow Connaught Drive north from town to the Yellowhead Highway. Drive east for 1.7 km to the Maligne Lake Road. Cross

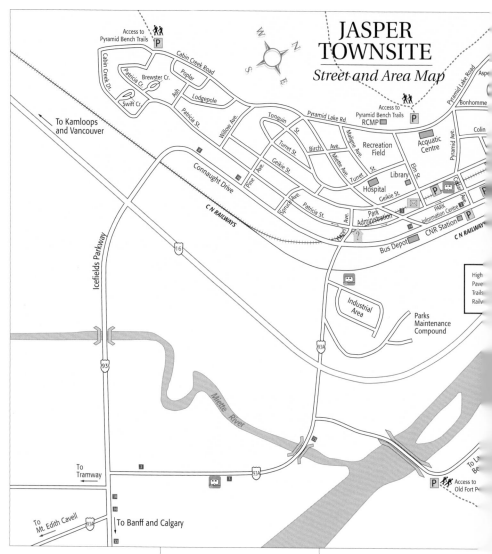

JASPER TOWNSITE
Street and Area Map

the bridge over the Athabasca River and turn right. The turnoff for Annette Lake and Edith Lake is encountered 1.4 km after. Keep straight ahead for Jasper Park Lodge and Lac Beauvert.

The Grand Trunk Pacific Railway was the brainchild of Charles Melville Hays. Hays was well aware of the Canadian Pacific Railway's successful mountain hotel business, and had grand plans for hotel development in Jasper. The GTPR intended to build one hotel in town and another at the mouth of the Fiddle River, near the park's eastern boundary. This second hotel, Chateau Miette, would capitalize on nearby Miette Hot Springs the way the Banff Springs Hotel had capitalized on hot springs at Banff. From Chateau Miette, patrons would be transported to Miette Hot Springs by a 15-km monorail. The waters of the springs would be piped to the hotel.

Hays drowned on the Titanic in 1912 and the impetus for these plans was lost. Financial problems plagued the young railway, and the townsite lodge never developed beyond a temporary settlement called "Tent City" on the

To Patricia ⊠ and
Pyramid Lakes ⊞ (7 km)
Horse Corrals 3km

Patricia
Circle

To Highway 16

Connaught Drive

To Edmonton/
Miette Hot Springs ⊞

To Jasper
Park Lodge ⊟

YEAR-ROUND ACCOMMODATIONS:

1 • Amethyst Lodge
2 • Astoria Hotel
3 • Athabasca Hotel
4 • Chateau Jasper
5 • Jasper Inn
6 • Jasper Park Lodge
7 • Lobstick Lodge
8 • Maligne Lodge
9 • Marmot Lodge
10 • Mount Robson Inn
11 • Pyramid Lake Resort
12 • Sawridge Lake Resort
13 • Tonquin Inn
14 • Whistler's Inn

SEASONAL ACCOMMODATIONS:

15 • Alpine Village
16 • Becker's Chalets
17 • Bonhomme Bungalows
18 • Jasper House Bungalows
19 • Miette Hot Springs Resort
20 • Patricia Lake Bungalows
21 • Pine Bungalows
22 • Sunwapta Falls
23 • Tekarra Lodge

Fairmont Jasper Park Lodge with Roche Bonhomme in the distance

Lac Beauvert with Mt. Edith Cavell in the background

shores of Lac Beauvert (bow-VAIR). Lingering plans for the Chateau Miette were finally dropped in 1916 when the railway line at that location was moved to the opposite side of the Athabasca River.

The Canadian government took over the GTPR in 1919, and in 1922 amalgamated it with the Canadian Northern, creating the Canadian National Railway. The CNR bought the lease for Tent City and constructed Jasper Park Lodge on the site. The main lodge building was claimed to be the world's largest log structure at the time. For $3.00 a day, guests could enjoy luxuries that equalled those available at the CPR's mountain hotels. By 1925, they could partake in golf on an 18-hole course as well. Reflecting Jasper's increasing popularity with visitors, expansion took place in 1927-28. The new lodge had a capacity of 600 guests. The CNR built a network of walking and horse trails along the east bank of the Athabasca River. Many are still used today.

Jasper Park Lodge burned on July 15, 1952. It was soon replaced by the present structure, built at a cost of $3 million. Today, Jasper Park Lodge is operated by Fairmont Hotels and Resorts, and accommodates 430 guests. When those staying in outlying cabins order room service, the food may be delivered by a waiter on bicycle.

Lac Beauvert, Edith Lake, Annette Lake

There are more than 800 lakes and ponds in Jasper National Park. More than 60 of these are within 15 km of Jasper townsite. Many of the small lakes are kettle ponds. These were created by melting blocks of glacial ice at the end of the

Jasper Information Centre

Operation Habakkuk

Winter 1942: The enemy had sunk more than 600 Allied ships. British prime minister Winston Churchill put out the word—any idea would be considered to cut the losses, no matter how far-fetched, no matter how expensive. Geoffrey Pyke, an inmate of an English mental hospital, put forward the idea of a monstrous aircraft carrier constructed of ice—a "bergship." It wouldn't burn if torpedoed, or melt in the chilly waters of the North Atlantic.

Desperate, the Allied Chiefs of Staff thought it over. Lord Louis Mountbatten demonstrated the merits of an ice boat to Churchill by playing with ice cubes in the bathtub at 10 Downing Street. They commissioned Pyke to draw up plans, and decided to build a 1,000-tonne prototype somewhere cold and remote…Canada would do.

Winter, 1943: The bizarre story shifted to the shore of Patricia Lake. Here, Geoffrey Pyke,

out on a pass, supervised the construction of the ice boat under the code name Operation Habakkuk. (Habakkuk was a Biblical prophet who promised "a work in your days which ye will not believe.")

Pyke invented pykecrete—ice that contained wood chips, moss, paper and sawdust. Experimentation proved that spruce chips gave more strength and flotation than pine chips. Still, pykecrete was not overly buoyant. The planned 650-metre-long, 20-storey-high, 2-million-tonne ice vessel would certainly bob below the surface, even without its complement of 2,000 crew members and 26 aircraft. It would also require all the commercially available wood chips in Canada. Pyke, true to form, suggested that the ice be filled with air. No one recorded whether tax dollars were spent pursuing this option.

The project employed

Doukhobors who were conscientious objectors and avowed pacifists. When they discovered the intent of their labours, they peacefully sat down on the job. Thus ended the first season of work.

The following winter, $75 million was budgeted for the project. The work was moved to other "cold Canadian places"—Lake Louise and Newfoundland. But pykecrete was a failure. As the Allies gained the upper hand in Europe, the idea of an ice boat melted into oblivion. Despite claims that a boat that can double as a refrigerator will revolutionize the fishing industry, the idea has never re-solidified.

Little remains at Patricia Lake of the zany industry of 1943. In 1988, divers placed a cairn and plaque on the lake bottom, where lie the remains of a shed that once housed the prototype of H.M.S. *Habakkuk*.

Jasper Tramway with the town of Jasper in the valley below

Wisconsin Glaciation. Lac Beauvert, Edith Lake and Annette Lake originated in this manner.

Lac Beauvert (bow-VAIR) means "beautiful green lake" in French. The lake is fed in part by underground discharges of the Maligne drainage system. (See page 237.) You can walk around the lake by following the trail that begins at the boat house. Canada geese and elk frequent the trail through the golf course. Please keep to the path.

Annette Lake and Edith Lake are popular for picnicking, swimming, and birdwatching. You may see common loons. The interpretive trail around Annette Lake is wheelchair accessible. Edith Lake was named for the wife of a railway superintendent, and Annette Lake for the wife of a park superintendent. The forest around these lakes contains stands of Douglas fir, white spruce, lodgepole pine and trembling aspen. Elk and mule deer are common.

Old Fort Point

To reach Old Fort Point, head south from the intersection of Hazel Avenue and Connaught Drive in town. Cross the Yellowhead Highway. Turn left onto Lac Beauvert Road and follow this one kilometre across the Athabasca River to the trailhead. You may also make the loop hike around Lac Beauvert from here.

Fur trade scout David Thompson was the first Euro-Canadian to cross Athabasca Pass, in the winter of 1810-11. While Thompson was away, his associate, William Henry, remained near the present site of Jasper to construct an outpost for the North West Company. Old Fort Point, directly east of Jasper across the Athabasca River, commemorates a possible location for this post. Named Henry House, it was the first permanent Euro-Canadian habitation in the Rockies.

There is no evidence that Henry House stood atop the knoll now called Old Fort Point. Most historians suspect

The Whistlers

The dome-shaped mountain southwest of Jasper is named The Whistlers. You can ride the Jasper Tramway to near the summit of this 2,464 m mountain, from which there is a spectacular view of the Athabasca and Miette valleys. To reach the Jasper Tramway, follow the Icefields Parkway 2.5 km south from town to Whistlers Road. Turn right and follow this road four kilometres. If you don't want to pay to get to the summit of The Whistlers, you can hike the 7.9-km trail that departs from km 2.7 on the Whistlers Road.

In its seven minute climb, the Jasper Tramway ascends 937 m, whisking you from forested valley bottom to the stark mountain top of The Whistlers. From the upper terminal, if you are well-shod and warmly-clothed, you can walk the rocky summit trail. This is the easiest way to a mountain summit in the Rockies.

The Whistlers is in the alpine ecoregion—the domain of strong winds, harsh sunlight, poor soils and brief summers. Your first impression may be of a mountain top devoid of life. However, the rocky soils of The Whistlers support a surprising array of vegetation.

Survival here is a precarious affair for plants. The harsh conditions dictate ingenious adaptive features. Alpine plants are minute, and hug the ground to reduce their exposure to wind. Leaves are frequently thick and waxy to assist in retaining moisture. The blooms, although colourful, are not long-lived, as energy must be conserved. Some plants are mat-like, and grow outwards in a circular fashion. Frequently, the centre of the mat will die off, as the plant prunes itself and directs its energy toward new growth. The mats, both dead and growing, help prevent soils from blowing away, and provide opportunities for other vegetation to take root.

The Whistlers exhibits hallmarks of a glacial landscape. Its domed summit was completely covered by ice during past ice ages. Huge blocks known as glacial erratics were left on the mountain top as the glaciers receded. Several bowl-shaped depressions called cirques were eroded by glaciers into the mountain's flanks.

Today, the repetitive freezing and thawing of moisture trapped in rocky crevices continues to lever apart the boulders on the mountain top, helping to create new soil. This subtle erosional process is part of a natural regime of slow transformation, whereby rock becomes soil, soil is stabilized by vegetation, and a small alpine meadow appears.

You may see Columbian ground squirrels, least chipmunks, golden-mantled ground squirrels, hoary marmots and white-tailed ptarmigan on The Whistlers. Mountain caribou sometimes frequent the slopes to the south and west. More than 150,000 people visit The Whistlers each summer. Snow patches frequently linger, making it difficult to find and stay on the trail. A single footstep off-trail can destroy an alpine plant, obliterating decades of growth in an instant. Please make every effort to stay on the trail.

"the fort" was located somewhere between the point and Edith Lake, possibly near today's Jasper Park Lodge. Some historians have ventured that Old Fort Point is a misnomer, and that Old *Ford* Point was the original name for this feature. A ford is a river crossing place.

The point is a *roche moutonée*—a landform carved by glacial ice. The streamlined, southwest slopes faced into the flow of ice, and the craggy northeast slopes faced away. The loop-hike at Old Fort Point travels through Douglas fir, aspen and pine forest, and provides a view of Jasper townsite and the Athabasca and Miette valleys. You may inspect the plaque unveiled when the Athabasca River was proclaimed a Canadian Heritage River in 1989.

Miette Hot Springs

A 120 km excursion that follows the Athabasca Valley to the northeastern part of Jasper National Park, with great opportunity to see elk and bighorn sheep. The Miette Hot Springs—hottest in the Rockies—are at the end of a 19 km sideroad. En route, you can explore the ruins of Pocahontas, a 1920s coal mining community. Strong hikers can ascend the Sulphur Skyline trail for a stunning overview of Jasper's front ranges.

Pyramid Lake Road

The 8 km Pyramid Lake Road climbs north from Jasper onto a forested bench, providing access to Patricia Lake and Pyramid Lake, and two trailheads. The road initially parallels the western edge of Jasper townsite. Follow any cross-street west to reach it, and then turn right (north). The road climbs steeply onto the bench, which is dotted with a myriad of tarns—lakes scoured from the bedrock during ice-age glaciations.

Cottonwood Slough is on the left at km 2, an excellent birdwatching location. The slough is the handiwork of beavers, who have dammed a slow moving stream. You may also see muskrat here. Large Douglas fir trees grace the grassy hillsides north of the slough. This Douglas fir savannah is one of the most uncommon habitats in the Rockies. Pyramid Lake stables is on the right at km 4. The Cottonwood Slough trailhead is on the left, opposite the stable turnoff.

The road follows the east shore of Patricia Lake, which was the setting for Operation Habbakuk (see box, p.222) during World War II. At km 6.5, you reach the south shore of Pyramid Lake. The road follows the lake's east shore for 1.5 km to a turnaround and picnic area. The 11 km Palisade Lookout trail begins here.

Pyramid Mountain forms the backdrop at the lake, its quartzite cliffs tinged red. The lake is a particularly pleasing destination in autumn, when aspen trees on the opposite shore add more colour to the scene. Pyramid Lake is on the only lake in Jasper on which power boats may be launched. Δ

Hoary Marmot

The Whistlers is named for the piercing whistle of the hoary marmot. Similar in appearance to the woodchuck, this large member of the rodent family lives in the quartzite boulderfields on the mountain top. Grasses, leaves, flowers and berries make up its diet. Grizzly bear, lynx and eagles are its predators. The marmot has the perfect answer to tough times in the alpine: when the snow flies and the going gets tough, it goes to sleep. Remarkably, it hibernates nine months of the year.

The Athabasca Parkway

T he Athabasca Parkway (Highway 93A) follows the route of the original Icefields Parkway from a point 7.5 km south of Jasper to Athabasca Falls, 33.1 km south of Jasper. When the Icefields Parkway was upgraded in the late 1950s, a different route for the improved road was chosen in this part of the Athabasca Valley. The Athabasca Parkway became an alternate route. You can combine it with the Mt. Edith Cavell Road and the Icefields Parkway to make an interesting loop drive from Jasper.

Athabasca Parkway to Mt. Edith Cavell Road

The Athabasca Parkway follows the west bank of the Athabasca River. As you climb away from the river, you can appreciate the breadth of the Athabasca Valley. The mountains on the opposite side of the valley are part of the Maligne Range. The most northerly summit is Mt. Tekarra (2,694 m), named for James Hector's Iroquois guide in 1859. At kilometre two, you cross Portal Creek. There is a picnic area nearby.

Marmot Basin is one of four commercial ski areas in the Rocky Mountain parks. You can reach it by following the 10.9-km access road from the Athabasca Parkway, 600 m south of the Portal Creek picnic area. The ski area and lifts are closed in summer, but the view of the Athabasca Valley from road's end is worth the excursion on a fair day. The Portal Creek trail begins at km 6.6 on the access road. This is one of the trailheads used by backpackers on the Tonquin Valley loop.

Downhill skiing at Jasper began when a few runs were cleared on The Whistlers in 1937. In 1949, slopes farther to the south at Marmot Basin began to attract skiers, who used snowmobiles instead of rope tows to reach the top. Development of the ski area began in 1962, and the paved road was completed in 1970.

Mt. Edith Cavell Road

The Mt. Edith Cavell Road is 5.2 km south along the Athabasca Parkway from the Icefields Parkway junction. Completed in 1924, the narrow, winding, 14.5-km-long road leads to the base of Mt. Edith Cavell. The road is not suitable for large RVs or camper trailers. A trailer drop-off is provided at the junction with the Athabasca Parkway. The Mt. Edith Cavell Road is generally closed by snow from October until late May.

Tonquin Valley

The Tonquin Valley is one of the most scenic upper subalpine environments in the Rockies, and one of the most popular backpacking areas in Jasper. The principal attractions are Amethyst Lakes and the imposing 1200-metre-high cliff of The Ramparts. The 44-km Tonquin Valley trail connects Astoria and Portal creeks, making a horseshoe from the Mt. Edith Cavell Road to the Marmot Basin road. You can see some of the high peaks of the Tonquin Valley from viewpoints on the Mt. Edith Cavell Road.

Astoria was a fur trade fort operated by the Pacific Fur Company at the mouth of the Columbia River in Oregon. *The Tonquin* was one of the company's boats. Some of the company's traders crossed Athabasca Pass, southwest of here, in the years following 1814.

To obtain a fine view of Mt. Edith Cavell and Cavell Lake, walk the short distance downhill from the Tonquin Valley trailhead at km 12.5, to the bridge at the lake's outlet. This

left: Mt. Edith Cavell and Cavell Lake

prospect is especially pleasing in early morning and late evening. There is a hostel opposite the trailhead.

Mt. Edith Cavell

Mt. Edith Cavell (3,363 m) is the highest mountain in the vicinity of Jasper townsite. Natives knew it as the "White Ghost," probably in reference to the snow-covered mountain's appearance in moonlight. The voyageurs of the fur trade called it "La Montagne de la Grande Traverse" (the mountain of the great crossing). When they saw Mt. Edith Cavell from the northeast, it meant that the long approach to Athabasca Pass was almost over, and that the "great crossing" of the Athabasca River lay just ahead.

In the early 1900s the mountain was for a short time known as Mt. Fitzhugh. In 1915, surveyor A.O. Wheeler was asked by the Geographic Board of Canada to recommend a mountain to commemorate nurse Edith Cavell. Remaining in Brussels after it fell during World War I, Cavell was executed for allegedly assisting Allied prisoners of war to escape. Wheeler chose "the beautiful mountain facing the Athabasca Valley," and the name was officially bestowed the following year. A memorial service is held for Edith Cavell each summer in Jasper. Climbers have taken a cross to the summit.

The road to the base of the mountain was one of the first constructed in Jasper, in 1924. At no other location in the Rockies do you drive so directly toward such an impressive mountain wall as

This photo from the 1920s shows Angel Glacier cascading into the valley floor

that of the north face of Mt. Edith Cavell. And so close too—the base of the cliffs is less than 1.5 km from the parking area, and the summit rises an equal distance above. A teahouse formerly stood near the parking lot at road's end. It operated from 1929 to 1972.

Mt. Edith Cavell is popular with mountaineers. The first ascent of the mountain occurred in 1915. The east ridge (left-hand skyline), first climbed in 1924, is considered one of the classic alpine rock climbs in the Rockies. The first ascent of the spectacular north face in 1961 marked the beginning of extreme alpine climbing in the Rockies. If you're wondering which is the mountain's highest point, it's the central bump on the nearly horizontal summit ridge.

The rock layers in Mt. Edith Cavell angle upward to the northeast. They are the western arm of a massive arch-shaped fold—an anticline. The Athabasca Valley has been

eroded downward through this fold, removing the crest of the arch.

A Disappearing Angel

The Path of the Glacier trail at Mt. Edith Cavell takes you through a recently glaciated landscape. Less than a century ago, the entire area traversed by the trail was buried under the combined ice of the Angel and Cavell glaciers. Today, hardy vegetation is in the process of recolonizing this area.

The Little Ice Age of 1200 to 1900 AD was a period of minor global cooling. Glaciers in the Rockies advanced significantly during this time—some as much as three kilometres beyond their present positions. When the first explorers arrived in the Rockies, most of the glaciers were near the maximum of the Little Ice Age advance. Their subsequent retreat has been well-documented. The rise just south of the parking lot is a terminal

This photograph of Angel Glacier shows the extent of its recession over the last 80 years

moraine, deposited by Cavell Glacier at the maximum of the Little Ice Age advance. Lateral moraines that were pushed up alongside the glacier are prominent on either side of the valley. By studying these moraines, you can get a sense of the former size of Cavell Glacier.

The pinnacles of ice on the upper cliffs of the Angel Glacier are called seracs (sair-RACKS). Angel Glacier formerly descended to the valley floor and merged with the ice of Cavell Glacier. In the 1940s, Angel Glacier broke contact with Cavell Glacier and began to retreat. Today, the hanging glacier frequently avalanches ice and snow onto the surface of Cavell Glacier. If conditions favouring glacial retreat persist, the "body" and "wings" of Angel Glacier will eventually disappear.

The Path of the Glacier leads to Cavell Glacier. The accumulation zone of this glacier is the north face of Mt. Edith Cavell. Snow does not usually bond to slopes steeper than 40°. As a result, most of the snow that falls on the north face slides off in avalanches. These avalanches are funnelled down couloirs and gullies onto the valley floor. Here, in the near-perpetual shade cast by the mountain, the snow accumulates and is transformed into the ice of Cavell Glacier.

In 1963, the retreating glacier uncovered a depression that has since filled with meltwater. You will often see icebergs or "growlers" floating in this marginal lake. The small niche glacier above and slightly left of Cavell Glacier is called Ghost Glacier—a reference to Mt. Edith Cavell's original native name "White Ghost."

Allow an hour to walk the Path of the Glacier trail. Lighting on Angel Glacier is best before midmorning.

Cavell Meadows

If you have half a day and want to explore the upper subalpine and alpine ecoregions, you will enjoy the 3.8-km Cavell Meadows trail. Dress warmly for this hike, and please stay on the beaten path.

The trail climbs steeply over an old lateral moraine of Cavell Glacier and abruptly enters ancient subalpine forest. This sudden transition from moraine to lush forest marks the trimline, the point where ice encroached into forest during the Little Ice Age advance of the glacier.

The damp, cool floor of this forest is carpeted with feathermosses, lichens and fungi. Dwarf dogwood (bunchberry) grows in patches. Tree lichens cling to the branches. Leaving the forest, the trail enters subalpine meadows. A variety of wildflowers blooms here during July and August. From this area, you have impressive views of Angel Glacier and the cliffs of Mt. Edith Cavell.

The trail continues through tree islands of stunted krummholz and emerges onto alpine tundra. The subsoil here is permanently frozen, so trees cannot take root. The topsoil thaws enough in summer to allow mats of heather, willow and mountain avens to grow, along with a host of other moisture-loving wildflowers. Caribou and grizzly bear sometimes visit these meadows.

Mt. Edith Cavell Road to Whirlpool River

Back on the Athabasca Parkway, the Wabasso Campground is four kilometres south of the Mt. Edith Cavell Road junction. *Wabasso* is Cree for "rabbit." Otto's

Cache picnic area is two kilometres farther south. The Otto Brothers—Jack, Bruce and Closson—were guides and outfitters at Jasper and Field in the early 1900s. Emergency assistance may be available at the Cavell warden station nearby.

The Athabasca Valley contains the largest area of montane habitat in the Rockies. Most of the valley burned in a tremendous fire in 1889. A fire-succession forest of lodgepole pine now towers over the sparse ground cover of juniper, bearberry, buffaloberry, twinflower, dwarf dogwood and wild strawberry. Here and there are stands of balsam poplar, trembling aspen and a few white birch. Black bears and grizzly bears frequent the valley floor, especially in July and August when the buffaloberry bushes are in

A mountaineer's view looking down Angel Glacier from the summit of Mt. Edith Cavell

fruit. The red and amber berries are a staple food. A grizzly bear may eat 200,000 berries in a day.

Whirlpool River

From the junction of the Whirlpool and Athabasca rivers, the westbound voyageurs of the fur trade ascended the Whirlpool Valley

Succession: From Ice to Forest

Although the forefield of Cavell Glacier may at first glance appear devoid of vegetation, hardy plants grow here. The process of succession—in this case, the transformation from barren moraine to subalpine forest—may take more than a thousand years. Less than one per cent of the area covered by ice a century ago is presently vegetated.

Soils in areas that have recently been uncovered by glacial ice are alkaline. After the ice retreats, it takes several decades for rainfall and snowmelt to leach the alkalinity from the soil. Then, the hardiest of alpine plants take root: willows, mountain avens, moss campion, mountain fireweed, mosses and sedges.

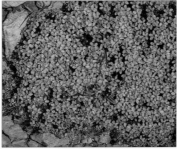

Moss campion

Mat-like and low in stature, mountain avens and moss campion anchor the thin soil. They fix nitrogen from the air into the soil, enriching it so that less hardy plants may grow. The pioneering plants take advantage of areas that receive the most sunlight and that are sheltered from wind. They also grow along stream

banks, although volatile glacial melt streams may wash them away or leave them high and dry.

After decades, small communities of vegetation may provide enough cover for seedlings of subalpine fir, Engelmann spruce and whitebark pine to grow. It takes centuries for these trees to mature in the harsh conditions close to glaciers. The scattered tree islands create a broken forest. If the glacier does not re-advance and if conditions favouring tree growth persist, the sheltered meadows between the tree islands eventually fill with seedlings, which grow to become a climax subalpine forest such as the one just north of the parking lot.

Mt. Edith Cavell

to Athabasca Pass on the continental divide. From the pass, they descended to the Columbia River and fur trade outposts in the Pacific northwest. A roadside display near the Whirlpool River describes the route of the fur trade.

The Athabasca River has the greatest volume of any river in the Rocky Mountain parks. From this vantage, you can well imagine the harrowing prospect that confronted the voyageurs. They were obliged to cross this river with their horses and loads. Sometimes, they constructed makeshift rafts or simply waded and swam towards the opposite bank. Not all of them survived.

Moab Lake

The graveled Moab Lake Road branches southwest from the Athabasca Parkway, and follows the north bank of the Whirlpool River for 7 km to a parking area. The short trail to Moab Lake offers the opportunity to trace a fraction of the voyageurs' fur trade route across the Rockies. From the parking area, follow the Athabasca Pass trail 300 m and turn right to reach the shore of Moab Lake. The lake is celebrated by anglers for its rainbow trout. Archeological evidence indicates it was frequented by natives in prehistoric times.

Leach Lake

When glacial ice receded from the Athabasca Valley at the end of Wisconsin Glaciation, large blocks of ice detached. These subsequently melted into slumps in the moraine on the valley floor, creating kettle ponds. Leach Lake is a kettle pond. Across the lake, you can see an unusual view of Mt. Edith Cavell.

As with most kettle ponds, Leach Lake has no surface outlet. Its waters leach through glacial sediments and rubble on the lake bottom. Δ

Horned Lark

Cavell Meadows is home to the only songbird in the Rockies that lives above treeline: the horned lark. Its fragile, melodious voice is a counterpoint to the harsh terrain of the alpine ecoregion. In flight, the horned lark is easy to recognize: It folds its wings between flaps. Two small, black tufts on the cap give the bird its name. The

horned lark eats insects, nests on the ground and migrates south in winter.

The Maligne Lake Road

T he-44 km-long Maligne Lake Road explores the Maligne Valley south-east of Jasper. Highlights include Maligne Canyon, Medicine Lake and Maligne Lake. The road is one of the best for viewing wildlife in the Rockies: bighorn sheep, deer, elk, moose, caribou, grizzly bear and

black bear. The author has even seen a cougar on this road.

The Maligne Lake Road is open year-round, although it may be closed in winter during times of avalanche hazard. The speed limit is 60 km per hour. You can easily spend a full day exploring the Maligne Valley. Camping is not permitted. If you would like to take a boat tour on Maligne Lake, you should make a booking before leaving Jasper, 852-3370.

The French word *maligne* (mah-LEEN) means "wicked." It was given to the river in 1846 by Jesuit missionary Pierre Jean de Smet, after he made a difficult crossing of the river at its mouth on the Athabasca River.

Jasper to Maligne Canyon

Follow the Yellowhead Highway, 4.4 km east from the Ice-

fields Parkway junction (1.7 km east from the east Jasper exit) to the Maligne Lake Road. Turn right (east) and cross the bridge over the Athabasca River. The bridge was built in 1940. In 1985, it was dedicated to Henry John Moberly, who was in charge of Jasper House from 1856-61, and who later became a pioneer settler of the Athabasca Valley.

Across the bridge, turn left (north). For the next two kilometres the Maligne Lake Road bisects one of the best examples of montane meadow in the Rockies. Only 5.5 per cent of Jasper National Park is in the montane ecoregion, and most of this area is lodgepole pine forest, so montane meadows are rare.

Montane meadows are sustained by localized ground fires. The fires prevent dense forest from developing. Fire-resistant Douglas firs form the islands of mature forest. Scattered stands of trembling aspen, balsam poplar and white birch rejuvenate after each fire.

In summer, these meadows are frequented by elk, coyote and Columbian ground squirrels. In winter, they receive little snowfall, and offer important winter habitat for elk, deer and bighorn

sheep, who desire the grasses. Unfortunately, most development in the Rockies has taken place in the montane ecoregion. The few montane meadows that exist have been fragmented by roads, railways and townsites. Suppression of natural fires has allowed forest to encroach on some of the meadows, further reducing their extent.

The turnoff for the Sixth Bridge of Maligne Canyon and the Jasper warden office is at km 2.3. There are six bridges across Maligne Canyon. The trail from the Sixth Bridge allows you to walk the entire length of the canyon. Back on the Maligne Lake Road, a sideroad at km 3.2 leads to the Fifth Bridge and a picnic area in the middle reach of Maligne Canyon. You may see bighorn sheep at the rock cuts nearby on the Maligne Lake Road.

You pass the northern terminus of the Skyline trail at km 5.5. In this vicinity, you can see Roche Bonhomme in the Colin Range, straight ahead. The mountain's name is French for "good fellow rock." The skyline ridge resembles the profile of a man's face, looking skyward. On the upper slopes, you can see the charred forest of a 1985 forest fire. The viewpoint at kilome-

left: Maligne Canyon

JOINS
PAGE
242

JOINS
PAGE
249

JOINS PAGE 212

JOINS PAGE

Maligne
Canyon

RANGE

2820 Sirdar
Mountain

Jacques
Lake

Maligne

1600

Summit
Lakes

Lake
Edith
Lake Annette

1018±

Beaver
Lake

JASPER PARK LODGE
GOLF COURSE

JASPER

Beauvert

Signal
2312 Mountain

Underground
Stream

Medicine

1436±

Whistlers Campground

Excelsior
Mountain

Wapiti Campground

Mount
Tekarra 2694

The
Watchtower

Centre
Mountain

PARC

Lake

Wabasso
Lakes

MARMOT
SKI AREA

1200

Amber
Mountain

·2628

Prairie de
la Vache

2200

Curator
Mountain

ATHABASCA

·1214

Antler
Mountain

Marmot
Mountain

Wabasso
Campground

93A

ICEFIELDS PARKWAY

MALIGNE

Lectern
Peak

River

1600

Hardisty

Aquila
Mountain

93

Franchère
Peak

2400

Mount
Hardisty 2716

N

Cavell
Lake

Leach
Lake

Horseshoe
Lake

RANGE

Angel
Glacier

Mount
Edith Cavell ·3368

Moab
Lake

Athabasca
Falls

2400

Verdant

2800

PROMENADE

Mount
Kerkeslin

2956

Pass

2879

DES

River

GLACIERS

N   T   A   G   N

·1215

1400

2400

Geraldine
Lakes

Mount
Fryatt ·3361

Honey

·3020

Diver gence

1828±

Mount
Christie

River

Dam
Ridge

·3103

Medicine Lake

tre six overlooks the Athabasca Valley and Jasper townsite. There is a hostel opposite the turnoff for Maligne Canyon, at km 6.3.

Maligne Canyon

At the end of the Wisconsin Glaciation, the mouth of the Maligne Valley was left hanging 120 m above the Athabasca Valley. Initially, the Maligne River cascaded into the Athabasca River as a waterfall. Over time, the river took advantage of weaknesses in the bedrock to erode Maligne Canyon—the longest, deepest, and most interesting limestone canyon in the Rockies. As one early visitor commented: "Any other canyon is like a crack in a teacup."

The bedrock here is Palliser limestone, and is being eroded by three processes: solution by naturally acidic rainwater and runoff, corrosion by the grinding effects of coarse glacial silt in the water, and sheer hydraulic force. These processes of erosion are relatively rapid in geological terms. Although two kilometres long and 55 m deep, Maligne Canyon is only 11,000 years old. But don't expect to see any changes during your visit—the canyon is being made deeper at the rate of half a centimetre each year.

The three trailheads at Maligne Canyon allow you to choose different experiences. The short loop from the Maligne Canyon teahouse is on a paved path, and provides quick access to the canyon's highlights. Part of this path is wheelchair accessible. The longer, uphill walks from Fifth and Sixth Bridge are on rougher trails, but allow a more complete appreciation of the canyon and its many interesting features.

The canyon is deepest in the vicinity of the Second Bridge. The highest waterfall, 23 m, is just above the First Bridge. Here, the entire volume of the river is forced through a narrow breach before plunging over the precipice. The airborne spray generated by this waterfall coats the canyon walls and edges and sustains moisture-loving plants. A canyon forest of Douglas fir and white spruce clings tenaciously to the canyon rim. The narrow, vertical world of the canyon is home to pack rats, mice and common ravens, whose nests are visible in places. Maligne Canyon is one of two nesting sites in Alberta for the black swift. You may also see the American dipper (water ouzel).

The rocks of Maligne Canyon contain fossils: snail-like gastropods, clam-like brachiopods, squid-like cephalopods, crinoids (related to starfish) and corals. Two prominent examples of fossils are displayed in the upper canyon between the tea house and the First Bridge. Please do not touch them.

If you carefully study some

of the boulders at trailside, you will notice that they are different in appearance from the rock of the adjacent canyon walls. These boulders are glacial erratics—rocks transported from elsewhere by glacial ice, and deposited here when the ice receded. Glaciologists use the presence of erratics to help determine the geographical origin of glacial ice.

There are good examples of potholes above the Second Bridge. A pothole is a circular depression that was drilled into the bedrock by the relentless action of eddies and backwaters. For a drill bit, the river used pebbles trapped in a slight depression, replacing them with boulders when the depression was enlarged.

When the river changed course, some potholes were left high and dry, frequently with the rounded pebbles and boulders in place. Some potholes have filled with silt and thin soils and have become hanging gardens on the canyon walls, where ferns, mosses, shrubs and even small trees take root.

More water flows out of Maligne Canyon than flows into it on the surface. Downstream from the Fourth Bridge, you can see where springs emerge from the canyon walls. These springs are outlets for the Maligne karst system. Water that drains underground at Medicine Lake, 17 km south, emerges here. (See page 237.)

If you are hiking downhill from the teahouse, remember: It's all uphill on the way back.

Maligne Canyon to Medicine Lake

Between Maligne Canyon and Medicine Lake, the Maligne Lake Road follows the Maligne River through lodgepole pine forest. The Maligne Valley is a strike valley, oriented along a fault in the earth's crust. This fault separates the front ranges to the east from the eastern main ranges the west. The steeply tilted front range mountains of the Colin Range and Queen Elizabeth Ranges are predominantly sawtooth mountains. The rounded summits of the Maligne Range are an unusual shape for eastern main range peaks. As with most other domed mountains

Moose

The wet meadows at roadside between Medicine Lake and Maligne Lake are frequented by moose. The moose is the largest antlered animal in the world, and is a circumpolar species—it also occurs in northern Europe and northern Asia. There is no mistaking this massive animal for other members of the deer family. The coat is dark brown or reddish-brown, sometimes verging on black, and lacks the light-coloured rump patch of other deer family members. There is often a loose flap of skin on the throat, known as a bell or dewlap. The legs are long and gangly with lighter-coloured fur than the rest of the coat.

The male (bull) carries pale antlers that fan outwards like outstretched hands. The muzzle is down-turned and the lips are large. An adult bull weighs up to

600 kg, and stands two metres tall at the shoulder. Aquatic plants are the favourite summer foods of moose. In winter, the moose moves to higher elevations, where it browses on shrubs that protrude through the snowpack.

Moose can run up to 55 km per hour, and are capable swimmers. Wolves are the principal

predator. Moose are in decline in the Rocky Mountain parks. Kills on the railway and highways and a parasitic liver fluke have taken a heavy toll in recent years. Seven moose were killed on Jasper's roads in 1990. In addition, active suppression of forest fires has reduced the extent of shrubland in the parks, forcing moose to look elsewhere for habitat.

Maligne Lake sunrise

of modest elevation in the Rockies, they were completely covered by glaciers in past ice ages. The ice removed the characteristic angles, towers and pinnacles.

The mountains of the eastern main ranges and front ranges differ in colour as well as in shape. The eastern main ranges near Jasper consist mostly of colourful quartzite. The front range peaks are drab, gray limestone.

You pass the Watchtower Valley trailhead at km 18.6. As you approach Medicine Lake at km 21, note the jumble of rocks on the east side of the road. This is debris from the rockslide that dammed the outlet of Medicine Lake.

Medicine Lake

The Maligne Valley contains what may be the longest underground river system in the world. This river system begins at Medicine Lake. Its outlets are in Maligne Canyon and in some of the lakes near Jasper Park Lodge.

Rainwater and runoff are naturally slightly acidic, and are able to dissolve limestone. Cracks in the bedrock are enlarged, creating deep fissures. When connected, these fissures may become subterranean waterways, known as karst.

The outflow from Maligne Lake flows on the surface via the Maligne River to Medicine Lake. In the bottom of Medicine Lake are a series of holes—karst features known as sinks. They allow the lake water to drain into an underground waterway at the rate of 24,000 litres per second.

During the runoff of spring and early summer, the capacity of the sink holes is exceeded and the lake level rises. In some years, the lake overflows into the normally dry riverbed beside the road at the northern end of the lake. By late summer, the volume draining through the sink holes exceeds that of the inflow to the lake, and the water level drops dramatically. By autumn, all that remains of Medicine Lake is a braided stream on an expansive mud flat—a good place to look for moose, elk and mountain caribou. The sink holes probably developed after the rockslide impounded the lake, when the waters were forced to find another outlet. In summer, it takes 20 hours for the water to flow underground from Medicine Lake to Maligne Canyon.

Before the road was constructed along the east shore of Medicine Lake, boats ferried tourists across its waters. The fluctuating lake level played havoc with boat traffic, and unsuccessful attempts were made to bring routine to the schedule by plugging the sink holes with newspapers and mattresses.

The Maligne karst system is one of the most studied in the world. However, the underground waterway, although 17 km long and capable of transporting an enormous volume of water, is too narrow to allow extended access to cavers. Dyes have been released into Medicine Lake, and by observing where they emerge, many of the karst outlets have been determined. However, the exact nature of the intervening system remains unknown.

Medicine Lake to Maligne Lake

The Maligne Lake Road follows the east shore of Medicine Lake beneath the steeply tilted slabs of the Queen Elizabeth Ranges. Watch for bighorn sheep on the road here. The Jacques Lake and Beaver Lake trailhead is at the picnic area at the far end of Medicine Lake. The 1.6-km walk to Beaver Lake is an excellent family outing.

From a pull-off just south of Medicine Lake, scan the mountainside above for the Natural Arch. Cracks in rock are enlarged by the repeated freezing and thawing of water in a process known as frost wedging. Eventually, the rock breaks along the weaknesses. The rock also expands and contracts with changes in temperature. This process of mechanical weathering breaks cliffs apart. Sometimes these erosive powers combine to create unusual features like the Natural Arch. If you look north from this vicinity, you can see the rockslide that dammed Medicine Lake.

Between Medicine Lake and Maligne Lake, the road crosses the Maligne River several times. The large boulders in the riverbed are glacial erratics that were transported by glaciers and left here when the ice receded. The river has many rapids, and is the mainstay of whitewater rafting companies near Jasper. Unfortunately, the river is also breeding and nesting habitat for the harlequin duck—a species in decline in western North America. Studies indicated that the rafting was negatively affecting these ducks.

Mary Schäffer—Mountain Woman

Henry MacLeod, a surveyor with the CPR, made the first recorded visit to Maligne Lake in 1875. It took him three days to travel the 40 km from the Athabasca Valley. Not impressed with the scenery, the trail, or the apparent dead end, he named Maligne "Sorefoot Lake."

Settlers from the Athabasca Valley probably frequented the lake in the late 1800s. However, the next recorded visit was in 1908 by Mary Schäffer and party. Schäffer was a Quaker from Philadelphia who had been visiting the Rockies annually since 1889. In 1907, she set out to find a large, mysterious lake known to the Stoneys as *Chaba Imne*—Beaver Lake. She failed on that attempt, but did manage to reach the headwaters of the Athabasca River.

Schäffer returned in 1908.

Using a map drawn by Sampson Beaver, a Stoney chieftain, Schäffer's party reached Maligne Lake from the south. They built a raft, *The Chaba*, and spent several days exploring, mapping and naming mountains and features. At the request of the Grand Trunk Pacific Railway, Schäffer returned again in 1911 to map the lake from its northern end.

Schäffer was a friend of the Stoneys. They called her *Yahe-Weha*—Mountain Woman. A talented writer and photographer, Schäffer gained fame with the accounts of her travels. She wrote *Old Indian Trails of the Canadian Rockies*. This book was out of print until 1980, when it was republished as *A Hunter of Peace*. It brings to life the experience of pack train travel and exploration in the early 1900s, and is highly recommended.

The river is now closed to rafting during the duck-breeding season. You may also see American dippers in the fast water of the river.

Maligne Lake

There are two parking lots at Maligne Lake. Park on the east side of the lake for the boat tours, Opal Hills trailhead and Schäffer Viewpoint trailhead. Use the parking lot on the west side of the lake for private boat launching, the Skyline trailhead, Bald Hills trailhead and Maligne Pass trailhead. There are picnic tables near both parking lots. Power boats are not permitted on Maligne Lake.

Maligne Lake is by far the largest natural lake in the Canadian Rockies. Fed by

Maligne Lake and Spirit Island

meltwaters from the Brazeau Icefield and other glaciers at its south end, the lake is 22 km long. It has an area of 20.66 square kilometres, an average width of about one kilometre, and a maximum depth of 96 m. Its waters are dammed by the second largest measured rockslide in the Rockies.

About two thirds of the way to the south end of the lake is an alluvial fan—a landform built by sediment transported by a glacially fed stream that descends from Maligne Mountain. This obstruction reduces the lake's width to 200 m. The channel is called Samson Narrows. Spirit Island is nearby, along with the postcard view of the glaciated peaks at the head of the lake.

In the view south from the lake's outlet, Mount Charlton (3,217 m) and Mt. Unwin (3,268 m) are on the west shore, with Leah Peak (2,801 m) and Samson Peak (3,081 m) on the east shore. Directly down the lake are some of the peaks at the lake's headwaters, 30 km distant. The low mountains flanking the lake's outlet on the east side are the Opal Hills, and on the west side, the Bald Hills.

The Skyline trail is a spectacular 44-km backpacking route along the crest of the Maligne Range from Maligne Lake to Jasper. Casual walkers can follow this trail 2.4 km from Maligne Lake to Mona Lake and Lorraine Lake. The Bald Hills and Opal Hills trails

involve more elevation gain, and each requires half a day. These destinations offer an overview of Maligne Lake. The easiest walk nearby is along the east shore of Maligne Lake to Schäffer viewpoint, and a good view of the lake.

The only way to reach the far end of Maligne Lake is by boat or on foot. Commercial boat tours on Maligne Lake began with Curly Phillips' operation in 1928. Phillips built the floating boat house that year. It is now a National Historic Building. Brook trout and rainbow trout are the two most common fish species in the lake. Emergency assistance may be available at the warden station on the west shore of the lake. ∆

239

The Yellowhead Highway

The Yellowhead Highway (Highway 16) is Canada's "other" transcontinental road. It runs east-west through Jasper National Park. As with Highway 1, the Yellowhead Highway follows the line of a transcontinental railway. Originally, two railways competed for

business through Jasper National Park—the Grand Trunk Pacific and the Canadian Northern. When these two lines merged, some of the railway grades were abandoned. The first cars driven from Edmonton to Vancouver in 1922 used the abandoned railway grades to get through Jasper National Park. The Jasper-Edmonton road opened in 1930. It was upgraded and dubbed the Yellowhead Highway in 1968.

The highway is named for Yellowhead Pass on the continental divide, 26 km west of Jasper townsite. The man nicknamed Yellowhead was probably Pierre Bostonais, a blond-haired Iroquois guide. He worked for the Hudson's Bay Company in the 1820s. In French, Yellowhead is *Tête Jaune,* and Bostonais is further commemorated in the village of Tête Jaune Cache (TET-

zjawn-cash), 102 km west of Jasper.

The Yellowhead Highway follows the Athabasca and Miette valleys through Jasper National Park. These valleys are in the montane ecoregion, and are home to elk, deer, moose, black bear, grizzly bear, coyote and wolf. The valleys include extensive wetlands that offer some of the best bird-watching locations in the Rockies.

Yellowhead Highway East: Jasper townsite to the eastern park boundary

Athabasca Valley

The Athabasca Valley is the largest valley in the Rocky Mountain parks. You can appreciate its breadth from the viewpoint on the Yellowhead Highway near Jasper townsite, 2.1 km east of the Icefields Parkway junction. Looking upstream, you can see the small hill on the opposite side of the river—Old Fort Point. Elsewhere in the Athabasca Valley, 72 native archaeological sites have been found. The peaks of the Maligne Range rise to the southeast.

Farther east, you pass the eastern entrance to Jasper townsite and the turnoff for the Maligne Lake Road. There is another viewpoint that overlooks the Athabasca Valley, 11.2 km east of the Icefields Parkway junction. Mt. Edith Cavell (3,363 m) is prominent in the view south from here, over the braided channels of the Athabasca River. The mountain was an important landmark for voyageurs of the fur trade in the 1800s. They called it *La Montagne de la Grande Traverse* (the mountain of the great crossing). Its appearance on the horizon signified that the long approach to Athabasca Pass on the continental divide was almost over, and that the hazardous crossing of the Athabasca River was just ahead. The original trail in the Athabasca Valley was on the opposite side of the river.

As in Banff, the front ranges of Jasper feature many sawtooth and overthrust mountains. Across the Athabasca River are the peaks of the Colin Range. You can see several spectacular folds in these mountains. Colin Fraser was an employee of the Hudson's Bay Company. He was in charge of Jasper House from 1835 to 1849. The forest

---

SuperGuide Recommendations

Sights/Attractions
- Mt. Robson
- Punchbowl Falls
- Miette Hot Springs

Hikes/Activities
- Pocahontas Trail at Miette Hot Springs Road

---

left: Mt. Robson and Robson River

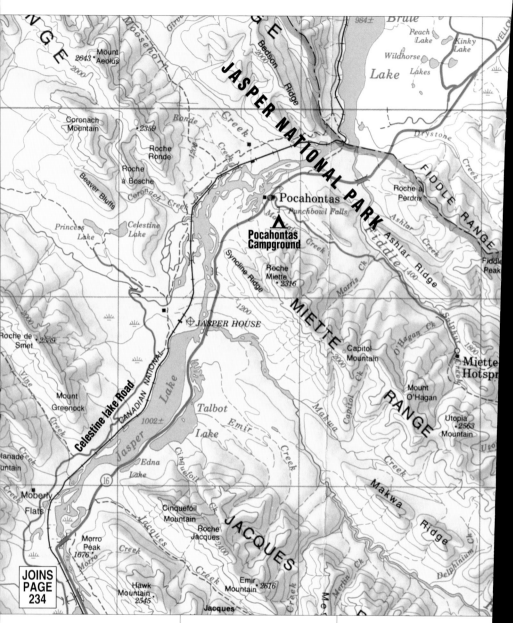

on the lower slopes of the Colin Range was consumed by a prescribed burn in 1989.

Snaring River and Cold Sulphur Spring

The Yellowhead Highway crosses the mouth of the Snaring River five kilometres east of the Celestine Lake Road. The river is named for the "Snare Indians." James Hector reported that this tribe lived in holes in the ground and hunted sheep, deer and moose with snares made of animal hide.

Four kilometres past the Snaring River, the Yellowhead Highway crosses the Athabasca River. The rocky knoll on the east side of the river is a glacially sculpted landform called a roche moutonée. This type of land-form is common in the

Athabasca Valley. A cold mineral spring issues from the base of the knoll, adjacent to the highway. The spring water has a temperature of 9 °C and a strong sulphur odour.

Jasper Lake and Talbot Lake

Much of this section of the Athabasca Valley was formerly occupied by a large lake, created at the end of the Wisconsin Glaciation when the Athabasca River was dammed by moraines. The lake was more than 100 m deep in places, and almost 100 km long. It extended from Yellowhead Pass to the foothills. Fine sediments accumulated on the lake bottom. When the Athabasca River eroded through the moraine

dam, the lake emptied.

Jasper Lake is a remnant of the ancient lake. Its level fluctuates annually. In summer, the Athabasca River floods Jasper Lake to a depth of one metre. In winter, the river level drops, the lake dries up and the exposed sediments are swept by strong winds. The winds deposit some of the sediment against vegetation and rocks, creating dunes.

One series of dunes separates Jasper Lake and Talbot Lake. The Yellowhead Highway travels along this natural causeway. Look for smaller dunes at roadside as you travel east.

As with most valley bottom lakes in the Rockies, the days of Jasper Lake are numbered. Eventually, the Athabasca

River will erode a deeper riverbed, and the annual flooding will cease.

The dunes are anchored by low-growing vegetation such as creeping juniper, bearberry, and Alberta's provincial emblem—prickly wild rose. Inactive dunes also support white spruce. Talbot Lake is in the lee of the dunes. The lake is a good place to look for Canada geese, common loon, osprey, bald eagle and waterfowl. There are beaver lodges at the north end of the lake. In early winter, the winds keep Talbot Lake snow-free, and its surface is popular for ice skating.

A trail from the Talbot Lake viewpoint leads south onto a knoll beneath Cinquefoil (SINK-foil) Mountain. The knoll is named for the five-

Swift's Place

The limestone bluff of The Palisade is 13.6 km east of Jasper townsite. The Palisade marks the division point between the eastern main ranges and the front ranges. The Palisade contains 360-million-year-old limestone of the Palliser Formation. The drab, gray cliff is in marked contrast to the colourful 570-million-year-old Gog quartzite of Pyramid Mountain, which typifies the eastern main ranges near Jasper townsite.

Lewis Swift settled in the Athabasca Valley in 1892 or 1893. At first, he lived in the ruins of Jasper House. Then he built a cabin beneath The Palisade. Here, he ran cattle and traded with the local natives. Before the Grand Trunk Pacific Railway was constructed, Swift's homestead was a

well-known stopping place for travellers in the Athabasca Valley. Explorer A.P. Coleman called it "a delightful oasis of prairie in the heart of the mountains." Swift offered accommodation and information to travellers, and operated a cable ferry across the Athabasca River. On his homestead he had a water-driven mill.

In 1908, Swift held surveyors of the Grand Trunk Pacific Railway at bay with a rifle for three days. The surveyors wanted to run the

rails right through his cabin, but then thought better of the idea and staked the line 10 m from the cabin. With the establishment of Jasper National Park, most natives and settlers were bought out by the federal government. Swift, however, declined; and was granted title to his land in 1911.

The Department of the Interior hesitated at Swift's offer to sell in 1935, so he sold the land privately. The two subsequent owners developed the leasehold as a tourist ranch. Swift's ranch was finally sold to the park in 1962 for $250,000. Most of the historic buildings are now gone. Swift's water wheel is among the artifacts at a site now used as a training centre and residence for park employees.

petalled flower borne by members of the genus *Potentilla*—of which shrubby cinqeufoil is common in the Rockies. From the crest of the knoll, you get a wonderful view of this part of the Athabasca Valley. Bighorn sheep frequent the area, attracted by two mineral licks nearby. Talbot Lake was named for Peter Talbot, a senator from the Alberta community of Lacombe.

Jasper House

In the winter of 1810-11, David Thompson of the North West Company travelled through the Athabasca Valley and crossed Athabasca Pass, establishing a fur trade route across the Rockies. Two years later, the company built a supply post called Rocky Mountain House on Brûlé Lake at the eastern edge of the Rockies. In 1817, the post was supervised by Jasper Hawse. It became known as Jasper's House to distinguish it from other outposts called Rocky Mountain House, on the North Saskatchewan River.

The North West Company and Hudson's Bay Company merged in 1821. Three years later, a new Jasper House was constructed just north of Jasper Lake. It was here that the men who packed the furs and supplies—the voyageurs—exchanged canoes for horses to continue the journey west. A tally of pelts traded at Jasper House in 1827 shows 899 beaver, 725 marten and one mink.

Jasper House sheltered many notable travellers: Sir George Simpson of the Hudson's Bay Company in

1824; botanist David Douglas in 1827; Jesuit missionary Jean Pierre de Smet and artist Paul Kane in 1846; James Hector of the Palliser Expedition in 1859; tourists Milton and Cheadle in 1863; and CPR engineer-in-chief Sir Sandford Fleming in 1872. Some travellers stayed forever at Jasper House—there are at least 23 graves nearby.

As the fur trade declined, Jasper House was used less frequently. The Hudson's Bay Company abandoned it in the early 1850s. Various settlers, including Henry John Moberly, subsequently operated Jasper House as a homestead and a hotel until 1884. Sadly, the building was destroyed in 1910 by a crew

Moberly Cabins

Jasper House

The Celestine Lake Road provides access to the North Boundary Trail and other hiking destinations at the mouth of the Snake Indian River. The Snaring campground is about five kilometres along the road. Beyond the campground, the road follows the west shore of the Athabasca River for 34 km, traversing the largest block of montane habitat in the Rocky Mountain parks. Access to this section of gravel road is controlled, with inbound and outbound traffic restricted to certain times of day. Trailers are not permitted. Check with the park information centre in Jasper for details concerning access.

Derelict cabins along the Celestine Road and on the east

bank of the Athabasca River record early settlement in the Athabasca Valley. Henry John Moberly ran nearby Jasper House for the Hudson's Bay Company from 1856-61. He married an Iroquois woman and had two sons, John and Ewan. After their father left the area, the sons built cabins in 1898—John on the east bank of the Athabasca River and Ewan on the west bank. The brothers sold their land in 1910 after Jasper National Park was established. The cabins were never removed. Ewan's cabin is at km 11 on the Celestine Road. John's cabin was largely destroyed by an illegal campfire in 1989. The ruins are seven kilometres along the Overlander Trail, which begins at Sixth Bridge at Maligne Canyon.

Jasper Lake and Talbot Lake

surveying the route for the Grand Trunk Pacific Railway. They used boards from Jasper House to construct a raft to cross the Athabasca River.

The name "Jasper" had become associated with the surrounding area, and was a logical choice for the new national park when it was established in 1907. The locale of Jasper House is now a special preservation area and a National Historic Site.

The French language of the voyageurs is retained in the names of many features in this part of the Athabasca Valley: Miette Range, Boule Range and Bosche Range. The de Smet Range commemorates Pierre Jean de Smet, the Belgian missionary who baptized 54 natives and performed seven marriages at Jasper House in 1846. It was de Smet who also who first coined the names "Maligne" and "Violin River." In keeping with the rustic musical style of the west, the Violin River soon became known as the Fiddle River. You'll cross it farther east along the Yellowhead Highway.

Complex Mountains

The de Smet, Bosche, Miette and Fiddle Ranges in the Athabasca Valley contain some of the best examples of complex mountains in the Rockies. Complex mountains are those in which the rock formations are neither horizontal nor uniformly tilted. They feature an array of U-shaped folds called synclines, and arch-shaped folds called anticlines. Some mountains also contain Z-shaped, over-turned folds.

The rocks in these mountains were originally in horizontal layers. As they were buried deep within the earth's crust, the rocks became warm and pliable. The tremendous compressive forces during mountain building warped the rocks, creating the folds.

The Athabasca Valley bisects four parallel mountain ranges between Jasper townsite and the park's east gate. These mountain ranges are oriented along the strike of the Rockies: northwest to southeast. It is thought that the course of the Athabasca River is older than these mountains. It was able to maintain its course by eroding downward as the front ranges were thrust skyward 85 million years ago.

Disaster Point

A spur of Roche Miette juts into the Athabasca River 40.5 km east of the Icefields Parkway junction. The original trail in the Athabasca River was along its east bank. Early travellers were forced to either ford the river here, or follow a difficult trail across the spur above. Either way, "disasters" were common. Another anecdote of disaster recounts that Sandford Fleming broke his brandy flask here in 1872. Presumably, the flask was full.

Dynamite and heavy equipment were used during the construction of the Yellowhead Highway to make the road bed at Disaster Point. Today, we pass this place with no difficulty. However, a disaster of a different sort is unfolding here.

Bighorn sheep that range on Roche Miette frequent several mineral licks near roadside at Disaster Point. The mix of wild animals and fast-moving vehicles is not a good one. Road-kills of sheep are common. Between 1945 and 1980, 236 sheep were killed on the Canadian National Railway in Jasper, and 167 sheep died on Jasper's roads.

Bighorn sheep are particularly vulnerable to this kind of drain on their population. When their range is threatened or becomes marginal, they tend not to relocate, but persist, either until matters improve, or they become locally extinct.

245

Many good bighorn sheep ranges elsewhere in Banff and Jasper are bisected by roads and railways. The overall population of this animal is dwindling. In the 1850s, there may have been 10,000 bighorn sheep in Jasper. By 1915, there were 3,000. In 1994, the population numbered in the hundreds. There is serious concern that some of the smaller flocks may not survive, particularly the ones that frequent roadsides, because they are also vulnerable to poaching. Please drive with extra care near Disaster Point.

Pocahontas Ponds

Pocahontas Ponds are on the north side of the Yellowhead Highway, 45.3 km east of the Icefields Parkway junction. These backwaters of the Athabasca River are excellent for bird-watching. Many of Jasper's more than 200 reported species may be seen here, including Canada goose, tundra swan, bald eagle, great blue heron, waterfowl and shorebirds. You may see beavers, too.

The coniferous trees in this part of the Athabasca Valley are almost all white spruce. Although this tree species is common in the montane ecoregion, pure stands seldom develop. Such stands are more typical of the boreal forest of central and northern Alberta.

Miette Hot Springs Road

The 14-km-long Miette Hot Springs Road is a narrow and winding route that is open in summer only. It leads to the hottest hot springs in the Rockies. Large RVs and trailers cannot be safely driven to the hot springs. Park them at the trailer drop-off, 150 m south of the Yellowhead Highway.

When the Grand Trunk Pacific Railway was under construction in 1910, there were elaborate plans for a resort involving Miette Hot Springs. Charles Melville Hays, the president of the railway, intended to build a luxury hotel at the mouth of the Fiddle River—Chateau Miette. Hot spring water would be piped to the hotel from Miette Hot Springs. If fate had not intervened, Chateau Miette may have become the principal settlement in Jasper National Park. Hays was on the Titanic in 1912, and his plans for Chateau Miette and other resorts along the GTPR went to the bottom of the Atlantic Ocean with him.

Pocahontas

Named after the noted mining town in Virginia, Pocahontas celebrated the dreams of a mining company that aspired to greatness after two prospectors discovered coal on the slopes of Roche Miette in 1908.

Beginning in 1910, Jasper Park Collieries worked four coal seams in its 40-square-kilometre claim at Pocahontas. The tracks of the Grand Trunk Pacific Railway were laid along the south side of the Athabasca Valley, and a spur line to the mine was

Osprey

The osprey or "fish hawk" lives along lakes and rivers in the montane and lower subalpine ecoregions. Its plumage is dark brown, with white feathers on the head and underside. A dark stripe encompasses the eye. Wingspan is 1.5 m. In flight, the underside reflects the colour of the water below, making the osprey less visible to prey. The osprey hunts by circling over water and diving to spear fish just below the surface with its talons. It has an opposable outer talon that works much the same way as the human thumb. The pads of its feet are covered in spines to help grip slippery fish. Rodents and smaller birds are also eaten.

Osprey mate for life and construct prominent treetop nests to which they return from migration each spring. They winter in Central America and Southern America. In recent years, osprey have been present in the Athabasca Valley, at Vermilion Lakes, in the Bow Valley, at Lake Louise, at Emerald Lake and in the Kicking Horse Valley. The osprey's likeness appears on the Canadian ten dollar bill.

Punchbowl Falls

Cadomin. You can explore the industrial section of Pocahontas from the Coal Mine Trail, which begins 150 m south of Pocahontas on the Miette Hot Springs Road.

Although the Pocahontas mining claim lay within the boundaries of the newly created Jasper National Park, the mine was permitted. It was not until the National Parks Act was passed in 1930 that new logging and mining claims were prohibited in national parks.

Punchbowl Falls

Punchbowl Falls marks the point where Mountain Creek encounters a resistant rock formation as it descends to the Athabasca Valley. The resistant rock is a conglomerate of pebbles and boulders—the natural concrete of the Cadomin Formation.

The constant pounding of the water at the base of each cascade has created plunge pools, from which the falls get their name. There is a seam of low-grade coal at the viewpoint, and archaeologists have inventoried a 3,500-year-old native campsite nearby. Modern-day campers can stay at Pocahontas Campground, one kilometre south of the falls.

Punchbowl Falls to Miette Hot Springs

The Miette Hot Springs Road climbs out of the valley of Mountain Creek and descends steeply to the Fiddle River. The mountain on the east side of the Fiddle Valley is Ashlar Ridge. Ashlar is a type of masonry dressed with thin stones. The tremendous cliff of Palliser limestone and the

constructed the following year. Production peaked in 1912, when more than 100,000 tonnes of coal were extracted and 250 people were employed.

The Pocahontas mine was plagued with bad management and bad luck. After a series of fatal accidents, mining inspectors demanded safety improvements. The company did not comply. When the Grand Trunk Pacific Railway and the Canadian Northern Railway amalga-

mated in 1916, the rails were moved to the other bank of the Athabasca River. This made access to the mine difficult. At the end of World War I, the market for coal collapsed and labour disputes disrupted operations. The final straw for Pocahontas came when the country's railways found that they could obtain coal more easily and more cheaply elsewhere. The Pocahontas mine closed permanently in April 1921. Many houses were moved to Jasper, Hinton and

Roche Miette

sawtooth mountain form inspired the name. The only stand of tamarack trees in Jasper National Park is at kilometre six on the Miette Hot Springs Road.

Roche Miette, Yellowhead Highway

The prow of Roche Miette (ROSH mee-YETT) (2,316 m) is a prominent landmark on the Yellowhead Highway in east-ern Jasper National Park. (The French name means "Miette's Rock.") There are three stories concerning the origin of the name. The most popular was related by artist Paul Kane, who stayed at Jasper House in 1846. A fur trader named

Miette Hot Springs—The Hottest of the Hot

Of the developed hot springs in the Rockies, Miette Hot Springs are by far the hottest, averaging 53.9°C. They are also the highest in dissolved mineral content, and the most pungent in sulphur odour. There are three outlets, with a combined flow of just over one million litres per day.

Hot springs form when groundwater seeps deep enough into the earth's crust to become heated and pressurized. In its return to the surface, the water dissolves minerals from the surrounding bedrock—in this case sulphur and calcium, with a trace of radium. Although we may now think otherwise, in Victorian

Miette Hot Springs in 1919

times the radioactive quality of the water was thought to be therapeutic.

These springs were well known to natives, traders of the Hudson's Bay Company and early settlers. However, it was miners from Pocahontas who began development here. They roughed out a track to the springs in 1910

and built a bathhouse and shelter in 1913. To fill idle time during a strike, the miners built the first pool in 1919. The Parks Branch completed the road in 1933, with full development of the springs taking place in 1937. The present bathing facility was built in 1986.

The Sulphur Skyline trail is recommended to strong hikers who have half a day to obtain a splendid view of remote valleys in Jasper's front ranges. A less strenuous outing is to walk the Miette Hot Springs boardwalk to the hot spring outlets, past the 1937 bathing pool. You may see bighorn sheep and mule deer at the hot springs parking lot.

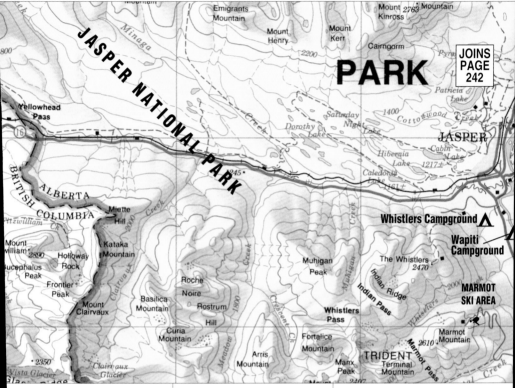

JOINS
PAGE
242

Miette made an ascent of the mountain and sat with his legs dangling over the abyss, contemplating life. Another story equates the crumbly nature of Roche Miette's limestone with the French word for crumb: *miette*. This is not particularly valid, as the Palliser Formation that comprises most of Roche Miette is one of the tougher limestones.

The story now widely accepted tells how the voyageurs corrupted a Cree word—*myatuck*—which means "mountain sheep." (Original spellings of Roche Miette are consistently "Myette.") The bighorn sheep is certainly common in the area, and was even more so in the early 1800s.

There is one other puzzle concerning the name Miette. The Miette River west of Jasper was originally called Caledonia River by traders of the North West Company. It is not clear how the name Miette was transferred from Roche Miette, 40 km west to this river. Perhaps there was a trader named Miette who travelled the Athabasca and Miette valleys.

The Yellowhead Highway reaches the eastern boundary of Jasper National Park 7.1 km east of Pocahontas. Ahead lie the foothills and boreal forest on the way to Hinton, Edson and Edmonton.

Yellowhead Highway West: Jasper townsite to Mt. Robson

Yellowhead Pass

Yellowhead Pass (1,143 m) is the lowest mountain pass on the continental divide in the Rocky Mountain parks. It was used by fur traders of the Hudson's Bay Company and North West Company between 1820 and 1826. They called it Leather Pass.

The man nicknamed "Yellowhead" was probably Pierre Bostonais, a fair-haired Iroquois guide and trapper. He was based on the west side of the Yellowhead Pass in the 1820s, near the present-day community of Tête Jaune

Cache (Yellowhead's Cache).

With its low elevation, Yellowhead Pass would seem to offer the best travel route across the Rockies. The approach from the east is relatively gentle. However, the valley of the Fraser River descends abruptly on the west side of the pass, and does not offer an easy travel route. After a few years of tackling the Fraser Valley, the voyageurs abandoned Yellowhead Pass and crossed the Rockies via the longer but easier Athabasca Pass route to the south.

Nonetheless, Yellowhead Pass was Sandford Fleming's preferred route for the Canadian Pacific Railway. Fleming was engineer-in-chief of the railway survey. By 1877, a survey line was staked, but full political commitment to the Yellowhead route was lacking. When Fleming left his position with the CPR in 1880, his influence quickly waned. Kicking Horse Pass was chosen as the route for the railway to prevent loss of trade to branch lines of American railways. The surveyors pulled

out, and Yellowhead Pass remained relatively unvisited for almost 30 years until the Grand Trunk Pacific Railway was proposed.

The Yellowhead Highway follows the Miette Valley to Yellowhead Pass. The Miette River is unusual for the Rockies—it is not glacially fed. The gentle river takes a meandering course, dropping only 83 m in the 26 km between Yellowhead Pass and its confluence with the Athabasca River, just south of Jasper townsite. The Miette Valley is a

A.O. Wheeler

Arthur Oliver Wheeler was a pioneering surveyor and mountaineer who had a strong influence on the exploration of the Canadian Rockies. As a land surveyor, Wheeler was trained in the use of photography in map making. His work typically involved occupying camera stations on mountain tops. As a consequence, he became an accomplished mountaineer.

In February of 1906, Wheeler presented the idea to establish an Alpine Club of Canada to an executive meeting of the CPR at Field. The railway immediately realized the tourism benefits that would accrue from such a club, and wholeheartedly supported the idea. The CPR provided assistance in staging annual mountaineering camps, and the attending mountaineers published widely read accounts of their exploits, thereby attracting more visitors to the Rockies. The first of these camps was at Yoho Pass in July of 1906.

Wheeler organized and led a scientific expedition to Mt. Robson in 1911. One of its unofficial

goals was to reconnoitre a location for an ACC camp. Almost all the pioneer mountaineering in the Rockies had been accomplished by British and American climbers, frequently in the company of Swiss guides. Wheeler was jealously determined that the highest peak in the Rockies would not be climbed by foreigners. The first ascent of Mt. Robson was made from the ACC camp at Robson Pass in 1913, by a party that included one Canadian. In the same year, largely as a result of the Wheeler's report of the 1911 expedition, Mt. Robson Provincial Park was established.

Wheeler was a crusty autocrat. He clashed with many of the freer spirits of the mountaineering community, and with the guides, outfitters and packers on whom he depended during both work and play. He had a strong interest in the Mt. Assiniboine area, and was instrumental in the creation of Mt. Assiniboine Provincial Park in 1922. A few years later, Wheeler oversaw the founding of Canada's first environmental group, the National Parks Association.

From 1913-25, Wheeler directed the British Columbia-Alberta Interprovincial Boundary Survey, during which he named many landscape features. A cairn dedicated to the achievements of the survey stands on the north side of Mt. Robson in Robson Pass. There is another display that details this survey at the Great Divide in Kicking Horse Pass in Yoho. Curiously, Wheeler's name is not commemorated in the Rockies, but in the name of Mt. Wheeler in the Selkirk Range to the west, which he also surveyed.

The First Ascent of Mt. Robson

Mt. Robson

Climbers on Mt. Resplendent

"Ever since I came to Canada and the Rockies, it was my wish to climb the highest peak." Austrian-born mountain guide Conrad Kain arrived in the Rockies in 1909. His wish was fulfilled just four years later, when he guided two Alpine Club of Canada members, W.W. Foster and A.H. MacCarthy, to Mt. Robson's summit. This difficult and dangerous ascent was the crowning achievement of Kain's guiding career, which included 50 first ascents in Canada and 30 first ascents in New Zealand.

During the 1911 ACC-Smithsonian expedition to Mt. Robson, it became apparent that expedition leader A.O. Wheeler was saving the big peaks for a future ACC camp. Kain stole away one afternoon on the pretence of visiting nearby Emperor Falls. When he returned the following morning, it was after a difficult, solo first ascent of Whitehorn Mountain. Wheeler was incensed, but Kain could not bear "being among beautiful mountains and not climbing one."

It was not the only time Wheeler and Kain clashed. During the same trip, Kain and expedition photographer Byron Harmon went for a stroll along Robson Glacier, stopping only when they had reached the summit of Mt. Resplendent—another mountain coveted by Wheeler. Still, Kain was too good a guide to be dismissed.

It was from the 1913 ACC camp in Robson Pass that Kain commenced the successful first ascent of Robson. The route, now called the Kain Face, lies out of view from the highway on the east side of the mountain. It represented a tremendous leap forward in Canadian mountaineering. A guide who led an unsuccessful attempt on this route four years earlier had commented: "I never before saw death so near."

Kain tirelessly chopped hundreds of steps in the steep ice of the mountainside to achieve the summit slopes. With customary modesty, he stepped aside just before the highest point and announced "Gentlemen, that's as far as I can take you." The descent by a different route required another full day.

James Monroe Thorington collaborated with Kain to produce the autobiography, *Where the Clouds Can Go*. Kain died in 1934 of encephalitis a year before this classic work on Canadian mountaineering was published.

mosaic of wetlands that are home to moose, beaver and wolf. It is excellent for bird-watching. You may see Canada goose, osprey, belted kingfisher, pileated wood-pecker and waterfowl. Mountain caribou sometimes cross the Yellowhead Highway near Yellowhead Pass. You can stop and enjoy the valley at several roadside, picnic areas.

The tracks of the Canadian National Railway are often in view. In places at roadside, you can see railway grades that were abandoned when the Grand Trunk Pacific Railway merged with the Canadian Northern Railway in 1916. The highway passes through prominent exposures of purple and brown slate of the Miette Formation.

The Decoigne warden station was named for François Decoigne, who was in charge of Jasper House in 1826. The montane meadows nearby are called Dominion Prairie. Archaeological sites here indi-cate that the meadows were a camping place on a native travel route across the Rockies. Shuswaps from the interior of B.C. crossed Yellowhead Pass to trade at Jasper House in the mid-1800s.

Yellowhead Pass is on the continental divide and on the boundary between Jasper National Park, Alberta and Mt. Robson Provincial Park, B.C. Waters flow east and north from here via the Miette, Athabasca and Mackenzie rivers to the Arctic Ocean; and west via the Fraser River to the Pacific Ocean. The pass is also the division point between the

Mt. Robson Provincial Park entrance

Mountain time zone and the Pacific time zone. Westbound travellers subtract one hour. Portal Lake is on the north side of the road at the pass. The lake is an excellent place to get

The Reverend and the Greenhorn

The first attempts to climb Mt. Robson were made by a party that included A.P. Coleman and Reverend George Kinney in 1908. In a story typical of Mt. Robson, poor weather prevailed and only four days out of 21 were con-ducive to climbing.

In 1909, members of the British Alpine Club, including L.S. Amery, mounted an expedition to Robson. At Jasper Lake, on their approach to the mountain, they encountered Kinney and outfitter Curly Phillips, returning from what Kinney claimed was the first ascent of Robson.

On his way to Mt. Robson earlier that summer, Kinney had met Phillips, who was prospect-ing in the Athabasca Valley. Phillips was a newcomer to the mountains, and had never seen Mt. Robson. His ignorance of the

dangers of mountaineering had allowed Kinney to convince him to join the venture. In reality, Kin-ney only wanted a good horse-man to get him to Mt. Robson. He was accustomed to climbing alone, having made the first solo ascent of Mt. Stephen near Field, in 1904.

What followed was one of the most intrepid episodes in the his-tory of Canadian mountaineering. Devoid of equipment and rations, the reverend and the greenhorn made four desperate attempts on the treacherous west face of the mountain. The last of these cul-minated in success, or so Kinney claimed.

Evidence, including Phillips' later testimony, indicated that the pair did not quite make the sum-mit. Still, their courage and perse-verance was remarkable. The dangerous west face of Mt. Rob-son is avoided by contemporary mountaineers, and has likely not been attempted since.

After this high adventure, Curly Phillips went on to become one of the most successful outfit-ters and guides in Jasper. He died in an avalanche on Elysium Mountain above the Miette Valley in 1938.

Mt. Robson and Berg Lake

out of your vehicle and stretch your legs.

Mt. Robson Provincial Park

Mt. Robson Provincial Park was the second provincial park established in B.C., in 1913. The park occupies 2,172 square kilometres. B.C.'s provincial parks have different objectives than national parks. The emphasis is on providing recreation and access, not on preservation.

Mt. Robson is the scenic focal point of the park. The Berg Lake Trail, which leads to the foot of Mt. Robson, is the most popular backpacking trail in the Rockies. The park's other backpacking trails are rugged and seldom visited. There are half a dozen short trails in the frontcountry that are suitable for families. Boating and canoeing are popular at Moose Lake and at Yellowhead Lake. In 1990, Mt. Robson Provincial Park was proclaimed part of the UNESCO Rocky Mountain Parks World Heritage Site. Campgrounds are located at Yellowhead Lake and near Mt. Robson.

Yellowhead Pass to Mt. Robson

There is a boat launch and picnic area at Yellowhead Lake, 6.8 km west of Yellowhead Pass. The Mount Fitzwilliam trailhead is on the south side of the highway. BC Parks' Lucerne campground is 2.8 km farther west, also on Yellowhead Lake.

Just beyond the outlet of the lake, the Yellowhead Highway crosses the Fraser River. There is a picnic area here. The 1,368-km-long Fraser is one of the major rivers of western North America. It begins in glaciers high on the west slopes of The Ramparts, 30 km southeast of Yellowhead Pass. These gentle beginnings are deceptive. Farther downstream is treacherous whitewater, including Hell's Gate and the Fraser Canyon.

In 1863, a year after the Overlanders made their crossing of the Rockies, the first tourists arrived—an unlikely pair named Milton and Cheadle. Viscount Milton was the sickly, 23-year-old son of the sixth Earl of Fitzwilliam (for whom Mt. Fitzwilliam is named). Dr. Walter Cheadle was his 27-year-old physician. At the Earl's request, Cheadle was to escort Milton through the wilds of the Rockies, where the clean air and hard work might restore his health. The misadventure nearly cost both Milton and Cheadle their lives.

By the time they had reached Yellowhead Pass, they were almost out of food. Marten, grouse, bear, porcupine and horse were added to the rations.

After three months on the trail, the entourage finally staggered into Kamloops.

The next celebrated journey across Yellowhead Pass could not have been more different in character. Railway mogul Sandford Fleming and Reverend George Munro Grant travelled the pass in 1872 as part of a cross-country journey on foot. The larder of this party was always full, and Sundays were a day off. Various food caches along the route contained enough brandy for a daily toast to everyone's health, and to set the weekly treat of plum pudding aflame. By contrast, this party reached Kamloops in two-thirds of the time.

For the next 18 km, the Yellowhead Highway follows the Fraser River to Moose Lake. The wet meadows at roadside provide habitat for moose, beaver, muskrat and waterfowl. The blooms of common fireweed colour the banks and ditches. Moose Lake is 13 km long. It is the largest lake in Mt. Robson Provincial Park, and one of the largest lakes in the Rockies. There is a boat launch and picnic area at its eastern end.

Five kilometres beyond the

Overlander Falls

outlet of Moose Lake, the Fraser River begins its westward plunge. In places, you can see the tracks of the Canadian National Railway as they hug

Cougar

The cougar is one of the most infrequently seen large mammals in the Rockies. But if you see this wild cat, there will be no mistaking it. A male cougar weighs up to 70 kg, has a body 1.5 m long, and a tail 75 cm long. It has a short-haired, tawny coat with a yellowish belly and white chin and throat. The kittens are spotted. Unlike the other wild cats in the Rockies—lynx and bobcat—the ears are not tufted.

In the Rockies, the cougar is most common in the front range valleys of Jasper and Waterton. This solitary animal ranges over a huge territory in quest of its favourite food: mule deer. The cougar hunts in the tradition of many big cats, stalking to within a few metres of its prey before lunging onto the victim's back. Then, it breaks the animal's neck and tears its throat. The cougar will also hunt many other mammals in the Rockies. Humans are its only predator.

Cougars only pair during mating. The female can conceive at any time of the year, but usually times her three-month gestation so that the kittens arrive in summer. In a switch, it is she who seeks out the male in order to mate, doing so every other year. Two to four kittens are born. They stay with the mother for at least one year, living in a sheltered den among boulders or under a cliff. One cougar gave birth to its kittens beneath a trailer in Jasper townsite.

A cougar can live 12 years in the wild. A major cause of premature death is injuries inflicted by prey. The cougar was formerly considered a pest, and attempts were made to eradicate it from the national parks. Its population has not recovered. Outside of the parks, the animal is also in decline because of hunting and a reduction in habitat.

Fraser River

the bank above the river. The Overlander Falls trailhead is 57 km west of Yellowhead Pass. It provides access to a 10-metre-high waterfall on the Fraser River. At Mt. Robson, 1.3 km further west, there is a park visitor centre, store, gas station and three campgrounds. And best of all, weather permitting, there's a view of Mt. Robson—eight kilometres to the northwest and concealed from view to westbound travellers until this point.

Mt. Robson

To Shuswap natives, Mt. Robson, the highest peak in the Canadian Rockies, was *Yuh-hai-has-kun*—the mountain of the spiral road. The huge ledges on the mountain angle upwards to the east like spiral ramps. Unfortunately for climbers, the spiral road does not reach the summit!

Mt. Robson (3,954 m) has the greatest vertical relief from valley floor to summit of any mountain in the Canadian Rockies and American Rockies—3,100 m. It is 207 m higher than Mt. Columbia, the second highest in the Canadian Rockies, and 528 m higher than Mt. Resplendent, its highest neighbour.

The summit of Mt. Robson is frequently obscured by clouds. As moisture-laden air rises to clear Mt. Robson's summit, the temperature and air pressure decrease, causing clouds to form. The Overlanders called Mt. Robson "Cloud Cap Mountain." Their native guide claimed to have seen the summit only once in his first 29 visits.

There is no easy climbing route to the summit of Mt. Robson. Fickle weather compounds the difficulty of climbing on steep snow and ice. Despite numerous attempts each year, the summit is not often reached.

Between 1939 and 1953, not a single party was successful. All things considered, you'll be fortunate if Mt. Robson stands unobscured during your visit.

Concealed from view on the north side of Mt. Robson is one of the most spectacular glacier systems in the Rockies. This area is a popular backpacking destination, reached by a 20-km hike along the Berg Lake trail.

Robson Junction to Tête Jaune Cache

The Yellowhead Highway leaves Mt. Robson Provincial Park three kilometres west of Robson Junction. You may stop here to admire the view of Mt. Robson. The Yellowhead Highway then crosses Swiftcurrent Creek, a tributary of the Fraser River that is the farthest point from the Pacific Ocean reached by migrating chinook salmon. The Mt. Terry Fox viewpoint is 8.7 km west of Robson Junction. It commemorates the young Canadian who, after having lost part of a leg to cancer, ran partway across Canada in 1980 to raise money for cancer research. Fox was a resident of B.C.

Rearguard Falls is the last point of interest before the junction with Highway 5 at Tête Jaune Cache. The falls are the final obstacle on the Fraser River that can be surmounted by chinook salmon. You can see them here from late August to mid-September, at the culmination of their 11-week migration from the Pacific Ocean. At the Highway 5 junction, turn south (left) for Valemount and Kamloops. Turn west (right) for McBride and Prince George. ∆

Waterton Lakes National Park

Established in 1895 as Canada's fourth national park, Waterton Lakes includes 525 square kilometres in the extreme southwestern corner of Alberta. The park's theme is "where the mountains meet the prairie." The dominant image in the park is the remarkable effect of the front ranges rising from the rolling plains. The three Waterton Lakes are among the largest in the Rockies. Bighorn sheep and mule deer will be seen by most visitors.

Waterton Lakes National Park is 264 km from Calgary via Highway 2 and Highway 5, and 130 km southwest of Lethbridge via Highway 5. The town of Waterton Park offers accommodation and services and has a park information centre. Most of the businesses operate during the summer only. The park has three front-country campgrounds with 391 sites: Townsite, Crandell and Belly River. The park information centre and warden office are just north of Waterton Park townsite, on Highway 5. There are no hostels.

SuperGuide Recommendations

Sights/Attractions
- Cameron Falls
- Red Rock Canyon
- Prince of Wales Hotel

Hikes/Activities
- Upper Waterton Lake shoreline trail
- Cameron Lake shoreline trail
- Red Rock Canyon
- Bear's Hump trail
- Boat trip on Upper Waterton Lake

Unlike the other Rocky Mountain parks which have through roads, Waterton Lakes is at road's end. Three sideroads explore the park: the Akamina Parkway (Cameron Lake Road), the Red Rock Canyon Parkway and the Chief Mountain International Highway. You can easily spend two full days driving these roads, visiting the townsite and walking a variety of short trails. For those interested in watersports or backcountry hiking, the park beckons you to stay longer. More than 600,000 people visit Waterton Lakes National Park each year. Many combine their visit with one to the adjacent Glacier National Park in Montana.

Upside Down Mountains

The processes that created the Rocky Mountains were identical throughout the range: deposition of sediments on ancient sea floors, the skyward thrusting of rock layers during mountain building and subsequent erosion by ice, water and wind. The mountains that you see in Waterton Lakes are the front ranges of the Rockies. However, they are very different from the front ranges of Banff and Jasper national parks.

Whereas the front ranges of Banff and Jasper are heavily faulted, the rock that comprises the mountains in Waterton was thrust northeastward during mountain building as a single sheet known as the Lewis Thrust. This thrust sheet was more than six kilometres thick, and slid 40 km atop underlying layers. Rocks 1.5 billion years old from near the sedimentary basement of the Rockies came to rest atop the undisturbed 60-million-year-old shales of the prairies. There is no transition zone between the older and younger rocks. Waterton is truly a place where mountains meet prairie.

Because older rocks are consistently found over younger ones, some people refer to Waterton's peaks as "upside down mountains." You can best appreciate the mountain-prairie contrast from the Bison Paddock viewpoint and from the viewpoint on Highway 6 just north of the park.

Geologists still don't know why the Lewis Thrust Sheet held together so well during mountain building. Similar thrust sheets elsewhere in the Rockies became faulted and broken. The integrity of the rocks of the Lewis Thrust has

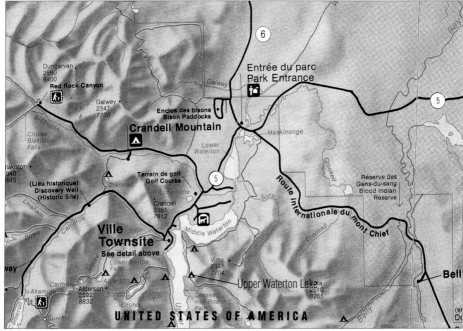

Overview of the main part of Waterton Lakes National Park

created an unusual front range landscape. Missing here are the steeply tilted sawtooth and overthrust mountains that occur in parallel ranges in Banff and Jasper. Instead, the peaks are irregular in shape, and the rock layers are horizontal. Although these mountains are oriented along the southeast/northwest axis of the Rockies, the network of valleys is haphazard. Average elevations of mountain summits in Waterton are lower than those further north in the Rockies. The highest peak in the park is Mt. Blakiston, 2,910 m.

Some of the rocks in Waterton are the oldest visible in the Rockies. Pale limestone and dolomite of the Waterton Formation can be viewed along the Akamina Parkway and at Cameron Falls. These rocks are 1.5 billion years old. Waterton's most beautiful rocks are argillites, hard mudstones that are sometimes stained red with iron oxide. The best examples are at Red Rock Canyon, but elsewhere, hikers will see many ridges of red argillite in the western part of the park. Examples of igneous rock— rock that was once molten— also occur in Waterton. As is always the case in the Rockies, these rocks are intrusions that flowed into existing sedimentary rock layers.

Although there are no significant glaciers in the park in the present day, the mountains and valleys of Waterton owe much of their appearance to the effects of glaciation. On several occasions in the past, a major glacier

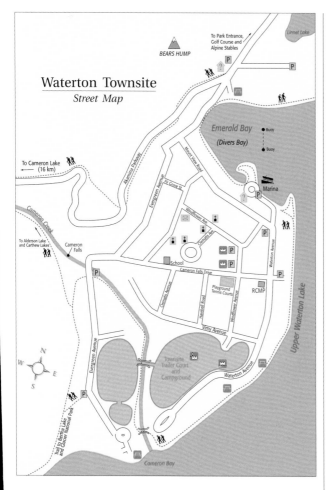

Waterton Townsite
Street Map

Waterton To Do List

Sights
- Buffalo Paddock
- Cameron Falls
- Cameron Lake
- Crandell Lake
- International Peace Park Pavilion
- Lower Bertha Falls
- Red Rock Canyon

Bike Rentals
- Pat's Cycle Rentals 859-2266

Boat Tours
- Waterton Shoreline Cruises 859-2362

Golf 859-2383

Horseback Riding
- Rocky Ridge Tours 653-2350

Entertainment
- Movies 859-2264
- Park interpretive programs 859-2224
- Waterton Heritage Centre 859-2624

Camping 859-5133
- Belly River
- Crandell
- Waterton Townsite

flowed northwards onto the prairie through the valley that now contains the Waterton Lakes. Upper Waterton Lake occupies this glacially scoured trough. With a depth of 157 m, it is the deepest lake in the Rockies. Middle Waterton and Lower Waterton lakes are kettle lakes that occupy ice-block depressions. They were created by the melting of a lobe of ice that detached when the glacier last receded 11,000 years ago.

Other evidence of glaciation abounds. Many of Waterton's backcountry lakes occupy glacially carved cirques. Hanging valleys empty into the main valleys. Waterfalls cascade from the mouths of these valleys. Near the bison paddock and along the Red Rock Canyon Parkway, you can see sinuous ridges of moraine called eskers that were deposited by streams underneath the glaciers. You can also see oval-shaped mounds of moraine called drumlins at the bison paddock. The Prince of Wales Hotel sits atop a kame terrace of glacial rubble that accumulated alongside the glacier that flowed through the Waterton Valley.

A Forgotten Corner

As elsewhere in the Rockies, natives were the first inhabitants in the Waterton Lakes region. In glacial times, they approached the area from the south along an ice-free corridor that bordered the eastern edge of the Rockies. With the retreat of glacial ice, natives began to hunt and fish in the valleys now included in Waterton. They followed the sea-

The Bison Paddock

To reach the Bison Paddock viewpoint, follow Highway 5 and Highway 6 to the north boundary of the park. The 300-metre viewpoint trail is wheelchair accessible.

The grasses and wildflowers of the bison paddock prairie represent the natural vegetation of the northern interior plains. There are only a few pockets of this vegetation left, and this partially explains the bison's demise.

As many as 60 million bison lived on the interior plains of North America in 1790. When horses and rifles were introduced onto the bison's range, the animal was subjected to a senseless slaughter. Habitat was also burned and put under the plough as the prairies were settled. Diseases imported by domestic cattle took a heavy toll. The net result of all this pressure? By 1890, the population of the plains bison had dropped to

1090. The decimation of this species was a double tragedy unparalleled in history, for it also spelled the end of the traditional way of life of plains natives.

The return of the plains bison from the brink of extinction can be attributed to a man named Walking Coyote, who captured bison in southern Alberta in 1874. Some of these animals were sold to two ranchers in Montana. In 1907, the Canadian government purchased 716 bison from the captive Montana herd. Descendants of these animals now constitute the exhibition herd at Waterton. This bison paddock was established in 1952 with one bull and five cows. Today, approximately two dozen bison live here.

The bison (BYE-sun) is the largest land mammal in North America. The popular name "buffalo" is more correctly applied to certain wild cattle of

Asia and Africa. Adult males stand 1.7 m tall at the shoulder and weigh 725 to 1,000 kg. There are two species: plains and wood. The bison in the Waterton paddock are plains bison.

You will notice that bison wallow in dust and dirt. The dirt reduces irritation from insects and from shedding skin. It is not uncommon for these mighty animals to tolerate the presence of birds on their backs. The birds bring relief by eating insects from their coats.

Bison have a heavy and clumsy appearance that belies their agility and speed. They can sprint 60 km per hour.

Bison are territorial and defensive, and will gladly take sport with tourists. If you drive through the bison paddock, remain in your vehicle. Bison can be long-lived. One of the original bison at the Banff paddock was 38 when he died.

Mountains and prairie

sonal migration of animals between the prairie and mountainsides, and crossed the backbone of the Rockies using Akamina Pass and "The Buffalo Trail" across South Kootenay Pass.

The plains bison was central to their livelihood. The meat of the animal provided sustenance. The natives fashioned clothing and shelter from the hide. There are more than 200 archaeological sites in Waterton—the highest density in the Canadian Rockies. The sites include a fishing camp at the Bosporous between Upper and Middle Waterton Lakes. It dates to 8,000 years ago. There are also bison jumps in the Blakiston Valley, where natives stampeded bison to their deaths.

The natives that the first Euro-Canadians encountered were members of the Blackfoot Confederacy: the Blood, the Peigan (pay-GAN) and the Blackfoot. Members of the Blood tribe now live on reserves near the park. The Blackfoot considered the Rockies to be the backbone of the world. Chief Mountain in Montana, southeast of Waterton, is a sacred site to the Blackfoot peoples. Young braves held their vision quests on the mountain's summit. Kutenai, Salish, Nez Percé and Flathead tribes from west of the Rockies made annual trips into Waterton to hunt bison, and occasionally to trade with the Blackfoot.

The recent human history of Waterton Lakes differs from that of the other Rocky Mountain parks. The "through traffic" that put the other parks on the map never developed here. Two fur trade scouts for the North West Company crossed South Kootenay Pass into Waterton in 1800. After that,

Charles Waterton

The Waterton Lakes were named by Thomas Blakiston of the Palliser Expedition for English naturalist and explorer, Charles Waterton. A member of the upper class, Waterton roamed South America, the Caribbean and the northwestern U.S. between 1812-29. He published several accounts of his expeditions, one of which details his riding on the back of an alligator. Waterton is best known for introducing curare (cure-RAH-ree) to western medicine, and for establishing the world's first bird sanctuary at his home in England. It housed more than 800 species. Charles Waterton never saw the lakes that were named for him four years after his death.

Waterton Lakes National Park

there were no recorded European visitors until 1858, when Thomas Blakiston's party from the Palliser Expedition crossed South Kootenay Pass and followed the creek now named for him. In his report, Blakiston commented favourably on the scenery and the abundance of wildlife. He was the first to note that Waterton is a windy place.

Obscurity followed. In the twenty-five years after the Palliser Expedition, while the young country of Canada schemed and dreamed of a railway linking sea to sea, the prairies and peaks of Waterton saw neither the railway surveyor nor hotelier. The only forays into the area were those of teams that surveyed and cleared the boundary between Canada and the U.S. along the 49th parallel. It was during this time that Waterton's most famous resident, John "Kootenai" Brown, arrived on the scene.

Brown was a character who

Windy Waterton

More often than not, it is windy on Upper Waterton Lake. The average daily wind speed at Waterton Park townsite is 32.5 km per hour. Gusts of 180 km per hour have been recorded in winter. At such times, spray from the lake collects on the windows of the Prince of Wales Hotel, 150 m away and 40 m above the lakeshore.

Many of the windy days in winter and spring are caused by chinooks. A chinook (shih-NOOK) occurs when a Pacific storm system sheds its moisture on the western slopes of the Rockies. The air is forced high to clear the crest of the range. As the dry air sweeps down the eastern slopes and its pressure increases, its temperature rises 1.5°C for each decrease in elevation of 100 m. The winds can be very strong. In 1926, when the Prince of Wales Hotel was being constructed, a chinook wind knocked one of hotel's wings 20

cm off its foundations.

Chinook is a native word that means "snow eater." In nearby Pincher Creek, the warm winds once raised the temperature 21° C in four minutes. Chinooks keep the mountain front snow-free for much of the winter, creating ideal winter habitat for elk, deer, sheep and goats, which require accessible grasses and browse. Some years, the winds also prevent the formation of ice on the Waterton Lakes.

Boating on Upper Waterton Lake

epitomized the "Wild West." For almost twenty years, he was in the thick of adventure and enterprise—serving with the British army in India, prospecting in the Cariboo gold rush, trapping furs, surviving life-and-death skirmishes with natives on the trail and serving as a police constable at Cranbrook. When he first saw the Waterton Lakes in 1865, he remarked: "This is what I have seen in my dreams, this is the country for me." He settled in 1878 on the shore of Middle Waterton Lake. (The Waterton Lakes were at that time known as the Kootenay Lakes, after the Kutenai natives who lived west of the Rockies.)

Brown supported his family by hunting, trapping, fishing, and guiding hunters and travellers. In the early 1890s, more outsiders were arriving each season, and settlement was approaching the mountain front. Brown and local ranchers became concerned that Waterton would soon be engulfed in uncontrolled development. One of the ranchers, F.W. Godsal, contacted the Department of the Interior and asked that a park be created at Waterton Lakes. In 1895, Kootenay Lakes Forest Park was set aside.

John Kootenai Brown continued to reside in the park, acting as its unofficial benefactor. In 1911, national park status was bestowed on Waterton Lakes and Brown became its first superintendent. Three years later, at Brown's request, the area of the park was increased thirty-fold to 1,095 square kilometres. Brown is buried near Middle Waterton Lake.

In its relatively remote setting, and with no transportation corridor bisecting it, Waterton Lakes has escaped many of the development pressures to which the other

The Waterton Lakes—Big Water

With a maximum depth of 157 m, Upper Waterton Lake is the deepest lake in the Canadian Rockies. It is 11.1 km long, has an area of 941 ha, and is by far the largest of Waterton's 80 lakes and ponds. It holds approximately 645 million cubic metres of water. The southern reach of the lake extends 4.5 km into Glacier National Park, Montana. The Blackfoot knew the Waterton Lakes by several names, one of which meant "big water."

There are 17 native species of fish in Waterton Lakes National Park, and eight introduced species. The largest fish on record in the park was a 23.2 kg lake trout caught in Upper Waterton Lake in July 1920. Reports from the early 1900s describe individuals taking 500 fish from Upper Waterton Lake in a day. Principally as a result of overfishing, fish are not as numerous today.

mountain parks have been subjected. Mining for coal, copper, silver and gold was attempted in the park, but did not prove commercially viable. However, drilling for oil sparked a brief boom in the early 1900s.

Natives and early settlers had long been aware of oily scum on the surface of Cameron Creek. One of the settlers devised a means of siphoning the oil off the water. He bottled it and sold it locally. Word of the oil soon spread. In 1900, a company was formed to drill for oil along Cameron Creek. In September of 1901, they struck oil at 311 m. It was Canada's second oil producing well.

"Oil City" sprang up nearby but the boom never came to fruition. The drilling technology of the day was not reliable, and the men were not experienced in operating it. The well became plugged after the first gush. It took three years to restore the flow, which turned out to be insignificant. Oil City disappeared. Today, it is a National Historic Site. You can see a few foundations along the Akamina Parkway. Other oil wells in the park also failed. In 1953, Shell Canada developed the Waterton Oil and Gas Field north of the park. Active wells there penetrate as deep as five kilometres.

Besides small-scale logging, the only other industrial activity that threatened the park's integrity was a plan to build a dam between the Middle and Upper Waterton lakes in the early 1920s. After much debate, the plan was abandoned.

After establishment of the national park in 1911, the town of Waterton Park evolved as a tourist facility. In the mid-1920s, the Great Northern Railway decided to run bus tours through the Rockies from Glacier National Park, Montana to Jasper. Waterton

Cameron Falls

Cameron Falls is located at the bridge on Evergreen Avenue, just south of town. The 10-m-high falls cascade over an outcrop of the Waterton Formation. This 1.5 billion-year-old limestone is the oldest rock visible in the Canadian Rockies.

Debris carried by Cameron Creek has created the alluvial fan where the townsite has been built. The creek has been known to exhibit a thousandfold increase in the volume of flow between winter and summer. Flash floods have inundated parts of the townsite. You can follow a short trail on the north side of the bridge to the rim of the canyon that has been carved by Cameron Creek. Mule deer are often seen near the falls.

Looking east over The Bosporus

43 species are rare in Canada, and 34 species are unknown in Alberta outside the park.

Waterton is home to 61 species of mammals, including most of the larger mammals of the Rockies: black bear, grizzly bear, elk, mule deer, bighorn sheep, mountain goat, cougar, coyote, beaver, porcupine and captive plains bison. The park's 80 lakes and ponds are near the major western migration flyways and serve as stopping places for a variety of songbirds and waterfowl during autumn and spring. There are 17 native fish species in the lakes, and eight species that have been introduced.

Recreation

Although it is a small park, Waterton has a lot to offer the outdoor enthusiast. Opportunities for extended backpacking are limited by the park's size, but 225 km of trails lead through valleys and along ridge crests. Popular short walks and hikes are: Blakiston Falls, Bison Paddock Viewpoint, Red Rock Canyon, Crandell Lake, Cameron Lake, Lower Bertha Falls, Waterton Townsite and Bear's Hump. The popular backcountry trails are: Bertha Lake, Crypt Lake, Carthew-Alderson and the Tamarack Trail. (See the *Altitude SuperGuides: Walks and Easy Hikes in the Canadian Rockies,* and *Classic Hikes in the Canadian Rockies.*)

Motorized boats may be launched on Upper Waterton Lake and Middle Waterton Lake. Commercial boat tours are available on Upper Waterton Lake. You can rent canoes and paddle boats at the town-

Park was considered an ideal place for an overnight stop. The railway constructed the Prince of Wales Hotel in 1926 to accommodate this venture. The hotel opened the following year, complete with a tour boat—*The International.* In 1997, this boat still plied the waters of Upper Waterton Lake.

Construction of the Akamina Parkway began in 1921. It was to connect with a new road in B.C., creating the opportunity for a circle tour of Waterton and Glacier national parks. The B.C. section of the road was never completed. The Chief Mountain International Highway was a Great Depression make-work project that opened in 1936. The park golf course was built in 1924, and enlarged to 18 holes in 1931.

A Place of Diversity

Waterton's climate and ecology can be summarized with a single word: diversity. After your visit, you might add the word "windy" too. Warm chinook winds are common in winter. At other times, winds are created by a difference in air pressure that persists between weather systems over southern B.C. and southern Alberta. There are no major mountain ranges immediately to the west, so these winds deliver more precipitation than falls at Banff and Jasper. The winds also bring plant seeds from the west. This gives rise to more than 100 plant species normally found in wet areas of B.C.'s interior.

In common with the other Rocky Mountain parks, Waterton features the montane, subalpine and alpine ecoregions. The northeastern part of the park includes three other ecoregions: prairie, aspen parkland and foothills transition. This results in a tremendous diversity of vegetation. There are 1,270 plant species in the park, including 870 vascular species—55 per cent of the total in Alberta. Of these, 113 species are rare in Alberta,

Red Rock Canyon

Red Rock Canyon is 17.5 km from Waterton Park townsite, at the end of the Red Rock Canyon Parkway. The paved trail at the canyon makes a circuit of one of the most colourful attractions in the Rockies. The red rock in the canyon is 1.5-billion-year-old metamorphic mudstone, known as argillite (ARE-jill-ite). This rock formed from iron-rich sediments deposited on ancient tidal mud flats. Where the mud flats were exposed to air, the iron oxidized and turned red. The green-and white-coloured rocks in the canyon are also argillite, but contain iron that did not oxidize.

Red Rock Canyon is 23 m deep. Its steep walls indicate rapid erosion. You can see potholes that were created by swirling rocks trapped in eddies. Red Rock Canyon also has some uncommon features. These include ripple rock that records wave action along a prehistoric shoreline. On the east side of the canyon, the trail crosses a honeycomb of mud cracks. These cracks opened when mud dried on the ancient tidal flat. The cracks were later filled with a different type of sediment. The entire formation subsequently lithified under the pressure of other sediments that accumulated above.

At trailside are examples of a fossil formation known as a stromatolite. These reef-like accumulations were created 1.5 billion years ago from calcium carbonate, produced by algae. Identical algae grow today, creating reefs in warm, shallow seas elsewhere in the world.

The last item of geological interest is an intrusion of igneous (once molten) rock near the mouth of the canyon. Virtually all rock in the Rockies was sedimentary in origin. However, blobs of molten rock sometimes found their way into cracks within the hardened sedimentary layers. The dark gray, igneous rock here is a lava known as basalt (BAY-salt).

Visitors have been coming to Red Rock Canyon for thousands of years. Natives from west of the mountains crossed to the prairies annually to hunt bison and trade with other tribes. One of their travel routes, known as The Buffalo Trail, crossed South Kootenay Pass and followed Blakiston Creek past the mouth of Red Rock Canyon. Seasonal native hunting camps have been found near the canyon. They date to 8,000 years ago.

site marina and at Cameron Lake. With its near-constant wind, Upper Waterton Lake is an excellent location for boardsailing. The water is cold and a dry suit is recommended. Scuba divers often explore the wreck of a sunken paddle steamer in Emerald Bay, adjacent to the Prince of Wales Hotel. There are attractive picnic areas throughout the park. Tennis, bicycle rentals and public swimming round out the summer activities. Winter access in the park is restricted by road closures. Cross-country skiing, snowshoeing and waterfall ice climbing are popular activities.

An International Peace Park and a Biosphere Reserve

The Canadian government was largely following the lead of the U.S. when it proclaimed the national park at Waterton Lakes in 1911. Glacier National Park in Montana had been established the previous year. There was an obvious opportunity to create an enlarged protected area.

The Canada-U.S. boundary runs through Upper Waterton Lake, 4.5 km from its southern end. The boat excursions from Waterton townsite could have posed a problem to the governments. However, a relaxed attitude prevailed toward the casual "border crossings" on these tours.

By 1930, locals were calling for the formal establishment of an international park to further demonstrate the goodwill between Canada and the U.S. The two governments agreed, and in 1932, created Waterton-Glacier International Peace Park, the first of its kind. Since then, park administrators have co-operated to integrate outlooks on preservation, interpretation and resource management.

In 1979, Waterton-Glacier and the surrounding lands were designated an International Biosphere Reserve— part of a worldwide United Nations program. A biosphere reserve acknowledges the arbitrary nature of the boundaries around a protected area, and encourages management of the surrounding lands to support the objectives within the protected area. Local industries, farmers, ranchers and governments participate in monitoring activities and impacts along the mountain front near Waterton. Biosphere Reserves have been established at 342 locations in 82 other countries. Δ

Cameron Lake

Cameron Lake is 17 km from Waterton Park townsite, at the end of the Akamina Parkway. The lake is 39 m deep and has an area of 17.2 hectares. It occupies a hollow excavated by glacial ice, and is dammed by a glacial moraine. The lake was named for Donald Cameron, who led the British party that surveyed the international boundary in 1874. The summit of Mt. Custer (2,708 m) at the south end of the lake lies entirely within Glacier National Park, Montana. The mountain was not named for the famous general, but for Henry Custer, a topographer with the U.S. Boundary Survey who worked in this area in 1860 or 1861.

The lake is surrounded by a dense subalpine forest that includes some of the oldest trees in the park. Red monkey flowers grow in places at trailside along the lakeshore. The avalanche paths at the south end of the lake are frequented by grizzly bears. The ridge to the west of the lake forms the B.C.-Alberta boundary.

Reference

Calgary, Edmonton and Vancouver have international airports with car rental agencies and bus transportation. There are daily shuttle buses direct from Calgary airport to Banff and Lake Louise. A passenger train service operates to Jasper from Vancouver and Edmonton. Calgary

does not have passenger train service. There are car rental agencies in Banff, Lake Louise and Jasper. There is daily bus service between Banff, Lake Louise and Jasper in summer, with less frequent service in winter. Bus tours to the major scenic attractions operate daily in summer from Banff, Lake Louise and Jasper.
For more information call VIA Rail: 1-800-564-8630 or Greyhound Bus: 1-800-661-6747.

Calgary to:
- Banff 129 km
- Jasper (via Banff) 415 km
- Waterton Park 264 km

Banff to:
- Calgary 129 km
- Edmonton (via Calgary) 423 km
- Edmonton (via Jasper) 657 km
- Field 85 km
- Golden 140 km
- Jasper 295 km
- Lake Louise 58 km
- Radium 132 km
- Red Deer 362 km
- Vancouver 858 km

Lake Louise to:
- Field 27 km
- Golden 82 km
- Jasper 237 km
- Radium 130 km
- Red Deer 304 km

Field to:
- Banff 85 km

- Golden 55 km
- Jasper 295 km
- Lake Louise 27 km
- Radium (via Golden) 160 km

Jasper to:
- Banff 295 km
- Calgary (via Banff) 415 km
- Edmonton 363 km
- Field 262 km
- Lake Louise 237 km
- Red Deer 413 km
- Vancouver 794 km

Edmonton to:
- Banff (via Calgary) 423 km
- Banff (via Jasper) 657 km
- Jasper 362 km
- Lake Louise (via Calgary) 481 km
- Lake Louise (Via Jasper) 599 km

Prince George to:
- Banff 671 km
- Jasper 376 km
- Lake Louise 613 km

Vancouver to:
- Banff 858 km
- Jasper 794 km

Driving in Canada
- Distances are measured in kilometres (km). Speeds are cited in kilometres per hour. Gasoline is dispensed and priced by the litre.
- Safety-belt use is mandatory.
- You must have vehicle insurance, including third party liability. You must carry proof of insurance

with you.
- You must be 16 or older to drive in Alberta and B.C.
- U.S. drivers' licences are valid in Canada for short visits. An International Driving Permit is valid when accompanied by your regular driver's licence.

Currency and Banking
- The Canadian money system is based on dollars and cents. 100 cents equal one dollar.
- Convert foreign currency into Canadian funds at a financial institution. There are banks in Banff, Canmore, Jasper, Golden, Invermere and Valemount. Most businesses will accept travellers cheques with identification. Major credit cards are usually honoured.
- Some hotels have currency exchanges. Some businesses have bank machines.
- The Goods and Services Tax (GST) will be added to most purchases and the cost of most services. However, some businesses include the GST in the posted price.
- Tipping is expected at most restaurants.

Liquor Laws
- The minimum age to pur-

chase alcohol in Alberta is 18; in B.C. it is 19.

- Do not carry open alcohol (including partially full cases of beer) in the passenger compartment of a vehicle. Transport it in the trunk.
- It is unlawful to drink liquor in an unlicensed public place. You may drink liquor at a residence or at a temporary residence.
- There are liquor stores in Banff, Canmore, Lake Louise, Jasper, Field, Golden, Invermere and Valemount.

National Park Regulations and Etiquette

- Vehicles stopping in national parks must pay the appropriate use fee at a park entry point or visitor information centre.
- Firearms may not be transported through a national park unless securely locked or dismantled.
- Hunting and trapping wildlife is not permitted.
- Anglers must obtain a national park fishing permit, and be familiar with closures and catch quotas for the waterbodies they intend to fish.
- It is illegal to disturb, remove or deface any natural, cultural or historic object.
- It is illegal to approach, feed or harass wildlife.
- Do not enter a closed area.
- Camp in designated campgrounds only.
- Light fires only in metal fire boxes provided. Use firewood sparingly.
- Mountain biking is permit-

ted only on specific trails.
- Keep to maintained trails when hiking. Do not short-cut switchbacks.
- Keep pets restrained at all times. There are restrictions on taking dogs into the backcountry overnight.
- Respect the rights of others to solitude. Hike and camp in small groups.
- Observe quiet hours at campgrounds between 10:00 p.m. and 7:00 a.m.

Safety

There are hazards in the Rocky Mountain national parks which may be unfamiliar to you. As anywhere, common sense is your best friend in the mountains. The following will help ensure that your visit is a safe one.

- Do not approach, entice or feed wildlife.
- Do not park or walk in posted avalanche or closed areas.
- Keep off snow-covered slopes. The snow in summer snow banks is abrasive and cuts skin easily. It may also conceal treacherous ice slopes.
- Keep off glacial ice.
- Stay on your side of the guardrail at viewpoints, waterfalls and canyons.
- Do not drink surface water from roadside or in heavily visited areas.

Metric/Imperial Conversions

Metric	Imperial
1 millimetre (mm)	0.0394 in
1 centimetre (cm)	0.394 inches
1 metre (m)	3.28 feet
1 kilometre (km)	0.62 miles
1 hectare (ha)	2.47 acres
1 square kilometre (km2)	0.386 square miles
1 kilogram (kg)	2.205 pounds
1 tonne (t)	0.9842 UK tons (1.102 US tons)
1 litre (L)	0.22 UK gallons (0.264 US gallons)
1° Celsius (C)	1.8° F

Imperial	Metric
1 inch	2.54 centimetres (cm)
1 foot	0.305 metres (m)
1 mile	1.61 kilometres (km)
1 acre	0.405 hectares (ha)
1 square mile	2.59 square kilometres (km2)
1 pound	0.4536 kilograms (kg)
1 UK ton	1.016 tonnes (t)
1 UK gallon	4.55 litres (L)
1 US ton	0.9072 tonnes (t)
1 US gallon	3.78 litres (L)
1° Fahrenheit	0.55° C

90 km per hour equals 56 miles per hour.
50 km per hour equals 31 miles per hour.
The freezing point is 0°C.
One hectare is 100 m by 100 m.

- Do not drive on paved shoulders. Park only in designated pull-offs. Observe the posted speed limit. Slow down in areas frequented by wildlife, or if you see wildlife at roadside. Be on the lookout for cyclists.
- Altitude increases the effects of sun and wind. Dress appropriately for walks and hikes. Use sunscreen. Wear sunglasses and a sun hat. Carry extra clothing and some food and water.
- Frost may develop on road surfaces at any time of the year, especially in the mountain passes. Be prepared for winter driving conditions between September and June, and equip your vehicle accordingly.
- Keep to the trails when hiking, Avoid taking "shortcuts."
- If you begin to tire excessively, retrace your route to the trailhead.
- A rough formula for converting distances and heights from metric to imperial is to multiply by 3 and add 10 per cent of the product. Example: 30 m x 3 = 90, plus 9 = 99. Therefore, 30 m equals approximately 99 feet.

Tips for 35 mm Photography

Good lighting makes good landscape photographs. If you have a particular destination in mind, carefully consider the time of day and the resulting angle of light. Many of the best-known scenes in the Rockies are lit best before mid-morning.

Lakes are usually calm at

Optimum Photography Times

Location	Time of Day
Banff	
Tunnel Mountain Hoodoos	any time
Lake Minnewanka	afternoon
Mt. Rundle	
(from Vermilion Lakes)	late afternoon and evening
Near Banff	
Sunshine Meadows	any time
Johnston Canyon	afternoon
Kootenay	
Marble Canyon	morning and early afternoon
Lake Louise	
Moraine Lake	early morning
Lake Louise	sunrise and early morning
Icefields Parkway	
Crowfoot Glacier	morning
Bow Lake	morning
Peyto Lake	morning and afternoon
Snowbird Glacier	early morning
Waterfowl Lakes	morning
The Weeping Wall	afternoon
Parker Ridge crest	morning
Athabasca Glacier	morning
Sunwapta Falls	afternoon
Athabasca Falls	afternoon
Mt. Edith Cavell	early morning and late afternoon
Jasper	
The Whistlers	any time
Pyramid Lake	morning
Mt. Robson	any time
Maligne Lake	
Maligne Canyon	midafternoon
Medicine Lake	any time
Maligne Lake	any, north shore at sunset
Yoho	
Natural Bridge	afternoon
Emerald Lake	morning
Takakkaw Falls	afternoon
Leanchoil Hoodoos	afternoon
Wapta Falls	afternoon
Waterton	
Cameron Falls	morning
Upper Waterton Lake	afternoon, evening

Bears and People–Avoiding Problems

Given that almost nine million people visit the Rocky Mountain parks each year, bear-human encounters are surprisingly few. Most of the incidents involve bears that have become habituated to garbage or unattended food. There is also a handful of encounters each year when hikers surprise a bear, and the bear charges. Still, as a rule, bears avoid humans.

By taking note of the following suggestions, you will help minimize the risk of an encounter with a bear, and you will also help prevent bears from becoming habituated to humans. A fed bear is a dead bear, as bears accustomed to food from humans are usually destroyed by park wardens.

1. Do not leave food unattended. Keep it locked in the trunk of your car or in a bear-proof container in campgrounds. Backcountry campers should store food at least five metres off the ground, strung between two trees at least five metres apart. Most backcountry campsites are equipped with bear poles, but you should carry enough rope for this purpose just in case.
2. Do not cook or eat in or near your tent. Eat everything you cook. Avoid aromatic foods. If fishing, do not dump fish cleanings at waterside or at your campsite. Pack them out, or burn them where fires are allowed.
3. Keep pets on leashes or enclosed in vehicles. Do not take pets into the backcountry. A dog will not protect you from a grizzly bear, and may provoke a bear to charge.
4. Travel in groups and stay on trails. Make noise while hiking—whistle, sing or shout. Avoid bear habitat. Make lots of noise on avalanche slopes and along streams. If you encounter fresh bear signs—scrapes, scats, carrion, scent—and have a choice, leave the area and

return to the trailhead. If you must continue, detour widely around the area and make even more noise.
5. If you see a bear while you are driving, remain in your vehicle. Take photographs with a telephoto lens. Never interfere with the relationship between a mother and her cubs or approach a bear that is feeding. Report your sighting to the nearest warden office or park information centre.
6. In the backcountry, an encounter with a bear can be a very complex situation. The first rule is: do not run. Avoid eye contact with the bear. Look for cubs and move away from them. Talk quietly to the bear while backing slowly away. Climbing a tree sometimes provides escape from an aggressive grizzly bear, but is less effective in an encounter with a black bear. If a grizzly bear attacks, play dead. If a black bear attacks, fight for your life. Consult a warden office or park information centre for more detailed theories on what to do and what not to do in a bear encounter. Or, read the section on bears in the *Altitude SuperGuide, Classic Hikes in the Canadian Rockies.*

HUMP

Grizzly bear

Black bear

dawn and dusk. These are the times to take reflection photographs. Direct sunlight disturbs the air and often causes the surface water to ripple.

The large mammals are most active at dawn and dusk in summer.

The horizon is blocked at most locations in the Rockies. At sunrise and sunset, the best effects are not obtained by including the sun in the photograph, but by capturing the colourful lighting opposite the sun. Called alpenglow, this lighting precedes sunrise and follows sunset. You may want to underexpose slightly, 1/2 to one stop, to saturate colours at these times of day.

Snow will often be present in your compositions. You will frequently encounter difficult lighting situations that incorporate opposing values of sunlit snow and shade. Bracket exposures. Shaded snowscapes will appear dull unless you overexpose. Take a light meter reading off your bare hand and use this for the scene.

To obtain details of people or objects in the foreground of bright landscapes, take a close-up light meter reading from the foreground subject and use this exposure for the scene. In some cases, the extraordinary contrast between foreground lighting and background lighting goes beyond the limits of film. Expose for the background and fill the foreground with flash, or use a neutral density filter to darken the brightest part of the scene.

If you have two camera bodies, dedicate each to a different kind of film. Load one with 25 ISO, 50 ISO or 64 ISO film. Load the other with 200 ISO or 400 ISO film. This will give you flexibility with regard to lighting, depth of field, colour saturation and tripod work.

At higher altitudes, film registers a bluish cast because of the greater incidence of ultraviolet light. Equip your lenses with UV filters. You can use a polarizing filter to cut glare in photos that involve water and ice.

Carry a selection of lenses from 24 mm to 300 mm and a sturdy tripod. Carry lots of film. Fingerless gloves take the chill out of cold-weather work.

Watch for condensation and frost on lens elements when you step from a warm vehicle into the cold outdoors. On really cold mornings, hold your breath when releasing the shutter so as not to get vapour in the foreground.

Keep your equipment lightweight, accessible and well organized. You will be more inclined to carry it with you. Ensure that your camera is ready with the lens best suited to the kind of photo you seek—telephoto for wildlife, or wide-angle for landscape. This will minimize set-up time when a good scene presents itself.

Carry your camera equipment over the shoulder in a case or bag rather than in your hands. You will tire less easily.

Campground Services

Full hook-ups
Tunnel Mountain Trailer Court, Whistlers, Redstreak, Waterton

Electricity hook-up only
Tunnel Mountain Village II, Lake Louise Trailer, Whistlers, Wapiti, Redstreak, Waterton

Hot showers
Tunnel Mountain, Two Jack Lakeside, Johnston Canyon, Lake Louise, Whistlers, Wapiti, Redstreak, Kicking Horse, Waterton

Walk-in sites
(cyclists and hikers)
Tunnel Mountain Village II, Waterfowl Lake, Pocahontas,

Snaring River, Wabasso, Jonas Creek, Columbia Icefield, Redstreak, Takakkaw Falls, Waterton

Year-round
(water may not be available in winter)
Tunnel Mountain Village II, Lake Louise Trailer, Mosquito Creek, Wapiti (Dolly Varden is open in winter only)

Group tenting
Banff, Jasper, Kootenay, Waterton, Yoho (contact in advance)

Handicapped restrooms
Tunnel Mountain Village II, Two

Jack Lakeside, Johnston Canyon, Lake Louise, Mosquito Creek, Rampart Creek, Pocahontas, Whistlers, Wabasso, Redstreak, Marble Canyon, McLeod Meadows, Kicking Horse, Waterton

Sani-stations
Tunnel Mountain, Two Jack Main, Johnston Canyon, Lake Louise, Waterfowl Lake, Whistlers, Wapiti, Wabasso, Wilcox Creek, Redstreak, Marble Canyon, McLeod Meadows, Hoodoo Creek, Kicking Horse, Waterton, Crandell

Campgrounds

Campgrounds in the Canadian Rockies national parks operate on a first come, first served basis. There are no reservations and check-out time is 11:00 a.m. In provincial parks, signs indicate the registration procedure. Because some provincial campgrounds are contracted out to private operators, these procedures vary. in Kananaskis, for example, six out of 35 campgrounds take reservations. Some have registration booths and some require self-registration. Also, check-out times vary from 11:00 a.m. to 2:00 p.m.

PARK/ CAMPGROUND	TYPE	OPENING DATE	CLOSING DATE
Kananaskis			
• Beaver Flats	Tents/RVs	mid-May	early Oct.
• Bluerock	Tents/RVs	mid-May	early Oct.
• Bluerock Equestrian	Tents/RVs	mid-May	late Nov.
• Bow River	Tents/RVs	early May	early Oct.
• Bow Valley	Tents/RVs	Year Round	
• Willow Rock	Tents/RVs	Year Round	
• Cataract Creek	Tents/RVs	mid-May	early Sept.
• Eau Claire	Tents/RVs	early June	mid-Oct.
• Etherington Creek	Tents/RVs	early May	late Nov.
• Gooseberry	Tents/RVs	early May	mid Oct.
• Lac des Arcs	Tents/RVs	early May	early Oct.
• Little Elbow	Tents/RVs	mid-May	late Nov.
• McLean Creek	Tents/RVs	Year Round	
• Mesa Butte Equestrian	Tents/RVs	Year Round	
• Mt. Kidd R.V. Park	Tents/RVs	Year Round	
• North Fork	Tents/RVs	early May	early Oct.
• Paddy's Flat	Tents/RVs	early May	early Oct.
• Boulton	Tents/RVs	Year Round	
• Canyon	Tents/RVs	mid-May	early Sept.
• Elkwood	Tents/RVs	mid-June	early Sept.
• Interlakes	Tents/RVs	mid-May	early Sept.
• Lower Lakes	Tents/RVs	late June	early Sept.
• Mount Sarrail	Tents/RVs	mid-June	early Sept.
• Sandy McNabb	Tents/RVs	Year Round	
• Sibbald Lake	Tents/RVs	early May	early Sept.
• Spray Lakes W. Shore	Tents/RVs	early May	late Nov.
• Three Sisters	Tents/RVs	early May	late Nov.
Banff National Park			
• Tunnel Mtn Trailer Court	Large RVs	early May	early Oct.
• Tunnel Mountain Village I	Tents/RVs	early May	early Oct.
• Tunnel Mountain Village II	Tents/RVs	Year Round	
• Two Jack Main	Tents/RVs	mid-May	late Sept.
• Two Jack Lakeside	Tents/RVs	late June	early Sept.

PARK/ CAMPGROUND	TYPE	OPENING DATE	CLOSING DATE
Banff National Park (cont'd)			
• Johnston Canyon	Tents/RVs	mid-May	mid-Sept.
• Castle Mtn.	Tents/RVs	late June	early Sept.
• Protection Mtn	Tents/RVs	late June	early Sept.
• Lake Louise Trailer	Large RVs/ winter	Year Round	Year Round
• Lake Louise Tent	Tents/RVs	mid-May	early Oct.
• Mosquito Creek	Tents/RVs/ winter	mid-June	early Sept.
• Waterfowl	Tents/RVs	mid-June	early Sept.
• Rampart Creek	Tents/RVs	late June	early Sept.
Jasper National Park			
• Pocahontas	Tents/RVs	mid-May	early Sept.
• Snaring River	Tents/RVs	mid-May	early Sept.
• Whistlers	Tents/RVs	early May	early Oct.
• Wapiti	Tents/RVs/	mid-May	late Sept.
	winter	mid-June	early Sept.
• Wabasso	Tents/RVs	late June	early Sept.
• Mt. Kerkeslin	Tents/RVs	mid-May	early Sept.
• Honeymoon Lake	Tents/RVs	early June	mid-Oct.
• Jonas Creek	Tents/RVs	mid-May	mid-Oct.
• Columbia Icefield	Tents	mid-May	mid-Oct.
• Wilcox Creek	Tents/RVs	early June	mid-Sept.
Kootenay National Park			
• Redstreak	Tents/RVs	early May	early Sept.
• Marble Canyon	Tents/RVs	late June	early Sept.
• McLeod Meadows	Tents/RVs	mid-May	mid-Sept.
Yoho National Park			
• Chancellor Peak	Tents/RVs	mid-May	early Oct.
• Hoodoo Creek	Tents/RVs	late June	early Sept.
• Kicking Horse	Tents/RVs	mid-May	early Oct.

Canadian Rockies SuperGuide

Banff To Do List

Bike Rentals
- BacTrax 762-8177
- Banff Adventures Unlimited 762-4554
- Gear Up 678-1636
- Performance Ski and Sports 762-8222
- Rebound Cycle 678-3668
- Ski Stop 762-5333
- Trail Sports 678-6764
- Wilson Mountain Sports, Lake Louise 522-3636

Boat Tours
- Lake Minnewanka 762-3473
- Canoe rentals, Chateau Lake Louise 522-3511
- Performance Ski and Sports 762-8222
- Western River Runners 762-3632

Golf
- Fairmont Banff Springs 762-6801
- Canmore 678-4785
- Kananaskis 591-7272
- Kananaskis Ranch 673-3737
- Silver Tip 678-1600
- Stewart Creek 678-2258

Horseback Riding
- Banff Springs Corral 762-2848
- Boundary Ranch 591-7171
- Brewster 762-5454
- Martin's Stables 762-2832
- Rafter Six Ranch 673-3622
- Sundance Stables 762-2832
- Warner Outfitting 762-4551

Hostels 762-4122
- Banff International Hostel
- Castle Mountain
- Hilda Creek
- Lake Louise
- Mosquito Creek
- Rampart Creek

Rafting
- Alpine Rafting Co. 1-800-663-7080
- Glacier Raft Company 762-4347
- Hydra-River Guides Ltd. 762-4554
- Kootenay River Runners 762-5385
- Mirage Adventure Tours 678-4919
- Rainbow Riders 673-3622
- Rocky Mountain Raft Tours 762-3632
- Western Canadian White Water 762-8256
- Wet 'N Wild 1-800-668-9119

Snocoach Tours
- Columbia Icefield 762-5454

Eco-Tours
- Good Earth Travel Adventures 678-9358
- MTW Guides Office Ltd. 678-2642

Camping 762-1500
- Castle Mountain
- Johnston Canyon
- Lake Louise
- Mosquito Creek
- Protection Mountain
- Rampart Creek
- Tunnel Mountain
- Two Jack Lake
- Waterfowl Lake

Jasper Park To Do List

Sights
- Athabasca Falls
- Athabasca Glacier
- Cavell Meadows
- Icefields Parkway
- Maligne Canyon
- Maligne Lake
- Miette Hot Springs
- Mt. Edith Cavell
- Mt. Robson
- Overlander Falls
- Patricia Lake
- Pocahontas Ponds
- Pyramid Lake
- Rearguard Falls
- Sunwapta Falls
- The Whistlers

Entertainment
- Interpretive programs 852-6176
- Library 852-3652
- Chaba Movie Theatre 852-4749
- Jasper-Yellowhead Historical Society 852-3013

Bike Rentals
- On-Line Sport and Tackle 852-3630

Boat Rentals
- Pyramid Lake Boat Rentals 852-3536

Boat Tours
- Maligne Lake Tours 852-3370

Golf
- Jasper Park Lodge 852-3301

Horse Riding
- Pyramid Stables 852-3562
- Skyline Trail Rides 852-4215
- Sunrider Stables 852-4215/852-3301
- Tonquin Valley Pack Trips 865-4417

Icefields Parkway
- Icewalks at Columbia Icefield 852-5595
- Johnston Canyon
- Mistaya Canyon
- Snocoach Tours 852-3332

Rafting
- Canadian Rockies Raft Trips 852-3370
- Jasper Raft Tours 852-3613
- Rocky Mountain River Guides 852-3777
- Rocky Mountain Voyageurs 852-5595

Swimming
- Horseshoe Lake
- Jasper Aquatic Centre 852-3663
- Lake Annette
- Lake Edith
- Miette Hot Springs 852-6176

Camping 852-6176
- Columbia Icefield
- Honeymoon Lake
- Jonas Creek
- Mt. Kerkeslin
- Pocahontas
- Snaring
- Wapiti
- Whistlers
- Wilcox Creek

Hostels 762-4122
- Athabasca Falls
- Beauty Creek
- Edith Cavell
- Maligne Canyon
- Whistlers

Think ahead to anticipate lighting. Linger a while if things are not initially favourable. As with most endeavours, patience with photography usually pays.

Downhill Skiing

There are four downhill ski areas in the Rocky Mountain parks and two in Kananaskis Country. Shuttle service is available from most Banff and Lake Louise hotels to these ski areas. You can purchase ski vacation packages that include lift tickets, instruction, accommodation and local transportation. For information contact:

Club Ski, Banff-Lake Louise
P.O. Box 1085
Banff, Alberta T0L 0C0
Marmot Basin
P.O. Box 1570
Jasper, Alberta T0E 1E0
862-3533
Nakiska
P.O. Box 1988
Kananaskis Village, Alberta
T0L 2H0
591-7777
Fortress Mountain
P.O. Box 720, Station E
Calgary, Alberta T3C 3M1

Contacts

Parks Canada welcomes comments on your experience in the mountain national parks. You can fill out comment forms at park information centres. Superintendents of the individual parks may be contacted using the addresses below.

The author and the publisher of the *Canadian Rockies SuperGuide* would also like to hear about your experience in the Rockies. If you have sug-

gestions, corrections or omissions concerning the *Super-Guide*, please forward them to the author in care of:

Altitude Publishing
1500 Railway Avenue
Canmore, AB
Canada T1W 1P6
403-678-6888

National Parks

Banff National Park

P.O. Box 900
Banff, AB T0L 0C0
403-762-1500
Park information centre,
Banff 762-4256
Park information centre, Lake Louise 522-3833
Banff warden office 762-1470
Lake Louise warden office
522-1220

Jasper National Park

P.O. Box 10
Jasper, AB T0E 1E0
403-852-6220
Park information centre,
Jasper 852-6176
Park information centre,
Columbia Icefield 761-7030
Park warden office 852-6560

Yoho National Park

P.O. Box 99
Field, BC V0A 1G0
250-343-6324
Park information centre
343-6783
Lake O'Hara bus and campground reservations 343-6433
Burgess Shale hikes 343-6783

Kootenay National Park

P.O. Box 220
Radium Hot Springs, BC
V0A 1M0
250-347-9615
Park information centre, west gate 347-9505
Park warden office 347-9361

Waterton Lakes National Park

Waterton Park, AB T0K 2M0
403-859-2224
Park information centre
859-5133

Parks Canada
520, 220 - 4 Ave. S.E.
P.O. Box 2989, Station M
Calgary, AB T2P 2M9
403-292-4401
To comment on overall policies affecting national parks:
The Hon. Minister of Canadian Heritage
House of Commons,
Parliament Buildings
Ottawa, ON K1A 0A6,
and your federal Member of Parliament

Provincial Parks

Kananaskis Country

Suite 412,
1011 Glenmore Trail S.W.
Calgary, AB T2V 4R6
403-297-3362
403-678-5508

Peter Lougheed Provincial Park

403-591-6344

Bow Valley Provincial Park

403-673-3985

Mt. Robson Provincial Park

P.O. Box 579
Valemount, BC V0E 2Z0
250-566-4325

Mt. Assiniboine Provincial Park

P.O. Box 118
Wasa, BC V0B 2K0
250-422-3212

Emergency Numbers

Banff National Park

Ambulance 762-2000
Fire 762-2000
Hospital 762-2222
Lake Louise Medical Clinic:
522-2184
RCMP 762-2226
Warden office 762-4506

Jasper National Park

Ambulance 852-3100
Fire 852-3100
Hospital 852-3344
Medical clinics 852-4885,
852-4456
RCMP 852-4848
Warden office 852-6156

Yoho National Park
Ambulance 344-6226
Fire 343-6028
Hospital 344-5271,
403-762-2222
RCMP 343-2221
Warden office 403-762-4506

Kootenay National Park
Ambulance 1-250-374-5937
Fire 347-9333
Hospital 342-9201
Medical Centre 342-9206
RCMP 347-9393
Warden office 347-9361

Waterton Lakes National Park
Ambulance 859-2636
Fire 859-2636
Hospital (Pincher Creek)
627-3333, (Cardston)
653-4411
Clinic (Pincher Creek)
627-3321
RCMP 859-2044

Kananaskis Country
Emergency Services 591-7767
RCMP: Ask operator for
Zenith 50,000

Mt. Robson Provincial Park
Ambulance 1-800-461-9911
RCMP 566-4466

Weather / Road Reports

Banff National Park
Weather office (24 hour
recording) 762-2088
Road report 762-4733
Avalanche forecast 762-1460
Trail conditions 762-1550

Jasper National Park and Mt. Robson
Weather office 403-852-3185
(24 hour recording)
Road report 1-800-222-6501
Avalanche forecast 852-6155

Yoho National Park
Weather report 343-6783
Road report 343-6783
Avalanche forecast 343-6783

Kootenay National Park
Weather report 347-9615
(summer)
Road report 347-9551

Avalanche forecast 347-9361

Waterton Lakes National Park
Weather report 328-3185
Road report 328-1181
Avalanche forecast 859-2224

Chambers of Commerce

Banff-Lake Louise Chamber of Commerce
Box 1298
Banff, AB T0L 0C0
403-762-3777, Fax 762-5758

Jasper Park Chamber of Commerce
Box 98
Jasper, AB T0E 1E0
403-852-3858, Fax 852-4932

Canmore, Bow Valley and Kananaskis Chamber of Commerce
Box 1178
Canmore, AB T0L 0M0
403-678-4094, Fax 678-2086

Waterton Park Chamber of Commerce
Box 556
Waterton Park, AB T0K 2M0

BC Rocky Mountain Visitor Association
(for Yoho and Kootenay)
495 Wallinger Ave., Box 10
Kimberley, BC V1A 2Y5
250-427-4838

Valemount Tourism and Recreation
Box 168
Valemount BC V0E 2Z0
250-566-4846

Environmental Organizations

These organizations actively participate in environmental issues that affect the Rocky Mountain parks:

Canadian Parks and Wilderness Society
401 Richmond St. W.
Suite 380
Toronto, ON M5V 3A8

Western Canada Wilderness Committee
20 Water St.
Vancouver, BC V6B 1A4

Bow Valley Naturalists
Box 1693
Banff, AB T0L 0C0

Jasper Environmental Association
Box 2198
Jasper, AB T0E 1E0

Alberta Wilderness Association
P.O. Box 6398, Station D
Calgary, AB T2P 2E1

Recommended Reading

General Reference and Recreation

Cameron, W. *Kananaskis Super-Guide.* Canmore: Altitude Publishing, 1996.

Fuller, M. *Mountains: A Natural History and Hiking Guide.* New York: John Wiley and Sons, 1989. An excellent overview of mountain building and mountain ecology, with tips for mountain travel.

Gadd, B. *Handbook of the Canadian Rockies.* Jasper: Corax Press, 1995. If it's not in the *Handbook,* it's not in the Rockies.

Helgason, G. and J. Dodd. *The Canadian Rockies Bicycling Guide.* Edmonton: Lone Pine Publishing, 1984.

Kavanagh, J. *Nature Alberta.* Edmonton: Lone Pine Publishing, 1991.

Patton, B. and B. Robinson. *Canadian Rockies Trail Guide.* Banff: Summerthought, 1994.

Pole, G. *Classic Hikes in the Canadian Rockies.* Canmore: Altitude Publishing, 1994. The best backcountry hiking trails, full colour photos and maps.

Pole, G. *Walks and Easy Hikes in the Canadian Rockies.* Canmore: Altitude Publishing, 2nd edition, 1996. A companion guide to *Classic Hikes,* packed with frontcountry outings.

Sandford, R.W. *The Book of Banff.* Banff: The Friends of Banff National Park, 1994.

Scott, C. *Ski Trails in the Canadian Rockies.* Calgary: Rocky Mountain Books, 1992.

Birding

Ehrlich, P., D. Dobkin and D. Wheye. *The Birder's Handbook.* New York: Simon and Schuster, 1988.

Gregg, Jack. *All the Birds of North America.* New York: Harper Collins, 1997

Holroyd, G.L. and Howard Coneybare. *The Compact Guide to Birds of the Rockies.* Edmonton: Lone Pine Publishing, 1990.

National Audubon Society. *Interactive CD-ROM Guide to North American Birds.* New York: Knopf New Media, 1996. Songs, still images, movies, range maps, field guide texts, in PC and Macintosh format on one CD. Highly recommended.

National Geographic Society. *Field Guide to the Birds of North America.* Washington: National Geographic Society, 2nd edition, 1987.

Scotter, G.W., Ulrich, T.J. and E.T. Jones. *Birds of the Canadian Rockies.* Saskatoon: Western Producer Prairie Books, 1990. Excellent photography.

Van Tighem, K., and A. LeMessurier. *Birding Jasper National Park.* Jasper: Parks and People, 1989.

Canadian Pacific Railway

Bain, D. *Canadian Pacific in the Rockies.* Calgary: The British Railway Modellers of North America. (In ten volumes)

Berton, P. *The National Dream.* Toronto: McClelland and Stewart, 1970.

Berton, P. *The Last Spike.* Toronto: McClelland and Stewart, 1971.

Berton, P. *The Great Railway Illustrated.* Toronto: McClelland and Stewart, 1972.

Cruise, D. and A. Griffiths. *Lords of the Line.* Markham: Penguin Books 1989.

Garden, J.F. *Nicholas Morant's Canadian Pacific.* Revelstoke: Footprint Publishing, 1991.

Hart. E.J. *The Selling of Canada.* Banff: Altitude Publishing, 1983.

Lamb, W. K. *History of the Canadian Pacific Railway.* Toronto: Collier Macmillan, 1977.

Lavallée, O. *Van Horne's Road.* Montreal: Railfare Enterprises, 1974.

Morris, J. *Trackside Guide to CP Rail.* Revelstoke: Friends of Mount Revelstoke and Glacier, Friends of Yoho, 1993.

McKee, B., and G. Klassen. *Trail of Iron.* Calgary: Glenbow-Alberta Institute, 1983.

Pole, G. *The Spiral Tunnels and The Big Hill.* Canmore: Altitude Publishing, 1996.

Turner, R. D. *West of the Great Divide: The Canadian Pacific in British Columbia 1880-1986.* Victoria: Sono Nis Press, 1987.

Yeats, F. *Canadian Pacific's Big Hill.* Calgary: The British Railway Modellers of North America, 1985.

Geology

Ferguson, S.A. *Glaciers of North America.* Golden, Colorado: Fulcrum Publishing, 1992.

Ford, D., and D. Muir. *Castleguard.* Ottawa: Minister of the Environment, 1985. A clear and lavishly illustrated description of natural processes at Castleguard Cave and Meadows, but relevant to the alpine throughout the Rockies.

Kucera, R.E. *Exploring the Columbia Icefield.* Canmore: High Country, 1987.

Sandford, R.W. *The Columbia Icefield.* Banff: Altitude Publishing, 1992.

Yorvath, C.J, and B. Gadd. *Of Rocks, Mountains and Jasper.* Toronto: Dundurn Press, 1995.

Human History

Boles, G., R. Laurilla and W. Putnam. *Place Names of the Canadian Alps.* Revelstoke: Footprint, 1990.

Cavell, E. *Legacy in Ice.* Banff; The Whyte Foundation, 1983. Photography and studies by the Vaux family.

Christenson, L. *A Hiker's Guide to the Art of the Canadian Rockies.* Calgary: Glenbow-Alberta Institute, 1996.

Engler, B. *A Mountain Life.* Canmore: Alpine Club of Canada, 1994.

Forster, M. *A Walk in the Past.* Jasper: Friends of Jasper National Park, 1987. Historical walking tour of Jasper.

Gadd, B. *Bankhead: The Twenty-year Town.* Banff: Friends of Banff National Park, 1989.

Hart, E.J. *Ain't It Hell.* Banff: EJH Literary Enterprises, 1995. A fictitious journal of Bill Peyto.

Hart, E.J. *Diamond Hitch.* Banff: Summerthought, 1979. Stories of trail life and an illustrated history of the guides and outfitters who opened up the Rockies.

Hart, E.J. *Jimmy Simpson: Legend of the Rockies.* Banff: Altitude Publishing, 1991.

Harmon, C. and B. Robinson. *Byron Harmon: Mountain Photographer.* Banff: Altitude Publishing, 1992.

Holterman, J. *Place Names of Glacier/Waterton National Parks.* Glacier Natural History Association, 1985.

Kauffman, A.J. and W.L Putnam.

The Guiding Spirit. Revelstoke: Footprint Publishing, 1986. A history of mountain guiding in the Rockies and Columbia Mountains.

Marty, S. *A Grand and Fabulous Notion.* Toronto: NC Press, 1984. The founding of Banff National Park and Canada's national park system.

Marty, S. *Men for the Mountains.* Toronto: McClelland and Stewart, 1978.

Nisbet, J. *Sources of the River.* Seattle: Sasquatch Books, 1994. Tracking David Thompson in the Rockies and western North America.

Patton, B. *Tales From the Canadian Rockies.* Edmonton: Hurtig, Publishers, 1984.

Pole, G. *The Canadian Rockies: A History in Photographs.* Banff: Altitude Publishing, 1991. Human history from 1884 to the 1950s, illustrated with 130 photographs.

Robinson, B. *Banff Springs: The Story of a Hotel.* Banff: Summerthought, 1988.

Sandford, R.W. and G. Powter. *Canadian Summits.* Canmore: Alpine Club of Canada, 1994.

Sandford, R.W. *The Canadian Alps.* Banff: Altitude Publishing, 1990. A history of early mountaineering in western Canada.

Sandford, R.W. *Yoho: A History and Celebration of Yoho National Park.* Canmore: Altitude Publishing, 1993.

Schäffer, Mary T.S. *A Hunter of Peace.* Banff: The Whyte Foundation, 1980. On the trail with Mary Schäffer, in quest of Maligne Lake.

Smith, C. *Jasper Park Lodge.* Jasper: Cyndi Smith, 1985.

Smith, C. *Off the Beaten Track.* Jasper: Coyote Books, 1989. Women explorers in western Canada.

Spry, I.M. *The Palliser Expedition.* Saskatoon: Fifth House, 1995.

Taylor, W.C. *Tracks Across My Trail.* Jasper: Jasper-Yellowhead Historical Society, 1984. The life and times of outfitter Curly Phillips.

Whyte, J. *Indians of the Rockies.* Banff: Altitude Publishing, 1985.

Vegetation

Anonymous. *Trees and Forests of Jasper National Park.* Jasper: Parks and People, 1986.

Bush, C. D. *Wildflowers of the Rockies.* Edmonton: Lone Pine, 1990. Colour illustrations.

Johnson, D., Kershaw, L., MacKinnon, A. and J. Pojar. *Plants of the Western Boreal Forest and Aspen Parkland.* Edmonton: Lone Pine Publishing, 1995.

Kershaw, Linda, MacKinnon, A. and J. Pojar. *Plants of the Rocky Mountains.* Edmonton: Lone Pine, 1998.

Kujit, J. *A Flora of Waterton Lakes National Park.* Edmonton: University of Alberta Press, 1982. Most of the species that occur in the Rockies are found in Waterton. An excellent reference for both novice and expert. Illustrations. Unfortunately, now out of print.

Lauriault, J. *Identification Guide to the Trees of Canada.* Toronto: Fitzhenry and Whiteside, 1989. The standard reference.

Little, E.L. *The Audubon Society Field Guide to North American Trees: Western Region.* New York: Alfred A. Knopf, 1980.

Moss, E.H. and J.G. Packer. *The Flora of Alberta.* Toronto: The University of Toronto Press, 1983. The standard technical reference. No illustrations.

Parish, R., Coupé, R. and D.

Lloyd. *Plants of Southern Interior British Columbia.* Edmonton: Lone Pine Publishing, 1996. Particularly useful for Yoho, Kootenay and Mt. Robson.

Parish, R. and S. Thomson. *Tree Book: Learning to Recognize Trees of British Columbia.* Victoria: B.C. Ministry of Forests and Canadian Forest Service, 1995.

Petrides, G.A. *A Field Guide to Western Trees.* New York: Houghton Mifflin, 1992. A Peterson Field Guide.

Porsild, A.E. and D.T. Lid. *Rocky Mountain Wild Flowers.* Ottawa: National Museum of Natural Sciences, 1979. Colour illustrations.

Potter, M. *Pocket Guide: Wildflowers of the Central Rockies.* Banff: Luminous Compositions, 1996.

Scotter, G.W. and H. Flygare. *Wildflowers of the Canadian Rockies.* Toronto: McClelland and Stewart, 1992. Good colour photographs.

Stanton, C. and N. Lopoukine. *The Trees and Forests of Waterton Lakes National Park.* Forestry Service and Environment Canada, undated. A free brochure available at Waterton Lakes National Park information centre.

Vitt, D.H., J.E. Marsh and R. Bovey. *Mosses, Lichens and Ferns of Northwest North America.* Edmonton: Lone Pine Publishing, 1988.

Whitney, S. *Western Forests.* National Audubon Society Nature Guides. New York: Alfred A. Knopf, 1985.

Wilkinson, K. *Trees and Shrubs of Alberta.* Edmonton: Lone Pine Publishing, 1990.

Zwinger, A. and B.E. Willard. *Land Above the Trees.* Tucson: University of Arizona Press,

1989. An excellent guide to ecology above timberline.

Wildlife

Barwise, J. *Animal Tracks of Western Canada*. Edmonton: Lone Pine Publishing, 1989.

Burt, W.H. and R.P. Grossenheider. *Mammals*. Boston: Houghton, Mifflin, 3rd edition, 1980. The standard Peterson reference for North America.

Chadwick, D. *A Beast the Colour of Winter*. The seminal work on the mountain goat.

Geist, V. *Mule Deer Country*. Minocqua, Wisconsin: NorthWord Press, 1990.

Geist, V. *Elk Country*. Minocqua, Wisconsin: NorthWord Press, 1991.

Geist, V. *Wild Sheep Country*. Minocqua, Wisconsin: NorthWord Press, 1993.

Herrero, S. *Bear Attacks: Their Causes and Avoidance*. Piscataway, N.J.: New Century, 1985.

Lynch, W. *Wildlife of the Canadian Rockies*. Canmore: Alpine Book Peddlers, 1995. Text and photographs by one of Canada's preeminent wildlife photographers.

McNamee, T. *The Grizzly Bear*. New York: Penguin Books, 1990. An enlightening examination of a year in the life of a grizzly bear.

Murie, O.J. *Animal Tracks*. Boston: Houghton and Mifflin, 1974. An excellent field guide with a wealth of information on animal behaviour.

Schmidt, D. and E. Schmidt. *Alberta Wildlife Viewing Guide*. Edmonton: Lone Pine Publishing, 1990.

Schmidt, D. and E. Schmidt. *Canadian Rockies Wildlife*. Canmore: Altitude Publishing, 1995.

Scotter, G. and T. Ulrich. *Mammals of the Canadian Rockies*. Saskatoon: Fifth House, 1995.

Stelfox, B., Wasel, S. and L. Hunt. *Field Guide to Hoofed Mammals of Jasper and Banff National Parks*. Jasper: Friends of Jasper National Park, 1992.

Ulrich, T.J. *Mammals of the Northern Rockies*. Missoula: Mountain Press, ca. 1988.

Van Tighem, Kevin. *Wild Animals of Western Canada*. Canmore: Altitude Publishing, 1992.

Photographic Credits

Shopping and Dining

Shopping

Although the towns in the Canadian Rockies are famous for their mountain settings, they are also home to many shops and services that cater to the international traveller. Waterton, Canmore, Banff, Lake Louise, Radium and Jasper all have grocery and convenience stores, pharmacies and gift shops.

Canmore

Canmore is bigger, and growing all the time. There are numerous service-type businesses and clothing shops, two grocery stores and a range of gift stores. There are a number of real gems — be sure to search out the small craft shops for which Canmore is famous.

Lake Louise

Shopping at Lake Louise is split between two locations: at the lake itself, there are numerous excellent gift, jewelry and clothing shops in the Chateau Lake Louise. A number of the other lodges in the Lake Louise area also have gift shops. Downtown, the shops are located in Samson Mall. Here, the gift and photo stores are supplemented by an excellent bookstore and an outstanding bakery.

Jasper

Jasper has a wide range of shops, including excellent craft stores, book stores, jewelry and gift shops. There are a couple of good bakeries and many service-type businesses. Jasper is slowly increasing the number of retail locations and new shops open each year. The downtown shopping area stretches along Connaught Drive and Patricia Street. A few more gift stores can be found across the river in the Jasper Park Lodge.

Banff

Banff is the largest town in the Canadian Rockies and has quite a cosmopolitan shopping area. The downtown centre is a maze of shopping malls that carry a wide range of goods from the cheap to the outrageously expensive, and from the mundane to the truly bizarre. As well as gift, clothing, jewelry and book stores, there are many unique specialty shops that can provide hours of browsing pleasure. There are, of course, drugstores and other service-related businesses, as well as some outstanding bakeries. The downtown area is supplemented by numerous shops at the Banff Springs Hotel, which also offer a wide range of high-quality goods.

Dining

Waterton

The restaurants in the various lodges in Waterton offer a range of culinary styles. You might try the Prince of Wales Hotel and the Kilmorey Lodge. Please ask around for further recommendations. A few downtown locations, such as the Waterton Park Cafe, are also excellent.

Canmore

Canmore boasts many excellent restaurants, especially for Italian, Swiss and French cooking. There are also a couple of excellent "country" style restaurants that provide wonderful food, and numerous family restaurants ideal for a casual meal.

Banff

People in Banff eat out very often and are quite demanding of their local restaurants. Consequently, there are a number of excellent places (you might want to ask some of the locals for their recommendations). The food choices range from Japanese and Chinese to Italian, French, Greek, Continental, Swiss, Mexican, "country" and fast food. There is fondue, seafood, hamburgers, pizza and deli. There is also a restaurant at the top of Sulphur Mountain. And of course, many family-style restaurants throughout Banff offer good food at reasonable prices in a casual atmosphere.

Lake Louise

Most of the restaurants in the Lake Louise area are connected with the hotels. The Chateau Lake Louise offers a wide range of dining rooms which appeal to different tastes and budgets. The Post Hotel houses one of the area's best-known restaurants. There is also a restaurant at Moraine Lake Lodge.

Field

There are two small sandwich shops and store in Field, but not a full-blown restaurant. Nearby, however, is Emerald Lake Lodge, which has a dining room and a coffee shop.

Radium

Like Lake Louise, most of the restaurants in Radium are connected to the hotels and motels. They offer family-style dining in a casual atmosphere.

Jasper

Like Banff (only on a smaller scale), there are plenty of restaurants to choose from in Jasper, including Greek, Japanese, Italian, French and deli. These are supplemented by a number of fine dining rooms in the Jasper Park Lodge. There is also a restaurant at the top of the Jasper Tramway.

Accommodations Listings

Accomodations key: First symbol "S" refers to summer rates (May to Oct.), second symbol "W" refers to winter rates (Nov. to Apr.). Winter rates do not apply to the period between Christmas (Dec 25) and the New Year. *Updated April, 2002.*

Summer rates (S)	Winter rates (W)
$=<100	$=<100
$$=100-200	$$=100-200
$$$=200+	$$$=200+
X=closed	X=closed

Waterton Lakes National Park

S	W	
$$$	X	Aspen Village Inn 403-859-2255
$$$	X	Bayshore Inn 1-888-527-9555
$$	$$	Crandell Mountain Lodge 859-2288
$	X	El Cortez Motel 859-2366
$$	$	Kilmorey Lodge 859-2334
$$	X	Northland Lodge 859-2353
$$	$$	Prince of Wales Hotel 236-3400/ 859-2231

Yoho National Park

S	W	
$$	$	Kicking Horse Lodge 250-343-6303
$$$	$$	Emerald Lake Lodge 1-800-663-6336 / 343-6321
$$	X	Cathedral Mountain Chalets 343-6442/403-762-0514
$$	$	West Louise Lodge 343-6311 / 1-800-258-7669
$$$	$$	Lake O'Hara Lodge* 343-6418 /403-678-4110

Guesthouse Suites

S	W	
$	$	Yoho Accommodations 343-6444/5
$	$	Mount Burgess Bungalow 343-6480
$$	$	Mount Stephen Guesthouse 343-6441
$$	$	Mount Van Horne Guesthouse 343-6380
$$	$	Otterhead Guesthouse 343-6034
$	X	Whiskey Jack Hostel 403-762-4122**

Lake Louise

S	W	
$$$	$$	Baker Creek Chalets 522-3761
$$	$$	Castle Mountain Village 522-2783/762-3868
$$	$	Deer Lodge 522-3991
$$$	$$	Fairmont Chateau Lake Louise 522-3511
$$	$$	Lake Louise Inn 522-3791
$$$	X	Moraine Lake Lodge 522-3733 /1-604-985-3456
$$	X	Mountaineer Lodge 522-3844
$$$	$$	Num-Ti Jah Lodge 522-2167
$$	X	Paradise Lodge & Bungalows 522-3595
$$$	$$	Post Hotel 522-3989
$$	$$	Skoki Lodge 522-3555
$$	$$	West Louise Lodge 250-343-6311

Canmore

S	W	
$	$	A-1 Motel 678-5200
$	$	Akai Motel 678-4664
$$$	$$	Banff Boundary Lodge 678-9555
$$	$	Bear Country Lodge 678-1000
$$	$$	Best Western Green Gables Inn 678-5488
$$	$$	Best Western Pocaterra Inn 678-4334
$	$	Bow Valley Motel 678-5085
$	$	Canmore Hotel 678-5181
$	$	Canmore Lodge 678-5528
$	$	Cee-Der Chalets 678-5251
$$	$	Chateau Canmore 678-6699
$$	$	Creekside Country Inn 609-5522
$$	$	Days Inn 609-0075
$$	$	Drake Inn 678-5131
$$	$	Four Points Sheraton 609-4422
$	$	Gateway Inn 678-5396
$$	$	Georgetown Inn 678-3439
$$	$	Howard Johnson 609-4656
$$	$	Kiska Inn 678-4041
$$$	$$	Lady Macdonald Inn 678-3665
$$	$	Mount Engadine Lodge 678-4080
$	$	Mountain View Inn 678-0992
$$	$	Paintbox Lodge 678-3956
$	$	Pigeon Mountain Motel 678-5756
$$	$$	Radisson Hotel & Conference Centre 678-3625
$$$	$$	Residence Inn by Marriot 678-3400
$$	$	Rocky Mountain Ski Lodge 678-5445
$$	$	Rundle Mountain Motel 678-5322
$$	$	Rundle Ridge Chalets 678-5387
$$	$	Stockade Log Cabins 678-5212
$	$	Westridge Country Inn 678-5221
$	$	Windtower Lodge 609-6600

Jasper

S	W	
$$	X	Aspen Lodge 852-5908
$$	$$	Amethyst Lodge 852-3394
$$$	$$	Astoria Hotel 852-3351
$$	$$	Athabasca Hotel 852-3386
$$	X	Bear Hill Lodge 852-3209
$$	$	Blue Lake Adventure Lodge 1-800-582-3305
$$$	$$	Charlton's Chateau Jasper 852-5644
$$$	$$	Fairmont Jasper Park Lodge 852-3301
$$	$$	Jasper Inn 852-4461
$$	$$	Lobstick Lodge 852-4431
$	$	Maligne Canyon Hostel 852-3215
$$	$$	Maligne Lodge 852-3143
$$$	$$	Marmot Lodge 852-4471
$$$	$$	Mount Robson Inn 852-3327

* Includes transportation, meals & tax
**Operates mid June to mid September

S	W	
$$$	$$	Overlander Mountain Lodge 852-866-2330
$$	$	Pyramid Lake Resort 852-4900
$$$	$	Royal Canadian Mountain Lodge 852-5644
$$	$	Sawridge Hotel Jasper 852-5111
$$$	X	Sunwapta Falls Resort 852-5215
$$$	$$	Tonquin Inn 852-4987
$$$	$$	Whistlers Inn 852-3361

Seasonal Accommodation (May to October)

S		
$$		Alpine Village 852-3285
$$		Becker's Chalets 852-3779
$$		Bonhomme Bungalows 852-3209
$$		Jasper House Bungalows 852-4535
$$		Miette Hot Springs Resort 866-3750
$$		Patricia Lake Bungalows 852-3560
$$		Pine Bungalows 852-3491
$$		Tekarra Resort 852-3058

Banff

Banff Central Reservations 762-5200

S	W	
$	$	Arrow Hotel 762-4496
$$	$	Beaver Suites and Cabins 762-5077
$$	$	A Good Night's Rest 762-2984
$$$	$$	Banff Avenue Inn 762-4499/1-800-772-0155
$$	$	Banff Bed and Breakfast 762-8806
$$	$	Banff Caribou Lodge 762-5887/1-800-563-8764
$$$	$$	Banff Douglas Fir Resort and Chalets 762-5591
$	$	Banff International Hostel
		762-4122 / 1-800-444-6111
$$	$$	Banff International Hotel
		762-5666/1-800-665-5666
$$$	$$	Banff Park Lodge 762-4433/1-800-661-9266
$$	$	Banff Ptarmigan Inn 762-2207/1-800-661-8310
$$$	$$	Banff Rocky Mountain Resort
		762-5531/1-800-661-9563
$$	$	Banff Voyager Inn 762-3301/1-800-879-1991
$$$	$$	Best Western Siding 29 Lodge
		762-5575/1-800-528-1234
$$	$	Bow View Motor Lodge 762-2261
$	$	Blue Mountain Lodge 762-5134
$$	$$	Brewster's Mountain Lodge
		762-2900/1-800-691-5085
$$$	$$$	Brewster's Shadow Lake Lodge 762-5454
$$$	$$$	Buffalo Mountain Lodge
		762-2400/1-800-661-1367
$$	$	Cascade Court Bed and Breakfast 762-2956
$$	X	Castle Mountain Chalets 762-3868
$$	$$	Charlton's Cedar Court
		762-4485/1-800-661-1225
$	X	Cottage Bed and Breakfast 762-0650
$$	$$	Dynasty Inn 762-8844/1-800-667-1464
$$	$$	Elk Ridge Guesthouse 762-3557
$$	$	Elkhorn Lodge 762-2299

S	W	
$$$	$$	Fairmont Banff Springs Hotel
		762-221/1-800-441-1414
$$	$	Hidden Ridge Chalets 762-3544/1-800-661-1372
$$	$	High Country Inn 762-2236/1-800-661-1244
$$	$	Holiday Lodge 762-3648
$$	$	Homestead Inn 762-4471/1-800-661-1021
$$	$$	Inns of Banff 762-4581/1-800-661-1272
$$	$	Irwin's Mountain Inn 762-4566/1-800-661-1721
$$	$	JR's Bed and Breakfast 762-2461
$$	$$	King Edward Hotel 762-2202/1-800-344-4232
$$	$	Misty Pines Bed and Breakfast 762-5496
$$$	$$	Mount Royal Hotel 762-8938/1-800-267-3035
$$	$	Mountain Lane Bed and Breakfast 762-2028
$$	$	Odenthal's Bed and Breakfast 762-2081
$	X	Park Avenue Bed and Breakfast 762-2025
$$	$	Red Carpet Inn 762-4184/1-800-563-4609
$$$	$$	Rimrock Resort Hotel
		762-3356/1-800-661-1587
$$	$	Rocky Mountain Bed and Breakfast 762-4811
$$$	$$	Royal Canadian Lodge 762-3307
$$	$	Rundle Manor Apartment Hotel 762-5544
$$	$$	Rundlestone Lodge 762-2201/1-800-661-8630
X	$$	Sunshine Village Inn 762-6555
$$	$	Timberline Inn 762-2281
$$	$	Traveller's Inn 762-4401/1-800-661-0227
$$$	$$	Tunnel Mountain Chalets
		762-4515/1-800-661-1859
$$	X	Welcome Friends Guest House 762-2196
$$$	$$	Woodland Village 762-5521

Mount Robson Provincial Park

S	W	
$	X	Mount Robson Lodge 250-566-4821
$$	$	Tijohn Lodge, west of park 250-566-9815

Mount Assiniboine Provincial Park

S	W	
$$	$	Mt. Assiniboine Lodge (a commercial facility near Lake Magog). Reservations needed; meals included 403-678-2883

Aside from backcountry camping, there are four alpine cabin shelters, the Naiset Huts, which house 31 people in total. They are located on the south side of Magog Creek, and you must pay a fee to use them.

For camping information in the area, call BC Parks District Manager 250-422-3212 or the Regional Director 250-371-6400.

Note from the Author

The enthusiastic response to the first edition of the *Canadian Rockies SuperGuide* was tremendously encouraging. This second edition has been completely rewritten and revised, not only to reflect the changes in the Canadian Rockies since 1991, but to include more of the information that readers find useful and interesting. A Recommended Reading section has been added, and key activities and destinations have been highlighted for each park. The index is expanded to allow you to cross-reference items in the text more easily.

Parks Canada's John Pitcher and Sophie Borcoman kindly reviewed passages of the text.

Obviously, in a book with the scope of the *Canadian Rockies SuperGuide*, my experiences and observations have been greatly enriched by the research, photography and writing of others. Enquiries, both formal and casual, have been too numerous to relate here, but there exists a multitude of informed and caring people who are passionate about the Canadian Rockies. They are the unofficial custodians of the Rocky Mountain Parks. In their energy, vision and commitment lies the promise of wilderness preservation.

I am particularly thankful to friends who have shared hiking trails, and ski and mountaineering adventures. Foremost among these is my wife Marnie, a near-constant companion in my mountain travels since 1989. Many of the photographs in this book and the observations of the landscape could not have been made without the companionship and enthusiasm of these people.

At the time of publication, Parks Canada was contemplating new use fees, the closure of some secondary roads and facilities and other alterations to services that affect visitors. Please contact a park information centre at the time of your visit to obtain the most current information on services, destinations and fees. See the Contacts section, p. 275.

If you have corrections or suggestions concerning the *Canadian Rockies SuperGuide*, please send them to me in care of the publisher. I sincerely hope you enjoy your visit to the Canadian Rockies.

Graeme Pole
Field, B.C., 1997

About the Author

Graeme Pole

Graeme Pole is the best-selling author of five non-fiction books that describe the human history and natural history of the Canadian Rockies. Three of his books have been finalists in the Banff Mountain Book Festival. *Classic Hikes in the Canadian Rockies* won the Mountain Exposition category in 1994. He has been a runner-up for the Andy Russell Nature Writers' Award, a finalist in the Crown of the Continent Nature Writing Award, a recipient of a Northwest Outdoor Writers' Association "Excellence in Craft Award," and a recipient of the Teddi Brown Award for Nature Writing. His first novel, *Healy Park*, was published in 1998.

Index

Index

Index

Index

Index

skiing
-contact addresses, 275
-cross-country, 48-50, 55, 126
-downhill, 40, 41, 48, 55, 80, 103, 123, 227, 275
-mountaineering tours, 47
Skoki Lodge, 123-24
Skoki Valley, 123-24
Skyline Trail, 238
sleigh rides, 50
Smith-Dorrien/Spray Road, 55-56
snakes, garter, 66
Snaring River, 242-43
Snocoach Tours, Columbia Icefield, 196
Snow Dome, 190
Snowbird Glacier, 172-73
snowmobiles, 49-50
spas, Banff Springs Hotel, 63
Spiral Tunnels, 39, 134, 135-37, 138
spruce, black, 214
spruce, Engelmann, 195
spruce, white, 246
squirrels, 174
Stanley Glacier Trail, 154
Stanley Peak, 155-56
Stephen Fossil Bed, 141
Stephen, Mount, 128, 131, 141-42
Storm Mountain, 101
Storm Mountain Lodge, 153
Stutfield Glacier, 207
subalpine ecoregion, 27-28
succession, 29, 230
Sulphur Mountain Gondola, 81
Sulphur Skyline Trail, 248
Sunshine Meadows, 102
Sunshine Ski Area, 40, 41, 48, 103
Sunwapta Falls, 210-12
Sunwapta Falls Lodge, 211
Sunwapta Lake, 190, 197
Sunwapta Pass, 184-85
swift, black, 235
Swift, Lewis, 243
Swift's Place, 243
swimming, 44, 63, 153, 165, 223
Swiss Guides, 120
sycline mountains, 23

Takakkaw Falls, 132, 139-40
Talbot Lake, 243-44
tamarack, 181, 247
Tangle Creek Trail, 205
Tangle Falls, 204, 205, 207
Taylor Lake Trail, 107
teahouses
-Lake Agnes, 121, 122
-Plain of Six Glaciers, 119-20
Temple, Mount, 101, 107, 126
Terrace Trail, 53
Terry Fox, Mount, 255
theatres, Banff Centre for the Arts, The, 85
Thompson, Charles, 170

Thompson, David, 207, 223
-National Historic Site, 207
Thompson, Mount, 170
Thorington, James Monroe, 178, 197
Three Sisters, 58
Timberline Trail, 171
time zone change, 129
Tonquin Valley, 227-228
tourist information.
See park information centres
Tower of Babel, 125
trail riding. See horseback riding
trails. See names of trails
train service, 86, 268
Trans-Canada Highway, 41, 53, 105-106
-See also car tours
trees, 29
-See also krummholz; names of trees
Tunnel Mountain, 63, 65, 86
Tunnel Mountain Hoodoos, 86-87

U-shaped valleys, 21
UNESCO World Heritage Sites
-Burgess Shale, 147
-Rocky Mountain national parks,61
Upper Hot Springs, Banff, 63, 65, 75, 77
Upper Spiral Tunnel Viewpoint, 138

V-shaped valleys, 21
Valley of the Five Lakes, 215
Valley of Ten Peaks, 126
Van Horne, William Cornelius, 57, 65-66, 78, 140
Vaux family, 114
vegetation
-by ecoregions, 27-28
-recommended reading, 278
Verendrye, Mount, 157-58
Vermilion Lakes, 92-93
Vermilion Pass, 151, 153, 155
Vermilion Pass Burn, 153-54, 155
Victoria Glacier, 118-20
Victoria, Mount, 47, 117-20
Vista Lake and Viewpoint, 151-52
vistor information centres.
See park information centres

Wabasso Lake, 214-15
walks, 46, 49
wapiti, 69
Wapta Falls, 146, 148-49
Wapta Lake, 134
Watchtower Valley Trail, 237
water, drinking untreated, 43, 116, 199, 269
waterfall ice climbing, 47, 140, 170, 183, 202
waterfalls
-Athabasca Falls, 213, 214
-Bow Falls, 77, 79, 81
-Helmet Falls, 157
-Sideway Falls, 183
-Sunwapta Falls, 210-11

-Takakkaw Falls, 132, 139-40
-Tangle Falls, 204, 205, 207
-Wapta Falls, 148-49
-Weeping Wall, The, 182
Waterfowl Lakes, 173, 177
watermelon snow, 199
Waterton, Charles, 261
Waterton Heritage Centre, 259
Waterton Lakes National Park, 256-67, 275
Waterton Townsite, 262, 263
-town map, 259
Waterton-Glacier International Peace Park, 41, 267
weasels, 32
weather, 50-51
-See also climate
weather reports, 276
Weeping Wall, The, 182
Wenkchemna Peaks, 101, 125-26
western main ranges, 17, 18
Wheeler, Arthur Oliver, 31, 39, 74, 163, 250-51
Whirlpool River, 230
Whirlpool Valley Viewpoint, 214
Whiskey Jack hostel, 139
Whistlers, The, 224
Whitehorn Lodge, 123
whitewater, 44, 253
whitewater rafting. See rafting
Whyte Museum of the Canadian Rockies, 41, 63, 85-86
Wilcox Pass Trail, 185
Wilcox, Walter, 38, 39, 114-15, 117, 124-27, 166, 182
wilderness pass, 43, 44
wildflowers see names of flowers
wildlife, 30-35, 270
-recommended reading, 279
-See also names of animals
Wilson, Mount, 181
Wilson, Tom, 30, 39, 70, 74, 101, 109, 137, 138, 143
wolves, 31, 108
Wood, Sharon, 201

Yale Lake Louise Club, 38, 115
Yamnuska Mountain, 55
Yellowhead Highway, 41, 240-55
-maps, 242, 249
Yellowhead Pass, 249-50, 252
Yoho Blow, 143
Yoho Blowdown, The, 149
Yoho National Park, 40, 128-49, 275
-map, 130
Yoho Pass-Iceline Trail, 139
Yoho Valley Road, 138, 139-40

zoos, 31, 83